CREATING WOMEN: AN INTERDISCIPLINARY ANTHOLOGY OF READINGS ON WOMEN IN WESTERN CULTURE

VOLUME ONE
RENAISSANCE TO THE PRESENT

Edited by

Linda Bennett Elder
Valdosta State University

Jean Gould Bryant
Florida State University

PEARSON

Prentice
Hall

Upper Saddle River, NJ 07458

Library of Congress Cataloging-in-Publication Data
Creating women : an anthology of readings on women in Western culture /
[edited by] Jean Gould Bryant, Linda Bennett Elder.—1st ed.
    p. cm.
  Includes bibliographical references and index.
    ISBN 0-13-759622-7 (v. 1)—ISBN 0-13-759630-8 (v. 2)
    1. Women—History. 2. Women—History—Sources. I. Bryant, Jean Gould.
II. Elder, Linda Bennett.

HQ1121.C67 2005
3054'09—dc22   2003056544

We dedicate this book to our husbands Jerry and Bob, our children Steven, John, Martha, and Peter, and to the creative women—past, present, and future—who enrich our world.

VP, Editorial Director: Charlyce Jones Owen
Executive Editor: Charles Cavaliere
Associate Editor: Emsal Hasan
Editorial Assistant: Shannon Corliss
Executive Marketing Manager: Heather Shelstaad
Senior Marketing Assistant: Cherron Gardner
Managing Editor: Joanne Riker
Production Editor: Jan H. Schwartz
Permissions Supervisor: Ron Fox
Permissions Researcher: Melinda Alexander, Carrie J. Hodges
Manufacturing Buyer: Tricia Kenny, Ben Smith
Cover Design: Bruce Kenselaar
Photo Researcher: Julie Tesser
Composition: PineTree Composition, Inc.
Printer/Binder: R.R. Donnelley
Cover Printer: Phoenix Color Corporation
Chapter opening art: Courtesy of the Women's Studies Program, Florida State University, Tallahassee, FL. Printed by permission of Donald Foss, Dean, College of Arts and Sciences, Florida State University.

Credits and acknowledgments borrowed from other sources and reproduced, with permission, in this textbook appear on appropriate page within text.

Pearson Education LTD.
Pearson Education Singapore, Pte. Ltd
Pearson Education, Canada, Ltd
Pearson Education–Japan

Pearson Education Australia PTY, Limited
Pearson Education North Asia Ltd
Pearson Education de Mexico, S.A. de C.V.
Pearson Education Malaysia, Pte. Ltd

10 9 8 7 6 5 4 3 2 1
0-13-759622-7

Contents

Preface

Our goal in writing this two-volume work is to provide students and instructors with a more comprehensive understanding of the history of humankind than has previously been available to the non-specialist. As the title suggests, these volumes document the significant part women have played in the development of Western civilization, from the Upper Paleolithic era (we begin ca. 35,000 B.C.E.) to the present. We have brought together a varied collection of primary source materials including archeological artifacts, images, and texts that reveal women's participation in all aspects of human culture, religion, the visual and performing arts, literature, philosophy, and public affairs.

We deliberately chose our title, *Creating Women,* because, in addition to its obvious reference to *creative* women, it reflects another important dimension of Western civilization: The ways in which societal notions of gender (masculine/feminine) and gender roles have in essence "created" and/or "constructed" women. A significant consequence of this social construction is that women's experiences and opportunities have often differed in significant ways from those of men. Together, the documents tell much about Western notions of sex differences and how and why "the woman question" continues to be among the most persistent controversies in Western thought and discourse.

Creating Women, like many other new texts, evolved from the need for reading materials for a new course. In 1985, a team of Florida State University faculty and graduate students from history, dance, theater, music, English, classics, religion, humanities, and art history received a university grant to develop an introductory course for women's studies that would also fulfill part of the university's liberal studies requirements. Jean Gould Bryant, director of the women's studies program, led that project and Linda Bennett Elder was a member of the development team from its inception.

The decision to develop an interdisciplinary humanities course was prompted by several considerations. We wanted a course to complement an existing humanities sequence that introduced students to the traditional canon of cultural developments of Western civilization but made few references to women's contributions. We also sought to fill curriculum gaps in classics, music, art history, theater, and European history and to provide a catalyst for the creation of courses on women and gender across the arts and sciences. We hoped as well to create incentives for faculty to include information related to women's accomplishments and experiences within existing courses. The course, Women in Western Culture: Images and Realities, was a vital addition to our women's studies curriculum that had previously focused almost exclusively on the Western world since the seventeenth century, with heavy emphasis on contemporary American society.

In 1986, as now, there were a few discipline-specific texts and anthologies of secondary articles and primary source readings, but no interdisciplinary text or anthology concerning women existed and no anthology spanned the entire history of Western civilization. As we proceeded to refine Women in Western Culture, we recognized not only the need for an interdisciplinary reader, but also a unique situation for developing such a text. Since 1986, we have used a variety of readings, audio-visual re-sources, and lecture material in our respective courses on women in Western humanities. We have also explored different configurations of chronology and course themes suggested by the critiques, ques-tions and responses of our students, and our mutual assessments. We discovered, for example, that al-though many contemporary feminist scholars ignore religion, religion is one of the most prevalent markers of women's participation in culture from prehistory through the medieval period, and it re-mained a critical factor through the nineteenth century. Over time we integrated the discrete multidis-ciplinary pieces of our examination of women into a coherent truly interdisciplinary course that highlighted major themes and patterns that emerged across disciplines and centuries.

The results have been exciting for us and for our students. We discovered that examining women's cultural achievements and struggles provides an innovative framework for discussing women's legal, socioeconomic, religious, and/or political status in different times and places. We found that the multi-disciplinary approach ensures that each student will discover some individuals whose life/work matches her or his personal interests or career aspirations and may indeed discover new role models or cultural icons for inspiration. We also learned that bringing women and their voices to the forefront sometimes radically changed our understanding of certain periods of Western civilization and often introduced provocative new cultural forms, alternative visions of society and its institutions, and chal-lenging critiques of values, ideas, and societal arrangements that many have regarded as "fixed" West-ern cultural traditions.

Creating Women is the product of an extended period of living with the material, adding to it and reconfiguring it in response to input from our students and colleagues. Both volumes integrate in-sights from an abundance of new scholarship that has enriched women's history in all fields over the last three decades. We believe that the interdisciplinary approach we have taken in these volumes and the expansive time-span that we have elected to cover will generate spirited discussion. Our approach will also add significantly to the reader's understanding of women and gender in Western civilization, thereby providing a more complete and realistic picture of the history of humankind.

CREATING WOMEN: STRUCTURE

Each volume consists of three parts with five chapters in each.

Volume one encompasses women and culture from prehistory through the middle ages:

Part I: **Women in Prehistory and the Ancient Near East**

Part II: **Women in the Mediterranean and Greco-Roman World**

Part III: **Women in the Roman Empire, Christian Origins, Late Antiquity, and the Middle Ages**

Volume Two encompasses women and culture from the Renaissance to the present:

Part I: **Women in Early Modern Europe**

Part II: **Women and Culture, 1750–1920**

Part III: **Women and Culture in the Twentieth Century**

CREATING WOMEN: FEATURES

• The narrative, biographical vignettes, and document introductions place women and their achieve-ments within the broader social-political context in which they lived and worked.

- Introductory narrative helps guide students' analysis of material and facilitates class discussion.
- Maps, charts, and narrative link women and their achievements with more familiar events and personages in Western civilization and also illustrate significant clusters of female creativity.
- Selected bibliographies facilitate student projects and enable instructors to enrich classes with audiovisual material.

ACKNOWLEDGMENTS

A work of this scope and magnitude is never a solitary effort and we are deeply indebted to the many individuals and institutions that made these two volumes possible. A 1985 grant from Florida State University underwrote the initial research for the interdisciplinary humanities course that was the genesis of these two volumes. The team of faculty and graduate students that developed the course, including, among others, Ellen Burns, Cynthia Hahn, and Catherine Schuler, introduced us to many of the women who appear in the pages that follow. In recent years, team members Nancy De Grummond, Tricia Young, and Karen Laughlin provided sage advice as we were selecting documents and writing these volumes. Our students have also shaped our work. Their questions, perceptive observations, and excitement when introduced to many of the women and documents that appear in these pages influenced our selections and introductory material. Lisa Beverly, Leah Cassorla, Cameron Cooper, Douglas and Berkay Grove, Tina Ports, Jan Richardson, and Maggie Willman provided invaluable assistance with the time-consuming mechanical details involved in tracking down documents, transcribing interviews and micro-materials, and obtaining permissions.

Creating Women would not have been possible without the scholarship of the women and men who recovered the works and lives of many who appear in the pages that follow and who placed women's history on a solid foundation. We are particularly grateful to those scholars who granted permission to include excerpts of their work in these volumes and who encouraged us, made suggestions, and shared our excitement about bringing the works of women who they had restored to history to a wider audience. Numerous archivists and publishers helped us locate elusive documents and obtain permissions. We are also indebted to the women who gave generously of their time to grant us interviews.

This book would not have been possible without the support of the History editors at Prentice Hall who believed in this project when we submitted our initial proposal and assisted us in its early stages: Sally Constable, Charlyce Jones Owen, and Todd Armstrong. During the arduous process of bringing these volumes to print, we have been blessed with the support and guidance of Charles Cavaliere, Executive Editor for History; Emsal Hasan, Associate Editor for History; Joanne Riker, Managing Editor for Production; Mirella Signoretto, Artist; Martha Williams, Copyeditor; Sharon Gonzales, Proofreader; and above all, our Production Editor, Jan Schwartz. The final product owes much to their patience and editorial assistance.

Finally, we thank our friends, colleagues, and relatives whose support and interest in this project sustained us through many years as we struggled to bring it to fruition. We are eternally grateful to Karen Laughlin, Dean of Undergraduate Studies at Florida State University, who interrupted an incredibly full schedule to give the entire manuscript a perceptive critique that helped us refine the book. Special thanks are due Gerald Bryant and Valerie Jean Conner who helped proof the final copy. In addition, special thanks go to Bob Elder, Vrnda Chaitanya, and Catherine Badura for their help in reviewing page proofs.

Introduction

As half of the human race, women have always been "making" history, yet their part in building Western civilization has been largely invisible. Until very recently, in fact, school and college courses and texts in the humanities, social and natural sciences, and the arts rarely mentioned women. Generations of students studied the activities, achievements, and ideas of men without realizing that the story was incomplete.

Why were women missing from our books and curriculum? And was their absence important? In the mid-1960s and early 1970s when some students and scholars began to question the invisibility of women, they met with widespread surprise that the question had even been raised. Women, the explanation went, were missing because they had not shaped major historical events and they had contributed little of significance to culture. Their lives revolved around the details of domestic routines and family concerns, whereas men dealt with matters of public import. There were, certainly, some exceptions, but those women were so rare and so exceptional that their visibility simply underscored the general rule.

To many of the scholars who began their professional careers in the 1970s, such explanations seemed highly suspect. This new generation included many women who owed their careers to the women's movement which had forced the removal of barriers that had long restricted women's access to graduate programs, academic positions, and male-dominated professions in Europe and North America. (In North America, it also included minorities who had benefited from the expanding Civil Rights movement.) These female scholars suspected that the real reason women were missing related to perspectives and assumptions of the male scholars who wrote and taught history. They also knew that women's (and minorities') historical invisibility had provided a rationale for their exclusion from an entire range of leadership positions, professions, and creative endeavors. The absence of a "female" Beethoven, Leonardo da Vinci, Shakespeare, Aristotle, or Einstein, for example was often cited as proof that women were incapable of producing great works.

WHAT IS HISTORY?

Not surprisingly, many challenged the traditional claims of scholarly objectivity and joined others in questioning the idea that written history was an accurate, complete record of events. History is not some abstract "Truth"; rather it is only what is recorded, interpreted, written, and disseminated as "history." It is the product of persons who have the education and resources to "write" history. It reflects their judgments regarding what and who is important, and the concerns of society as they experience it. History also reflects the interests of those who support its writing and dissemination. Until very recently, the "written history" of Western civilization has been almost exclusively *androcentric* or male-centered and *ethnocentric*. That is, it has been written and supported by men of the privileged class and has reflected their experiences and values.

REDISCOVERING AND RECREATING WOMEN'S HISTORY

Knowing this, the new scholars concluded that women's history needed to be told. Like their male colleagues and predecessors, these academic women drew on their life experiences and personal interests as well as the concerns and values of their generation and culture as they selected topics of inquiry and framed the questions that guided their research and teaching.

Scholars dedicated to research on women's history found evidence of talented women who were highly respected during their lifetimes. Proof of women's cultural contributions consisted of art, music, and literary works by women and a wide variety of artifacts discovered or re-analyzed by historians, archeologists, and anthropologists. Evidence was also abundant in records of male contemporaries who corresponded with women or wrote about them and their work. Early "histories," in fact, turned out to be important sources of information about women's activities, as did well-known texts by men whose works comprised the canon of Western civilization. As more scholars joined the search and documents became more widely accessible (in translations, microform, and databases for manuscript collections), it became evident that the "exceptional" women in Western culture were not such anomalies after all.

PATTERNS AND THEMES IN WOMEN'S HISTORY

The evidence gathered in the last three and a half decades has revealed some intriguing patterns. Clusters of creative women or women who fostered cultural developments, for example, turned up in unexpected places. Some time periods, geographical locations, and/or societies known for significant male achievements seemed to produce few women of note. In contrast, evidence of significant female creativity and leadership often appeared in times and geographical places not commonly thought of as culturally vibrant.

References to prominent women often disappeared from the historical record and their works vanished. Sometimes a once-famous woman was forgotten, then rediscovered as much as a century or more later, only to disappear from history again until her more recent "recovery" in the late twentieth century. Occasionally, when a woman's work was rediscovered, it was attributed to a male contemporary while she remained invisible. Experts sometimes pronounced work signed by a woman as a plagiarism or a fraud perpetrated by the discoverer. Typically, however, creative women were omitted from the historical record on the grounds that their works were inferior to the works of men or failed to address topics of "universal" concern.

We also find that, despite their virtual absence from the historical record as creators and artists, women were quite visible as subjects or objects of male attention through much of Western history. Women appear in the dramas, literature, art, songs, legal codes, and religious and philosophical treatises written by men far more frequently than they appear in person as performers or creators of these cultural artifacts. In many documents, men seem preoccupied with a need to define the differences between men and women. They focus on women's physical attributes, mental and moral limitations, and their societal roles. Indeed, the "woman question" has been a persistent theme in male discourse throughout Western history.

Finally, although men and women shared much in common, it is evident that their life experiences, perspectives, and creative contributions often differed, sometimes dramatically. Women's creative endeavors frequently addressed different topics, gave a different slant to a popular theme, used a different language style, or exhibited a different vision of the world. Women often pursued their creative work and exercised leadership within a very different context than men. Women also relied upon different support systems and created separate institutions and networks. Even as they perpetuated and supported existing societal values and structures, women often voiced discontent and disagreement with prevailing standards. In both direct and indirect ways, they challenged male depictions of women and restrictions on women's lives and opportunities. Through their work, many also sought to discover and tell their own history.

GENDER AS A PRIMARY COMPONENT OF SOCIAL ORGANIZATION

The patterns summarized in the preceding section reveal the centrality of a more fundamental pattern in Western civilization: the role of gender as a major element of social organization and determinant of human experience. One of the major contributions of the new scholarship of the last 30 or more years has been to advance our understanding of the complex ways in which gender (intersecting with social class, ethnicity, race, and religion) shapes human experiences and serves as a central organizing principle in human culture.

Gender is a social construct. It is how a particular group or culture defines the roles of males and females based on their biological sex. Gender roles vary from culture to culture and also vary over time within cultures. Particular circumstances and societal needs may bring temporary changes in how gender is constructed, as when women fill male jobs during wartime. The rigidity of gender roles and definitions of gender may also fluctuate from time to time. Wrenching societal changes often produce pressure for rigid adherence to prescribed gender roles, whereas prosperity and security permit more flexible roles.

The social construction of gender roles and ideology does not necessarily mandate a particular gender structure. Some societies or organizations construct a complementary system of gender where, though the duties of men and women might differ, all are regarded as of equal importance. Others, in contrast, construct a hierarchical social order in which one sex is deemed innately inferior to the other and the roles and activities of the dominant sex are naturally believed to be more important. Gender-based power relationships may also undergo periodic changes within a given society.

In *Creating Women,* as the title suggests, we examine women's contributions to Western civilization from prehistory to the present through primary sources. Focusing primarily on the cultural aspects of Western civilization, the anthology documents the roles and achievements of women in religion, art, music, drama, dance, discourse, and literature and their impact on Western cultural traditions as patrons and leaders. Equally important, we also examine the ways in which Western societies "created" or shaped women by their definitions of womanhood and prescribed gender roles.

In selecting the documents for the anthology, we have sought to include a broad sampling of the rich evidence that demonstrates women's varied and significant contributions to culture. We have also included selections that illustrate the complex relationships between men and women that affected female creativity: their friendships, partnerships, and collaborations; familial ties; and rivalries and conflicts. In addition, we have included some of the works by men that were instrumental in creating and perpetuating images of women and gender ideology that inhibited female creativity and women's full participation in society throughout much of Western civilization. Above all, we have selected documents that bring women's voices to life. Through the documents we learn about female experiences, what women thought about their work, their creative processes, their dreams, self doubts, and frustrations. We learn how they negotiated their multiple social roles, as well as their class, race, ethnic, religious, and gender identities, and how they defined and created their own institutions and support systems. We also learn how women themselves often helped perpetuate traditional notions of gender. Finally, we learn much about women's resistance, as we see how some women challenged societal barriers and developed a feminist critique of Western patriarchal values and a vision of a new and more inclusive society.

We hope that you will share the excitement we felt as we discovered the fascinating women who appear in the pages that follow—that you, too, will be moved by their lives, their struggles, and their work, and be inspired by their courage and achievements to follow your own dreams, however impossible they might seem to be. It is our dream that you, in turn, will tell others about these women and strive, as so many of them did, to ensure that the work of our foremothers is passed on to the generations to come. Perhaps you will rediscover others yet unheralded and restore them to their rightful place in human history!

INTRODUCTION TO VOLUME ONE

Volume One is divided into three parts and covers a chronological framework that extends from ca. 35,000 B.C.E. to ca. 1500 C.E. Texts included in Volume One represent the most expansive geographic and chronological scope in *Creating Women,* and the most diverse and complex methods for analyzing the materials that are presented. Among numerous challenges that emerged in formulating materials for Volume One, a few are noteworthy to the reader.

Our commitment to beginning our inquiry into prehistory, at the genesis of human culture, has meant that for earliest human communities where symbol systems had not yet been formalized into a written language (e.g. Neolithic Anatolia), images of art, iconography, and artifacts are presented as texts. We also elected to devote considerable attention to the earliest societies that meet traditional criteria as historical, especially in Ancient Near Eastern Mesopotamia. Selections that were written by women in the Ancient Near East have customarily been available only to scholarly specialists. Many of these texts are fragmentary, and require considerable contextualization from secondary sources, but they *are* texts penned by women and thus are indispensable to the historical record of women's contributions to culture. Parallel evidence for so many texts written by women does not emerge again until the early Middle Ages of the Common Era nearly four thousand years later.

One further note concerning challenges in designing Volume One pertains to Religion as a featured category for highlighting women's contributions to culture. Since the Enlightenment, and especially in the past century or so, to the extent that history has come to identify itself as a *social science,* religion has received only a cursory address in historical analysis. Religion is among the first social institutions in human culture, and, for good or ill, it is *the* social institution in which there exists the most extensive, hard evidence of women's participation and contributions to culture from prehistory to the Early Modern period.

Each of the three parts in Volume One is preceded by an introduction that places primary source selections in historical and cultural context. Part I of Volume One explores Paleolithic and Neolithic Old Europe, Neolithic Anatolia, the Ancient Near East, Egypt, and texts from the Hebrew Bible.

Part II addresses texts and images from the Mediterranean basin that are representative of Minoan Crete and ancient Etruria. It concentrates principally, however, on texts by and about women from Greece and Rome through the Hellenistic period. Part II concludes with texts from Hellenistic Judaism. The ordering process adopted for materials representing such diversity and scope is quite simple. Reading selections within each chapter in Parts I and II are organized as representative of such fundamental categories as: Social Organization, Legal Status of Women, Religion, Women in the Aristocracy, and Women Outside the Aristocracy, in order to facilitate clarity. This organizational structure also permits the reader to observe distinct and decisive differences among women's experiences across cultures and across the centuries.

The focus in Part III is on women in the Early Roman Empire, Christian Origins, and Late Antiquity in the Greco-Roman World and in the Middle Ages in Western Europe. The final chapters in Volume One serve as a precursor to Volume Two. The reader will notice that for various reasons discussed in this introduction, Volume One is characterized as *expansive* and Volume Two is *intensive.* These last five chapters mark the transition. In Part III of Volume One, we encounter a rich profusion of texts written by women. The elemental categories used in Parts I and II are abandoned. Readings in Chapters 12 through 15 of Part III bring the reader into social and historical contexts that are more familiar as representative of *western* civilization. The individual selections emerge from various genres and are arranged along lines of thematic interests within discrete chronological periods. Each major selection is prefaced with an introductory paragraph which discusses particular themes and provides biographical data where available. Smaller selections include a brief introductory comment. Suggestions for further reading are included at the end of most chapters throughout the volume.

PART I

WOMEN IN PRE-HISTORY
AND THE ANCIENT NEAR EAST

Part I of Volume One is by far the most *expansive,* geographically and chronologically, in this two-volume anthology. In Part I we investigate women's contributions to culture in Paleolithic and Neolithic Old Europe, Neolithic Anatolia, the Ancient Near East, and Egypt and texts from the Hebrew Bible. The time line for Part I extends from ca. 35,000 B.C.E. to the fifth century B.C.E. A few comments about the perspectives advanced in Part I clarify our intentions for this first section of *Creating Women, An Interdisciplinary Anthology of Readings on Women in Western Culture.*

The advent of the social sciences in the mid-nineteenth century marked the beginnings of extensive research among scholars and social scientists in Western civilization to determine what can be known about the history of *Homo sapiens sapiens* (one who knows that she or he knows). Succeeding generations have broadened and deepened insights into our past. *Eurocentric* culture is based upon Western European intellectual, social, political, economic and religious values. It is based on a patriarchal pattern of social organization characterized by the dominance of a male perspective. Scholarship throughout Western civilization has, thus, also been advanced from a perspective that was *androcentric* (male centered). During the last quarter of the twentieth century in particular, however, research and scholarship about pre-history began to emerge that suggests a far more balanced picture of early human existence. The process of incorporation of such new perspectives into the *canon* (texts representative of dominant cultural norms) and knowledge that is *traditioned* (handed down) to future generations is often met with resistance. In a book designed to present interdisciplinary texts about women in the Western culture, however, it is important to begin specifically by considering research on women in the earliest human communities.

Any discussion of women in prehistory needs to note at the outset that an increasing number of articles and books on the subject have been published in the recent past in both scholarly *and* popular literature. These books and articles represent viewpoints shaped by a variety of academic disciplines and different ideological perspectives, including the history of religions, art history, depth psychology, classics, archaeology, anthropology, history, and feminist spirituality. Formal conversation across these disciplines that would encourage in-depth assessment and critical analysis of scholarly findings in this area of inquiry could be immensely helpful and will, hopefully, be forthcoming in the future. In the interim, many students and scholars/educators do not discern the complexity of the situation and many choose neither to examine nor to evaluate hypotheses advanced during this ongoing process of discovery. We suggest that scholars and educators who inform themselves of current theories about prehistory, with an understanding that they emerge from diverse ideological perspectives, will recognize their value for a more comprehensive understanding of human origins.

Part I of Volume One begins in the Upper Paleolithic, ca. 35,000 B.C.E. In Chapter 1, "Paleolithic, Neolithic, and Proto-Historic Cultures," we discuss archaeological and anthropological evidence for women's contributions at one of the earliest points in the cultural record of our species and mark transitions in the human experience as agriculture became the primary mode of subsistence. Evidence is demonstrated for women's contributions and participation in Neolithic Old Europe and Anatolia. In Chapter 1 we present some of the representative findings recently proposed by scholars concerning women from pre-history to proto-history. We introduce "texts" in the form of archeological artifacts, images, and *mobilary art* (art that can be transported) that emerged from cultures characterized in our interpretive framework as predominately *egalitarian,* with equal rights and privileges across lines of gender, and *matrifocal,* with cultural emphasis focused on the female. Lines of descent were not through the father as they are in the West in the present day but through the mother (*matrilineal*). The most detrimental event for women's participation in pre-historic culture began ca. 3500 B.C.E. to 2400 B.C.E. as egalitarian social-organizational patterns in Neolithic societies began a gradual transition to a *patriarchal* (male dominant) model.

Chapter 2, "Ancient Near Eastern Mesopotamia: The Religious Context," and Chapter 3, "Ancient Near Eastern Mesopotamia: The Social Context," on women in ancient Mesopotamian societies, address transformations in culture that are stimulated by increased population, urbanization, and the understanding of property as private that culminate in patriarchal models of social organization. Reading selections about women in Ancient Near Eastern and Egyptian civilizations offer compelling insights into women's experience as transformations in social institutions occur. Transformations in social, economic, and political spheres gradually uprooted and supplanted egalitarian models of social organization that had prevailed for millennia.

These transformations are first described in literature and artistic imagery from about 3200 B.C.E. in Mesopotamia in the Ancient Near East. Chapter 4, "Ancient Egypt," addresses women in Egypt in the Dynastic periods beginning ca. 2500 B.C.E. and Chapter 5, "Ancient Israel," reviews texts about women from the Hebrew Bible written from ca. 1000 B.C.E. Historical and cultural contexts for writings from the complex societies in which they emerged are discussed in detail in their respective chapters.

A principal theme throughout Parts I and II of Volume One is the significance for women's experience of the model of *social organization* adopted within a particular society. In earliest cultures *religion* functioned as an organizing and ordering framework in society. As time went on, however, transitions and transformations are observed in this pattern. Political agendas, the concepts of property as private, women as property, the institution of slavery, emphasis on military might, among numerous factors, shaped dominant models of cultural organization. We identify the impact on women's lives of these significant transitions both in the move toward the institutionalization of patriarchal cultural norms and in the resistance to those norms.

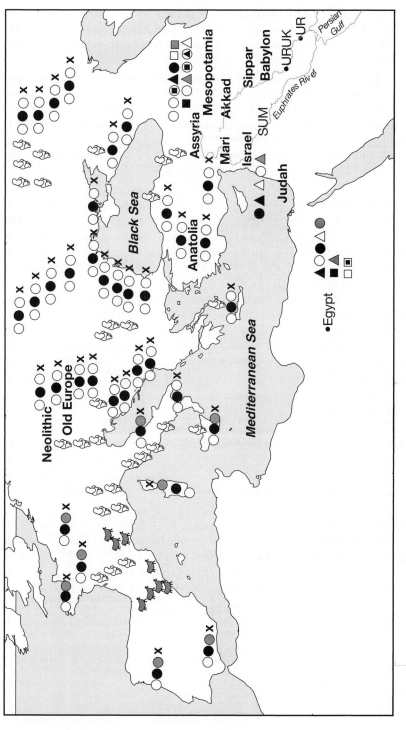

Female Entrepreneurs □

Female Poet ▣

Females in the public sphere ▣

Female Slaves ■

Females of the Aristocracy ▲

Females Outside the Aristocracy △

Female Merchants and Artisans ▲

Educated Females ◉

Hetairae/Courtesans ◭

Zoomorphic and Anthropomorphic 🐂

Female Agriculturalists ✕

Female Deities ○

Female Priests ◉

Female Religious Functionaries ●

Map 1–1

Time Lines and Constituents of Culture

Archaeologists suggest dates for at least 100,000 B.C.E. before homo sapiens appears in Europe. Earliest artifacts designated as art in Upper Paleolithic Old Europe are dated between 35,000 and 25,000 B.C.E. Chronological designations for culture groups, and acquisition of various skills in the Neolithic periods discussed in Chapter 1 moved from East to West and vary from location to location beginning in ancient Anatolia (modern day Turkey) and across the European continent). Chart material for Chapters 2–5 relates to Patriarchal cultures in the Ancient Near East and Egypt, and provides names of women represented in texts in these cultures (*attested in sources that appear in this book).

Upper Paleolithic Old Europe 35,000 to 10,000 B.C.E.	Neolithic Anatolia 6,000-4,500 B.C.E	Ancient Mesopotamia. ca. 3,400-1,700 B.C.E	Dynastic Egypt ca. 3,100 1,200 B.C.E.
Social Organization Egalitarian, nomadic, nonmilitaristic	**Social Organization** egalitarian, matrifocal, matrilineal, matrilocal, nonmilitaristic	**Social Organization** Patriarchal, patrilocal, patrilineal, stratification: male and female high priests, kings, military elite, merchants, artisans, serfs, slaves.	**Social Organization** Patriarchal, monarchy, scribal "class" for palace and temple. Social stratification: less emphasis on military, some gender equity in certain
Subsistence hunting and gathering, division of labor by gender (gathering mostly by women, hunting mostly by men).	**Subsistence** Nonhierarchic division of labor by gender. Agriculture developed by women, herding by men. Both men and women domesticated animals, bartered and traded.	**Named women in the Aristocracy** *Queens and Princesses* Kubau, Nin-netabarre, Bara-irnun, Ku-Baba, Summuramat, Naqui'a, Adad Guppi, Sibtu,	spheres (laws, property ownership). **Women in the Aristocracy** *Female Kings* Meryt-neith, Nitocris Sobeknofu, Hatshepsut, Nefertiti,Twosret.
Technology Women created tools such as slings and baskets, constructed clothing, and protected spaces for base camps, tools of stone, bone, and wood.	**Technology** Site suggests *city-planning* (ca.6,000 residents at its zenith). Constructions of mud-brick dwellings, walls of plaster. Women created jewelry, cosmetic items, kilim tapestries,	*Governor's Wife* Inibsina **Royal Concubines** Addu-duri	*Queens* Queen Ankhesenamun, Queen Tiye, *God's Wife* Ahmose-Nefretary, Hatshepsut
Religion Reverencing of zoomorphic and anthropomorphic *fertility* as female in ritual, art, and symbols.	textiles, and ceramics. **Formal Religion** Mother Goddess, Mistress of Animals, Maiden Goddess, Bucrania (bull horns–male and female fertility),	**Law Codes** Specify rights of women in all strata of society **Formal Religions** Pantheons emerge for Goddesses and Gods. *Principal female deities:	Nefrure, Nitocris, Princess Ankhnesneferibre **Formal Religions** *Principal Female Deities:* Ma'at Cosmic Principle of Order/
Mesolithic and Neolithic Old Europe 9,000-3,500 B.C.E.	Androgynous deities, shrines, priestesses, and their grave goods. Myths, rituals, and symbol systems. Images relating to birth, death, and rebirth.	Inanna and Ishtar. Large Temples are the hub of major cities; palaces emerge later. **Myths, Rituals, Sacred texts, Symbol systems, and Female**	Wisdom, Neith, Isis, Hathor. **Sacred Texts, Myths, Rituals, and Female Religious Functionaries** Educated (Priests and) Priestesses.
Social Organization Egalitarian,matrifocal,matrilinal, matrilocal, nonmilitaristic, permanent villages, and towns. Multiple cultural groups spread from East to West.	**Proto-History to ca. 3,400 B.C.E.**	**Religious Functionaries** *High Priestess-"En/Entu"* Enheduanna *Priestesses-"Ugbabatu"* Sippirtum, Inibsina, Tasuba,	Female singers, musicians, dancers, and scribes. **Women Artisans Merchants, Serfs, and Slaves** Attested in poetry, legal contracts,
Subsistence Ca.5,500 B.C.E. Agriculture developed by women, herding by males. Both fished, bartered, traded, and domesticated animals,	**Social Organization** Shift begins toward patriarchy; patrilocal, patrilineal family structures. Property comes to be considered private. Defense of	Ummiya *Consecrated women-* "Naditu"Aja-Belet,matum, AjaSitti, Aja-Talik, Aja Taribu, Aja Tillabi, Awat Aja, Belti-Aja,	literature, archives, epigrams, and lists. **Ancient Israel ca. 1,800-550 B.C.E.**
Technology Constructions of thatch, wood, and stone; many villages and towns are *planned;* making of tools for subsistence; women create *linear band* ceramic in jewelry. Travel by water and land.	property leads to armed combat. Cultural diversity and a move toward social stratification increases. **Subsistence** Same as Old Europe. Greater division of labor according to gender.	Eristi-Aja, Sat-Aja, Serikti-Aja, Aia-belet-nisi, Aja-rimtu, Aja-kuzzub-matim,Aja-ka-gi-na **Women Prophets, Hierodules** *Women Scribes* Sat Aja, Nin Azu, Mana, Amat	**Social Organization** Patriarchal, nomadic, confederacy, monarchic. Shifts radically over centuries. *Women Of The Patriarchs* Sarah and Hagar, Rebecca, Rachel Leah, and Dinah.
Formal Religion. Goddess creates, wields death, and regenerates. Labyris was a tool for farming, later used to symbolize transformation. Goddess represented in zoomorphic and anthropomorphic	**Technology** The same as Old Europe, but accommodates greater diversity of culture groups. Proto-writing system highly stylized.	Samas, Amat –Mamu *Named Woman Poet* Enheduanna *Women Entrepreneurs* Hussutum, Iltani, Ibni Samas,	*Women In The Aristocracy* Queens Bathsheba, Maacah, Jezebel, Athaliah, Esther, Princess Tamar, **Formal Religion**
vessels, mobilary art, and visual art. Elaborate symbol systems celebrate and reverence all aspects of life. Temples and priestesses, rituals, myths and symbols of fertility, grave goods. Symbols evolve into proto-writing system.	Formal Religions Number of "specialized" deities increase. Myths of the Goddess transformed to incorporate heroes, sons of the Goddess and her consorts as Gods.	Amat-namu, Inanna-amamau **Women Artisans Merchants, Serfs and Slaves** Mentioned by occupation in Law Codes	Myth, Ritual, The Holy in Sacred Texts: *Hochmah: Divine Wisdom; Female at Creation Gen. 1 and 2. *Female Religious Functionaries and Prophets* Miriam, Deborah, Huldah Wise Women of Tekoa and, Abel; Hierodule: Gomer

Chapter 1

Paleolithic, Neolithic, and Proto-Historic Culture's

PALEOLITHIC OLD EUROPE

Present research indicates that the hominid species *Homo sapiens* that is a precursor of our species emerged in Africa between 400,000 and 200,000 B.C.E. Artifacts from archaeological research indicate that their *traditioning* (handing down) and transmitting of customs, knowledge, and patterns of behavior that constitute culture are traceable for many thousands of years. Our species probably emerged around 130,000 B.C.E. By at least 40,000 B.C.E., in what is now modern-day Europe, *Homo sapiens sapiens,* or one who knows that she or he knows, had all but supplanted the Neanderthals (*Homo erectus*). We have evidence in Old Europe during the Upper Paleolithic for the creation of art between ca. 40,000 and 35,000 B.C.E. In this chapter we investigate vestiges of the art and culture of *Homo sapiens sapiens* that represent women's earliest contributions to humanities in Western culture. We intend our discussion of women in the Upper Paleolithic to provide a context for the artifacts and images related specifically to the female. Because there are no formal *written* texts from the Paleolithic and Neolithic to aid our understanding, the artifacts and images in Chapter 1 are presented as our available *texts* for this period of pre-history. To facilitate us in comprehending early human beings, we have arranged intensely interrelated information into four distinct but overlapping categories: social organization, subsistence, technology, and religion.

SOCIAL ORGANIZATION

Scholars have advanced various theories to suggest what the social organization of our earliest human ancestors might have been. For many years "Cave Man" or "Man the Hunter," and an understanding that all tribal groups were dominated by males, were characteristic descriptions. Scholarship on the Upper Paleolithic has advanced significantly in recent years and includes rigorous analyses of evidence from the period. These data are also cross-referenced with current primate studies and with intensive analysis of contemporary tribal peoples. The gender-inclusive field studies conducted by primatologists, archaeologists, and anthropologists that inform current scholarship on the Upper Paleolithic make clear that the issue of social organization among our earliest human ancestors poses far more

Figure 1–1   Cave painting of a pregnant cow found in Lascaux, France. *Art Resource, N.Y.*

questions than answers. For example, where evidence for divisions of labor along lines of gender is apparent, this information does not indicate patterns of dominance on the basis of gender.

Among the few tribal peoples in the present day whose subsistence is based on foraging, anthropologists sometimes discover clothing differences according to gender, and different tools according to different tasks, nonetheless contemporary foragers have equal status within their communities. Egalitarian models of social organization, with no hierarchical stratification on the basis of gender, prosper among foragers because all adult male and all adult female members in the group, which may number as few as 10 or 12 adults and their offspring, are equally important to the group's survival. Anthropologist Margaret Ehrenberg suggests examples of how this equality works out in daily life.

In lieu of the term *matriarchal* (Greek: *mater* means mother; *arche* means "head" or "authority") that in current parlance translates as female dominant, we use the term *matrifocal*. For several reasons this word, that is translated as *"women focused,"* more clearly depicts prepatriarchal, egalitarian social organization than does women's dominance. In the Paleolithic all higher primates, including Homo sapiens, among whom the relationship with the mother is the central relationship in the lives of her offspring, could be designated as matrifocal. Dependency on the mother is not limited to physical nurturing in infancy and early childhood, but persists into strong relationships among siblings and their mother up to and including adolescence. Some theorists suggest that before the domestication of animals, women's capacity to bleed regularly and not die and their ability to re-create the species endowed the female with *mana,* a supernatural power. This theory assumes that few cognitive

Figure 1–2   "Woman of Willendorf", ca. 30,000-25,000 B.C. *"Venus of Willendorf", c. 30,000-25,000 B.C. Limestone. H. 4 3/8 in. Naturhistorisches Museum, Vienna.*

connections would have existed in the Paleolithic between the incidence of sexual intercourse and the occurrence of pregnancy.

The term *matrifocal* is also instructive in the discussion that follows about the significance of fertility, in all of its aspects, among earliest expressions of human religiousness. Suggestions that our human ancestors were matrifocal and traced lines of descent through the mother are founded on the number of matrifocal cultures among present-day tribal peoples.

Chart 1–1   Ehrenberg's Theory on Egalitarian Social Organization among Foragers

1. All can put forward suggestions and have them considered. Individual decisions are respected.
2. Special skills or knowledge or wisdom are acknowledged until they are no longer viable.
3. There is no private property.
4. There is a fairly fixed division of labor between the sexes in subsistence tasks, especially on the provision of food.
5. Women provide as much or more labor as men, have equal knowledge of the territory and contact with other people. Their importance as food producers and bearers of the next generation is greatly appreciated. Females are as important as males.

Data adapted from Margaret Ehrenberg, Women in Pre-history *(Norman and London: University of Oklahoma Press, 1989), p. 65.*

SUBSISTENCE

Ninety percent of humans in the Paleolithic were foragers. The isolated, remaining hunting and gathering societies in the present day are a vital resource for anthropological studies and provide a basis for theories about earliest foraging peoples. Scholars today recognize that numerous factors, especially those dictated by natural disasters and variations in the environment, required adaptations to various ecosystems and sources of subsistence over thousands of years. At times these factors may have helped determine the patterns or models of social organization adopted by individual tribal groups. Data available from research among present-day hunters and gatherers suggest obvious parallels with customs and practices shared among hunters and gatherers in the distant past. Anthropologist Margaret Ehrenberg points out that for insights into the Upper Paleolithic in Europe, studies of the Inuit habitations provide valuable comparisons. Similarly, indigenous !Kung and Australian habitations are comparable to the East African Paleolithic, and Mbuti pygmies would be similar to hot phases of the inter glacial Mesolithic (Ehrenberg, 1989, 50–51).

When studies of foraging societies in the present day are brought together with data from archaeological studies of Paleolithic sites, new insights emerge concerning women's participation in culture. Among hunting and gathering peoples we now understand that gathered foods constitute between 60 and 80 percent of the diet. Females and children, and among some tribes also males, are responsible for gathering roots, berries, legumes, nuts, fruit, wild cereals, and grains. The ingenuity of converting these "raw materials" into edible foods as well into "teas" and poultices used for medicinal purposes would have been the responsibility of those who were gatherers. Whereas customarily studies of contemporary hunter-gatherers show that females are responsible for gathering and males for hunting, it is important to note that there are tribes in which both males and females are engaged in hunting. In the early Paleolithic, scavenging available portions of meat from kills made by larger predators most likely constituted "hunting." This form of hunting was done by both females and males until, over several thousand years, more strategies and tools for hunting evolved. At this point hunting became more dangerous and women of childbearing age ceased to participate. It is interesting to note, however, that among the Agata (Philippines) women continue to hunt with men. Australian indigenous women gather, but they also hunt small game and kangaroos with small dogs that they have trained. These indigenous women in Australia sometimes also hunt and fish with males (Ehrenberg, 1989, 53–55). It is also not uncommon that all members of a tribe might be engaged in fishing and the acquisition of mollusks, clams, frogs, and the like from the streams, lakes, rivers, or ocean within a particular habitat. Archaeological excavations, for example, found fish hooks buried with both males and females in Scandinavia.

TECHNOLOGY

Ancient and present-day tribes whose subsistence is based on gathering and hunting find shelter in natural caves and rock shelters or construct a lean-to that is adequate for foraging within a particular region. According to Udo Hirsch, there is evidence for primitive constructions that provided shelter from the elements among our hominid ancestors in southern France as early as 300,000 B.C.E. (Hirsch, Vol. III, 1989, 2).

Evidence of technology developed for long-term storage and preservation of foods is characteristic of a sedentary lifestyle that begins in the Neolithic. Among gatherers on the other hand, slings and containers used by women for carrying gathered foods and for holding infants on the mother's front or back constitute important technological advancements for hunters and gatherers. Containers used for food storage, such as reed baskets, and sticks and axes for digging and severing branches are vital technological

Figure 1–3   Forager woman gathering honey.
Library of Congress

contributions within communities of foragers in the present, and by inference and analogy also in the past. Containers permit gathering for the group instead of self; food and water can be taken to home base where constant sharing of foods invites living in larger and regular social groups. (Ehrenberg, 1989,55)

RELIGION

All religions include a concept of the Holy, creation myths and sacred stories, rituals, symbols/symbol systems, sacred functionaries (male and/or female shamans, prophets, sages, priests), and worshiping members of a community (*cultus*). The following discussion considers evidence for the presence of each of these categories in the Paleolithic.

The Holy

There have been numerous theories to explain the source of religion in the human community. It is important to state at the outset that no theories on this topic are definitive. Many early theories tended to be reductionistic. Recent explanations, on the other hand, become more plausible the more inclusively and cogently they represent human experience rooted in the context of physical, social, and cultural environment. The following hypothesis incorporates elements of several current theories concerning religion in pre-history. These theories suggest that in pre-history, fertility, a power of the abundant production of offspring of flora and fauna, was consciously and subconsciously associated with human hopes and fears about the past, the present, and future existence. Although as human beings we are always dependent upon nature for our continued existence as a species, it is difficult, especially from perspectives shaped in an urban environment, to imagine the immediacy and urgency of dependence upon nature for all of our needs, each day, throughout a lifetime. The continuation of life depended (and still does depend!), literally, upon fertility. We can never know with certainty the interior fears, longings, expectations, joys, or sorrows of another human being. Certainly no one can presume to know the interior life of Paleolithic Homo sapiens and how these women and men related to their environment. It is possible, however, to surmise that, over time, our human ancestors recognized that they possessed neither the power to ensure fertility nor the power to control natural disasters. Yet they experienced consciousness of the need for provisions and protection. Most scholars who address this subject consider it highly unlikely that early Homo sapiens made connections between sexual intercourse and human fertility until the domestication of animals in the Neolithic period. For this reason many scholars consider that certain art and artifacts from the Paleolithic represent the earliest expressions of human religiousness and the quest to identify a source of provision and protection. Although much scholarly debate continues to surround questions about pre-history, increasing evidence of art and artifacts from the Upper Paleolithic lends credibility to the hypothesis outlined earlier for the origins of early forms of religious expression. Continued research promises to yield significant insights into this compelling dialogue. A synopsis of theories suggesting that human religiousness originated among men and women in the Paleolithic is based upon assumptions about their increasing consciousness of aspects suggested in Chart 1-2.

Chart 1–2   Synopsis of Contemporary Theories for Origins of Human Religiousness

1. The need for fertility, including human offspring and fertility in nature, was recognized essential for survival.
2. The power to ensure fertility in all of its aspects did not reside within human communities.
3. Over time, people came to appeal to a source of power, outside themselves, that they hoped would ensure their continued survival.
4. The female in each species within their ecosystem was the bearer of life.
5. Symbol systems developed that represent female fertility in the form of images that were *zoomorphic* (forms of animals important for subsistence within the tribe, e.g., bison, mammoth, mountain lions, birds, serpents) or *anthropomorphic* (such as the Woman of Willendorff). The symbol systems also included abstracted markings of female fertility such as triangles, V's, chevrons, ovoids, zigzags, and wavy parallel lines.
6. Representations and abstractions of the fertile female associated with the source/power of fertility were *perceived* in pre-history in a manner that corresponds to what a contemporary Westerner might refer to as sacred.

Symbol Systems

Mobilary art (an art object) that can be carried in one's hand or portaged easily is most strikingly represented by images of the female figure that, like the Woman of Willendorf, have large breasts, and large bellies and thighs. (See Figure 1-2.) Such images are found in prehistoric sites around the globe and may indeed relate to earliest religious traditions that venerated fertility. If this is so, the theory suggests, figurines of the pregnant female represented an abstraction for *all* fertility that came to be considered holy and were among the earliest expressions of the Great Earth Mother Goddess.

If fertility comes from the "earth as mother" then caves and caverns are symbolically situated inside the mother, in the womb of the mother. Many cultures buried the dead within the earth as a symbolic return to the mother. In this context it is hypothesized that early burials sprinkled with *red ochre* (a red pigment that symbolized the blood of life) and accompanied by *cowerie shells* (shaped like the entrance to the birth canal) suggested themes of life, death, and rebirth. Similar symbolic significance is suggested for the magnificent paintings of pregnant cows, mammoths, bison, and horses discovered inside caves in Western Europe at Lascaux, Chateauneuf-les-Martiques, Cova Fosca, Chauvet, et al.; and scholars discuss these paintings in the context of religious ritual. (See Figure 1-4.) A rudimentary symbol system related to fertility that first emerged in the Upper Paleolithic is also evidenced in representations of eggs, vulvas, triangles, and wavy lines representative of the water of life. These symbols were inscribed on rocks, walls of caves, entrances of caves and on implements used for hunting.

Myth and Ritual

There were no written texts as a source for religious myth and sacred stories in the Paleolithic period. It is possible, however, that the cave paintings at Lascaux and at other caves in southwestern Europe from the Paleolithic and Mesolithic provide evidence of religious ritual. It is interesting to note that the ritual caves were not used as dwelling places; rather, most scholars who address the issue have assumed that these caves were reserved for ritual celebrations. (See Figure 1-5.)

Religious Functionaries

The image of a masked human figure at Lascaux may indicate the presence of a religious functionary, that is, a person who is formally engaged in religious ritual in the person of a male or female Shaman. The sacred *work* of a Holy Woman is ratified by the community. This person serves as an intermediary between

Figure 1–4   Cave painting, from Lascaux, France, of a horse and a pregnant cow. *Pearson Education/PH College*

Figure 1–5   Women in ritual dance. *© 1991 by Marija Gimbutas. Reprinted by permission of HarperCollins Publishers Inc.*

the Holy and the human community and often also functions as a transmitter of myth in oral tradition, ritual, and healing arts. It may indeed be that a *shamanic* figure led ritual dances or dramas within the decorated caves to appeal to the zoomorphic "Power" or "Source" that was embodied in the bison, mammoths, and horses. The likelihood of this theory for assuring continued fertility is especially viable considering the large number of pregnant female mammals represented in the cave paintings.

NEOLITHIC OLD EUROPE

The Mesolithic or Proto-Neolithic Period (ca. 10,000-8,000 B.C.E.) discussed earlier in this chapter marks the transition from the Old Stone Age. Subsistence patterns of hunting and gathering are superceded by the advent of the Neolithic period when agriculture became the primary mode of subsistence. It should be understood that this transition was gradual and that it occurred at different periods in different locations. By as early as ca. 8,000 B.C.E., however, the transition to agriculture was established in some locations. The following pages present evidences for commonalities in culture in Neolithic Old Europe, an area that comprises much of Eastern Europe and extends south into Macedonia and Greece. We shall also consider site-specific data from Catal Huyuk in Mesolithic and Neolithic Anatolia (present-day Turkey). Substantial evidence and archaeological data provide significant insights about women's contribution to and participation in culture in the Neolithic period.

The development of agriculture, the chief defining characteristic of the Neolithic, is recognized as one of the most significant technological developments in human history. Scholarly consensus supports the position that women had a critical role in the transition to agriculture as a primary mode of subsistence. Our interest here is to investigate available data concerning women's participation in Neolithic

Chart 1–3   Summary of Functions and Images of the Neolithic Great Goddess

A. LIFE-GIVING, DEATH WIELDING, REGENERATION (lunar: rising, dying, self-renewing)

I. "Giver of All": Giver of life and health, foreteller of spring, increaser (or decreaser) of material goods, and protectress of human and animal life and household

1. Birth-Giver
   a. Anthropomorphic Giver of birth
   b. Primeval Mother in the shape of bear, deer doe or elk doe
2. Giver of Life Water and Health
   a. Standing stone (menhir) as epiphany of the Goddess, guardian of life water
   b. Vessel: anthropomorphic or bird-shaped. Aquatic images ("parallel line square Goddess" and others)
3. Spring and Future Foreteller
   a. Young (Artemis type) Goddess
   b. Spring birds: cuckoo, oriole, swallow, lark, dove
4. Increaser (or Decreaser) of Material Goods and Happiness
   a. Water-fowl/woman hybrid
   b. Epiphanies: duck, goose, crane, swan, stork, snake
   c. Sacred animal: ram
5. Embodiment of Life Energy, Healer, and Regenerator, Protector of Household
   a. Serpent-woman
   b. Crowned or horned snake
   c. Genii or penates of household, humans and animals in the shape of snakes or phallic men
6. Protectress of Young Life
   a. Nurse (carrying a pouch), hunchback figurines
   b. Madonna (holding baby), both anthropomorphic and zoo-pomorphic (bird, snake, bear)

II. Death Wielder

1. Death Foreboder and Killer
   a. Vulture-woman, owl-woman, snake-woman
   b. Epiphanies: owl, raven, crow, other birds of prey; boar, white dog, poisonous snake
2. Death Goddess
   a. Bone (bone phalange with or without owl eyes)
   b. Anthropomorphic Stiff Nude "White Lady" sometimes with bird of prey or snake features
   c. Frightening mask (with features of a poisonous snake), antecedent of the Gorgon head

III. Regeneratrix

1. As Regenerative Vulva
   a. oval or seed-shaped
   b. triangle
   c. axe
2. Anthropomorphized as:
   a. triangle with breasts
   b. hourglass-shaped with vulture's/owl's feet or hands
3. As Regenerative Uterus
   a. zoomorphic shape: bucranium, fish, frog, toad, hedgehog, turtle, lizard, hare
   b. anthropomorphized as fish-woman, frog-woman, hedgehog-woman
4. As transformed into:
   a. bee, butterfly or moth, usually portrayed rising from the head or between the horns of a bull
   b. anthropomorphic bee, butterfly and other insects
5. As Life Column: In the shape of aquatic column (wavy lines, concentric arches), vertically rising snake, phallus or tree, associated with or flanked by symbols of becoming (uteri, horns, spirals, crescents, a moon cycle, dogs, he-goats, ithyphallic men)

Adapted from Marija Gimbutas, Language of the Goddess, *Harper San Francisco, 1989, 328–329.*

culture. We are also interested in the implications of female iconography and various images of the female, both *zoomorphic* and *anthropomorphic,* for the expression and transmission of this culture. In discussing the Paleolithic we looked first at Social Organization and Subsistence. Discussion of Neolithic Old Europe, however, begins with Religion, which, we suggest, functions specifically as an organizing/ordering framework in Neolithic society. We will then look at Social Organization and Subsistence.

Theories developed by archaeologist Marija Gimbutas influence several aspects of our discussion of Old Europe in the Neolithic. Her extensive research as an anthropologist and archaeologist in Old Europe over a 40 year period included an interdisciplinary approach that incorporated comparative mythology, linguistics, early historical sources, folklore, and historical ethnography. A number of Gimbutas's hypotheses concerning Neolithic culture are challenged by more conservative archaeologists who study the period. Our decision to include Gimbutas' theoretical perspectives is precisely that her research on Old Europe provides the most *comprehensive* analysis of the archaeological data that are available at this point. This is especially true of her attention to and analysis of female imagery and iconography, some of which is referenced in the following pages.

RELIGION

Intensification and expansion of evidence for Mother Earth as the Great Goddess that flourished in the Neolithic has been acknowledged by scholars of Western civilization since the nineteenth century. In Volume One of *Creating Women,* the implications of recent scholarship on religion in pre-history, approached from a *gynocentric* or female-centered perspective, challenge traditional views of religion from the past and the present. We consider in what ways investigation of The Holy, Myth, Ritual, Symbols and Religious Functionaries enhance understanding of women in Neolithic Old Europe following the model for religion in our discussion of Paleolithic Old Europe.

The Holy

It is important to recognize that in preliterate cultures no distinction between religion and secular (nonreligious) life exists as it does in Western culture in the present day. Living in dependence upon, and acknowledgment and appreciation of, the Sacred is characteristic of preliterate peoples. Just as in the Paleolithic we discussed the Sacred in terms of *zoomorphic* (animal form) and *anthropomorphic* (human form) manifestations, both forms, and abstractions that incorporated combinations of the two are found in expressions of the Great Mother Goddess in Old Europe. One factor that differs distinctly, however, is that *zoomorphic* images now incorporate features of the human female. In *Language of the Goddess,* Gimbutas' classification of the essence and functions of the Great Goddess proposes the categories noted in Chart 1-3, Essence and Functions of the Great Goddess (Gimbutas, 1989, 328–329). Varieties of artifacts at all Neolithic sites suggest that the female, symbolized in images that were *zoomorphic* and *anthropomorphic* as well as abstract combinations of these forms, represented the source of fertility in a manner that in the present day would be equated with the Holy/Divine. A Great Mother Goddess was the most common expression of this source and she was the subject of formal religious worship including shrines and temples, female priests, sacred vessels, rites, and rituals.

Ritual

Temples and shrines constructed in Neolithic Old Europe to celebrate and revere the Goddess were a central social force. Models from temples in various culture groups indicate a tradition of temple

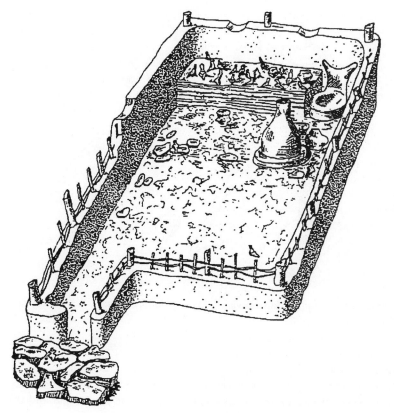

Figure 1–6   Reconstruction with ovens in the courtyard. © *1991 by Marija Gimbutas. Reprinted by permission of HarperCollins Publishers Inc.*

building that began in the seventh millennium B.C.E. The reconstructions provide considerable examples of architecture, furnishings, and various religious activities associated with the Temples/Shrines.

Religious Functionaries

Reconstructions of a temple and the grounds surrounding the temple suggest that much time and energy were devoted to religious activity among female religious functionaries who supervised the preparation and performance of rituals. These women would have served as transmitters of myth, legend, ritual, custom and tradition. Artifacts discovered in close proximity to the Temples/Shrines suggest the production of religious equipment and votive gifts, grinding of grain and baking of sacred breads, pottery used for rituals, and the creation of sacred masks and vestments.

Myth

Sacred stories among peoples in the Neolithic would have been transmitted in oral tradition. It is possible that some of the legendary and mythological figures who comprised their heroines, heroes, and deities had origins in sacred stories of earlier times that were transmitted over the millennia. Fertility

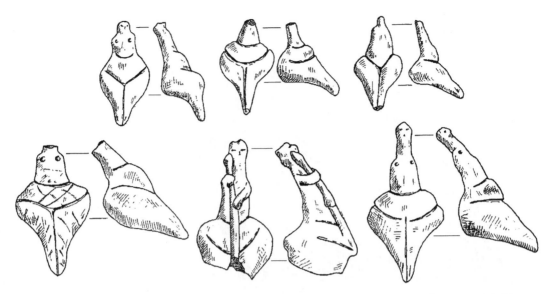

Figure 1–7   Female figurines found in the temple of Sabatinivka. © *1991 by Marija Gimbutas. Reprinted by permission of HarperCollins Publishers Inc.*

themes of life, death, and rebirth are an integral feature of the symbols and symbol systems in Neolithic Old Europe. In the Neolithic the association of the earth as mother is explicit not only in subterranean caves, but also in many subterranean graves designed to imitate the birth canal and the womb. Many graves are sprinkled with *red ochre,* the red pigment assumed to be associated with lifegiving blood.

Symbol Systems

It is important to recognize that earliest efforts in the modern period to decipher and translate ancient Egyptian hieroglyphs and Ancient Near Eastern cuneiform tablets demanded the development of strategies, techniques, and technologies. It also involved the systematic assignment of symbolic significance to carved or incised pictures and figures called "glyphs" that had been generated in the context of ancient temples, tombs, or the court. Basic vocabularies were identified and then decided and agreed upon by scholars as they observed relationships among symbols. Decisions were established by scholars about what was meant, or inferred, by particular patterns and groupings of glyphs. Among current studies of pre-history, tensions and disagreements arise in the face of data that could radically transform present understandings about the early development of writing. Among the most radical speculations under review at present is evidence to suggest that a "pictorial script" was embedded in the religion of the Old European Great Goddess. Marija Gimbutas contends that signs, symbols, and images of zoomorphic and anthropomorphic divinities are raw materials for reconstructing a model of the lifestyle and the world view in Neolithic Old Europe (Gimbutas, 1989, xxii; 1991, 303–320.) Gimbutas analyzes the symbols preserved in the actual artifacts and suggests that they constitute "the grammar and syntax of a kind of meta-language by which an entire constellation of meanings is transmitted. They reveal the basic world view of Old European culture."

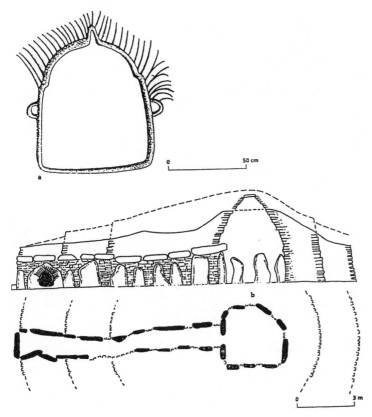

Figure 1–8   A womb–shaped tomb. *© 1991 by Marija Gimbutas. Reprinted by permission of HarperCollins Publishers Inc.*

She proposes that the symbols can best be understood in their own context and grouped by their inner coherence. The symbols constitute a complex system in which every unit is interlocked with every other. Gimbutas suggests that these systematic associations indicate the extension of the Goddess religion as a cohesive and persistent ideological system.

SOCIAL ORGANIZATION

Analysis of grave goods in Old Europe supports the thesis that social organization was *egalitarian* (equality in social, economic, and political affairs). Neolithic societies were *matrifocal* throughout Old Europe and the acquisition and distribution of material goods appears to have been *egalitarian* and was constituted along lines of age rather than gender. In addition to women's participation in the religious sphere, and in agriculture, evidence for women's participation in culture from Neolithic Old Europe is apparent in a variety of contexts. Arguments for the persistence of *matrifocal* lines of descent include evidence from historical, nonIndo-European cultures in the regions that made up Old Europe. There was, in the early Neolithic, apparently no stratification of classes of rulers and laborers but, rather, a comfortable "middle class" which arose as a result of metallurgy and trade. Division of labor between the sexes was demonstrated by differences in grave goods, but Gimbutas contends that, even though culture was *matrifocal*, in Old Europe superiority of one sex

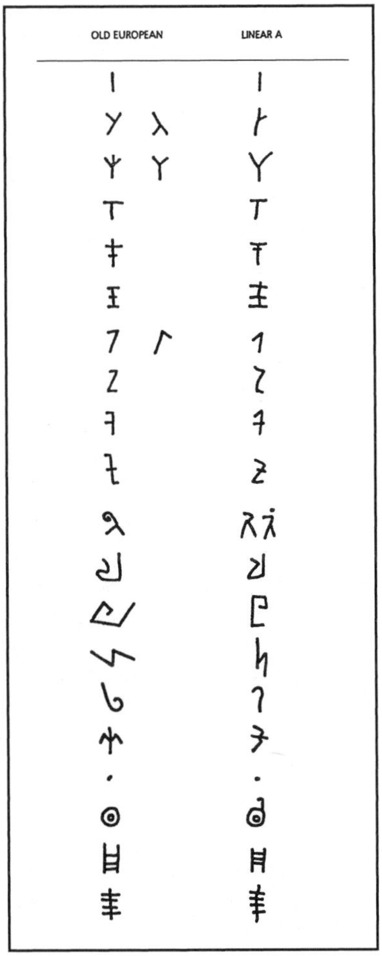

Figure 1–9   Parallels between Old European and Linear A symbols.
© 1991 by Marija Gimbutas. Reprinted by permission of HarperCollins Publishers Inc.

in relation to the other is absent. In Old Europe, as the division of labor within villages became increasingly complex, responsibilities in healing arts such as midwifery and specialists in making poultices, medicinal teas, etc., may have become increasingly diversified. From the time that sheep and goats were domesticated, female grave goods included spindles and loom weights suggesting that the creation of textiles became the province of females. Grave goods of both males and females included jewelry and tools; gender designations are not specified among specialists in metallurgy for the creation of tools and jewelry.

SUBSISTENCE

In the previous section on the Paleolithic we discussed the role of women as the primary gatherers within societies of hunters and gatherers. Over thousands of years, gatherers would have observed which edible plants grew in specific locations within their particular ecosystems. They would have had to learn in what regions a particular root could be found and in what particular locations, for instance, in sunlight or shade, under rock shelters or among particular types of mosses. Gatherers would have observed when, during different seasons, various edibles in their ecosystem would achieve the most desirable stage of maturity for human consumption for various uses. For example, certain herbs can be poisonous during a particular stage of their maturity but when picked at another stage can be used effectively for medicinal purposes.

Scholarly agreement that women were responsible for the development of agriculture is based upon the skills and observations required in their role as gatherers. Differing versions of the following premise support the hypotheses: at some point between 10,000 and 8000 B.C.E. women collected seeds for grains and cereals, planted the seeds at their "home base," observed their growth cycles, harvested the grains and cereals and then used the seeds to plant again. Over time it became apparent that various crops could be planted and cultivated. The development of technology to cultivate a sufficient number of crops for sustaining their communities through annual weather cycles made it possible to adopt a sedentary lifestyle. As the semi-nomadic lifestyle required by foraging was abandoned the first villages and towns were established. The size of villages and towns ranged from 50 to 300 households (Hirsch, 1989, Vol. III, 7). Toward the end of the Neolithic and into the Copper and Bronze Ages towns had up to 4,000 persons and sometimes more.

In many villages agriculture was supplemented by fishing, occasional hunting, and, as the domestication of animals increased, animal husbandry and herding. The development of textiles and metallurgy prompted trade and the beginnings of commerce. The earliest trade connections are known from Anatolian obsidian found in Jericho from around 9000 B.C.E. (Hirsch, 1989, Vol. III, 4) There is little evidence for *martial* (warlike) activity or fortifications at early Neolithic sites discussed here; rather, data suggest considerable production, trade, and commerce among Neolithic peoples from the seventh and sixth millennia B.C.E. into the Bronze Age, ca. 2400 B.C.E.

NEOLITHIC ANATOLIA

The archaeological site at Catal Huyuk from ancient Anatolia in Asia Minor is situated in present-day Turkey and is among the most exciting Neolithic projects under excavation in recent times. The first excavations were directed by James Mellaart beginning in 1961.

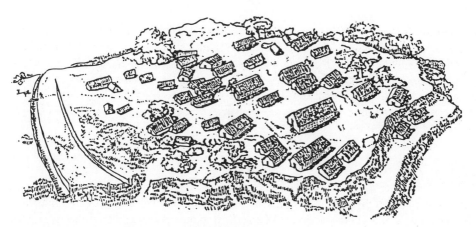

Figure 1–10   Reconstruction of a village from the Vinca culture. © *1991 by Marija Gimbutas. Reprinted by permission of HarperCollins Publishers Inc.*

His approach to the part of the site that he excavated, and that of his colleagues who have addressed the continuing excavations, shapes the perspectives advanced here. Current research at Catal Huyuk has expanded to include several different parts of the site and researchers explore a variety of different perspectives in their analysis of data. Far more questions than "answers" emerge about this fascinating project.

As the time line for habitation of ancient Anatolia suggests, there have been several cultural influences in this region. Focus for the present chapter extends from the earliest habitation in the Proto Neolithic, ca. 9000 B.C.E., which was *aceramic* (wooden and stone vessels) with hunting as a primary mode of subsistence.

In the Neolithic period, culture was sustained primarily by agriculture, and ceramics were introduced ca. 6500–6000 B.C.E. down through ca. 5500 B.C.E. This site is significant for the study of women principally because of women's crucial participation in, and defining of, culture throughout the centuries the site was inhabited. *Cultural continuities* (e.g., earliest strata reveal images of hunting; some images of the Goddess are the same as those in the Paleolithic) and *discontinuities* (e.g., more complex division of labor and implied high status of women) are noted in the move toward urbanization among the communities that inhabited Catal Huyuk. In the areas excavated by Mellaart the evidence from burials suggests *matrifocal* emphasis, *matrilineal* descent and the higher status of women, especially in the religious sphere at Catal Huyuk. Note that Catal Huyuk, a community covering 32 acres, sustained transitions from the time that hunting was an integral part of subsistence to what can most appropriately be called a city with extraordinary economic and cultural diversity.

RELIGION

The Holy

At Catal Huyuk additional and more complex abstractions of the Mother Goddess appear than we observed in Old Europe. Within 40 shrines excavated by Mellaart there were some 35 different iconographic or sculpted anthropomorphic representations; many of these images were unquestionably female.

Many images, however, though identical in contour, shape, size, outline, substance, and cultic context to representations of the Great Goddess, had neither breasts nor pubic triangle. These images appear

Figure 1–11   Early hunters at Catal Huyuk. *James Mellaart*

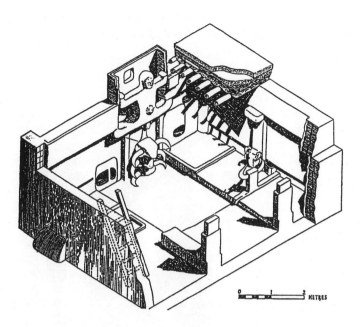

Figure 1–12   Shrine of the goddess giving birth. *James Mellaart*

to be abstractions of the female, although the possibility exists that they may also have been intentionally abstracted as *androgynous* (male and female combined). Numerous *bucrania* (head of a bull with horns) can be interpreted as representing both the female womb and fallopian tubes of the female as well as the fertility of the male. Female images include representations of the Goddess as Mother giving birth.

Male fertility is represented almost exclusively in zoomorphic iconography by horns and heads of bulls. Most shrines incorporate different combinations with the Goddess/Androgyne and *bucrania* as

Figure 1–13   Goddess with hair flying in the wind. *James Mellaart*

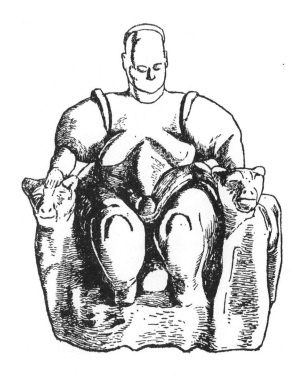

Figure 1–14   Goddess seated on a throne flanked by leopards. *James Mellaart*

the focal and primary images. Some shrines include the Goddess/Androgyne and *bucrania* in concert with images of animals. Themes of life, death, and rebirth abound at Catal Huyuk as they do throughout all of the *matrifocal* cultures that characterize the Neolithic period.

Myth

Symbols of life, death, and rebirth embodied in the Mother Goddess from Anatolia are attributed to the Goddess Cybele in later times in Hatti culture during the first millennium B.C.E. Sacred stories about Goddesses such as Cybele, her consort Attis, and their themes of *life, death,* and *rebirth* occur throughout the Ancient Near East, Greece, and Egypt in historic periods. During the Roman Empire worship of Cybele constitutes a major *Mystery Religion* (see Chapter 11, "The Roman Empire") associated with the dying and rising divinity.

Ritual

Of 139 dwellings that were examined in early excavations by Mellaart's team, 40 were designated as shrines. Iconography (images and artistic renderings that are incised, in relief, and/or painted on surfaces) and artifacts within the shrines speak boldly to the matrifocal orientation at Catal Huyuk. Traditions of the Great Goddess that are apparent in the Paleolithic survive at Catal Huyuk (including a Goddess flanked by lions that may be the earliest form of the Goddess Cybele) as do new and different artistic representations.

Texts selected in this Reader that represent extant sources for women's contributions to culture in the earliest historic societies proceed almost exclusively from writings and the arts among women associated with the religious *cultus* (worshiping community) and, after societies became socially stratified, women among the nobility.

Religious Functionaries

At Catal Huyuk it is grave goods and an analysis of the religious cultus that most emphatically attest to women's agency as participants in the cultus as priestesses and other religious functionaries.

Based upon evidence from graves, shrines, and the art and artifacts excavated by his team of archaeologists, Mellaart advanced compelling arguments for the status of women at Catal Huyuk. Burials at Catal Huyuk occurred in two stages: first *excarnation* (removal of flesh from bones) and then burials of the bones that had been polished and placed under the platforms within the dwellings. Excavations of graves conducted by Mellaart's teams at Catal Huyuk reveal a significantly greater number of female burials in relationship to male burials. Red ochre burials occur only in shrines and are virtually all female remains. Grave goods in shrine burials were not the richest but were marked by differences that imply ritual significance. For example, green pigment and azure blue pigment were applied around the neck of females and one male in shrines (at two levels of the excavation). Two objects that occur only in shrines are finely polished mirrors of obsidian (found at two levels) and bone belt-fasteners, possibly connected with ceremonial leopard dress. Mellaart suggests that these were presumably used by priestesses (and priests) and would explain their rarity and their discovery in shrines. Fine flint daggers and spouted stone vases also appear only as gifts in shrines or with the few male burials beneath shrines (Mellaart, 1967, 227).

In burials beneath houses the grave goods tend to consist of items used in daily life irrespective of the sex of the person buried. There are vast differences, however, in the intricacy and richness of grave gifts along lines of gender. Female burials included cosmetic sets that had a small spoon, a fork, and a pallette. There were also shells filled with red ochre, ointment sticks of bone, baskets with rouge, obsidian mirrors, and jewelry, including necklaces, bracelets, armlets, anklets of beads of a large variety of stones, shell, clay, animal bones, and teeth and beads of copper and lead. (Mellaart 1967, 228–229) Finger rings, amulets, and pins made of various substances are sheathed in copper, tools are less frequent but include awls for sewing, bodkins for basketry work, knives, and hoes. Female children were also buried with necklaces, pendants, and rings but had no other grave goods. (Mellaart, 1967, 228–229) Male burials include virtually no jewelry. Tools included maces, daggers, knives, flints for striking fire, a scraper, groups of arrowheads, and hooks and eyes for fastening belts. Metal in male burials is all but nonexistent. One male burial included a ceremonial dagger, a stone bowl, green paint, ointment sticks, and a bone scoop. (Mellaart, 1967, 200)

SOCIAL ORGANIZATION

At this point there are still many questions about social organization at Catal Huyuk. The principal issue is that with extensive excavation in progress considerably more information is needed before responsible theories can be advanced without qualification. Mellaart, however, affirms for the early excavations the significantly greater number of female than male burials at the site, and the importance of the female presence as administrators in the religious sphere and as priests. Innovations created and implemented by women in establishing agriculture and animal husbandry as the primary mode of subsistence assured the importance of their status. Reference to more extensive and elaborate grave goods in female burials also attests to women's status at Catal Huyuk. Yet, despite compelling evidence, it is still too early to verify the move from strictly egalitarian social organization to one in which members of the priestly class enjoyed a privilege of status related to the religious *cultus.* Burials under the female sleeping platform and the richness of female burials demonstrate *matrifocality.* The present teams of excavators have proposed DNA testing of these skeletons to verify *matrilineage.* The relatively small size of the houses that have been excavated does not suggest matrilocal residence of large, extended families but some matrilocal pattern that permits for habitation of smaller groups.

The discussion about social organization at Catal Huyuk can also be enhanced by reference to Udo Hirsch's theory of a consciousness of "belonging together" and what he refers to as a "we" mentality (Hirsch, 1989, Vol. III, 7). It appears obvious that the small tribal groups in the Paleolithic possessed this consciousness. Hirsch argues, however, that the dramatic population increase that followed the transition to a sedentary lifestyle resulted in an intensification in the concept of "belonging together" within these larger groups. This "we" consciousness, Hirsch contends, would also have been experienced by members of one culture group in relationship to members of a "different" group suggesting the emergence and intensification of a "we/they" dichotomy. This concept becomes important when, at the close of the Neolithic, there is a flourishing in the emergence of cities throughout the Ancient Near East. (Hirsch, 1989, Vol. III, 9)

SUBSISTENCE

Over time, in addition to agriculture and animal husbandry, numerous industries developed. With the exception of what appears to be a "bakery" in the courtyard of the area excavated by Mellaart, other locations at the site housed the workplaces for metallurgy, stone industry, woodworking, woolen textile production, ceramic production, and the production of stone, copper, and gold jewelry. Trade and commerce would also have been conducted in a different part of the site. Catal Huyuk was a remarkable civilization and definitely marks a transition from the concept of village and town to the emerging concept of "city."

Among the most stunning aspects of Anatolian women's contributions to culture is the production of Kilim tapestries and rugs that were used to ornament and insulate shrines and houses where they were placed on the raised platforms used for sleeping, working, and conversation. These rugs were characterized by a color pallette dictated by berries, roots, and the like, available for making dyes in the region. Sacred myths and stories are depicted on the rugs with figures of ancient deities and symbolic images first generated ca. 7000 B.C.E. and passed down in culture from the Neolithic to the present day. Images discovered on walls at Catal Huyuk are the same images used on Kilim rugs that are exported from this same region today, seven to eight thousand years later.

Division of labor at Catal Huyuk became more complex as the site became more densely populated. It is suggested that as the site grew, inhabitants represented members from numerous and diverse tribal groups from diverse regions. This is an aspect of cultural development that points toward urbanization.

TECHNOLOGY

It is immediately apparent that Catal Huyuk was an orderly and very well planned settlement. Mellaart identified twelve successive building levels representing 12 habitation periods. Each building in this first "condominium" complex had its own walls and was hemmed in by the others. Dwellings were replastered continually on the inside and the outside to keep out damp and rain. The built-in furniture, walls, floors, and ceilings were coated with white clay.

Sections of the site excavated by Mellaart between 1961 to 1963 covered approximately one acre of the site and included houses and shrines that are primarily distinguished by wall decorations that indicate mythic and ritual themes. All habitations contained platforms and ovens and were accessible by ladders; the positions of the platforms, the oven, and the ladder never changed in the buildings at Catal Huyuk (Mellaart, 1967, 6). Movement from one part of a dwelling to another was through small

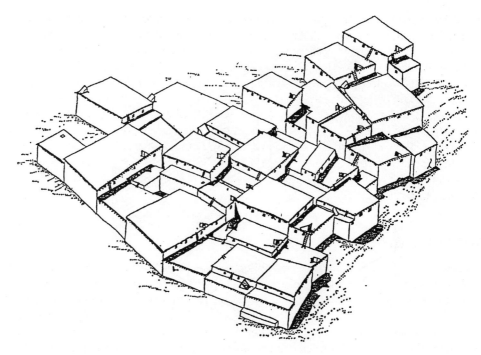

Figure 1–15 Reconstruction of an excavated site. *James Mellaart*

porthole-like doorways but with no doors. Each house or shrine usually also had storage spaces. Because each dwelling had its own walls, small openings for light and air were strategically placed under the eaves of outside walls. Disposal of waste products and sanitation were outside the dwelling proper, possibly in courtyards designated for that purpose. The interiors of houses and shrines were fastidiously clean. Shrines were inhabited, and it is probable that they were inhabited by members of the religious cultus. The platforms found in each house or shrine are the prototype for the Turkish sofa (and divan) and served for sleeping, sitting, and working. They are often covered with reed matting as a base for cushions, textiles, and bedding. Below these platforms the bones of the dead were buried.

Studying burial customs and grave contents, it has been affirmed that the small corner platform belonged to the male. The largest platforms were for females, and were located in a consistent position within both houses and shrines. Children's bones were buried with the females. Most compartments had two platforms but none had more than five. Mellaart suggests that families within a single dwelling consisted of fewer than eight people (Mellaart, 1967, 60).

THE PROTO-HISTORIC PERIOD

Proto-historic is a suitable term for identifying factors that characterize an astonishing number of transitions in human culture at the close of the Neolithic period. A principal objective here is to note how the convergence of these transitions impacted the lives of women. Our interest to identify, organize, and clarify what can reasonably be proposed is enhanced by recent theories and methods from anthropology and archaeology.

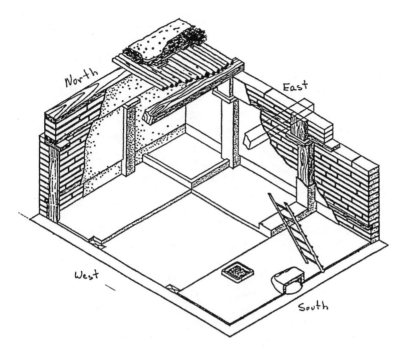

Figure 1–16   A drawing of an apartment with a ladder in place. *James Mellaart*

The single most significant factor for women's experience in the proto-historic period was the gradual transition in social organization from societies that were egalitarian, matrifocal, matrilineal, and matrilocal to patriarchal, patrilineal, and patrilocal societies. In the early twentieth century theorists J. J. Bachofen (1948) and Robert Briffault (1931) advanced hypotheses to explain these transitions. Since that time numerous theories have been suggested. It is very important to note at the outset of this discourse that no single theory is adequate. Relevant insights emerge, however, from reviewing prominent theories and assessing ongoing discoveries in several academic disciplines that address questions about prehistory. Chart 1-5 suggests the most significant factors that generated changes in social organization.

By the latter part of the Neolithic period, the distinctiveness, homogeneity, and self-sufficiency of the "we" consciousness that characterized the Neolithic began to shift to a different mode. In the tribal society of the early Neolithic village changes were necessitated by requirements that were internal to the

---

Chart 1–5   Changes in Social Organization

1. The hierarchical stratification of society based upon the use of power for dominance by those with accumulated wealth
2. Determination or understanding of acquired and/or inherited possessions as "private property"
3. Development of martial weaponry
4. Martial strategies to protect and expand private property
5. Dramatic rise in population
6. Move toward urbanization

Data adapted from U. Hirsch, vol. 3.

tribe. Decision-making processes must involve all of a tribe's members and the scope of change is limited. Udo Hirsch notes "as the most significant orientation guide, the 'we' feeling creates a belief in the uniqueness and validity of its value system among *all* the group's members." (Hirsch, 1989, 7) Economic factors in particular influence a shift to an "I" mentality that is characteristic of an urban society.

Many of the theories advanced to explain the radical shifts in social organization are related to developments in the economic sphere. The following scenarios represent some of the ideas that are proposed in present scholarship.

Scenario One

During the millennia of the Neolithic period, as hunting became less necessary, males became more consistently involved in advancing technologies for agriculture and animal husbandry. As production increased, some families used excess crops and goods to expand their holdings. The beginnings of an "I" mentality develop around an understanding of property as private and of a need to protect and expand private property. Females had value as producers of children who would become workers to further expand and inherit property. Weaponry that had been used for hunting and protection from predators was now used to protect private property from members of other tribes or villages/towns. The begetting of progeny increased potential of the work force for further accumulation of private property. Warfare and raids were conducted in which women were taken as property from "out" groups. These captive women were brought back to the villages of their captors, taken as wives, concubines, or slaves and used as workers and as begetters of children (a means of production). Increase in a mind-set of territoriality led to warfare to protect the "in group" and to prevail over an "out group."

Scenario Two

One of the theories that describes the transitions in social organization that took place by at least 3500 B.C.E. is based on evidence of several waves of invasions. Some *pastoralists* (subsistence from grazing of animals) have a lifestyle that is seminomadic. Males leave home base to graze cattle or sheep and are gone for long periods. Other pastoralists adopt a fully nomadic lifestyle. The invasion theory holds that nomadic peoples from areas that were peripheral to permanent agricultural settlements in Old Europe and the Ancient Near East were driven into these regions by numerous factors, including climatic conditions. The nomadic invaders were presumably martial peoples who used weaponry to overtake peaceful Neolithic settlements. Many of the invaders had domesticated the horse. The nomadic peoples worshiped a male sky deity and were organized socially on a *patriarchal* (male dominant) model with lines of descent *patrilineal* (through the father). Social stratification was on a strict hierarchal model and included a military elite. Over many centuries, as history attests, the male-dominant model prevailed.

Variations and combinations of the two scenarios outlined above provide helpful insights into the perplexing questions about transition in social organization from the Neolithic Period in pre-history into the period designated as historic. Numerous factors that inform questions about transitions in social organization from matrifocal to patriarchal continue to be discussed and debated. These debates raise provocative questions and suggest that further developments in this area of scholarship might introduce

Chart 1–6   Conditions for the Emergence from a "Basic culture" to "High culture"

1. A complex economy with broad natural resources and basic raw materials that leads to the emergence of professions within which rural and urban artisans are represented.
2. Barter replaced by professional trade, with currency as a value.
3. Society is stratified along class lines that represent particular economic and social pursuits.
4. The exploitation of human labor resources (including slaves) increases production with surplus appropriated by the power elite.
5. A society with an ideological foundation that reaches beyond the tribal unit and is capable of incorporating foreign ethnic characteristics.
6. The society often includes a warrior aristocracy.
7. There exists a binding legal order in which the authority of a central government prevails.
8. A penal authority replaces self-help, individual responsibility replaces collective responsibility.
9. The city is the center of action and integration, the seat of religion and political and religious authority and a corresponding civil service administration.
10. A polytheistic pantheon incorporates individual tribal deities, giving each a new name and a specific function. These names may relate closely to the deity's previous name and/or function.
11. In most cases there was also a corresponding hierarchy of female and/or male priests.
12. The new script or script substitute enabled the transmission of news and statistical involutions.

Data adapted from H. Nachtigall, Vokerkunde, *Stuttgart, 1979, 117–18.*

greater balance to an understanding of human history. As increasingly thorough analyses and substantive arguments are advanced it is important to guard against a tendency to posit one theory in distinct opposition to another; rather we do well to hold in a dynamic tension the variety of theories that emerge.

The move from a "we" consciousness to an "I" consciousness that is characteristic of urban culture in the historic period is generated in environments where a shift in culture from "Basic" to "High" culture can take place. Complexity and diversity of populations bring the need to tolerate diversity of ideas. It is during this period of cultural transitions that we also find the formalization of symbol systems into a "written" language whereby culture can be transmitted across lines of diverse cultural populations and to future generations.

H. Nachtigall (*Vokerkunde,* Stuttgart, 1979, 117–18) defines pre-conditions for the emergence from a "Basic culture" to "High culture" as seen in Chart 1-6.

At present the earliest records of texts in formalized and phoneticized written language are found in the city of Uruk in Ancient Near Eastern Sumer, at ca. 3200 B.C.E. Ancient Near Eastern Mesopotamia is the site of Chapter 2.

SUGGESTED READINGS

Barbar, Elizabeth. *Women's Work: The First 20,000 Years.* Norton Publishers, 1994.

Biaggi, Cristina. *Habitations of the Great Goddess.* Manchester, CT: Knowledge Ideas and Trends, 1994.

Claassen, Cheryl, and Joyce, Rosemary, editors, *Women in Pre-History in North America and Mesoamerica,* Philadelphia: Penn Press, 2001.

Ehrenberg, Margaret. *Exploring Gender Through Archaeology: Selected Paper from the Boone Conference.* Madison, WI: Pre-history Press, 1992.

Engels, Fredrick. *The Origin of the Family, Private Property, and the State.* New York: International Publishers, 1972.

Gero and Conkey. *Engendering Archaeology.* Oxford: Blackwell Publishers, 1991.

Marcus, Joyce. *Women's Ritual in Formative Oxaca: Figurine Making, Divination, Death and the Ancestors.* Ann Arbor, MI: University of Michigan Museum of Anthropology, 1998.

Ortner, Sherry. *Making Gender.* Boston: Beacon Press, 1996.

Valcarenghi, Dario. *Kilim: History and Symbols.* Translated by Huw Evans. Milan and New York: Electra/Abbeville Book, 1994.

Yakar, Clak. *Pre-Historic Anatolia: The Neolithic Transformation and the Early Chalcolithic Period.* Tel Aviv: Institute of Archaeology of Tel Aviv University, 1991.

Sources Cited

Skira, Albert, and Georges Bataille. *Lascaux; or the Birth of Art: Prehistoric Painting.* Austryn Wainhouse. Translateed by Lausanne: Skira, 1955; republished Cleveland: The World Publishing Co., 1962.

Ehrenberg, Margaret. *Women in Pre-History.* Norman and London: University of Oklahoma Press, 1989.

Gimbutas, Marija. *Civilization of the Goddess.* San Francisco: Harper, 1991.

_____. *Language of the Goddess.* San Fransisco: Harper, 1989.

Hirsch, Udo. *Environment, Economy, Cult and Culture,* Vol. III, in *Goddess from Anatolia,* James Mellaart, Udo Hirsch, and Belkis Balpinar, editors. Milan: Ezkanazi, 1989.

Mellaart, James. *Catal Huyuk: A Neolithic Town in Anatolia.* New York: McGraw-Hill, 1967.

Nachtigall, H. *Vokerkunde.* Stuttgart, 1979.

Chapter 2

Ancient Near Eastern Mesopotamia: The Religious Context

In the present day, despite numerous advances in women's status in society arguments persist about "woman's place." There is a vocal constituency throughout all social classes in Western civilization that continues to argue against the appropriateness of women in leadership roles in the government and in religious institutions. Chapter 2 and Chapter 3, "Ancient Near Eastern Mesopotamia: The Social Context," include more extensive text offerings than other chapters in Volume One. We include two chapters on the Ancient Near East precisely in order to address a large, representative number of texts that attest to women's agency as leaders and participants in the religious hierarchy and in government from the earliest written records in human history. Mesopotamian cultures under review in this chapter and in Chapter 3 include Sumer, Mari, Akkadia, Babylonia, and Assyria.

As populations exploded and the tendency to *urbanization* expanded at the beginnings of the Bronze Age, Mesopotamia, the land between the Tigris and Euphrates rivers had abundant natural resources to sustain the development of "high" culture. Over the centuries *patriarchal* social organization, described in the discussion on Proto-history, was established and institutionalized. The process, however, happened gradually over a long period of time and demanded a drastic reordering of foundational elements of culture. Texts we have selected from the earliest societies in the Ancient Near East exemplify transformations to the historic period and represent new political and religious realities.

Written sources for this chapter and the next include letters, hymns, financial records, poems, historical writings, wisdom texts, laws and epigraphic (inscription, especially on tombs or buildings) evidence. Selections in Chapters 2 and 3 attest that some women enjoyed alternative lifestyles that transcended boundaries of gender. Other texts indicate patterns of women's subjugation specifically on the basis of gender. Religion provided a principal component of continuity in transitions from Proto-history to the historical period and is the theme for Chapter 2. Foundational elements of religion, that had been primary in human culture for millennia, continued to function as an ordering process within the new societies. A second area of continuity from the past concerning women, in the beginning of transitions to a patriarchal ordering of society, is evidenced in the authority ascribed to female deities and to women's leadership roles in the religious *cultus*. The number, genre, and content of Ancient Near Eastern texts from earliest written records that are pertinent to religion are vast and varied.

We begin with readings from Ancient Sumer from ca. 3200 to 2300 B.C.E. Representations of the Female Principle of the Divine are among the most prominent in this oldest Ancient Near Eastern civilization that is characterized as having "high culture." Much of the literature from later Mesopotamian societies including Babylonia, Akkadia, and Assyria is based upon myths and stories from this earlier epoch.

A great deal of information included in this chapter, and the next, about women in early periods of human history has not previously been made available in formats outside the literature of the scholarly disciplines. Despite laudable progress in making scholarly information on this period available, especially through electronic media, much of the research on ancient texts from the Near East has not yet been made accessible in English and is not included in this reader. Some of the research describes and interprets ancient texts in scholarly publications but does not make available English translations of the texts that are described. Scholarly resources on the Ancient Near East also include books and articles that publish translated fragments of texts as examples of a type, circumstance, event, or relationship that is described in the author's narrative. In this chapter, and the next, we have included selections from a variety of sources, some of which are translated only in fragments. We also include readings in this chapter in which a contemporary scholar of women in the Ancient Near East discusses her research and her interpretation of her findings. Descriptive categories for various dimensions of religion become more complex as culture becomes more complex. We can, however, continue to use categories of The Holy, Myth, Ritual, and Religious Functionaries to situate the reading selections in this chapter.

RELIGION

The principal Sumerian cities of Uruk, Ur, Lagash, and Eridu were each constructed around a temple that was the center of worship. It is assumed that Uruk, the earliest city in Sumer, was inhabited from at least 4000 B.C.E. In the original Sumerian city-states the deity was understood to be the owner of the city-state, and the ruler as High Priest/ess served the deity as the intermediary between the deity and the people. The principle deity and owner of Uruk was the Goddess Inanna, Queen of Heaven; the temple and seat of worship was the Eanna, "The House of Heaven." (Hallo and Simpson, 1971, 44)

Texts selected about Inanna attest to the powerful cultural significance of this Goddess in patriarchal Sumerian culture. While many interpretations of this deity retain the integrity of a *matrifocal* perspective, it is instructive to note that interpretations of Inanna that correspond to a patriarchal agenda transform her myth.

The Holy/Myth

Among the significant rituals in the Ancient Near East, Egypt, and, later in Greece and the Mediterranean Basin, was the *hieros gamos* or sacred royal marriage. This ritual is integrally related to fertility with its life, death, and rebirth themes, and the dying and rising God themes that constitute one of the pervasive myths in the ancient world. We include the best-known sacred stories related to the dying and rising God in each major culture group discussed in Volume One. These sacred stories and the rituals in which they are reenacted are woven into the fabric of the societies from which they emerged. They are a way of expressing the vital significance of fertility for life in the human community, and in the life-sustaining crops and herds and fields. They provide explanation for the months when the ground lies fallow by identifying the king with the vegetation God, whose annual death, resurrection, and reunion with his spouse were accepted as doctrine.

Dumuzi was a historical Sumerian king whose death profoundly affected the theological thinkers of his day. According to the ancient sacred myth-makers, Dumuzi's wife, the Goddess Inanna, had relegated Dumuzi to the underworld because of his pride and ingratitude. When Dumuzi saw the error of his ways, Inanna decreed that he could spend half of each year on earth. The sacred marriage between Inanna and the king, as the resurrected Dumuzi, was celebrated in Sumer as the culmination of the New Year festivities. The king as the risen God and the Goddess who was his wife were sexually re-united, making fields and flowers and crops bloom and blossom once again. The concept of the immortality of the king is perhaps the most long-lasting legacy of the *heiros gamos* but in reading the following hymn of Inanna and Dumuzi consider as well the implications of the ongoing significance of fertility, celebration of human sexuality within a sacred story, friendship and nurture in the male/female relationship, independence in relationship, mutual respect across lines of gender, and some of the tensions between those engaged in herding and those in farming. This hymn was read/chanted at the equinox during the sacred marriage.

THE SACRED MARRIAGE OF INANNA AND DUMUZI[*]

. . . Inanna, at her mother's command, Bathed and anointed herself with scented oil. She covered her body with the royal white robe. She readied her dowry. She arranged her precious lapis beads around her neck. She took her seal in her hand. Dumuzi waited expectantly.

Inanna opened the door for him. Inside the house she shone before him Like the light of the moon.

Dumuzi looked at her joyously. He pressed his neck close against hers. He kissed her.

Inanna spoke

"What I tell you Let the singer weave into song. What I tell you, Let it flow from ear to mouth, Let it pass from old to young:. . .

Inanna sang: "He has sprouted; he has burgeoned; He is lettuce planted by the water. He is the one my womb loves best.

My well-stocked garden of the plain, My barley growing high in its furrow, My apple tree which bears fruit up to its crown, He is lettuce planted by the water.

My honey-man, my honey-man sweetens me always

My lord, the honey-man of the Gods, He is the one my womb loves best. His hand is honey, his foot is honey, He sweetens me always.

My eager impetuous caresser of the navel, My caresser of the soft thighs, He is the one my womb loves best, He is lettuce planted by the water."

Dumuzi sang:

---

*The Sacred Marriage of Inanna and Dumuzi, translated by D. Wolkstein and S.N. Kramer, Cambridge and San Francisco: Harper and Row, 1983, 30–51 excerpts.

"O Lady, your breast is your field. Inanna, your breast is your field. Your broad field pours out plants. Your broad field pours out grain. Water flows from on high for your servant. Bread flows from on high for your servant. Pour it out for me, Inanna. I will drink all you offer."

Inanna sang:

"Make your milk sweet and thick, my bridegroom. My shepherd, I will drink your fresh milk. Wild bull, Dumuzi make your milk sweet and thick. I will drink your fresh milk.

Let the milk of the goat flow in my sheepfold. Fill my holy churn with honey cheese. Lord Dumuzi I will drink your fresh milk. . . .

"The bed is ready!" She called to her bridegroom:

"The bed is waiting!"

I bathed for the shepherd Dumuzi,

I perfumed my sides with ointment,

I coated my mouth with sweet-smelling amber,

I painted my eyes with kohl

He shaped my loins with his fair hands, The shepherd Dumuzi filled my lap with cream and milk, He stroked my public hair, He watered my womb. He laid his hands on my holy vulva, He smoothed my black boat with cream, He quickened my narrow boat with milk, He caressed me on the bed.

Now I will caress my high priest on the bed, I will caress the faithful shepherd Dumuzi, I will caress his loins, the shepherdship of the land, I will decree a sweet fate for him."

The Queen of Heaven, The heroic woman, greater than her mother, Who was presented the me by Enki, Inanna, the First Daughter of the Moon, Decreed the fate of Dumuzi:

In battle I am your leader, In combat I am your armor-bearer, In the assembly I am your advocate, On the campaign I am your inspiration. You, the chosen shepherd of the holy shrine, You, the king, the faithful provider of Uruk, You, the light of An's great shrine, In all ways you are fit:

To hold your head high on the lofty dais, To sit on the lapis lazuli throne, To cover your head with the holy crown, To wear long clothes on your body, To bind yourself with the garments of kingship, To carry the mace and sword, To guide straight the long bow and arrow, To fasten the throw-stick and sling at your side, To race on the road with the holy sceptre in your hand, And the holy sandals on your feet, To prance on the holy breast like a lapis lazuli calf.

You, the sprinter, the chosen shepherd, In all ways you are fit. May your heart enjoy long days.

Ninshubur, the faithful servant of the holy shrine of Uruk, Led Dumuzi to the sweet thighs of Inanna and spoke: "My queen, here is the choice of your heart, The king, your beloved bridegroom. May he spend long days in the sweetness of your holy loins. Give him a favorable and glorious reign. Grant him the king's throne, firm in its foundations. . . .

Let his shepherd's staff protect all of Sumer and Akkad.

As the farmer, let him make the fields fertile, As the shepherd, let him make the sheepfolds multiply, Under his reign let there be vegetation, Under his reign let there be rich grain.

In the marshland may the fish and birds chatter,
In the canebrake may the young and old reeds grow high,
In the steppe may the mashgur-trees grow high,
In the forests may the deer and wild goats multiply,
In the orchards may there be honey and wine,
In the gardens may the lettuce and cress grow high, In the palace may there be long life. May there be floodwater in the Tigris and Euphrates, May the plants grow high on their banks and fill the meadows, May the Lady of Vegetation pile the grain in heaps and mounds.

O my Queen of Heaven and Earth, Queen of all the universe, May he enjoy long days in the sweetness of your holy loins."

The king went with lifted head to the holy loins. He went with lifted head to the loins of Inanna. He went to the queen with lifted head. He opened wide his arms to the holy priestess of heaven.

Inanna spoke:

"My beloved, the delight of my eyes, met me. We rejoiced together. He took his pleasure of me. He brought me into his house.

He laid me down on the fragrant honey-bed. My sweet love, lying by my heart, Tongue-playing, one by one, My fair Dumuzi did so fifty times.

Now, my sweet love is sated. . . .

The following selection is an example of a ritual supplication/appeal to a female deity by her female subject. Pudu-hepas is queen to Hattusilis in Hatti country. This land of the Hittites was formerly Anatolia. A Hittite queen such as Pudu-hepas was an official of the court as a partner with her husband, and shared with him administrative and cultic duties and rights. (Lesko, W E R, 1987, 44) She begins her prayer by identifying herself, her faithfulness to Arinna and to Hattusilis, the subject of her supplication. Pudu-hepas reminds the Goddess that she was "reared" by Arinna, implying that she has been devoted to her since childhood. The queen also promises to see that the worship of Arinna that was interrupted during the military siege will be restored among the people. She asks for the Goddess's intervention and protection for her husband.

Pudu-heppas' Prayer to Arinna the Sun Goddess[*]

To the Sun-Goddess of Arinna, my lady, the mistress the Hatti lands, the queen of heaven and earth. . . I Pudu-hepas, am a servant of thine from of old, a heifer from thy stable, a foundation stone (upon which) thou (canst rest). Thou, my lady, reardest me and Hattusilis, thy servant, to whom thou espousedst me, so closely associated with the Storm-God of Nerik, thy loved son. . .

[*Pudu-hepas recounts her profound faithfulness in her devotion to all of the Gods and Goddesses.*]

. . . thus we shall attend to the ordinances (and) celebrations due to you, the Gods. The festivals of you, the Gods, which *they* had stopped, the old festivals, the yearly ones and the monthly ones, they shall celebrate for you, the Gods. Your festivals,

*"Pudu-Heppas" Prayer, translated by Albrecht Goetze, *ANET,* 1950, 393.

O Gods, my lords, shall never be stopped again! For all our days will we, your servant (and) your handmaid, worship you.

[*Pudu-hepas makes her plea to Arinna*]

. . . Among men there is a saying: "To a woman in travail the God yields her wish." [Since] I, Pudu-hepas, am a woman in travail (and since) I have devoted my-self to thy son, yield to me, Sun-Goddess of Arinna, my lady! Grant to me what [I ask]! Grant life to [Hattusilis, thy serv]ant! Through [the Good-women] (and) the Mother-Goddesses [long (and) enduring] years (and) days shall be [given to him. . . . In [the assembly] of all the Gods request thou the life [of Hattusilis]! May [thy] re-quest be received with favor! Because thou, [Sun-Goddess of Arinna, my [lady], hast shown favor to me and (because) the [g]ood of [the land] and of its realm [is close to thy heart], thou shalt enjoy the reverent [worship] of [my family. Where[as I have now pacified] thy soul, Sun-Goddess of Arinna, my lady, hearken to what-ever I lay before thee in prayer on [this] day! [Do something] for this cause! Let not the Gods re[ject my] request. (Puduheppas'). . . .

Religious Functionaries

Before palaces and courts for monarchs were established, the seat of governance and administration of a city resided within the Temple complex. Even though tribal and kinship loyalties from the Neolithic were replaced by political loyalties, earliest sources for rulership in the Ancient Near East are traced to religion rather than military leadership. (Halo, 1971, 44) The myths and legal texts cite the role of *Entu* (High Priest: female) and *En* (High Priest: male). Sometimes females are also designated as En, which was the first attested royal title. The En or Entu held considerable power and influence consistent with the norms of the culture.

En, Entu : High Priestess

In the priestly class women served in various capacities that included En or Entu/High Priest and as fe-male priests, prophets, and *hierodules* (embodiments of sacred fertility), scribes, musicians, and other religious functionaries. The *Naditu* were women consecrated to a deity and also lived within the Tem-ple complex. Stratification within the Temples was ordered as follows: Temple elite, high officials, bu-reaucrats (e.g., record keepers). As the stratification continued there were blurring distinctions between state and private entrepreneurs, free laborers, conscripted laborers, and female slaves in large numbers for textile manufacture and grain milling.

Enheduanna, Entu of the God Samas, the daughter of Sargon, King of Akkad, discussed previ-ously, is the earliest female poet and scribe whose works we have in translation. Enheduanna, High Priestess of the Moon God, Nanna, devotee of the Goddess Inanna was later High Priestess in Inanna's own city Uruk. As of the present writing Enheduanna is the earliest named female poet in history. Her father Sargon of Akkad (ca. 2350 B.C.E) was the son of a High Priestess to Inanna and his successful victories at Ur and Uruk may indeed have owed something to the fact that he installed Enheduanna as High Priestess at Uruk.

In the hymns, Enheduanna petitions Inanna to restore her to priestly office from which she was removed during a coup against her father. Poems of Enheduanna have been translated into English since at least 1968, yet most students of history and humanities continue to be taught that Sappho of Lesbos, from the sixth century in Greece, was the first female poet.

THE HIGH PRIESTESS ENHEDUANNA'S HYMN TO INANNA[*]

THE EXALTATION OF INANNA

Inanna and the divine attributes

Lady of all the divine attributes, resplen-
dent light,

Righteous woman clothed in radiance,
beloved of Heaven and Earth,

Hierodule of An, (you) of all the great
ornaments,

Enamored of the appropriate tiara, suitable for the high-priesthood,

Whose hand has attained (all) the
"seven" divine attributes,

Oh my lady, you are the guardian of all
the great divine attributes!

You have picked up the divine attributes, you have hung the divine attributes on your hand,

You have gathered up the divine attributes, you have clasped the divine attributes to your breast.

Inanna and An (Heaven)

Like a dragon you have deposited
venom on the foreign land.

When you roar at the earth like Thunder,
no vegetation can stand up to you.

A flood descending from its mountain,

Oh foremost one, you are the Inanna of
heaven and earth!

Raining the flaming fire down upon the
nation,

Endowed with divine attributes by An,
lady mounted on a beast,

Who makes decisions at the holy command of An.

(You) of all the great rites, who can
fathom what is yours?. . .

Inanna and Mt. Ebih

In the mountain where homage is with-
held from you vegetation is accursed.

Its grand entrance you have reduced to
ashes.

Blood rises in its rivers for you, its people have nought to drink.

It leads its army captive before you of its
own accord.

It disbands its regiments before you of
its own accord. . . .

Inanna and Uruk(?)

Because the city has not declared "The
land is yours,". . .

You have spoken your holy command,
have verily turned it back from your
path,

Have verily removed your foot from out
of its byre. . . .

Invocation of Inanna

You of the appropriate divine attributes,
great lady of ladies,

Issued from the holy womb, supreme
over the mother who bore you,

Omniscient sage, lady of all the foreign
lands,

Sustenance of the multitudes, I have verily recited your sacred song!

True goddess, fit for the divine attributes, it is exalting to acclaim you.

Merciful one, brilliant, righteous
woman, I have verily recited your divine attributes for you!

The Banishment from Ur

Verily I had entered my holy cloister at
your behest,

I, the high-priestess, I, Enheduanna!

I carried the ritual basket, I intoned the
acclaim.

(But now) one has placed me in the
leper's ward, I, even I, can no longer
live with you!. . .

Let me, Enheduanna, recite a prayer to
her.

My tears like sweet drink

Let me give free vent to for the holy
Inanna, Let me say "Hail!" to her!. . .

[*]*Hallo*, COS, 1997, 519–21.

Oh lady, the (harp of) mourning is placed on the ground.

One had verily beached your ship of mourning on a hostile shore.

At (the sound of) my sacred song I am are ready to die.

The Indictment of Nanna

As for me, my Nanna takes no heed of me.

In murderous straits, he has verily given me over to destruction.

Ashimbabbar has not pronounced my judgment.

Had he pronounced it: what is it to me? Had he not pronounced it: what is it to me?

(Me) who once sat triumphant he has driven out of the sanctuary.

Like a swallow he made me fly from the window, my life is consumed.

In the bramble of the mountain he made me walk.

The crown appropriate for the high-priesthood he carried off from me.

He gave me dagger and sword—"it becomes you," he said to me.

Second (?) Appeal to Inanna

Most precious lady, beloved of An,

Your holy heart is lofty, may it be assuaged on my behalf!

Beloved bride of Ushumgal-anna

Of the heavenly foundations and zenith you are the "senior" queen.

The Anunna have submitted to you.

From birth on you were the "junior" queen.

Over the great gods, the Anunna, how supreme you are!

The Anunna with their lips kiss the ground (in obeisance) to you.

(But) my own sentence is not concluded, a hostile judgment appears before my eyes as my judgment.

(My) hands are no longer folded on the ritual couch.

The pronouncements of Ningal I may no longer reveal to man.

(Yet) I am the brilliant high-priestess of Nanna,

Oh my lady beloved of An, may your heart take pity on me!

The Exaltation of Inanna

That one has not recited as a "Known! Be it known!" of Nanna, that one has recited as a "Tis Thine!":

"That you are lofty as Heaven (An)—be it known!

That you are broad as Earth—be it known!

That you devastate the rebellious land—be it known!

That you roar at the land—be it known!

That you smite the heads—be it known!

That you devour cadavers like a dog—be it known!

That your glance is terrible—be it known!

That you lift your terrible glance—be it known!

That your glance is flashing—be it known!

That you are ill-disposed toward the defiant—be it known!"

That one has not recited (this) of Nanna, that one has recited it as a "Tis Thine!"—

(That,) oh my lady, has made you great, you alone are exalted!

Oh my lady beloved of An, I have verily recounted your fury!

The Composition of the Hymn

One has heaped up the coals (in the censer), prepared the lustration.

The nuptial chamber awaits you, let your heart be appeased!

With "It is enough for me, it is too much for me!" I have given birth, oh exalted lady, to (this song) for you.

That which I recited to you at (mid)night

May the singer repeat it to you at noon!

(Only) on account of your captive spouse, on account of your captive child,

Your rage is increased, your heart unas-
suaged.
The Restoration of Enheduanna
The first lady, the reliance of the throne-
room,

Has accepted her offerings.
Inanna's heart has been restored.
The day was favorable for her, she was
clothed sumptuously, she was garbed
in womanly beauty.

Contexts of Correspondence From Mari

A large number of the texts that follow in this chapter are derived from *Studies on Women at Mari*, by Bernard Frank Batto (Batto, 1974).

Excavations of the Middle Euphrates kingdom of Mari from the Old Babylonian period yielded numerous cuneiform tablets from the royal archives that tell us about women in politics and religion. The majority of these documents concern people in the aristocracy, and whereas references to women in the lower classes do give us insight into their occupations, they do not provide insight into their experience. The Mari documents of the Old Babylonian period are from the reigns of the Assyrian, Yasmah-Addu (1790–1779 B.C.E.) and Zimri-Lim (1745 B.C.E.), a local king.

Batto tells us that the position of women in the Old Babylonian period was far superior to that in the succeeding periods; ". . . [the] legal position of the woman at Mari was as good as women in Babylonia. Women had equal powers with men before the law in such transactions as adoption, loans, and deposits. Women at Mari could contract in their own name and serve as a witness to a contract, they could also sue in court and share in an apportionment of goods. Some women were well educated and some women served as scribes. Women had the power to seal legal and official documents." (Batto, 1974, 3–5).

Until texts from Mari are translated and published in their entirety, our insights into the secrets they hold are limited to "glimpses." By this we mean that we are able to provide only small excerpts from translated passages of these primary texts and insights into their contexts. It is frustrating not to have the translations in their entirety. It is, nonetheless, very much worthwhile to see texts verifying women's capabilities and ingenuity as significant contributors to culture in the Ancient Near East. In the source material, the translator sometimes gives us only the reference number of the text as it is catalogued; for example Batto's translations of Sibtu's correspondence with her family reveals her continued interest in a former attendant (X 151), and announcement of the birth of her twins (X 26); at other times he gives us a translated sentence or paragraph fragment from the Mari writings. Batto provides particularly interesting information about the *Ugbabatum* priestesses. His texts refer variously to the King of Mari, Zimri-Lim, his primary Queen, Sibtu, their daughters, concubines of Zimri-Lim, and various officials of the court of this king.

The Ugbabatum Priestess

In general the Mari materials concerning the *Ugbabatum* agree with what is known of this priestess from elsewhere. She was of high social status and apparently not married. Knowledge of her cultic function remains vague. The status of an *Ugbabatum* Priestess is somewhere between that of an Entu (High Priestess) and a Naditu. She followed rules of celibacy and customarily lived within a cloister, but in some circumstances she could live in the home of her father. When an Entu died, an *Ugbabatum* priestess might be elevated to the status of Entu in that particular cloister.

The first group of texts from which we have translated excerpts are letters between Kibri-Dagan and Zimri-Lim who wishes Kibri-Dagan to oversee the restoration of a residence for an *Ugbabatum* Priestess of Dagan and to assist in installing the newly appointed priestess (Batto, 1974, 79–88). Selections from Batto include the catalog number for the document from which a quote is taken.

ZIMRI-LIM TO KIBRI-DAGAN RE: UGBABATUM PRIESTESS OF DAGAN[*]

Kibri-Dagan writes that he is undertaking this restoration at the direction of Zimri-Lim, "in accordance with what my lord wrote me previously, concerning the house in which the *Ugbabatum* of Dagan is to live. . . " (III 42.7–10)

Kibri-Dagan had omens taken and that they were favorable for beginning "to put that building in order"

The question also came up whether, because of its close proximity to a seller of pastries, this location was appropriate for the residence of the priestesses.

Kibri-Dagan informs Zimri-Lim concerning the location of the cloister. To show that the God approves "he (the God) is in complete accord over the dwelling-place of the '*Ugbabatum*.'" Kibri-Dagan encourages Zimri-Lim to bring the priestess to her new residence.

"May my lord, out of the goodness of his heart come up and himself kiss the feet of Dagan, the one who loves him! (Meanwhile) I will complete the work (here). I cannot possibly come!"

The second group of letters about the Ugbabatum priestesses are addressed to Sibtu, Queen of Zimri-Lim.

ZIMRI-LIM TO QUEEN SIBTU RE: UGBABATUM PRIESTESS OF DAGAN[**]

Zimri-Lim writes: "To Sibtu, say, thus (says) your lord: Perhaps you have heard some rumor and have become alarmed. No armed enemy has withstood me! All is well; there is no reason for you to be alarmed. Now Adad of Kulmi; has caused this disturbance because of his *Ugbabatum!* In the tablet of the prisoners-of-war which I sent, the *Ugbabatum* of (Adad of) Kulmi; and the *Ugbabatum* of the (other) Gods were separately listed, each one individually, in (that) tablet. Now then, let them pick out the *Ugbabatum* of (Adad of) Kulmi by themselves (i.e., as a separate group) for [. . .]. You clothe them with garments. Then they shall put them aboard(?) two-wheeled wagons(?) and. . . . Let the servants who brought them from here now conduct them back safely to me; [not] a single one of them [is to be injured"] (X 123) (Batto, 1974, 81–82)

In a letter to Sibtu, Zimri-Lim writes: "Now I have sent you some female weavers; there are some *Ugbabatum* among them. Pick the *Ugbabatum* and assign the others (literally, them) to the textile factory" (X 126.4–7).

*(Batto, 1974, 80–81)

**(Batto, 1974, III, 84.11–12)

"To Sibtu say, thus (says) your lord: Concerning what I previously wrote you, (namely) the selection of girls for the veil from among the booty which I have sent-now then, they are not to select any girls for the veil from among that booty. (Rather) let those girls be set aside as female weavers. There is (other) booty here before me; I myself will select girls for the veil from among the booty which is here and I will send (them) to you."

A proposed location for a dwelling for the *Ugbabatumm* of Dagan brought objections because of the close proximity of "female weavers, fullers, and artisans."

These passages suggest a class distinction whereby the priestesses should not be housed so close to the working women. Other *Ugbabatum,* are known to us by name. Foremost among these is Inibsina, who is identified as an *Ugbabatum* of Adad and also as a king's daughter. Ibal-Addu, the king of Aslakka, mentions two other priestesses in the Mari documents. It is reasonable to suggest that they are from that city and may have functioned there. We may also speculate that these last two priestesses may even be princesses. Yahdun-Lim evidently had a daughter who was a priestess and whose name seems to have been Inibsina. She might, however, be the un-named daughter of Zimri-Lim who was dedicated to Adad. The first daughter, Tasuba, is listed among those bringing a sheep as a gift to the palace (VII 225.1–226.50). The second daughter is listed as Ummiya. "Let . . . before Ummiya and [Proper name], the ugbabatum" (X 170.9–11).

The Naditu

This love song is the earliest example we have that is written by a woman to honor and celebrate a king. S.N. Kramer attributes the poem to a Sumerian *Lukur* (same as an Akkadian *Naditu*). The poem is written to thank the king for a beautiful gift he has given her. Kramer, who translated this ancient poem, tells us that it is dedicated to Shu-Sin, the fourth ruler of the Third Dynasty of Ur, who reigned sometime about 2000 B.C. Noteworthy are reverence to the mother of the king, and, as found throughout the marriage hymn between the Goddess Inanna and her human spouse Dumuzi, the inclusion of fertility imagery in alluding to sexual intimacy. It was excavated in Nippur and dates from the first half of the second millennium B.C.E.

LOVE SONG TO A KING[*]

She gave birth to him who is pure. . .
The queen gave birth to him who is pure,
Abisimti gave birth to him who is pure,
. . . O my (queen) who is favored of limb,
O my (queen) who is dark of head, my queen Dabbatum,'
O my (lord) who is dark of hair, my lord Shu-Sin,
O my (lord) who is . . . of word, my son of Shulgi! Because I uttered it . . .
the lord gave me a gift, Because I uttered a cry of joy, the lord gave me a gift,

A pendant of gold, a seal of lapis lazuli, the lord gave me as a gift,
A ring of gold, a ring of silver, the lord gave me as a gift.
lord, thy gift is brimful of. . . . [lift] thy face [unto me],
Shu-Sin, thy gift is brimful of. . . . [lift] thy face unto me.
The city [lift]s its hand like a cripple, O my lord Shu-Sin,
It lies at thy feet like a lion-cub, O son of Shulgi.

*"Love Song to a King," translated by S.N. Kramer, *ANET,* 1964, 494.

O my God, of the wine-maid," sweet is
   her date wine,
Like her. . . " sweet is her vulva, sweet is
   her date wine,
Sweet is her diluted drink, her date wine.
O my Shu-Sin who hast favored me,

O my (Shu-Sin) who hast favored me,
   who hast fondled me,
O my Shu-Sin who hast favored me,
O my beloved of Enlil, (my) Shu-Sin,
O my king, the God of his" land!

The research of Professor Rivkah Harris on the Naditu provides the most extensive, detailed, and thorough contribution concerning the world of female religious functionaries in the Ancient Near East. The Naditu women were consecrated (set apart) and dedicated their lives to the devotion of a particular deity. They lived celibate, cloistered lives within the Temple complex of the deity they served. Naditu were often from the most influential wealthy families. They were permitted to own property in their own names. In many instances they bequeathed properties to other Naditu. We will see this practice again among Beguines in Europe in the eleventh to thirteenth centuries C.E. Many Naditu owned properties outside the cloister; some who owned farms and other properties hired administrators who managed the properties and engaged in commerce at the Naditu's instruction. Letters from Naditu to family members and benefactors indicate that their primary duties consisted in praying for their loved ones. The excerpts that follow are taken from three of Professor Harris' works: "Women in Ancient Mesopotamia" (1989, in *Women's Earliest Records: from Ancient Egypt and Western Asia,* Barbara Lesko editor; and *The Naditu Woman,* (Harris, 1965). The next excerpt is from "The Cloister in Babylonia," R. Harris, 1953, Journal of the Social and Economic History of the Orient, Leiden: Brill, vol. 6 no 2, 1953

HARRIS' DESCRIPTION OF NADITUS

Theirs [the Naditus'] was a unique institution, a strange blend of characteristics, probably based on an earlier prototype but transformed radically, it would seem, to meet the new challenges of this period. Before focusing on our topic of independence and autonomy, I will briefly describe the institution of Naditu women of Shamash who lived in the *gagu* (cloister). The term Naditu derives from the root, nadu, meaning, "to leave fallow" (the comparison of women to fields is common in ancient Near Eastern texts). The Naditu was then a "fallow woman"; she was prohibited from sexual relations throughout her life. This was a basic prohibition for all Naditu women dedicated to different Gods as well and therefore possibly living under different regulations. (For example, the Naditu of Marduk of Babylon might marry, but she too was forbidden to bear children and so had to provide or permit her husband a secondary wife for that purpose.)*

The *gagu* (cloister) of Sippar was apparently the most prestigious of all the cloisters of Mesopotamia because women went there from Dilbat even though the Kish cloister was closer. More importantly, princesses of the royal house of Babylon and Mari were installed in Sippar. In the midst of Sippar, surrounded by a wall, was the cloister where some one to two hundred Naditu and Entu and cloister officials

*Harris, 1965, 108.

lived in private dwellings, some owned, others leased by their residents. The girl would be brought by her father or guardian at an age when girls ordinarily married, that is, in her mid-teens. Here she would live away from the "outside" or kidu as the Naditu referred to the world outside, until her death when she would be buried in the gagu cemetery alongside her sister Naditus. Though there were times when the Naditu of Shamash might have the freedom to leave for short family visits or have her relatives visit her, she lived until death in the cloister, viewed by later lexicographers as a gloomy prison.*

But the life of the Naditu was by no means a passive one. In crucial and striking ways the gagu and Naditu women bear no resemblance to the medieval nunnery and its nuns. Each Naditu as I have noted, lived in her own private house within the cloister compound. She had her own slaves or slave girls to take care of the household tasks. A life of poverty was no ideal. On the contrary, many, if not most of them, were born into the wealthiest and most respectable families. Among them were princesses, even a sister of King Hammurabi, the daughters of temple, military, and cloister officials, members of the top echelon of the bureaucracy. Some were daughters of city administrators, of wealthy scribes, judges, physicians, and diviners.

When these girls were brought to the cloister they did not come empty-handed. Most received as a dowry fields, plots of land, slaves, jewelry, and prized household furniture and utensils. The Code of Hammurabi even stipulated that the Naditu was not given a dowry before her father's death she was (quite exceptionally) to receive a full share of the inheritance equal to that of her brothers.**

Excerpt 2

In my view herein lies one of the major reasons for the establishment of the cloister at this particular point in Mesopotamian history. Celibacy was not unknown before the Old Babylonian Period. "There was the earlier institution of the Entu priestess," who was a princess selected for life to participate in the annual sacred marriage, the hieros-gamos and remain unmarried and live in the giparu residence. But the Old Babylonian Period was the only time when a community of women lived as celibates and virgins.

What is remarkable is what I. J. Gelb referred to as "the uniquely capitalistic development of the Naditum institution at Sippar . . . [which] seems beyond anything that can be connected with the aims and activities of cloisters and monasteries of all times." The hundreds of Naditu texts are mainly business documents: contracts of sale, lease and hire. With few exceptions it is a Nadtitu who buys houses and fields, leases out fields, houses, and plots of land, and hires out her slaves as farm hands to Sipparian farmers or as menials in their households. What emerges then is the amazing picture of a community of female celibates acting throughout the Old Babylonian Period as a significant economic power in their community.***

By providing a most respectable alternative to marriage for their daughters, wealthy families also found the means to conserve their wealth. It was perhaps at the instigation of these affluent individuals

---

*Harris, 1989, 151.

**Harris, 1953, "The Cloister in Babylonia."

***Harris, "Independent Women in Ancient Mesopotamia", 152.

that the transformation of the already existing cloister was effected and a new form and character given to it to meet the new social and economic conditions.

The Naditu in a sense entered the household of the father-in-law, the God Samas, in the Cloister. Here the simile ends; there was no later marriage to a son. But just as the relationship between the daughter-in-law and her future mother-in-law was of great importance to the girl, perhaps even taking precedence over her relationship to her father-in-law, so too the Naditu seems to have a more intimate relationship with Aja, the consort of Samas and thus her "mother-in-law," than she has to Samas. (Harris, 1965, Naditu Woman, 113). Chart 2-1 illustrates several of the Naditu priestesses who took the name of Aja, the wife of Samas.

Information concerning the social location of the fathers of Naditu reveals that many were the daughters of military officials, and two were daughters of overseers of the merchants in Sippar. There were daughters of scribes, a doctor, an official in the Samas temple, a judge, and a diviner. And there are records that show relatives of Naditu who were artisans. (Harris, 1965, 124)

Batto's work on women in Mari indicates that Zimri-Lim placed several of his daughters as Naditu in the service of different deities. A daughter of Zimri-Lim, Eristi-Aya, the author of eight letters in the Batto collection (X 36–43), was a Naditu at the Temple in Sippar dedicated to the God Samas and his consort Aya. The letters indicate that her chief duties consisted in praying continually for the life/welfare of her royal father. The texts also provide insight into the personal struggles of this young woman who is accustomed to great privilege and who expresses consternation and frustration when she feels that her needs are not being met appropriately.

ERISTI-AYA, A DAUGHTER OF ZIMRI-LIM, LETTER EXCERPTS[*]

In this letter to her mother she protests that she has been insulted. "Why have you not put on my garment (which I sent you)? (Instead) you have returned (it) to me and (so) inflict slander and curses upon me!"

She seems to have also felt ignored her father for she writes to him: "I presented (to you) a garment like your (own) clothing, but he paid no attention to me."[**]

Even if Eristi-Aya is imagining things or exaggerating, she evidently felt certain estrangement from the royal court, which could only have been reinforced by the distance that separated Mari and Sippar. In Sippar it was customary for Naditu to own

Chart 2–1	Names of Naditu in which the theophoric name is Aja		
	Aja-belet-matim	Awat-Aja	Aja-damqa Aja-ellet
	Aja-sarrat	BeIti-Aja	Aja-inib-matimrnatiln
	Aja-sitti	Eristi-Aja	Aja-inib-resetim
	Aja-tallik	Sat-Aja	Aja ka..gi.na
	Aia-tariba	SeriktiAja	Aja-kuzubbb-matim
	Aja-tillati	Aia-belet nisi	Aia-rimtu

[*]X 43.7–11.

[**]X 39.29–31.

slaves for carrying out household tasks and for nursing and companionship when the Naditu was older. It is highly probable that every Naditu owned at least one slave, and many had several. Eristi-Aya's slaves were supplied to her by her father. "Last year you sent two female slaves and one (of those) slaves had to go and die!"

Batto notes that in only one place does she address Zimri-Lim as abiya, "my father" (X 42.1–2). However, she normally does address him as "my Star" (kakkabiya), a term of respectful familiarity given the king and reserved, it seems, to members of the royal family. Her mother was undoubtedly Sibtu, Zimri-Lim's chief wife and queen, for one of her letters is addressed "to the queen my mother." (X 42.1f.)

The letters of Naditu of Sippar customarily begin with the stereotyped saluta- tion: "May my lord and my lady preserve your life permanently for my sake!" or "May my lord and my lady, for my sake, guard you like the heavens and the earth!" (X 36.4–7; 37.4–6; 41.4). "May my lord be everlasting as the heavens and the earth are everlasting" Eristi-Aya as a Naditu writes that she is the king's special "emblem" who habitually prays for him in Samas' temple, Ebabbar (X 38.9–11).

In a manner that differs considerably from enclosed convents for many consecrated religious nuns in contemporary religious traditions, a Naditu was allowed to leave the cloister to visit her relatives and also to have her relatives visit her. Eristi-Aya's letters that reveal her feelings of isolation probably have to do with the fact that Sippar is located so far from her home in Mari. She states that her father has sent certain items that she has in turn offered to the Goddess Aya, her "mistress."

Batto mentions an un-published text affirming that this daughter of Zimri-Lim was cloistered at the Temple of Samas in Sippar. "To Zimri-Lim say this: Thus (says) the prophet of Samas this is what Samas, the lord of the country, says: 'Let them send quickly to me to Sippar for (your own) life the throne destined for my residence of splendor—as well as your daughter which I have (already) requested of you.' "*

Sometimes when Eristi-Aya writes to her father to assure him that she is praying for him she also informs him of her need for supplies. "To my Star, my father, say thus (says) Eristi-Aya, the one who prays for you" (X 42.1–4). "Now the daughters of your house . . . are receiving their rations of grain, clothing, and good beer. But even though I alone am the woman who prays for you, I am not provisioned! I dedicated a sun (disk) and my ring (money) for your life but then Ermi-Addu [took] my ring (money) and the sun (disk) [for] his servant." (X 40.1–10). "I am the emblem of your father's house. Why am I not provisioned? They have not given me honey or oil!" "Am I not your praying emblem who constantly prays for your life? Why am I not provisioned with oil and honey from my father?" (X 37.7–12); "Am I not your praying emblem who gives you a good reputation in Ebabbar?". . . (X 38.9–11)

As noted earlier Rivkah Harris has pointed out that the Naditu of Sippar had a closer attachment and a more personal relationship with Aya than with Samas. Batto notes that in one letter Eristi-Aya writes that she has given a garment and a jar (of ointment?) from Zimri-Lim "to my lady (Aya), who preserves your (Zimri-Lim) life." (X 38.24–25) In another letter she asks her father to "send me oil. I have to go and anoint the body of my lady." (Aya) It was the parent's responsibility to send their

*Batto, 1974, 93.

Chart 2–2   Named Naditus Whose Documents Attest To Their Activities as Religious Functionaries for a Period of over Twenty-five Years

Iltani, the daughter of Apil-ili;u	54 years
Ina-libbini-erset, the daughter of lpiq-ilisu	52 years
Iltani, the princess	50+ years
Aja-resat, the daughter of Il su-ibni	48 years
Mannatum, the daughter of Jassi-el	44 years

---

daughter to the cloister: "Your husband and you made me enter the cloister." (X 43.15–17)

In an impassioned letter to her mother, complaining of neglect, Eristi-Aya states: "I am a king's daughter! You are a king's wife! Even disregarding the tabets with which your husband and you made me enter the cloister—they treat well soldiers taken as booty! You, then, treat me well!" (X 43.12–22) "My rations of grain and clothing, with which father keeps me alive, they (once) gave me, so let them give me (them lest I starve)." (X 36.22–26)

Batto notes that Eristi-Aya's complaints are undoubtedly exaggerated but, despite having several servants, there does seem to be a sense of estrangement from her family.*

Two letters from Lamassi

In the two Letters from Lamassi (PBS 7 105 and 106) to her father mention is made many times to My Lord (Samas) and My Lady (Aja): "May your well being last forever and ever before my Lord and my Lady. May the guardian of your welfare and life never depart from you. I make morning and evening offerings before my Lord and Lady, I constantly pray for your well-being." (R. Harris, "The Cloister in Babylonia, *Journal of the Social and Economic History of the Orient* 6, no. 2 (1963):5)

Chart 2–2 has the name of Naditus who served over 25 years or more as well as the names of their fathers. (Harris, 1965, 116–17)

Female Scribes and Entrepreneurs

It is not surprising to find that the complex organization of the cloister had its own scribes. Nor is it astonishing to find that many of the scribes were Naditus themselves. That there were women who were able to undertake this work attests to the high social status of the women who entered the cloister. It is even possible that these women scribes were taught and trained in their profession in the temple school of Ebabbar. Female scribes are mentioned in the very earliest Naditu texts. Scribes too, like other cloister officials, appear as witnesses, usually the last witness in the many documents of a sister Naditu.

Among named Naditu scribes, Harris mentions Inanna-amamu, who served during the reigns of three different rulers, as well as Sat-Aja, Nin-azu, Amat-Samas, Mana, Ajatum, Amat-mamu, who served for over forty years during the reigns of three different rulers from Hammurabi to Abi-esuh, and Aja kuzub matim.

---

*Batto, 1974, 59, 80, 81, 82, 84, 93, 94, 95, 96, 98, 100, 104.

AMAT-SAMAS, SCRIBE[*]

Among the most interesting accounts of Naditu are the records assembled by Rivkah Harris that describe a number of extremely wealthy Naditu. These are women who Harris suggests are probably the wealthiest people in Sippar. One of these women is Amat-Samas, the daughter of Arbi-Ea, who is cited numerous times as a creditor who lends barley to various people. She contracts loans for the barley, and all of these contracts date from the reign of Hammurabi. Amat-Samas even acts as guarantor for a man who is indebted to another Naditu.

HUSSUTUM, THE DAUGHTER OF SIN-PUTRAM[**]

Hussutum appears frequently as the lessor of fields. She lived to be an old woman, her documents attest to her activities for thiry-nine years, from the thirteenth year of Sin-muballit to the thirty-second year of Hammurabi. During the period of Sin-muballit the field she leases out is located in Taskun-Istar, an area where many other Naditu women owned property. Another lease text, which only states that the lessor is Hussutum, also belongs to this same Hussutum. Three of the witnesses to this transaction also appear in another of her lease texts. In the reign of Hammurabi, Hussutum leases out a field located in the region of Pahusum. Apparently Hussutum leased out this field over and over again for in the thirteenth and thirty-second year of Hammurabi she leased out the very same field. She undoubtedly did the same thing in the intervening years. It is relevant to note that in the thirty-second year Hussutum received a greater percentage of the harvest than she had in the thirteenth year of Hammurabi.

ILTANI THE PRINCESS, EXCERPTS***

This Iltani is the only Naditu to whom some attention has been paid. By the time of Iltani's latest text she was already an old woman of perhaps more than 70 years. Her activities were manifold. Her many texts clearly show she was a woman of great wealth and affluence and one can unhesitatingly state that she was the wealthiest of all the Naditu women known thus far. Iltani was an important landowner. We find her leasing fields from other Naditu women. She leases a field from the Naditu Melulatum in the vicinity of Ugartabu adjacent to a field that is hers. She leases a field from Ina-libbim-erset, in another region. Further evidence of her vast holdings is found in her many texts, which deal with the hiring of harvest workers to work her fields.

Ibni-Samas, the Sabra official, through Sin-eribam and Marduk-muballit, also officials and all three part of Iltani's household staff, received 1 mina of silver in order to hire workers "for harvesting the field of Iltani, the Naditu of Samas, the

---

*R. Harris, "The Organization and Administration of the Cloister," *Journal of the Economic and Social History of the Orient*, Leiden: E.J. Brill, 138.

**R. Harris, "Biographical Notes on the Naditu Women of Sippar," *Journal of Cuneiform Studies*, vol. 16, 1962, 5.

***Harris, 1962, 6–7.

princess." Another index of Iltani's importance as a landowner is to be seen in her having issakku farmers manage her fields. Only one other Samas is known to have had an issakku farmer. The issakku farmer was responsible for supervising the work in the fields and was in charge of the field workers. He was a wealthy man in his own right because he received a substantial share of the harvest from the owner of the field as his wages.

It was not surprising to find Iltani acting as a creditor lending barley to different people. In one text she lends barley to Anum and Namramsarur the sons of Sin-iddinam. We mention the debtors by name because it seems that the latter man and his father are mentioned in a letter written by one Iltani to two women. Although it is highly likely that this Iltani is the famous Iltani, it is surprising that the writer of the letter complains bitterly about her financial straits and this is certainly at variance with the other texts of Iltani. One can explain this discrepancy by saying that the letter represents a certain stylization that did not necessarily reflect the true situation.

Iltani in addition to being a landowner was also a cattle owner, an occupation which was rare among the Naditu women. An administrative account of the cattle belonging to Iltani, mainly under the care of her herdsman Awel Nabium is given. . . . The text which most strikingly speaks of Iltani's wealth lists the number of cattle owned by Iltani and the names of the herdsmen in charge of them. Altogether she owned 1085 head of cattle in [under the] charge of six different men.

INANNA-AMAMU, SCRIBE, DAUGHTER OF ABBA-TABUM[*]

Inanna-amamu is the earliest of the Naditu women known to have acted as a scribe for her sister Naditus. She appears in a text dating from the period of Buntahun-ila, a time when Sippar had not yet come under the rulers of the First Dynasty of Babylon. She also appears in texts dating from Immerum, and Sumu-la-el. It is significant to note that the father of Inanna-amamu, Abba-tabum, was also a scribe. And Inanna-amamu like several other Naditu women had a sister named Abaja who also entered the cloister as a Naditu of Samas.

Female Prophets

At Mari, Batto's findings indicate that women participated equally in all types of prophetic activity, whether professional or lay, public or private. There were male respondents and female respondents, male ecstatics and female ecstatics, in addition to the female speaker (*qabba-tum*). Women were as likely to receive divine revelations through dreams as were men.

Batto investigates what can be gleaned from the Mari texts about the prophetesses and the role of women in prophetic activity. Professional prophetesses are almost always associated with a Temple and include the female respondent, the female ecstatic, and the female speaker. Female prophets, like their male counterparts, were associated with specific deities as mediators between that deity and the people. There did not seem to be hard and fast rules about the different categories of prophets at a single Temple. Batto reports that "Dagan of Terqa had a male ecstatic and a female speaker; and Dagan of

[*]Harris, 1962, 8.

Tuttul had a male respondent and male ecstatic. And if Innibana is to be attached to the temple of Annunitum then that temple had both a female respondent and female ecstatic." (Batto, 1974, 122) It is also possible that prophetic respondents functioned at several Temples. "They may go into ecstasy in the temple and deliver a public oracle (X 8), or they may deliver their oracle privately." (XIII 114; X 100). Most frequently, however, their prophetic experience is in the form of a dream. (X 10, 12, 50, 94, 117)

ORACLES[*]

> "The wife of a free-man came to me and spoke as follows . . . " (XIII llf. 8)
> Sibtu writes to Zimri Lim
> "For a report of the campaign which my lord is on, I waited(?) on signs. I asked a man and a woman, and the word is very favorable to my lord. Similarly, with regard to Isme-Dagan I asked the man and the woman, and his prognosis is not favorable." (X 4.3–11)
> "I am not making them speak. On their own they speak; on their own they agree!" (X 11. 37–39)

Correspondence between Sibtu and Zimri-Lim also appears in Chapter 3, "Ancient Near Eastern Mesopotamia: The Social Context," as we consider the social, cultural, and political texts related to women in ancient Mesopotamia.

SUGGESTED READING:

Harris, Rivkah. "Biographical Notes on the Naditu Women of Sippar." *Journal of Cuneiform Studies* (American Schools of Oriental Research) 16 (1962): 1–12.

Leick, Gwendolyn. *Sex and Eroticism in Mesopotamian Literature.* London and New York: Routledge, 1994.

Lesko, Barbara, editor. *Women's Earliest Records: From Ancient Egypt and Western Asia.* Edited by Brown Judaic Studies. Atlanta: Scholars Press, 1989.

Meador, Betty de Shong. *Inanna, Lady of the Largest Heart: Poems of the High Priestess Enheduanna.* Austin: University of Texas Press, 1989.

Van Buren, Elizabeth Douglas. "The Rain Goddess as Represented in Early Mesopotamia." *Analecta Biblica* 12 (1959): 343–55.

Wolkstein, D., and S. N. Kramer, translators. *Inanna: Queen of Heaven and Earth.* Cambridge and San Francisco: Harper and Row, 1983.

Sources Cited

"The Sacred Marriage of Inanna And Dumuzi," translated by D. Wolkstein. In S.N. Kramer, *Inanna: Queen of Heaven and Earth.* Cambridge and San Francisco: Harper and Row, 1983. 30–49.

"'Pudu-Heppas' Prayer to Arinna the Sun Goddess," translated by Albrecht Goetze. In *Ancient Near Eastern Texts Relating to the Old Testament,* edited by James B. Pritchard. Princeton, N.J.: Princeton University Press, 1950. 393.

[*]Batto, 1974, 119–25.

"The Exaltation of Inanna," translated by William W. Hallo, *Contexts of Scripture: Canonical Compositions from the Biblical World,* Vol. 1, Leiden. London, Koln: Brill, 1997.519–521.

Batto, Bernard Frank. *Studies on Women at Mari.* Baltimore and London: Johns Hopkins University Press, 1974. 59, 80, 81, 82, 84, 93, 94, 96, 97, 98, 99, 100.

"Love Song to a King," translated by S.N. Kramer. In *Ancient Near Eastern Texts Relating to the Old Testament,* edited by James B. Pritchard. Princeton, NJ: Princeton University Press, 1969. 494.

Harris, Rivkah. "Independent Women in Ancient Mesopotamia." In *Women's Earliest Records: From Ancient Egypt and Western Asia,* edited by Barbara Lesko, Atlanta: Brown Judaic Studies, Atlanta Scholars Press, 1989. 151–152.

——"The Naditu Woman." In *Studies Oppenheim.* Chicago: University of Chicago, 1965. 106–35.

——"The Cloister in Babylonia." *Journal of the Social and Economic History of the Orient* 6, no. 2 (1963): 5.

——"Biographical Notes on the Naditu Women of Sippar." *Journal of Cuneiform Studies* (Cambridge, MA) 16 (1962): 1–12.

Chapter 3

Ancient Near Eastern Mesopotamia: The Social Context

As was demonstrated in Chapter 2, "Ancient Near Eastern Mesopotamia: The Religious Context," the most informative texts concerning women's experience in Mesopotamia, from ca. 4000 B.C.E. to ca. 2400 B.C.E., pertain to institutional religion, either directly or indirectly. In the present chapter, however, texts representative of life defined by political and legal institutions are the source of our inquiry. We have noted previously that in a patriarchal society, hierarchical social stratification, and male-centered values shape culture. The reading selections in this chapter demonstrate the gradual institutionalization of hierarchical stratification and male-centered values.

Education was a matter of privilege, and the great majority of all texts that have been excavated from archaeological sites in the Ancient Near East reflect the interests and activities of the upper echelons of society. Texts generated by males, for males, written exclusively from the point of view of male experience became increasingly normative over the centuries as patriarchal values were institutionalized. The section on Women in the Aristocracy includes fragments of translations that attest to female leadership within the royal court and the government. Unlike some of the Naditu women, female scribes, and En/Entus/High Priestesses whose personal agency and autonomy often benefited women, we find in the aristocracy women whose agency was shaped by the agendas of the males with whom they are associated as mothers, wives, concubines, and daughters.

Numerous legal texts, arranged in a chronological order, are intentionally included in this chapter. These examples show how laws pertaining to women became increasingly severe over time. They are also selected to illustrate significant references to women that diminish their status as autonomous individuals. In the earliest legal texts many laws concerning women tended to be designated on the basis of a woman's vocation (e.g., Naditu, Entu, Ugbabatu) or occupation (e.g., scribe, shopkeeper, tavern owner, landlady, barkeeper). As patriarchal values became increasingly institutionalized over the centuries, women were referenced almost exclusively in terms of their relationship to males (daughter, wife, mother, sister, concubine, slave). However, despite the evidence that laws during the time of Hammurabi were written from the point of view of males, Sibtu exhibits considerable autonomy in the political sphere within a patriarchal ethos and was, according to some scholars, a half sister of that same Hammurabi. It is important to recognize that there apparently have always been diverse interpretations of the patriarchal ethos that eventually governed the basic social institutions among most human communities.

There is very little information on women outside the aristocracy in the Ancient Near East with the exception of the legal codes. Scholarly inquiry into this area of research continues and we note some of the findings in the latter part of the chapter.

SOCIAL ORGANIZATION

Cosmology Shapes Culture

Transitions to formal, inherited kingship by royal succession was not institutionalized until the Early Dynastic III period (ca. 2500 to 2300 B.C.E.) in Sumer (Hallo, 1976, 49). This transition demanded considerable cooperation between religious and royal interests. An entirely new way of defining governance required a new understanding of the relationship between the Ruler and The Holy (Hallo, 1976, 49). That is, there was a need to develop an understanding of deity/God/Goddess that reflected the new patriarchal, hierarchical social organization within a formal monarchy. If we understand these dynamics in the context of thousands of years of matrifocal culture that was being transformed to a patriarchal model it should not be surprising to discover texts that represent a struggle in power between male and female deities. This is especially apparent in myths such as the Tiamat-Marduk story.

The creation story of the Babylonians, *The Enuma Elish,* was inscribed on clay tablets as early as 1000 B.C.E., though it was probably composed during the reign of Hammurabi (1728-1686 B.C.E.). This text facilitates a new theology among the Babylonians. The Babylonian God, Marduk, represents the political ascension of the Babylonians over other Mesopotamian kingdoms. The battle that ensues in the story is interpreted as a means to formally institute the male deity Marduk as the chief God. Marduk's defeat of the powerful Mother Goddess Tiamat functions also as a means of instituting male supremacy over the female. The rewriting of mythology to reflect new social and political agendas can be found in the sacred texts of all religious traditions. The interpretive framework used by theologians who created *The Enuma Elish* depicts the Goddess Tiamat as the primordial chaos, thus associating disorder with the female while Marduk is depicted as bringer of law and order that are subsequently associated with the male. In the brief excerpts that follow, notice that both deities are portrayed as fierce warriors and consider the contrast with the descriptions of the Mother Goddess in Chapter 1, "Paleolithic, Neolithic, and Proto-Historic Culture."

THE ENUMA ELISH: THE BABYLONIAN GENESIS[*]

[*Tiamat Responds Personally to Marduk's Challenges*]
When Tiamat heard this,
Tiamat cried out loud (and) furiously. . .
Tiamat (and) Marduk, the wisest of the Gods, advanced against one another;
They pressed on to single combat, they approached for battle.
[*after a vicious battle*]
The lord spread out his net and enmeshed her;

The evil wind, following after, he let loose in her face.
When Tiamat opened her mouth to devour him
He drove in the evil wind, in order that (she should) not (be able) to close her lips.
He shot off an arrow, and it tore her interior;
It cut through her inward parts, it split (her) heart.

The Enuma Elish: The Babylonian Genesis, translated by E.A. Speiser, 1955, *ANET.* 39–42 excerpts.

When he had subdued her, he destroyed
　her life;
After he had slain Tiamat, the leader,
Her band broke up, her host dispersed.
As for the Gods [who were] her helpers. . .
　They trembled for fear. . .
(But) they were completely surrounded,
　(so that) it was impossible to flee.
[*Marduk's Strategies*]
He imprisioned them and broke their
　weapons
And then he returned to Tiamat, whom
　he had subdued.
The lord trod upon the hinder part of
　Tiamat,
And with his unsparing club he split
　(her) skull.

He cut the arteries of her blood
And caused the north wind to carry (it)
　to out-of-the-way places.
[*The Patriarchs rejoice at Tiamat's
　defeat*]
When his fathers saw (this), they were
　glad and rejoiced. . . .
He split her open like a mussel(?) into
　two (parts);
[*Marduk Creates Heaven and Earth from
　the Body of Tiamat*]
Half of her he set in place and formed
　the sky (therewith) as a roof.
He fixed the crossbar (and) posted
　guards;
He commanded them not to let her wa-
　ters escape.

WOMEN IN THE ARISTOCRACY

Women of the Royal Household

Royal palaces that were physically separate from the Temples did not begin to become a norm until at least 2800 B.C.E. As monarchies were institutionalized, the ruler's duties were divided between religious spheres, demands of trade and commerce, and military duties. The gradual redistribution of wealth from egalitarian models of the Neolithic period to the accumulation and acquisition of private property by the Temple, Palace, and estates of the nobility resulted in sharp social stratification.

Written documents from Mesopotamia were generated by members of the nobility from the point of view of their own experience and represented their interests and concerns exclusively. Texts created in this social setting represented a distinct minority of men, and (sometimes) women, of privilege.

Within the framework of a life, death, rebirth mythology that prevailed in the Ancient Near East, the king was the child of a sacred marriage (*heiros-gamos*), that is a sexual union between the ruler and the priestess of a given God or Goddess. Thus a king was seen as the son of a particular God or Goddess. At the birth of a king several additional deities would also be invoked to give strength and wisdom to the infant king. A prince was "suckled by the goddess" and when he was old enough to take the throne he became a "representative" for the deity. (Hallo, 1976, 49) Other children of royal and noble parentage would become Ens and Entus. Thus, although kingship became a separate profession it continued to be authorized and legitimated by the religious cultus. Similarly, female and male members of the priesthood, as well as religious functionaries within the temple complex, were endowed by the ruler and the court. Ens and Entus were considered appointees of the deity and shared in the wealth of the nobility. Ancient Near Eastern texts have been discovered that attest to women's contributions to culture in leadership positions not only within the religious sphere, but also in newly defined administrative roles that were part of the patriarchal bureaucracy.

Queen Adad-Guppi whose tomb inscription follows, embodied roles both as Queen and as the mother of a king.

QUEEN ADAD-GUPPI, A BURIAL INSCRIPTION[*]

INTRODUCTION

I am Adad-guppi, mother of Nabunaid, king of Babylon, a worshipper of Sin, Ningal, Nusku, and Sadarnunna, my gods, for whose divinity I have cared since my youth.

AUTOBIOGRAPHICAL NARRATIVE

Whereas in the sixteenth year of Nabopolassar, king of Babylon, Sin, the king of the gods, became angry with his city and his house, and went up to heaven (with the result that) the city and its people were transformed into a ruin. During that time I cared for the sanctuaries of Sin, Ningal, Nusku, and Sadarnunna, since I revered their deity. Sin, the king of the gods, I was constantly beseeching. I daily, without fail, cared for his great deity. I was a worshipper of Sin, Shamash, Ishtar, and Adad all of my life (whether) in heaven or on earth. My fine possessions that they gave to me, I gave back to them, daily, nightly, monthly, yearly. I was continually beseeching Sin. Gazing at him prayerfully and in humility, I knelt before them. Thus (I said): "May your return to your city take place. May the black-headed people worship your great divinity." In order to appease the heart of my god and my goddess, I did not put on a garment of excellent wool, silver, gold, a fresh garment; I did not allow perfumes (or) fine oil to touch my body. I was clothed in a torn garment. My fabric was sackcloth. I proclaimed their praises. The fame of my god and goddess were set (firmly) in my heart. I stood their watch. I served them food.

From the twentieth year of Assurbanipal, king of Assur, in which I was born, until the forty-second year of Assurbanipal, the third year of Assur-etilluili, his son, the twenty-first year of Nabopolasser, the forty-third year of Nebuchadnezzar, the second year of Awel-Marduk, the fourth year of Neriglissar—for ninety-five years I cared for Sin, the king of the gods of heaven and earth, and for the sanctuaries of his great divinity. He looked upon me and my good deeds with joy. Having heard my prayers and agreeing to my request, the wrath of his heart calmed. He was reconciled with Ehulhul, Sin's house, located in the midst of Harran, his favorite dwelling.

Sin, the king of the gods, looked upon me. He called Nabunaid, my only son, my offspring, to kingship. He personally delivered the kingship of Sumer and Akkad, from the border of Egypt and the upper sea, to the lower sea, all the land.

I lifted my hands to Sin, the king of the gods, reverently in prayer: [Thus (I said): "Nabunaid is (my) son, my offspring, beloved of his mother]. II:1 You are the one who called him to kingship and have spoken his name by your own divine utterance. (Now) may the great gods go at his side. May they fell his enemies. Do not forget Ehulhul but complete and restore its rites."

When, in my dream, Sin, the king of the gods, had set his hands (on me), he said thus: "Through you I will bring about the return of the gods (to) the dwelling in Harran, by means of Nabunaid your son. He will construct Ehulhul; he will complete its

[*]"Tomb Inscription of the Mother of King Nabonidus," translated by Tremper Longman III, in *Contexts of Scripture: Canonical Compositions from the Biblical World,* Vol. 1, Leiden, London, Koln: Brill, 1997. 519–521

work. He will complete the city Harran greater than it was before and restore it. He will bring Sin, Ningal, Nusku, and Sadarnunna in procession back into the Ehulhul."

[*The narrative continues with only minor breaks. The text concludes with an exhortation to observe the worship of Sin.*]

FINAL EXHORTATION

[Whoever] you are—whether king, prince [ ] in the land. [Continually stand watch] for Sin, the king [of the gods], the lord of the gods of heaven and earth, his great divinity and reverence [the divinities of heaven and] earth who [ ] dwell in Esagil and Ehulhul and pray (to the divinities) in heaven and earth and [ ] the command of Sin and Ishtar who saves [ ] keep your seed safe forever and ever.

Ancient Near Eastern cuneiform writings that have been translated and published thus far verify Ku-Baba from Kish as a ruling female monarch in ancient Mesopotamia. As cuneiform translations continue to be published, we discover a number of women who also had considerable influence and power in political affairs, including High Priestesses Baranamtara and Shag-Shag from Lagash and Neo-Assyrian queen-mothers Sammuramat and Naqi'a. The translations of women's correspondence discovered from the archaeological excavations of Mari help to give us further insight into the influence of particular women as leaders in the Ancient Near East in the 1700s B.C.E

Correspondence: Personal and Political

Bernard Batto affirms that the identity of Sibtu, as the principal wife of Zimri-Lim, has long been established from the inscription of her seal: "Sibtu, the daughter of Yarim-Lim, the sister of Hammurabi, was the wife of Zimri-Lim." (Batto, 1974, 5) Zimri-Lim, who had sought asylum at the court of Sibtu's father, won his favor and returned to Mari with the daughter of Yarim-Lim as his bride. In the following excerpts we provide an abbreviated context for passages and fragments of translated material from Batto's research. Where Batto has referenced an untranslated text, or a text that he does not include in the book, we supply his references for identification of the primary documents. Correspondence to Zimri-Lim constitutes the majority of the documents from Sibtu and reflects the various aspects of her relationship to him.

QUEEN SIBTU OF MARI, CORRESPONDENCE EXCERPTS[*]

On a personal note, for example, in sending him clothing when he is away on campaign she notes that she wants him to wear proudly the garments "which I have made" (X 17.9-13; Batto, 1974, 9)

Sibtu was always deeply concerned for the protection of her husband. She often consulted female and male prophets to determine their revelations about his well being (X 11; 12017; 124.18-2118), and she fervently hoped he would soon return home: "May my lord conquer his enemies, And may my lord enter Mari in safety and happiness" (X 17.5-8). (Batto, 1974 10). Zimri-Lim wrote to assure her: "Perhaps you have heard some rumor and your heart is disturbed, no armed enemy has withstood me! All is well. There is no need to be concerned." (X 123, 4-9). (Batto, 1974, 10)

*(Batto, 1974, 19–20).

Most of Sibtu's correspondence that has been preserved addresses issues that pertain to her official duties and responsibilities as queen. These include her mention that the palace, the temples, the workshops, and the city are functioning well. "The palace is fine" (II 116.5; X, 6.4; etc.). "The palace is fine; the temples and workshops are fine" (X, 11.4-6; see also 10.3-4); "The city of Mari is fine" (X 23.5; cf. 22.5). (Batto, 1974, 11)

Sibtu had authority to supervise administrators and officials in charge of the harem. (X, 126.32) and (X, 125.33) (X 126.16-21). In a letter from Zimri-Lim (X, 10) the queen is given the charge to see that controllers are shown particular documents in the archives in order to examine them. Sibtu supervises the controllers' examination and then reseals the door of the archives with her own seal thus guaranteeing the integrity of the whole operation. The queen is in this case the king's personal deputy in a matter of some importance. In this letter the queen reports the success of one of the king's pet projects, the recently constructed reservoir: "On the 24th day (of this month) it rained heavily in Mari. In the middle of the reservoir, which my lord built, the water stood 1 'rod' deep." This project was of great personal interest to Zimri-Lim, (XIII 27–28; 48.4). (Batto, 1974, 14).

The queen's conduct indicates her fervent attention to all matters of the king's concern. It was also widely understood that Sibtu had great influence with Zimri-Lim and there are texts that indicate high officials sought her intervention. Batto suggests that Tablet X 154 is an example of several texts written to secure the queen's favor. This one is addressed to the queen by Itur-Asdu, governor in Nahur, later governor in Mari. Itur-Asdu writes to Sibtu for a favor concerning the government's appointment of household staff for the governor. "If it pleases my mistress, let them expel (. . .) that slave from my house" (X .154 lines 5–7). (Batto, 1974, 15).

In X 153 Kibri-Dagan, the governor of Terqa, writes to the queen, "his mistress," that he will personally see to the case of a certain woman named Partum, about whom the queen had written. Batto includes another letter of the queen's directives involving Terqa that is included in X 27. Sibtu's favor could also influence the advance of a political career. Similarly, a governor named Meptum sends Sibtu an intelligence report about the movements of the enemy and their strength (X, 155). Batto tells us that "Meptum reports on the safety of his district to the queen (line 3), just as he does to the king" and that Itur-Asdu as the governor of Nahur (X, 152.50) and Buqaqum, another provincial governor (X, 158.51) send to Sibtu what also seem to be political or military reports. The king himself also kept Sibtu posted on political developments (X, 121.5–17; 122; 132), just as the queen surely kept the king informed of political news that came to her attention. Ili-eli, a merchant who is late in delivering the goods that Sibtu has purchased apologizes for his lateness: "Although they have been paid for in full, the boats have not yet arrived. For this reason I am late. May my lady not be upset."

Whereas Sibtu was committed to carrying out responsibilities as the king's agent in a great variety of functions she also used her personal initiative in a number of independent decisions. Sibtu was often engaged in cultic affairs. Sometimes this involved her omens taken for the king that reflect her personal concerns. At other times she serves as a "stand in" for the king. On one occasion Zimri-Lim calls upon Sibtu to escort the statue of Hisametum back to the city Hisameta and there offer sacrifice to the Goddess: "With regard to conducting Hisametum who has written

me. Now then, go to Hisamta and conduct Hisametum, and offer that sacrifice."
(X, 128.59) In another letter Sibtu asks Zimri-Lim whether he would arrive at Mari
in time for the sacrifice in honor of Ishtar; Zimri-Lim replied in the affirmative
(X, 120.17–20). The implication appears to have been that if the king would not arrive in time, then Sibtu, as Zimri-Lim's representative, would oversee the performance of the sacrifice. When Sibtu relays to the king various oracular happenings in
Mari (X, 6–10), she again functions very much like other officers of the crown, particularly in requiring the symbols of authenticity, the hem and the lock of hair, from
the Asum (X, 7.23–27). "Asum the temple administrator brought to Sibtu the oracle
along with the hem and the lock of hair from a woman who delivered an ecstatic
oracle in his temple" (X, 8.19–28). It was in an official capacity, not just as a concerned wife, that Sibtu sought out the God's will concerning the king's campaigns
(X, 6.101–16'; 4.6) and had omens taken for the safety of the king (X, 11.8–11; X,
120). Provincial governors provided perhaps the closest parallel. Babdi-Lim, as governor of Mari, commissioned the taking of omens for the safety of the troops and
the king (VI 75; cf. 67.7). He also accepted in the name of the king the legal symbols
of the hem and the lock of hair from a female ecstatic from the temple administrator
Asum (VI 45). "It may be concluded, then, that in all these matters dealing with the
cult, the overseeing and even offering of sacrifice, the commissioning of omen-
taking, the supervision of oracular events, Sibtu was acting in her quasi-official capacity as a representative of the king. She could and did perform all the actions the
lesser officer did, but she was not limited along jurisdictional lines as were these
lesser officers in state affairs."

POLITICALLY PROMINENT WOMEN ADMINISTRATORS OF ZIMRI-LIM, LETTER EXCERPTS

Texts related to two different aristocratic women at Mari parallel to some extent
Sibtu's cultic role, just in a lesser capacity. The first was the governor's wife Inibsina
and the other was a powerful woman administrator Addu-duri. Ranking to determine a person's importance is sometimes surmised from lists that designate dis-
bursement of supplies, such as oil and woven fabric. Immediately after Sibtu, on one
list (VII 206,4,7') and on another immediately after a list of princesses (C 1.18) is
Dam-hurasi. The latter text further witnesses to her rank by recording that Dam-
hurasi, along with one Yatar-Aya listed with her, receives a significantly larger ration
of oil than any of the other women, including the king's own daughters and sister.
The king's affection for her, his trust in her abilities, and her importance to the king
are attested in letters from and abundant correspondence (X. 62–72). Her letters reveal her to be both beloved by the king and an important woman charged with responsibility over a palace.

As we will continue to see, dynastic marriages were common throughout the
Ancient Near East as a means of forming or strengthening political alliances. Zimri-
Lim regularly employed political marriage in his own imperial policy to secure patronage and increase his boundaries. He married his daughter Tizpatum to Ili-I;tar,
king of Guna, another daughter Kiru to Haya-Sumu of Ilansura. Ibbatum was given

to Himdiy the ruler of Andariq, and, possibly a fourth daughter to Ibal-Addu of Aslakka. Whereas we know that some daughters of Zimri–Lim were consecrated as Naditu, the daughters of Zimri-Lim who married were invested with considerable responsibility related to the interests of their father and the prosperity of Mari. (Batto, 1974, 52–53) Samsi Addad, a later king at Mari, who perhaps did not have affection for royal wives at Mari, warns his son against too harsh treatment of his wife.

A POLITICAL MARRIAGE[*]

"Did not the previous kings install their spouse in the palace? Yahdun-Lim honored his women-friends but his own wife he put aside, installing her in the desert. Now perhaps you, in the same manner, wish to install in the desert the daughter of Ishi-Addu. Her father will learn of it and he will be upset. This will not do. There are many rooms in the 'palace of palms.'" Let a room be selected and install her in this room, (but) do not install her in the desert." (A.2548.)69.

LEGAL STATUS OF WOMEN

Legal Codes

The codified laws concerning women that are selected in the present section pertain to marriage, divorce, women's behavior in the public and private spheres, sexual behavior, and ownership of property. A quasi-chronological listing of extant legal texts indicates that a marked decline in women's agency (initiative, freedom to act) and autonomy (ability to be self-governing) is apparent as culture becomes increasingly patriarchal. Over the centuries women's status came to be increasingly dependent upon the social class into which they were born and the status of the men to whom they *belonged* as daughters, wives, or concubines. Always however, there were exceptions. Social status as a female member of the nobility or as a religious functionary of the priestly class continued to provide many privileges for women and such privileges are reflected in the legal codes.

The following text is from the Early Post Sumerian period some time in the first half of the second millennium B.C.E. This code precedes the code of Hammurabi (from which we have extensive entries toward the end of this chapter) by over a century. The Lipit-Ishtar Law Code has three main parts: a Prologue, the legal texts, and an Epilogue. Note that, like Uruk, this city "belonged" to a Goddess. Although all of the prologue is not preserved, what remains lists some of Lipit-Ishtar's accomplishments. King Lipit-Ishtar, the fifth ruler of the Dynasty of Isin, recounts the historical events during which the leading Sumerian and Babylonian Gods and Goddesses and the Goddess Ninisinna of Isin determined that he would reign and establish justice in Sumer and Akkad. Some thirty-eight laws are preserved. The following laws concerning women are representative of and pertain to marriage and inheritance. Note that consideration is made for the well-being of the female and although equity is, by this time, influenced by social status, the well-being of all females is taken into account.

*(Batto, 1974,52-53)

Law Codes from Lipit Ishtar 3000–2500 b.c.e.[*]

[PROLOGUE]

[When] the great [Anu, the father of the Gods, (and) [Enlil, [the king of all the lands, [the lord who determines ordinances, had . . . [Nini]sinna, [the daughter of A]nu . . . when they had given her the kingship of Sumer (and) Akkad (and) a favorable reign in her (city) Isin. Anu (and) Enlil had called Lipit-Ishtar, the wise shepherd whose name had been pro-nounced by Nunamnir'-to the princeship of the land in order to establish justice in the land, to banish complaints, to turn back enmity and rebellion by the force of arms, (and) to bring well-being to the Sumerians and Akkadians, then I, Lipit-Ishtar, the humble shep-herd of Nippur, the stalwart farmer of Ur, who aban-dons not Eridu, the suitable lord of Erech [king] of Isin], [kin]g of Sum[er and Akkad], who am f[it] for the heart of Inanna, established [jus]tice in [Su]mer and Akkad in accordance with the word of Enlil. Verily, in those [days] I procured . . . the [free-dom of the [so]ns and daughters of [Nippur], the so]ns and daughters of Ur, the sons and daughters of [I]sin, the [sons and daughters of [Sumer (and) Akkad upon whom slaveship had been imposed.

Lipit-Ishtar Lawcode[**]

¶b If a man dies without male offspring, an unmarried daughter shall be his heir.

¶c If [a man dies] and his daughter [is married(?)], the property of the pa-ternal estate [. . .], a younger sister, after [. . .] the house [. . .]

¶d If [a . . .] strikes the daughter of a man and causes her to lose her fetus, he shall weigh and deliver 30 shekels of silver.

¶e If she dies, that male shall be killed.

¶f If a . . . strikes the slave woman of a man and causes her to lose her fetus, he shall weigh and deliver 5 shekels of silver.

¶12 If a man's female slave or male slave flees within the city, and it is con-firmed that the slave dwelt in a man's house for one month, he (the one who harbored the fugitive slave) shall give slave for slave.

¶18 If the master or mistress of an es-tate defaults on the taxes due from the estate and an outsider assumes the taxes, he (the master) will not be evicted for three years; (but after three years of defaulting on the taxes) the man who has assumed the tax burden shall take possession of the estate and the (original) master of the estate will not make any claims.

¶21 (B) [If . . .] marries, the (marriage) gift which is given by(?) her/his pa-ternal estate shall be taken for her/his heir. [. . .] (O) [If . . .] is given to a wife, her/his brothers will not include for division (among their inheritance shares) the (marriage) gift which had

[*]Prologue: *Law Codes of Lipit Ishtar,* translated by S.N. Kramer, 1955, *ANET,* 159.

[**]"Lipit-Ishtar Lawcode" translated by Martha T. Roth, in *Law Collections from Mesopotamia and Asia Minor,* edited by Pitor Michaelowski, Writings from the Ancient World Series, Society of Biblical Literature (Atlanta: Scholars Press, 1995), 23–36 Excerpts

been given by(?) her/his paternal estate, but [. . .]

¶22 If, during a father's lifetime, his daughter becomes an *ugbabtu,* a *nadītu,* or a *qadištu,* they (her brothers) shall divide the estate considering her as an equal heir.

¶23 If a daughter is not given in marriage while her father is alive, her brothers shall give her in marriage.

¶25 If a man marries a wife and she bears him a child and the child lives and a slave woman also bears a child to her master, the father shall free the slave woman and her children; the children of the slave woman will not divide the estate with the children of the master.

¶26 If his first-ranking wife dies and after his wife's death he marries the slave woman (who had borne him children), the child of his first-ranking wife shall be his (primary) heir; the child whom the slave woman bore to her master is considered equal to a native freeborn son and they shall make good his (share of the) estate.

¶27 If a man's wife does not bear him a child but a prostitute from the street does bear him a child, he shall provide grain, oil, and clothing rations for the prostitute, and the child whom the prostitute bore him shall be his heir; as long as his wife is alive, the prostitute will not reside in the house with his first-ranking wife.

¶28 If a man's first-ranking wife loses her attractiveness or becomes a paralytic, she will not be evicted from the house; however, her husband may marry a healthy wife, and the second wife shall support the first-ranking wife.

¶29 If a son-in-law enters the household of his father-in-law and performs the bridewealth presentation, but later they evict him and give his wife to his comrade, they shall restore to him twofold the bridewealth which he brought, and his comrade will not marry his wife.

¶33 If a man claims that another man's virgin daughter has had sexual relations but it is proven that she has not had sexual relations, he shall weigh and deliver 10 shekels of silver.

Ur Nammu Law Code 2000s b.c.e.*

¶4 If a male slave marries a female slave, his beloved, and that male slave (later) is given his freedom, she/he will not leave (or: be evicted from?) the house.

¶5 If a male slave marries a native woman, she/he shall place one male child in the service of his master; the child who is placed in the service of his master, his paternal estate, . . . the wall, the house, [. . .]; (any other) child of the native woman will not be owned by the master, nor will he be pressed into slavery.

¶6 If a man violates the rights of another and deflowers the virgin wife of a young man, they shall kill that male.

¶7 If the wife of a young man, on her own initiative, approaches a man and initiates sexual relations with him, they shall kill that woman; that male shall be released.

¶9 If a man divorces his first-ranking wife, he shall weigh and deliver 60 shekels of silver.

¶10 If he divorces a widow, he shall weigh and deliver 30 shekels of silver.

*Ur Nammu Law Code, translated by Martha T. Roth, *LCMAM,* 1995, 17–20

¶11 If a man has sexual relations with the widow without a formal written contract, he will not weigh and deliver any silver (as a divorce settlement).

¶14 If a man accuses the wife of a young man of promiscuity but the River Ordeal clears her, the man who accused her shall weigh and deliver 20 shekels of silver.

¶17 If [a slave or(?)] a slave woman [. . .] ventures beyond the borders of (his or) her city and a man returns (him or) her, the slave's master shall weigh and deliver [x] shekels of silver to the man who returned (the slave).

¶25 If a slave woman curses someone acting with the authority of her mistress, they shall scour her mouth with one sila of salt.

Eshnunna was one of the numerous Amorite-controlled states of the period. The city of Eshnunna itself is located at Tell Asmar, a site that was excavated by the Oriental Institute of the University of Chicago. Note the attention to a variety of particular situations in which the female bears responsibility and instances where the laws function for her well-being. Note also laws in which social status has a distinct bearing on the extent to which a woman's well-being is considered.

Eshnunna Law Code 2000s b.c.e.[*]

¶15 A merchant or a woman innkeeper will not accept silver, grain, wool, oil, or anything else from a male or female slave.

¶17 Should a member of the *awīlu*-class bring the bridewealth to the house of his father-in-law—if either (the groom or bride then) should go to his or her fate, the silver shall revert to its original owner (i.e., the widower or his heir).

¶23 If a man has no claim against another man but he nonetheless takes the man's slave woman as a distress, detains the distress in his house, and causes her death, he shall replace her with two slave women for the owner of the slave woman.

¶24 If he has no claim against him but he nonetheless takes the wife of a commoner or the child of a commoner as a distress, detains the distress in his house, and causes her or his death, it is a capital offense—the distrainer who distrained shall die.

¶26 If a man brings the bridewealth for the daughter of a man, but another, without the consent of her father and mother, abducts her and then deflowers her, it is indeed a capital offense—he shall die.

¶27 If a man marries the daughter of another man without the consent of her father and mother, and moreover does not conclude the nuptial feast and the contract for(?) her father and mother, should she reside in his house for even one full year, she is not a wife.

¶28 If he concludes the contract and the nuptial feast for(?) her father and mother and he marries her, she is indeed a wife; the day she is seized in the lap of another man, she shall die, she will not live.

*Eshnunna Law Code, translated by Martha T. Roth, *LCMAM* 1995-57-71 Excerpts

¶29 If a man should be captured or abducted during a raiding expedition or while on patrol(?), even should he reside in a foreign land for a long time, should someone else marry his wife and even should she bear a child, whenever he returns he shall take back his wife.

¶30 If a man repudiates his city and his master and then flees, and someone else then marries his wife, whenever he returns he will have no claim to his wife.

¶31 If a man should deflower the slave woman of another man, he shall weigh and deliver 20 shekels of silver, but the slave woman remains the property of her master.

¶32 If a man gives his child for suckling and for rearing but does not give the food, oil, and clothing rations (to the caregiver) for 3 years, he shall weigh and deliver 10 shekels of silver for the cost of the rearing of his child, and he shall take away his child.

¶33 If a slave woman acts to defraud and gives her child to a woman of the *awīlu*-class, when he grows up should his master locate him, he shall seize him and take him away.

¶34 If a slave woman of the palace should give her son or her daughter to a commoner for rearing, the palace shall remove the son or daughter whom she gave.

¶35 However, an adoptor who takes in adoption the child of a slave woman of the palace shall restore (another slave of) equal value for the palace.

¶41 If a foreigner, a *naptaru*, or a *mudû* wishes to sell his beer, the woman innkeeper shall sell the beer for him at the current rate.

¶59 If a man sired children but divorces his wife and then marries another, he shall be expelled from the house and any possessions there may be and he shall depart after the one who . . . , [. . .] the house . . .

The small selection of texts that follow are from Hittite culture established ca. 1800 B.C.E. by Indo-European tribes to the west of Mesopotamia in the area of (the former) Anatolia (see Chapter 1). The Hittites are definitely a martial people and the laws concerning women represent more severe treatment of women than in the codes we have looked at from Mesopotamia. Be aware, however, that as patriarchal models of social organization become more firmly entrenched, laws pertaining to women become increasingly stringent and repressive.

HITTITE LAW CODES CA. 1800 B.C.E.*

26 (A): If a woman send away a man[. . .], and the man shall get his children.

26 (B): If a man divorces a woman, and he may sell her; whoever [buys her] shall give 12 shekels of silver.

27: If a man takes a wife and carries her [to his house], he takes her dowry with her. If the woman dies, they turn her property into the property of the man and the man also receives her dowry.

But if she dies in the house of her father and there are children, the man will not receive her dowry.

*"The Hittite Laws," excerpts, translated by A. Goetze, *ANET*, 1955, 190.

31: If a free man and a slave-girl (are) lovers and they cohabit, he takes her for his wife, they found a family and have children, but subsequently, either (as) they quarrel or (as) they reach a friendly agreement, they break up the family, the man receives the children, but the woman receives one child.

32: If a slave takes a free woman, the provision of the law is the same for them.

34: If a slave brings the bride-price for a woman and takes her for his wife, no one shall change her social status.

The extensive and elaborate law code from the reign of Hammurabi in the latter part of the eighteenth century B.C.E. is the best-known legal document among students introduced to the building blocks of Western civilization. Selections that follow pertain specifically to the status of women. Note however, from whose perspective the majority of these texts are formulated. In instances where the female is the subject, not the object of the law, her status is a clear determinant. Note that unless designated differently reference to the male indicate any free man of standing.

Law Code of Hammurabi, 1700s b.c.e.[*]

¶17 If a man seizes a fugitive slave or slave woman in the open country and leads him back to his owner, the slave owner shall give him 2 shekels of silver.

¶40 (However), a *naditu*, a merchant, or a holder of a field with a special service obligation may sell her or his field, orchard, or house; the buyer shall perform the service obligation on the field, orchard, or house which he purchases.

¶108 If a woman innkeeper should refuse to accept grain for the price of beer but accepts (only) silver measured by the large weight, thereby reducing the value of beer in relation to the value of grain, they shall charge and convict that woman innkeeper and they shall cast her into the water.

¶109 If there should be a woman innkeeper in whose house criminals congregate, and she does not seize those criminals and lead them off to the palace authorities, that woman innkeeper shall be killed.

¶110 If a *naditu* or an *ugbabtu* who does not reside within the cloister should open a tavern or enter a tavern for some beer, they shall burn that woman.

¶118 If he should give a male or female slave into debt service, the merchant may extend the term (beyond the three years), he may sell him; there are no grounds for a claim.

¶119 If an obligation is outstanding against a man and he therefore sells his slave woman who has borne him children . . .

¶127 If a man causes a finger to be pointed in accusation against an *ugbabtu* or against a man's wife but cannot bring proof, they shall flog that man before the judges and they shall shave off half of his hair.

¶128 If a man marries a wife but does not draw up a formal contract for her, she is not a wife.

¶129 If a man's wife should be seized lying with another male, they shall bind them and throw them into the

*Law Code of Hammurabi. Translated by Martha T. Roth, *LCMAM*, 1995. 23 ff.

water; if the wife's master allows his wife to live, then the king shall allow his subject (i.e., the other male) to live.

¶130 If a man pins down another man's virgin wife who is still residing in her father's house, and they seize him lying with her, that man shall be killed; that woman shall be released.

¶132 If a man's wife should have a finger pointed against her in accusation involving another male, although she has not been seized lying with another male, she shall submit to the divine River Ordeal for her husband.

¶135 If a man should be captured and there are not sufficient provisions in his house, before his return his wife enters another's house and bears children, and afterwards her husband returns and gets back to his city, that woman shall return to her first husband; the children shall inherit from their father.

¶137 If a man should decide to divorce a *šugītu* who bore him children, or a *nadītu* who provided him with children, they shall return to that woman her dowry and they shall give her one half of (her husband's) field, orchard, and property, and she shall raise her children; after she has raised her children, they shall give her a share comparable in value to that of one heir from whatever properties are given to her sons, and a husband of her choice may marry her.

¶138 If a man intends to divorce his first-ranking wife who did not bear him children, he shall give her silver as much as was her bridewealth and restore to her the dowry that she brought from her father's house, and he shall divorce her.

¶141 If the wife of a man who is residing in the man's house should decide to leave, and she appropriates goods, squanders her household possessions, or disparages her husband, they shall charge and convict her; and if her husband should declare his intention to divorce her, then he shall divorce her; neither her travel expenses, nor her divorce settlement, nor anything else shall be given to her. If her husband should not declare his intention to divorce her, then her husband may marry another woman and that (first) woman shall reside in her husband's house as a slave woman.

¶142 If a woman repudiates her husband, and declares, "You will not have marital relations with me"—her circumstances shall be investigated by the authorities of her city quarter, and if she is circumspect and without fault, but her husband is wayward and disparages her greatly, that woman will not be subject to any penalty; she shall take her dowry and she shall depart for her father's house.

¶143 If she is not circumspect but is wayward, squanders her household possessions, and disparages her husband, they shall cast that woman into the water.

¶145 If a man marries a *nadītu,* and she does not provide him with children, and that man then decides to marry a *šugītu,* that man may marry the *šugītu* and bring her into his house; that *šugītu* should not aspire to equal status with the *nadītu.*

¶150 If a man awards to his wife a field, orchard, house, or movable property, and makes out a sealed document for her, after her husband's death her children will not bring a claim against her; the mother shall give her estate to whichever of her children she loves, but she will not give it to an outsider.

¶152 If a debt should be incurred by them after that woman enters the man's house, both of them shall satisfy the merchant.

¶153 If a man's wife has her husband killed on account of (her relationship with) another male, they shall impale that woman.

¶154 If a man should carnally know his daughter, they shall banish that man from the city.

¶155 If a man selects a bride for his son and his son carnally knows her, after which he himself then lies with her and they seize him in the act, they shall bind that man and cast him into the water.

¶157 If a man, after his father's death, should lie with his mother, they shall burn them both.

¶162 If a man marries a wife, she bears him children, and that woman then goes to her fate, her father shall have no claim to her dowry; her dowry belongs only to her children.

¶167 If a man marries a wife and she bears him children, and later that woman goes to her fate, and after her death he marries another woman and she bears children, after which the father then goes to his fate, the children will not divide the estate according to the mothers; they shall take the dowries of their respective mothers and then equally divide the property of the paternal estate.

¶170 If a man's first-ranking wife bears him children and his slave woman bears him children, and the father during his lifetime then declares to (or: concerning) the children whom the slave woman bore to him, "My children," and he reckons them with the children of the first-ranking wife—after the father goes to his fate, the children of the first-ranking wife and the children of the slave woman shall equally divide the property of the paternal estate; the preferred heir is a son of the first-ranking wife, he shall select and take a share first.

¶172 . . . If that woman should decide on her own to depart [from her husband's house], she shall leave for her children the marriage settlement which her husband gave to her; she shall take the dowry brought from her father's house and a husband of her choice shall marry her.

¶173 If that woman should bear children to her latter husband into whose house she entered, after that woman dies, her former and latter children shall equally divide her dowry.

¶177 If a widow whose children are still young should decide to enter another's house, she will not enter without (the prior approval of) the judges. When she enters another's house, the judges shall investigate the estate of her former husband, and they shall entrust the estate of her former husband to her later husband and to that woman, and they shall have them record a tablet (inventorying the estate). They shall safeguard the estate and they shall raise the young children; they will not sell the household goods. Any buyer who buys the household goods of the children of a widow shall forfeit his silver; the property shall revert to its owner.

¶178 If there is an *ugbabtu*, a *nadītu*, or a *sekretu* whose father awards to her a dowry and records it in a tablet for her, but in the tablet that he records for her he does not grant her written authority to give her estate to whomever she pleases and does not give her full discretion—after the father goes to his fate, her brothers shall take her field and her orchard and they shall give to her food, oil, and clothing allowances in accordance with the value of her inheritance share, and they shall thereby satisfy her. If her brothers should not give to her food, oil, and clothing allowances in accordance with the value of her inheritance share and thus do not satisfy her, she shall give her field and her orchard to any agricultural tenant she pleases, and her agricultural tenant shall support her. As long as she lives, she shall enjoy the use of the field, orchard, and anything else which her father gave to her, but she will not sell it and she will not satisfy another person's obligations with it; her inheritance belongs only to her brothers.

¶179 If there is an *ugbabtu*, a *nadītu*, or a *sekretu* whose father awards to her a dowry and records it for her in a sealed document, and in the tablet that he records for her he grants her written authority to give her estate to whomever she pleases and gives her full discretion—after the father goes to his fate, she shall give her estate to whomever she pleases; her brothers will not raise a claim against her.

¶182 If a father does not award a dowry to his daughter who is a *nadītu* dedicated to the god Marduk of the city of Babylon or does not record it for her in a sealed document, after the father goes to his fate, she shall take with her brothers her one-third share from the property of the paternal estate as her inheritance, but she will not perform any service obligations; a *nadītu* dedicated to the god Marduk shall give her estate as she pleases.

WOMEN OUTSIDE THE NOBILITY

The majority of women in Ancient Near Eastern civilizations were women whose social location resided outside the nobility. For all but a minute percentage of women the demands and responsibilities of marriage and child rearing, work related to the creation of fabric for their families, farming and tending of flocks defined, in great measure, women's experience. Some women, however, did work in the public sphere.

Female Scribes

Precursors to writing in Old Europe, and in areas to the west of Mesopotamia are attested from perhaps as early as the eighth millenium B.C.E. Cuneiform tablets from Sumer dated at 3200 B.C.E. are among the earliest, if not the earliest, bodies of literature that have been translated and published. Mythological texts are assumed to reflect an earlier time. The Sumerian Deity of writing is the Goddess Nidubana. Scribal education was basic to all careers including clergy, military leaders, and civil servants. Among administrative positions held by women in the Ancient Near East is that of Scribe. Early cuneiform texts have also been discovered at Ebla and Mari.

Female Merchants and Artisans

Seals from Uruk and Jedmet Nasr provide evidence that female merchants and artisans included potters and many women engaged in the textile industry. Laws about women tavern owners and female owners of properties affirm women's participation in the public sphere. (See Legal Codes).

Female Serfs

Women in the lower classes would have been involved in agriculture, some aspects of animal husbandry, creation of textiles and clothing, commerce, making of pottery, and perhaps the creation of ornamentation such as jewelry, the managing of their households, and the rearing of children.

Female Slaves

Female slaves were employed in the textile industry in great numbers. They were domestic servants and were engaged in many of the same areas of work as women outside the aristocracy. Female domestic slaves to aristocratic families and their households may have experienced less overt oppression than female slaves in other occupations.

SUGGESTED READINGS

Lerner, Gerda. *The Creation of Patriarchy.* Oxford: Oxford University Press, 1986.

Lesko, Barbara. "Women in Egypt and the Ancient Near East." In *Becoming Visible: Women in European History.* Boston: Houghton Mifflin Company, 1987.

Seibert, Ilse. *Women in the Ancient Near East.* New York: Abner Schram, 1974.

Sources Cited

"The Enuma Elish: The Babylonian Genesis," translated by E. A. Speiser. In *Ancient Near Eastern Texts Relating to the Old Testament,* edited by James B. Pritchard, Princeton N.J., Princeton University Press, 1955. 39–42 Excerpts.

"Tomb Inscription of the Mother of King Nabonidus," translated by Tremper Longman III in *Contexts of Scripture: Canonical Compositions from the Biblical World,* Vol. 1, Leiden. London, Koln: Brill, 1997. 519–521.

Batto, Bernard Frank. *Studies on Women at Mari,* Baltimore and London: Johns Hopkins University Press, 1974. 9, 10, 11, 13, 14, 15, 17, 18, 19, 20, 21, 22, 23, 38, 59.

"Lipit-Ishtar Lawcode," translated by Martha T. Roth in *Law Collections from Mesopotamia and Asia Minor,* edited by Pitor Michaelowski, Writings from the Ancient World Series, Society of Biblical Literature, Atlanta: Scholars Press, 1995. 23–36 Excerpts.

"Laws from Ur Nammu," translated by J.J. Finklestein, *Ancient Near Eastern Texts Relating to the Old Testament,* edited by James B. Pritchard, Princeton, N.J. Princeton University Press, 1969. Supplement, 524.

"Laws from Eshnunna," translated by Martha T. Roth in *Laws Collections from Mesopotamia and Asia Minor,* edited by Pitor Michaelowski, Writings from the Ancient World Series, Society of Biblical Literature, Atlanta: Scholars Press, 1995. 57–71 Excerpts.

"The Hittite Laws," translated by Albrecht Goetze, *ANET,* 1955, 190.

"Laws of Hammurabi," translated by Martha T. Roth in *Law Collections from Mesopotamia and Asia Minor,* edited by Pitor Michaelowski, Writings from the Ancient World Series, Society of Biblical Literature, Atlanta: Scholars Press, 1995. 71–143.

Chapter 4

Ancient Egypt

In recent years a number of controversial issues have informed new interpretative frameworks for studies of the history and culture of Egypt. The majority of these controversies emerge from challenges to Eurocentric and Darwinian perspectives that dominated scholarship on the subject in the nineteenth century and most of the twentieth century. These challenges pertain especially to linguistics, writing, population theories, and Egyptian and Near Eastern influence on Greek culture and the reverse. Questions emerging from scholars in women's studies have not received a great deal of attention but as this chapter attests they are beginning to be addressed.

A principal issue in historical research in any area of inquiry is the accuracy of chronological records. Apparently, until the composition of historical chronologies assembled by Mantheo, a scribe and priest in the Ptolemaic dynasty (322-30 B.C.E.), it was customary for historical periods in Egypt, and in other ancient societies to be configured beginning with the rule of a particular monarch and concluding at the end of that individual monarch's reign. Thus we might read: in the third year of a king's reign, in the eighteenth year of his reign, and so on, until his death was recorded, at which point time was then designated as the first year of the next monarch's reign. Mantheo's chronological system provided a continuous chronology, arranged into kingdoms (representing periods of order and prosperity) and intermediate periods (periods of disturbance and chaos) where the dynasties were numbered according to this schema. Historical Egypt thus begins at the end of the Predynastic period, ca. 3100 B.C.E., with the double kingship of the First Dynasty that included a monarch from both Lower and Upper Egypt. Scholarly research on the pre-dynastic period is sparse but contains evidence for cultural development similar in many respects to that discovered in Upper Paleolithic and Neolithic sites attested in earlier chapters. Egyptian settlements along the Nile River were, as already noted, divided into Lower Egypt and Upper Egypt (Lower Egypt is actually north of Upper Egypt). Upper Egypt extended roughly 700 miles from the south up into the Nile Delta. Lower Egypt occupied the more fertile delta land and also had the advantage of the Mediterranean seacoast that facilitated Egyptian trade and commerce.

Two additional problems that influence the study of Ancient Egypt have to do with the nature of the source material and the interests and biases of the Egyptologists. Earliest excavators were interested in the spectacular wealth of artifacts discovered in the tomb burials of the pyramids. And, whereas today every stage of the excavation process is carefully noted and recorded, ordinary artifacts that early excavators exhumed were not considered important and were simply not catalogued.

Many textual, archaeological, and iconographic artifacts have been excavated from the desert areas in Egypt. The area of the Nile Delta, however, which was the economic center of the land, is much more difficult and expensive to excavate. Due to fewer excavations in the Delta area, the record of what we do know about Egyptian culture in antiquity is limited. It is important to recognize that there are vast gaps in the whole of our knowledge about ancient Egypt, especially in areas concerning women's experience.

SOCIAL ORGANIZATION

Scholarship concerning women and social organization in Pre-dynastic Egypt is limited. Evidence for women's status is inferred by the importance of female deities (in a manner similar to that of Mesopotamia) and by the evidence for matrilineal lines of descent. The single most important deity in the first two dynasties is the Goddess Neith whose presence surpasses that of Horus (the titular deity of the king). A survey of the literature from the first two dynasties yielded 107 references to Neith which constitutes over 40 percent of the listings of a single deity from this period. Neith, like Ma'at, discussed as we proceed, is also perceived as one who orders the cosmos. Hollis suggests that the dominance of Neith in the early period indicates she may indeed have been considered a creator deity in earliest times. However, because her city, Sais, had no political importance this probability has not yet received notable scholarly attention (Hollis 1992, 6). Theophoric names (names that make a statement about the deity or deities incorporated in it) for Neith include those related to her cultus, namely, beneficial behavior, geographical location, warrior spirit, spiritual relationship, and names affirming the individual's attitude or action toward her. There were kings in Predynastic Egypt, and the decorations on their uraeus (crowns) included the cobra serpent symbolism of the Goddess Wadjet of Lower Egypt and her Upper Egyptian counterpart Nekhbet, the vulture goddess. This symbolism that incorporates iconography of a female deity as integral to the regal "crown" attests to the importance of the Female Principle of the Divine (Hollis 1992, 11). The persistence of this symbolic imagery associated with the ruling king, and eventually the queen, conveys a strong female element in royalty. It is not until the dynastic periods, however, that substantive evidence concerning historical women is available. Consistent with findings from the Ancient Near East, the majority of information available from Egypt pertains exclusively to women in the upper strata of Egyptian society.

Hierarchical social organization prevailed in Ancient Egypt. The world of the Gods was predominant. The Pharaoh or king, the highest member of the human population, was considered to be the personification of Egypt and believed to intervene between the Gods and the people. Members of the Pharaoh's family also occupied a position at the apex of the earthly sphere. As writing was instituted, and culture became more complex, an elite class of scribes and priests evolved who administered Egypt's powerful male bureaucracy. These men (and occasionally women), who represented a minuscule percentage of the total population, generated the majority of the source material that we have for Ancient Egypt. They, along with their families, ranked under the royal family but above the rest of society. Merchants, minor professionals, and artisans were next in the hierarchy. In each of the socially stratified societies we have examined thus far, the great majority of the population was comprised of a peasant class. Slaves comprised the lowest echelon of society.

It is estimated that fewer than 2 percent of the population were literate and this group of men virtually ran the country. It is probable that women of the elite scribal class were also literate and had learned both reading and writing (Robins 1993, 16). There are not at the present stage of research any early dynastic sources that were, like Enheduanna's hymn to Inanna (Chapter 2), composed and written by a woman.

RELIGION

Relationship to the Holy, being in the favor of the Goddesses and Gods, and hope for a prosperous life after death were central themes among the elite classes who produced the written accounts of life in Ancient Egypt. Despite the stability that is a characteristic of Egyptian culture, the history of religion in Egypt is extensive and complex. There came to be over millennia countless myths, legends, and stories about deities in the vast pantheon that were sometimes represented as *zoomorphic,* sometimes *anthropomorphic,* and sometimes as hybrid combinations.

Different deities enjoyed favor in different periods depending upon the theological (and sometimes political) propensities of the Pharaoh and the ruling elite. Although it is not a topic of discussion in the present volume, among the most fascinating aspects of Egyptian religion is the emphasis on both monumental and intricate, intensive preparations for the afterlife. Readings selected in the present section on religion, however, are limited to categories of the Holy in myth and ritual and evidence for female religious functionaries.

The Holy/Myth: Female Principle of the Divine

As previously noted, the Egyptian pantheon was vast and varied. Unlike Indo-European pantheons with male sky Gods as the chief deities, among the earliest Egyptian sky Gods was the Goddess Nut whose consort was the earth God, Geb. There are numerous creation stories in Egyptian mythology and the most popular stories have acquired myriad variations as they have been transmitted over time. In Egyptian mythology, the divine and human worlds came into being at the same time and there is a complex interaction between them. Both male and female principles of the divine functioned to energize the structure and substance of the universe and both also functioned to bring about cosmic renewal.

Ma'at is a Divine Principle of Cosmic Order. This complex concept that encompassed truth and justice represented the ideal state of the universe. All of the order in the universe and in society is sustained by Ma'at. As the Source of Wisdom Ma'at is depicted as a Female Principle of the Divine. Succeeding chapters in this anthology reveal that many patriarchal cultures designated and assigned characteristics of Wisdom to female deities. Ma'at is honored in Egypt's Wisdom literature and some scholars propose that the defining characteristics of Hockhmah, in the Wisdom literature of Ancient Israel, are influenced by this Divine Principle in Egyptian mythology. Ma'at is acknowledged as a governing principle in this hymn of praise to Aten and the King.

MA'AT, COSMIC FEMALE PRINCIPLE OF WISDOM AND JUDGMENT OF THE DEAD*

Adoration of Re-Harakhti-who-rejoices-in-lightland. In his name Shu-who is-Aten, who gives life forever; by the king who lives by Ma'at, the Lord of the Two Lands (and of) the King of Upper and Lower Egypt: Neferkheprure, Sole-one-of-Re, the

*From "Hymn to Aten and the King." In *Ancient Egyptian Literature: A Book of Readings, Vol. II, The New Kingdom.* Edited by Miriam Lichtheim. Published under the auspices of the Gustave E. von Grunebaum Center for Near Eastern Studies. Berkeley, Los Angeles, London: University of California Press, 1973, 124–125.

Son of Re: who lives by Ma'at, the Lord crowns Akhenaten, great in his lifetime;
(and) the great Queen Nefer-Nefru-Aten Nefertiti, living forever,
Praises to you when you dawn in lightland, O living Aten, lord of eternity!
Kissing the ground when you dawn in heaven, To light all lands with your beauty,
The Ruler of Ma'at who came from eternity,
The Son of Re who exalts his beauty,
Who offers him the product of his rays, The King who lives by Ma'at,
The Lord of the Two Lands, Neferkheprure, Sole-one-of-Re,
    (And) the great Queen, Nefer-Nefru-Aten Nefertiti

One of the most ancient and important Egyptian myths is that of Isis and Osiris. This myth, the essence of which is discussed here, has numerous variations. The principal components of its life, death, and rebirth themes are for the most part consistent. The creator deity, Heiropolis, who produced male and female pairs of deities, contained both male and female potential (this female potential was later known as Hathor) (Robins 1993, 17). The principal deities created were generated in male/female pairs: Shu (air)-Tefnut (moisture) and Geb (earth)-Nut (sky) who produced Isis and Osiris and their sister Nepthys and brother Seth. Seth murdered his brother Osiris in a jealous rage. Isis and Nepthys mourned their brother Osiris and searched throughout Egypt for his dismembered body. When they had retrieved all of the parts, Isis reconstructed Osiris' body and conceived a son by him. This son, Horus, would eventually avenge his father. Isis protected Horus with her magic and ingenuity. She was known from very ancient times as a protectress and as a Goddess who brought hope related to the afterlife. By the close of the first century B.C.E., Isis was the most powerful deity in the Greco-Roman world. The selection that follows is an early example (ca. 1250–1300 B.C.E.) that illustrates her wit and wisdom.

In the ancient world one's name was integral to personality and power. A name might be so charged with divine potency that it could not be pronounced. In this case the God Re kept a name hidden in order to keep an element of power and supremacy over all other Gods and humankind. The Goddess Isis plotted to learn this name and thus to secure power for herself. Isis, using persuasion and knowledge of ancient lore, outwitted Egypt's most powerful God.

THE GODDESS ISIS DISCOVERS RE'S UNKNOWN NAME OF POWER[*]

SPELL of the divine god, who came into being by himself, who made heaven, earth, water, the breath of life, fire, gods, men, flocks, herds, reptiles, birds, and fish, the kingship of gods and men altogether, with limits beyond numerous years, [. . .] and with numerous names. One did not know that (name); one did not know this (name).

Now, Isis was a wise woman. Her heart was more devious than millions among men; she was more selective than millions among the gods; she was more exacting than millions among the blessed dead. There was nothing that she did not know in heaven or earth, like Re, who made the substance of the earth. The goddess planned in her heart to learn the name of the noble god.

Now, Re entered every day in front of the crew (of the solar bark), being established on the throne of the two horizons. A divine old age had weakened his mouth

*The Legend of Isis and the Name of Re. Translated by Robert K. Ritner, COS, 1997, 519–521.

so that he cast his spittle to the earth. He spat out, it lying fallen upon the ground. Isis kneaded it for herself with her hand, together with the earth that was on it. She formed it into a noble serpent; she made (it) in the form of a sharp point. It could not move, though it lived before her. She left it at the crossroads by which the great god passed in accordance with his heart's desire through his Two Lands. The noble god appeared outside, with the gods from the palace in his following, so that he might stroll just like every day. The noble serpent bit him, with a living fire coming forth from his own self. It raged(?) among the pines. The divine god worked his mouth; the voice of his majesty reached up to heaven. His Ennead said: "What is it? What is it?" His gods said: "What? What?" He could not find his speech to answer concerning it. His lips were quivering, and all his limbs were trembling. The poison seized upon his flesh as the inundation seizes what is behind it. The great god regained his composure and cried out to his followers: "Come to me, you who have come to be from my body, gods who came forth from me, so that I might let you know its development. Something painful has stabbed me. My heart does not know it. My eyes did not see it. My hand did not make it. I cannot recognize it among any of the things that I have made. I have not tasted a suffering like it. There is nothing more painful than it."

"I am a noble, son of a noble, the fluid of a god come forth from a god. I am a great one, son of a great one. My father thought out my name. I am one who has numerous names and numerous forms. My form exists as every god. I am called Atum and Horus of Praise. My father and mother told me my name. I have hidden it in my body from my children so as to prevent the power of a male or female magician from coming into existence against me. I went outside to see what I had made, to stroll in the Two Lands that I created, and something stung me. I do not know it. It is not really fire; it is not really water, though my heart is on fire and my body is trembling, all my members giving birth to a chill."

"Let the children of the gods be brought to me, whose words are magically effective, who know their spells, whose wisdom reaches up to heaven!"

The children of the god then came, each man of them bearing his boasting. Isis came bearing her effective magic, her speech being the breath of life, her utterance dispelling suffering, her words revivifying one whose throat is constricted. She said: "What is it, what is it, my divine father? What, a serpent has inflicted weakness upon you? One of your children has raised his head against you? Then I shall overthrow it by efficacious magic, causing him to retreat at the sight of your rays."

The holy god opened his mouth: "It was the case that I was going on the road, strolling in the Two Lands and the deserts. My heart desired to see what I had created. I was bitten by a serpent without seeing it. It is not really fire; it is not really water, though I am colder than water and hotter than fire, my entire body with sweat. I am trembling, my eye unstable; I cannot see. Heaven beats down rain upon my face in the time of summer!"

THEN SAID Isis to Re: "Say to me your name, my divine father, for a man lives when one recites in his name."

(Re said:) "I am the one who made heaven and earth, who knit together the mountains, who created that which exists upon it. I am the one who made the water, so that the Great Swimming One came into being. I made the bull for the cow, so that sexual pleasure came into being. I am the one who made heaven and the mysteries of the horizons; I placed the *ba*-spirits of the gods inside it. I am the one who opens his two eyes so that brightness comes into being, who closes his two eyes so that darkness comes into being, according to whose command the inundation surges, whose name the gods do not know. I am the one who made the hours so that the days came into being. I am the one who divided the year, who created the river. I am the one who made living fire, in order to create the craft of the palace. I am Khepri in the morning, Re at noon, and Atum who is in the evening."

The poison was not repelled in its course; the great god was not comforted.

Then Isis said to Re: "Your name is not really among those that you have said to me. Say it to me so that the poison might go out, for a man lives when one pronounces his name."

The poison burned with a burning; it was more powerful than flame or fire.

Then the majesty of Re said: "May you give to me your two ears, my daughter Isis, so that my name might go forth from my body to your body. The most divine one among the gods had hidden it, so that my status might be broadened within the Bark of Millions. If there occurs a similar occasion when a heart goes out to you, say it to your son Horus after you have bound him by a divine oath, placing god in his eyes." The great god announced his name to Isis, the Great One of Magic.

"Flow out, scorpions! Come forth from Re, Eye of Horus! Come forth from the god, flame of the mouth. I am the one who made you; I am the one who sent you. Come out upon the ground, powerful poison! Behold, the great god has announced his name. Re lives; the poison is dead. NN, born of NN, lives; the poison is dead, through the speech of Isis the Great, the Mistress of the Gods, who knows Re by his own name."

Words to be recited over an image of Atum and of Horus-of-Praise, a figure of Isis, and an image of Horus, DRAWN (ON) THE HAND OF THE SUFFERER AND LICKED OFF BY THE MAN; DO LIKEWISE ON A STRIP OF FINE LINEN, PLACED ON THE SUFFERER AT HIS THROAT. THE PLANT IS SCORPION PLANT. GROUND UP WITH BEER OR WINE, IT IS DRUNK BY THE MAN WHO HAS A SCORPION STING. IT IS WHAT KILLS THE POISON—TRULY EFFECTIVE, (PROVED) MILLIONS OF TIMES.

The Holy/Ritual

In envisioning religious rituals in the ancient world it is important to remember that the sites for ritual were predominately the temples and shrines of specific deities. These temples were not like present-day churches, mosques, and synagogues with preachers/rabbis/imams and sermons. Priests and priestesses attended the deity in rituals that included feeding and dressing the images of the deity; they officiated in ritual celebrations and feasts; and offered rituals of praise, sacrifice, intercession, and supplication for worshipers.

Dendera Lunet in Upper Egypt was the center for the worshiping community of the Goddess Hathor. Among the many texts that accompany the ritual scenes, a number of hymns (including this hymn) were translated with commentaries by H. Junker in 1906. Hathor was a bearer of fertility in all of its aspects. She was also a funerary deity who was concerned with rebirth into the afterlife. The sense of joy in this poem reflects Hathor's good side and contrasts vividly with her warrior aspect. The text accompanies a scene showing the king offering a wine jug to the enthroned Goddess.

Hymn to Hathor[*]

The King,
Pharaoh, comes to dance, he comes to
    sing;
Mistress see the dancing,
Wife of Horus see the skipping!
He offers it to you, This Jug;
Mistress see the dancing,

Wife of Horus see the skipping
its heart is straight, his inmost open, No
    darkness is in his breast;
Mistress see the dancing,
Wife of Horus see the skipping.
Golden one, how good is this song Like
    the song of Horus himself.

Female Religious Functionaries

The historical record shows that as early as the Fourth Dynasty women served as priestesses in temples and shrines. Priestesses attended female deities such as Neith and Hathor as well as Gods such as Amun. In the Hathor cult during the Old Kingdom a priestess who bore the title *mrt* was in charge of the management of the estates of the Goddess and her High Priest was sometimes a woman. Whereas earliest priestesses came from the highest echelons of society, by the New Kingdom numerous women of all classes were permitted to serve as religious functionaries. A priestly title carried prestige and respectability for the woman who bore it and was an indication of her intellectual capabilities (Watterson 1991, 139).

Although many women did hold high priestly office, it was not a general practice to appoint priestesses as administrators. They did, however, function significantly in the worship of the divinity. Among the most important tasks was the impersonation of the Goddess in rituals, and in the mortuary cult performing the same services in the tomb-chapel that were performed in the temple.

There is also substantial textual and iconographic evidence for women who served in the liturgical sphere as dancers, chantresses, and bearers of sacred imagery in processions. As in earlier periods, some of these positions were permanent and some were temporary. Education for permanent members of the priesthood was extensive and included the study of medicine, astronomy, and astrology in addition to the sacred myths and rituals of the deities to whom the individuals were consecrated. Many scribes were also members of the priestly class and were dedicated to specific deities.

The office of the God's Wife first appears in the Middle Kingdom and was apparently occupied by royal and nonroyal women. In the Eighteenth Dynasty it was a high priestly office and was occupied by women such as Ahmose, Nofretary, Hatshepsut, and Hatshepsut's daughter Nefrure, all of whom were commanding figures. The God's Wife position continued to be a seat of power for some 50 years for King/Queen Nitocris and for another 60 years for her niece who was invested with the title after the death of Nitocris. Compared to data about women in ancient Mesopotamia, for example, the En, Naditu, and Scribe, Egyptian records published thus far provide very little narrative textual evidence for the corresponding religious structures for women. We do have records however, confirming that the God's Wife/the Divine Adoratrice, like an En (High Priestess)

---

[*]Hymn to Hathor, translated by H. Junker, *Zeitschrift fur Ägyptische Sprache und Altertumskunde* 43 (1906), *ANET,* 1955, 101–127, 131.

or like a Naditu priestess, owned land and fields and buildings. She also had a retinue of officials who attended her that was headed by the First Majordomo (Menu, 1989, 193–205).

First Prophet of Amun

The office of First Prophet of Amun was conferred upon Princess Ankhnesneferibre by her great aunt Nitocris, who had maintained the title of God's Wife as the Divine Wife of Amun for over 50 years. By holding this office Nitocris, who had also served as a king of Egypt, ensured that the subsequent kings of Egypt could not send their men into Thebes as part of the retinue of The God's Wife Apparent. In 595 B.C.E. when she was in her seventies, Nitocris adopted her niece and installed her as the First Prophet of Amun, which was the High Priest of Amun, an office that was not accorded to any other God's Wife. When Nitocris died the stele used the same phrases used to mark the passing of a King of Egypt. Twelve days after the death of Nitocris, Ankhnesneferibre was invested with the office of the God's Wife of Amun. The office of Divine Wife or God's Wife was, without question, a position of exceptional power. Nitocris and her niece reigned as The God's Wife of Amun for over 130 years. (Watterson 1989, 170)

STELE OF NITOCRIS AT MEDINET HABU[*]

> Year 4 of Apries, 4th month of Shomu, day 4, the Divine Wife Nitocris, justified, was raised up to heaven, being united with the sun's disk, the divine flesh being merged with him who made it.

WOMEN IN THE ARISTOCRACY

Women of the aristocracy are represented as King, Queen, God's Wife, King's Mother, King's Principal Wife, King's Wife, and/or in the Priestly class as religious functionaries. The majority of what we know about women in Ancient Egypt represents women in the royal family and the women who were the wives, daughters, mothers, and sisters of the men in the bureaucracy who administered the country. It is important to remember that what was written represented the point of view of the scribal elite and reflects their interests, perspectives, and agendas.

Female Kings of Egypt

Six women are recognized as having been a king of Egypt: Meryt-Neith, Nitocris, Sobeknofru, Hatshepsut, Nefertiti, and Twosret. There is substantive evidence to support a claim that three of these women did in fact serve as kings in Egypt, although only Hatshepsut's reign was lengthy enough to significantly influence the monumental, iconographic, and textual records. J. Tyldesley notes that all six women were queen-consorts and thus were probably of royal blood, and with the exception of Meryt-Neith, all of the six produced only daughters. The reigns of each of these women would have been facilitated by the support of men who were advanced in the Egyptian hierarchy (Tyldesley 1994, 112–14, 221).

*Watterson 1989, 170

Meryt-Neith

The sumptuous burial of Queen Meryt-Neith first identified her as a king when her tomb was excavated in 1900. The burial is from the First Dynasty and she may have been the third ruler of the dynasty. The spacious tomb of Meryt-Neith is significant because when it was discovered among the burials of kings at Abydos with 44 attendants buried with her and 77 servants buried in a U-shape around her monument, it was assumed she was a man. Later, however, it was discovered that he was actually she. It is important to note that interpreters of the burial site found it difficult to confront hard evidence of Meryt-Neith's status as a monarch.

Nitocris

Nitocris is listed in the historical record as the first female king of Egypt. Nitocris's reign followed as the second or third successor after the death of her husband King Pepi II, who had ruled the Sixth Dynasty for 90 years. Mantheo, who developed the Egyptian chronology, remarked that Nitocris was the noblest and loveliest woman of her time. Her reign is reported to have lasted anywhere from two and a half years to twelve years at the beginning of the First Intermediate Period. When her reign as king ended, Nitocris maintained the powerful title and position as the God's Wife of Amun for over 50 years at Thebes.

Sobeknofru

Queen Sobeknofru held power as the king of Egypt briefly at the close of the Twelfth Dynasty, from ca. 1789 B.C.E., for almost four years. Her reign also occurred at a time of disintegration in the state at the close of the Middle Kingdom. She was a royal princess who was the sister of her husband Amenemhat IV and daughter of his father Amenemhat III. Scholars now assume that she became king in order to continue the dying royal line. Sobeknofru, unlike Hatshepsut, never dressed as a male, and her celebrity as a female ruler includes inscription of her name in the major lists of kings.

Hatshepsut

It is in the Eighteenth Dynasty that Hatshepsut assumed the throne as king of Egypt. This powerful and remarkable figure was the daughter of King Tuthmosis I and Queen Ahmose. During this especially prosperous dynasty the royal family in Egypt produced a shortage of sons and when it was deemed necessary, Pharaohs brought nonroyal males, such as Tuthmosis, into marriages with their daughters to serve as kings and, hopefully, to beget male heirs (Tyldesley, 1994, 221). Hatshepsut began her career as the undistinguished wife and queen consort of her half brother Tuthmosis II. She held the customary titles of King's Daughter, King's Great Wife, King's Sister, and God's Wife, and bore her half-brother two daughters, Neferure and Meritre-Hatshepsut. Tuthmosis II, having no male heir with Hatshepsut, designated his son from a concubine to succeed him. Titles of God's Wife, and Great Royal Wife were sufficient for Hatshepsut in the transitional period after her husband's death. By the seventh year after his demise, however, wearing the male costume of a king, Hatshepsut assumed the throne as King of Egypt as co-ruler with her stepson. Tuthmosis III apparently did not contest the arrangement. Her rule of 22 years was characterized by a flourishing economy and impressive building projects. Scholars continue to puzzle over the complexities of Hatshepsut's assertions about her divine and human designation as king. The selection that follows elucidates her perspective on her own commitment to the Deities.

OBELISK INSCRIPTIONS OF QUEEN HATSHEPSUT IN THE TEMPLE OF KARNAK[*]

[*Speech of the Queen* Dedicated to Her
 Father]
I have done this with a loving heart for
 my father Amun;
Initiated in his secret of the beginning,
Acquainted with his beneficent might,
I did not forget whatever he had
 ordained.
My majesty knows his divinity,
I acted under his command;
It was he who led me,
I did not plan a work without his doing.
It was he who gave directions,
I did not sleep because of his temple,
I did not stray from what he commanded.
My heart was Sia' before my father,
I entered into the plans of his heart.
I did not turn my back to the city of the
 All-Lord,
Rather did I turn my face to it. . . .
His favored place that bears his beauty,
That gathers in his followers.
It is the King himself who says:
I declare before the folk who shall be in
 the future,
Who shall observe the monument I
 made for my father,
Who shall speak in discussion,
Who shall look to posterity-
It was when I sat in the palace,

And thought of my maker,
That my heart led me to make for him
Two obelisks of electrum,
Whose summits would reach the heavens,
In the august hall of columns,
Between the two great portals of the
 King, . . .
Now my heart turns to and fro,
In thinking what will the people say,
They who shall see my monument in
 after years,
And shall speak of what I have done.
Beware of saying, I know not, I know not:
Why has this been done?
To fashion a mountain of gold through-
 out,
Like something that just happened.
I swear, as I am loved of Re,
As Amun, my father, favors me,
As my nostrils are refreshed with life
 and dominion,
As I wear the white crown,
As I appear with the red crown,
As the Two Lords have joined their por-
 tions for me,
As I rule this land like the son of Isis,
As I am mighty like the son of Nut, . . .
As sky endures, as his creation lasts,
As I shall be eternal like an undying star,
As I shall rest in life like Atum-

So as regards these two great obelisks, wrought with electrum by my majesty for my
father Amun, In order that my name may endure in this temple, For eternity and
everlastingness. . . .

Not shall he who hears it say,
"It is a boast," what I have said;
Rather say, "How like her it is,
she is devoted to her father!"
Lo, the God knows me well,
Amun, Lord of Thrones-of-the-Two-
 Lands;

He made me rule Black Land and Red
 Land as reward,
No one rebels against me in all lands.
All foreign lands are my subjects,
He placed my border at the limits of
 heaven, What Aten encircles labors
 for me.

*Excerpts from Hatshepsut's Stele Publication: *Ancient Egyptian Literature,* edited by Miriam Lichtheim, The New Kingdom: Published under the auspices of The Gustave E. von Grunebaum Center for Near Eastern Studies, University of California, Los Angeles, *Ancient Egyptian Literature,* 1973, Volume II, 25–28.

He gave it to him who came from him,
    Knowing I would rule it for him.
I am his daughter in very truth,
Who serves him, who knows what he
    ordains. My reward from my father is
    life-stability-rule,
On the Horus throne of all the living,
    eternally like Re.
All foreign lands are my subjects,
He placed my border at the limits of
    heaven,
	What Aten encircles labors for me.
	He gave it to him who came from him,
	    Knowing I would rule it for him.
	I am his daughter in very truth,
	Who serves him, who knows what he
	    ordains.
	My reward from my father is life-
	    stability-rule,
	On the Horus throne of all the living,
	    eternally like Re.

Nefertiti

The Egyptian queen who is most noted for her beauty, Nefertiti, also reigned in the Eighteenth Dynasty as Principal Wife of King Amenhotep IV, who assumed the name Akhenaten during his attempt to institutionalize radical religious reform. Nefertiti was supportive of her husband's commitment to a monotheistic religion, Aten or the Aten, founded on the worship of the sun. She took as a *theophoric* name Neferneruaten-Nefertiti (beautiful are the beauties of the Aten) and was a prominent figure in ritual celebrations. Eventually both she and her husband were included as objects of devotion among their faithful subjects. During this period (known now as the Armana period) transitions in art and fashion consciously de-emphasized sexual distinction and adopted a more leisurely and informal style. These new conventions heighten our sense of mutuality and equality between Nefertiti and Akhenaten and between other males and females represented in art.

Twosret

In the Nineteenth Dynasty, Twosret was the last woman to serve as king of Egypt. Her ascent to the throne was effected by a gradual seizing of power as she mentored the stepson who became king at the death of her husband Seti II. Despite great chaos during the reign of her stepson, Twosret managed to secure the full rights and recognitions of a male king of both Lower and Upper Egypt.

Female Queens of Egypt

This next text is taken from the *Annals of Suppiluliumas* compiled by his son Mursilis. The queen who writes the letter is Ankhesenamun, one of the six daughters of Nefertiti and Akhenaten.

QUEEN ANKHESENAMUN OF EGYPT AND KING SUPPILULIUMA[*]

While my father was in the land of Carchemish, he sent Lupakki and Tarhunta(?)-zalma into the land of Amqa. They went to attack Amqa and brought civilian captives, cattle and sheep back to my father. When the people of Egypt heard of the attack on Amqa, they were afraid. And since their lord Nibḫururiya (=Tutankhamun) had just died, the Queen of Egypt (=Ankhesenamun), who was the

---

[*]From "Deeds of Suppiluliuma," translated by Harry A. Hoffner Jr., *COS,* 1990, vol. 1, 190.

king's wife, sent a messenger to my father saying: "My husband has died, and I have no son. They say you have many sons. If you will give me one of your sons, he will become my husband. I do not wish to choose a subject of mine and make him my husband . . . I am afraid." When my father heard this, he convened the Great Ones for council (saying): "Nothing like this has ever happened to me in my whole life." My father sent Ḫattuša-ziti, the chamberlain, to Egypt (with this order): "Go bring back the true story to me. Maybe they are trying to deceive me. Maybe (in fact) they do have a son of their lord. Bring back the true story to me." . . .

When spring arrived, Ḫattuša-ziti [came back] from Egypt, and the messenger of Egypt, Lord Hani, came with him. Now, since my father—when he sent Ḫattuša-ziti to Egypt—had given him these orders: "Maybe they have a son of their lord. Maybe they deceive me and do not want my son for the kingship."—therefore the queen of Egypt wrote back to my father as follows: "Why did you say 'they deceive me' in that way? If I had a son, would I have written about my own and my land's embarrassing predicament to a foreign land? You did not believe me and have dared to speak this way to me. My husband has died, and I have no son. I do not wish to take one of my subjects and make him my husband. I have written to no other land, only to you. They say you have many sons. Well then, give me one of them. To me he will be a husband, but in Egypt he will be king." So, since my father was kindhearted, he granted the woman's wish and set about choosing the son he would send.

Queen Tiye

Queen Tiye, the Great Royal Wife of Amenhotep III in the fourteenth century B.C.E., reigned as queen and queen mother for over half a century. This great Nubian monarch, who bore four daughters and two sons, was the mother of two Pharaohs, Akhenaten and Tutankhamen, and mother-in-law of Nefertiti. In what began as a political alliance to quell military invasions in Nubia, the northern portion of the Nubian-Kushite stronghold on the Nile (present day Ethiopia, Chad, Niger, Mali, and Senegal), Amenhotep demonstrated high regard and affection for his queen. When Egyptian officials contested his marriage to a woman who was outside the royal family, Amenhotep persisted. Tiye was an educated woman, the daughter of High Priests, and her personal library reflected religious, historical, and scientific texts. Tiye acquired wealth, power, and respect and was a significant stabilizing force in Egypt during the years that her husband's health declined, when her son Akhenaten devoted his energies to religious reform and when her two youngest sons Smenkhare and Tutankhamen reigned.

A PROCLAMATION BY AMENHOTEP III[*]

The Princess, the most praised, the lady of grace, sweet in her love, who fills the palace with her beauty, the Regent of the North and of the South, the Great Wife of the King who loves her, the lady of both lands, Tiye.

*(Simon 1984, 64)

WOMEN OUTSIDE THE NOBILITY

We learn very little about the experiences of either men or women outside the aristocracy until the New Kingdom. Categories of literature that contribute to our knowledge of women's experience include legal status, professions, and occupations. Wisdom literature and love poetry are categories of inquiry that tell us more about male ideas about women than about women's experience.

Legal Status of Women

Despite the rigid class system in Ancient Egypt, upward social mobility was possible for women. Iconographic, inscriptive, and textual evidence indicates what women living in the New Kingdom could and did advance their social status.

Women in all social strata could and did engage in activities without the need of a male representative. In dynasties of the New Kingdom, women's equality to men under the law across lines of social class is unquestionably attested.

Women's participation in legal transactions declined in the Twenty-fifth to Thirty-first Dynasties and did not increase again until the Ptolemaic period. Nonetheless, contracts have been preserved in the following categories: loans, renting of fields, selling of land, houses, offices, provisions to be furnished or supplied, tombs, domestic animals, thread, and transfer of services. (Menu 1989, 201)

Women's Occupations

In the Thirteenth Dynasty (mid-eighteenth century B.C.E.) there is evidence for the presence of numerous women from the Ancient Near East serving in Egyptian households. Whether they should specifically be called slaves is not certain, even if probable. Since there is no contemporaneous evidence for military capture of lands specifically in these regions and considering the number of Semitic names, the biblical Joseph story (Gen. 37:28, 36) may supply the solution. This story suggests

---

Chart 4–1   Legal Rights of Women

Own and administer land and property
Inherit in their own name
Will their property to others
Initiate and/or conclude legal cases
Be a contracting partner for marriage and divorce
Engage wet nurses
Free slaves
Contract themselves as a slave (e.g., at a temple)
Make adoptions
Bring lawsuits against anyone
Serve as witness in legal disputes

Data adapted from Bernadette Menu, "Women in Business Life in the First Millenium B.C." In Women's Earliest Records: From Ancient Egypt and Western Asia, *edited by Barbara Lesko. Atlanta: Brown Judaic Studies, Scholars Press, 1989, 193–205.*

Chart 4–2   Females from the Ancient Near East in Egyptian Household Service

Female Hairdresser, Weavers and Warpers
The maidservant, Iy's daughter Sat-Gemeni-it is her name-hairdresser.
Her daughter Renes-seneb-it is her name-child.
The Asiatic woman, Rehui-she is called Kai-pu-nebi -warper of cloth.
The Asiatic woman, Haiimmi-she is called . . . -weaver of linen.
The Asiatic woman, Menahem-she [is called . . . weaver of linen.
The Asiatic woman, Sekrat'-she is called Wer-dit-ni-Nub- weaver of linen.
(The Asiatic woman), Immi-Sukru5-(she is called) Seneb-[Sen]-Usert-[weaver of] linen.
The Asiatic woman, Aduttu-(she is called) Nub . . . -[weaver of li]nen.
(The Asiatic woman), [Se]kratu-(she is called) Sen[eb . . .]-weaver of cloth.
The Asiatic woman, Akhati-mer'-she is called Henuti-pu-Wadjet-warper of linen.
The Asiatic woman, Shepra-she is called Senebhenutes weaver of linen.
The Asiatic woman, Sukra-iputy- she is called Merit Nub-warper of cloth.
The Asiatic woman, Asher-[she is] called Wer-Intef. -weaver . . .
Her daughter, Senebtisy-it [is her name]—child.
The Asiatic woman, An[ath . . .]-she [is called] Nub-em-mer-Kis-weaver of linen.
The Asiatic woman, Shamashtu~-she is called Seneb-henut . . . warper of linen.
The maidservant, Wewi's daughter, Irit-it is her name- . . .
The Asiatic [woman,]i-huti- she is called Men—hesut- . . .
Her daughter, Dedet~-Mut . . . [it is her name]-child.
The Asiatic [woman], Akh . . . -linen.
The Asiatic [woman], Aduna-she is called Seneb-he[nut . . .]- . . .
The Asiatic woman, Baaltuya-she is called Wah-Res-seneb-

ANET Supplement, *1969, 117*

---

a trade in persons from the Ancient Near Eastern territories north and east of Egypt carried on by inhabitants of those territories. This list provides specific names of women and descriptors for their occupations.

Table 4–2, in its entirety, deals with more than 80 servants of a single Theban household, of whom more than 40 are stated to be from the Ancient Near East. There are many more women than men. Among the males are housemen, cooks, a brewer, and a tutor. The majority of the women worked in the weaving rooms. The translator of the text refers to the women as Asiatics, by which this is meant Western Asia, more commonly referred to in present-day scholarship as the Ancient Near East.

Education

The Hellenistic period discussed in Chapter 9, "The Hellenistic World," presents considerable evidence for the education of women in Egypt from 322 B.C.E. In the centuries that precede the Ptolemaic Dynasty in Egypt we have argued for the likelihood that women in the royal family and women of the scribal class were not just literate but educated. Among women outside this sphere Menu cites five areas of endeavor in which women in Ancient Egypt participated as professionals: priesthood, midwifery, mourning, dancing, and music (Menu, 1989). Training was demanded for each of these professions that practiced in both sacred and secular contexts. Training in the temples was administered by temple personnel. There is also evidence for training in secular contexts.

Wisdom Literature

Composed in the New Kingdom, almost certainly in the Eighteenth Dynasty, this text is unusual because it is addressed to members of the middle class and pertains to the life of the average young man. Conventions for wisdom literature of this type are in the form of a father's instructions to his son when the young man reaches adulthood. The values represented reflect the evolution of the rising middle class in Egyptian society. The following excerpts pertain to instructions concerning the appropriate attitudes toward the women with whom the young man can anticipate relationships. In patriarchal cultures such attitudes traditionally shaped the framework of propriety between men and women of the nobility among whom the norms are set. These texts are especially significant because they illustrate one of the ways in which those same norms are transmitted to affect the lives of middle-class women.

THE INSTRUCTION OF ANI FROM THE REIGN OF QUEEN NEFERTARI[*]

[*Beginning of the educational instruction
    made by the Scribe Ani of the Palace of
    Queen Nefertari.*]
Take a wife while you're young,
That she make a son for you;
She should bear for you while you're
    youthful,
It is proper to make people.
Happy the man whose people are many,
He is saluted on account of his progeny.
Beware of a woman who is a stranger,
One not known in her town;
Don't stare at her when she goes by,
Do not know her carnally.
A deep water whose course is unknown,
Such is a woman away from her hus-
    band.
I am pretty, she tells you daily,
When she has no witnesses;
She is ready to ensnare you,
A great deadly crime when it is heard.
Double the food your mother gave you,
Support her as she supported you;
She had a heavy load in you,
But she did not abandon you.
When you were born after your months,
    She was yet yoked (to you),

Her breast in your mouth for three
    years. When she sent you to school,
And you were taught to write, She kept
    watching over you daily, With bread
    and beer in her house. When as a
    youth you take a wife, And you are
    settled in your house, Pay attention
    to your offspring, Bring him up as
    did your mother. Do not give her
    cause to blame you, Lest she raise her
    hands to God, And he hears her cries.
Do not control your wife in her house,
When you know she is efficient; don't
    say to her: "Where is it? Get it!"
    When she has put it in the right
    place. Let your eye observe in silence.
    Then you recognize her skill; it is joy
    when your hand is with her. There
    are many who don't know this. If a
    man desists from strife at home, He
    will not encounter its beginning.
    Every man who founds a household
    should hold back the hasty heart. Do
    not go after a woman let her not steal
    your heart.

Egyptian Secular Love Poetry

The love poetry in this section, like the contracts for inheritance and property rights, honors both the male and the female. The poetry is written as if from the perspective of both the males and the females. The terms "brother" and "sister" do not designate a familial relationship but do allude to intimacy. Some of the selections are written by scribes, however, we do not know whether any of the poems were penned by female poets/scribes. It is interesting to compare this love poetry to the hymns about Inanna and Damuzi in Chapter 2, "Ancient Near Eastern Mesopotamia: The Religious Context," and love poems from the Song of Songs in Chapter 5, "Ancient Israel."

POEMS FROM *PAPYRUS HARRIS 500 11*[*]

[*From The First Collection*]
I fare north in the ferry
By the oarsman's stroke,
On my shoulder my bundle of reeds;
I am going to Memphis
To tell Ptah, Lord of Truth:
Give me my sister tonight!
The river is as if of wine, its rushes are
    Ptah,
Sakhmet is its foliage, Iadet its buds,
Nefertem its lotus blossoms.
[*The Golden*] is in joy
When earth brightens in her beauty;
Memphis is a bowl of fruit
Placed before the fair-of-face!
vi
I shall lie down at home
And pretend to be ill;
Then enter the neighbors to see me,
Then comes my sister with them.
She will make the physicians unneeded,
She understands my illness.
[*From The Second Collection*]
Beginning of the delightful, beautiful
    songs of your beloved sister as she
    comes from the fields.
The voice of the wild goose shrills.

It is caught by its bait;
My love of you pervades me.
I cannot loosen it.
I shall retrieve my nets,
But what do I tell my mother,
To whom I go daily,
Laden with bird catch? I have spread no
    snares today,
I am caught in my love of you!
vi
The voice of the dove is calling,
It says: It's day! Where are you?'
O bird, stop scolding me!
I found my brother on his bed,
My heart was overjoyed;
Each said: I shall not leave you,
My hand is in your hand;
You and I shall wander
In all the places fair.'
He makes me the foremost of women,
He does not aggrieve my heart.
My heart thought of my love of you,
When half of my hair was braided;
I came at a run to find you,
And neglected my hairdo.
Now if you let me braid my hair,
I shall be ready in a moment.

---

[*]Poems from *Papyrus Harris 500 11, AEL,* 1973 Vol. 1, 2, 193

SUGGESTED READINGS

Allen, S. "Women as Owners of Immovables in Pharonic Egypt." In *Women's Earliest Records: From Ancient Egypt and Western Asia.* Edited by Barbara Lesko. Brown Judaic Studies. Atlanta: Scholars Press, 1989.

Menu, Bernadette. "Women in Business Life in the First Millennium B.C." In *Women's Earliest Records: From Ancient Egypt and Western Asia.* Edited by Barbara Lesko. Brown Judaic Studies. Atlanta: Scholars Press, 1989.

Robins, Gay. *Women in Ancient Egypt.* Cambridge, MA: Harvard University Press, 1993.

Tyldesley, Joyce. *Daughter of Isis: Women of Ancient Egypt.* London: Viking Press, 1994.

Watterson, Barbara. *Women in Ancient Egypt.* New York: St. Martin's Press, 1991.

Women's Earliest Records: From Ancient Egypt and Western Asia. Edited by Barbara Lesko. Atlanta: Scholars Press, 1989.

Sources Cited

Ma'at, Cosmic Female Principle of Wisdom and Judgment of the Dead. "Hymn to Aten and the King." In *Ancient Egyptian Literature: A Book of Readings, Vol. II, The New Kingdom.* Edited by Miriam Lichtheim. Published under the auspices of the Gustave E. von Grunebaum Center for Near Eastern Studies. Berkeley, Los Angeles, London: University of California Press, 1973, 124–125.

The Goddess Isis Discovers Re's Unknown Name of Power. *The Legend of Isis and the Name of Re.* Translated by Robert K. Ritner. *Contexts of Scripture: Canonical Compositions from the Biblical World*, Vol. 1. Leiden, London, Koln: Brill, 1997, 519–521.

Hymn to Hathor. Translated by H. Junker. *Zeitschrift fur Agypitische Sprache und Altertumskunde* 43 (1906): 101–27, 131.

"A Penitential Hymn to the Goddess Meres-Ger: Lady of Heaven." Translated by B. Gunn. *Journal of Egyptian Archaeology,* III (1916) 86–87. In *Ancient Near Eastern Texts Relating to the Old Testament Supplement.* Edited by James B. Pritchard, Princeton University Press, 1950, 381.

Obelisk Inscriptions of Queen Hatshepsut in the Temple of Karnak. In *Ancient Egyptian Literature: A Book of Readings, Vol. II, The New Kingdom.* Edited by Miriam Lichtheim. Published under the auspices of the Gustave E. von Grunebaum Center for Near Eastern Studies. Berkeley, Los Angeles, London: University of California Press, 1973, 25–28.

Queen Ankhesenamun of Egypt and King Suppiuliumas. From "Deeds of Suppiluliuma." Translated by Harry A. Hoffner, Jr. *Contexts of Scripture: Canonical Compositions from the Biblical World,* Vol. 1. Leiden, London, Koln: Brill, 1997, 190.

"The Instruction of Ani," from the Reign of Queen Nefertari translated by J.N. Erman. In *Ancient Egyptian Literature: A Book of Readings,* Vol. 1, 2, *The New Kingdom.* Edited by Miriam Lichtheim. Published under the auspices of the Gustave E. von Grunebaum Center for Near Eastern Studies. Berkeley, Los Angeles, London: University of California Press, 1973, 192.

Papyrus Harris 500 11. In *Ancient Egyptian Literature: A Book of Readings,* Vol. 1, 2, *The New Kingdom.* Edited by Miriam Lichtheim. Published under the auspices of the Gustave E. von Grunebaum Center for Near Eastern Studies. Berkeley, Los Angeles, London: University of California Press, 1973, 193.

Chapter 5

Ancient Israel

Because the Hebrew Bible is so significant to interpretations of women in Western culture, this introduction provides a more detailed context for reading selections taken from the Biblical texts. Judaism is one of the most ancient "living" religions in the world. One of its principal sacred texts, the Hebrew Bible, is a foundational text in Christianity and informs the sacred history of Islam. The three primary religions in Western civilization are instructed by representations of women described in the bible.

Interpretations of women in biblical texts have been used in religious, social, economic and political contexts to legitimate the subjugation of women. These interpretations have not been limited to Western European cultures but have influenced in varying degrees all societies that were colonized by Western European Christian countries. In recent years, portrayals based upon reconstructions of women in the biblical texts are also a significant contribution to efforts toward women's liberation from oppression.

The earliest versions of the Hebrew Bible/Old Testament represent the story of Israel from its mythical past at the creation of the universe to stories that precede the Monarchy. Scholarly consensus argues that the initial version was first compiled and edited during the United Monarchy under kings David and Solomon (1000-ca. 922 B.C.E.). Final redaction of the Hebrew Bible including the histories, psalms, writings, wisdom, and prophetic texts was not completed until about 200 of the Common Era (C.E.). Numerous writings produced in the midst of early Judaism that were not included in the final version of the bible will be discussed in readings for the Hellenistic period.

Chart 5-1 is included to assist in determining a time line for ancient Israel and notes as well the particular pattern of social organization Israel adopts during that period. The chart also includes the female subjects of readings under the appropriate time period that their stories are intended to reflect.

SOCIAL ORGANIZATION

Social organization throughout biblical history is patriarchal. The particular structure within which the male is dominant, however, varies in each of the major cultural transitions among the ancient Hebrews. Families of Abraham, Sarah and Hagar, Isaac and Rebekah, and Jacob, Leah, and Rachel in the book of Genesis represent a seminomadic patriarchal social organization. During the period of the

---

Chart 5–1   Ancient Israel

Primeval Literature-Mythopoeic Time—Time-Outside -of -Time:
Story of Eve, Genesis 2:4 ff.
1600–1400 B.C.E. Patriarchs: Abraham, Isaac, and Jacob
Social Organization: Semi-nomadic tribal peoples with a Patriarch at the head of the tribe. Little or no social stratification.
    Women's experience represented during this period include Sarah, Hagar, Rebekkah, Rachel, Leah, Dinah, Tamar, and the woman who was raped, divided into parts, and distributed to the tribes.
ca. 1200 B.C.E. Exodus
Reformulation of tribes under leadership of Moses who is neither warrior, priest, nor king; tribal patriarchs give allegiance to Moses. Moses is assisted by his sister Miriam, who is a prophet, and his brother Aaron who is made a priest.
    Readings about Miriam.
1200–1020 B.C.E. Occupation of Canaan/Judges
The 12 tribes of Israel live within a confederacy. Judges are sometimes permanent. Early on they were chosen to serve during times of particular problems, often demanding military skill; at other times judges serve as prophets, as counselors, and as functionaries who perform ritual sacrifices. Important women in this period include Deborah, Ja'el, Jepthah's daughter, Delilah.
    Readings about Deborah and Ja'el, Delilah.
1020–931 B.C.E. United Monarchy
Saul 1020–1000. David 1000–965/961; Solomon 961–922 or 965–931. Monarchy based upon a patriarchal heirarchy. Readings about Queen Bathsheba; Solomon and the daughter of Pharoah, the Queen of Sheba; the rape of Princess Tamar; the Wise Women of Tekoa and Abel; the Woman of Endor.
922–586/587 B.C.E. Divided Monarchy
Two monarchies, Judah/Jerusalem in the South and Israel, the monarchy in the North. Readings about queens of Israel, Jezebel and Athaliayah, Queen Mother, Queen Esther, female prophet Huldah, Ruth and Naomi, Gomer the prostitute or hierodule.
587/586 B.C.E. Babylonian Exile
The Temple at Jerusalem was destroyed and Judah was taken into captivity by the Babylonians. Many prophetic writings were generated during this period and the Deuteronomists composed, compiled, and edited many texts.
    Readings about Jeremiah's references to the Queen of Heaven.
538 B.C.E. Post Exilic Israel/Judah
From the point of the exile in 586 B.C.E. Israel until the Hasmonean Dynasty in the Hellenistic period, Israel was under the domination of foreign powers.
    The return took place in four stages beginning in 538 B.C.E.
358 B.C.E.
Readings include the first woman in Genesis 1: Hockhmah, the Female Principle of Divine Wisdom, the Female as Dame Folly, the Perfect Wife, Job's Daughters.

---

judges and the occupation of Canaan. The Haiparu or Hebrews were a loosely organized confederacy of tribes. Each tribe was headed by a patriarch and by judges. Many judges were charismatic leaders who arose to lead the tribes in times of a crisis. The Book of Judges attests to at least one female judge, Deborah, who functioned also as a counselor and advisor as well as a leader in worship.

The monarchy in Ancient Israel began in ca. 1000 B.C.E. and extended to the Babylonian exile in 586 B.C.E. Religion continued to be an organizing/ordering framework in society until the period of the monarchy. From that point until the Babylonian exile, political, economic, and military issues at court assumed increasing importance, yet religious validation of the court continued as did governmental support of religious institutions. The Post-Exilic period and the rebuilding of Israel began ca. 530 B.C.E. at the time that Israel was the subject of Persia until the late fourth century in the Hellenistic period and the establishment of the Hasmonean Dynasty. Writers and interpreters of the Hebrew Bible incorporate women as transmitters of myth and patriarchal tradition.

Reading selections in this chapter represent many aspects of women's experience as they are documented and interpreted by the male scribes. These scribes composed and edited the texts for the male rulers to whom they were subject and within the male-centered culture they advanced, sustained, and perpetuated. In Ancient Israel, as in its counterparts in Mesopotamia, Egypt, and the Levant, intrinsic and complex associations between political and religious spheres defined characteristics of culture.

WOMEN OF THE PATRIARCHS

The following selections provide insights into women's status in the context of patriarchal social organization. Some of the women in these readings used their wit, wisdom, and knowledge of the "system" to ensure their own safety and the well-being of their children. Other women, regardless of their social status were abused and objectified.

In this selection note the rights of Sarah as wife of Abraham, the first Patriarch among the Hebrews, to assign a slave to her husband, to be a wife for the purpose of begetting a child, to name children, to challenge her husband, and to dismiss her servants. Sarah's Egyptian slave, Hagar, had no voice in the matter of whether or not to submit to Sarah's plan. However, through Divine intervention, Hagar was promised that if she were obedient to Yahweh, her son Ishmael would become the father of many nations. In Islam, Ishmael is a spiritual father as Jacob/Israel (son of Abraham and Sarah's son Isaac) is in Judaism. Rebekkah, Rachel, and Leah, wives of the patriarchs Isaac and Jacob (Gen. 24–39) had the same rights as Sarah.

SARAH AND HAGAR, MOTHERS OF TWO NATIONS*

> Now Sarai, Abram's wife, bore him no children. She had an Egyptian slave-girl whose name was Hagar, and Sarai said to Abram, "You see that the Lord has prevented me from bearing children; go in to my slave-girl; it may be that I shall obtain children by her." And Abram listened to the voice of Sarai. So, after Abram had lived ten years in the land of Canaan, Sarai, Abram's wife, took Hagar the Egyptian, her slave-girl, and gave her to her husband Abram as a wife. He went in to Hagar, and she conceived; and when she saw that she had conceived, she looked with contempt on her mistress. Then Sarai said to Abram, "May the wrong done to me be on you! I gave my slave-girl to your embrace, and when she saw that she had conceived, she looked on me with contempt. May the Lord judge between you and me!" But Abram said to Sarai, "Your slave-girl is in your power; do to her as you please." Then Sarai dealt harshly with her, and she ran away from her. [*Hagar flees to the desert.*]
>
> The angel of the Lord found her by a spring of water in the wilderness, the spring on the way to Shur. And he said, "Hagar, slave-girl of Sarai, where have you come from and where are you going?" She said, "I am running away from my mistress Sarai." The angel of the Lord said to her, "Return to your mistress, and submit to her." The angel of the Lord also said to her, "I will so greatly multiply your offspring that

The New Oxford Annotated Bible. Edited by Bruce M. Metzger and Roland E. Murphy. New Revised Standard Edition. New York: Oxford University Press, 1991. Excerpts from Genesis 16.

they can not be counted for multitude." And the angel of the Lord said to her, "Now you have conceived and shall bear a son; you shall call him Ishmael, for the Lord has given heed to your affliction. Hagar bore Abram a son. Abram named his son, whom Hagar bore, Ishmael. Abram was eighty-six years old when Hagar bore Ishmael.

Sarah conceived and bore Abraham a son in his old age, at the time of which God had spoken to him. Abraham gave the name Isaac to his son whom Sarah bore him. And Abraham circumcised his son Isaac when he was eight days old, as God had commanded him. Now Sarah said, "God has brought laughter for me; everyone who hears will laugh with me." And she said, "Who would ever have said to Abraham that Sarah would nurse children?" The child grew, and was weaned; and Abraham made a great feast on the day that Isaac was weaned. But Sarah saw the son of Hagar the Egyptian, whom she had borne to Abraham, playing with her son Isaac. So she said to Abraham, "Cast out this slave woman with her son; for the son of this slave woman shall not inherit along with my son Isaac." The matter was very distressing to Abraham on account of his son. But God said to Abraham, "Do not be distressed because of the boy and because of your slave woman; whatever Sarah says to you, do as she tells you, for it is through Isaac that offspring shall be named for you. As for the son of the slave woman, I will make a nation of him also, because he is your offspring."

So Abraham rose early in the morning and took bread and a skin of water, and gave it to Hagar, putting it on her shoulder, along with the child, and sent her away. And she departed, and wandered about in the wilderness of Beersheba. When the water in the skin was gone, she cast the child under one of the bushes. Then she went and sat down opposite him a good way off, about the distance of a bowshot; for she said, "Do not let me look on the death of the child."

And as she sat opposite him, she lifted up her voice and wept. And God heard the voice of the boy; and the angel called to Hagar from heaven, "What troubles you, Hagar do not be afraid; for God has heard the boy where he is. Come, lift up the boy and hold him fast with your hands for I will make a great nation of him." Then God opened her eyes and she saw a well of water. She went, and filled the skin with water, and gave the boy a drink. God was with the boy and he grew up; he lived in the wilderness and became an expert with the bow. He lived in the wilderness of Param and his mother got a wife for him from the land of Egypt.

WOMEN IN THE ARISTOCRACY

Queens, Princesses, Queen Mothers

Women in this category were primarily identified as wives, daughters, concubines, and slaves in relationship to the dominant men in their lives. The readings about these women, who had the privilege and status that attends being associated with powerful men at the top of a patriarchal hierarchy, give insights about their subjugation and in many instances the strategies they devised and the agency they carved out for themselves as participants in the culture of their times.

David, king of Israel, was a profoundly complex and charismatic man. His accomplishments as the second king of Israel were responsible for Israel's considerable status as a nation among nations. He was brilliant. David was and continues to be so revered as a heroic figure that the moral and ethical implications of his relationship to Bathsheba receive little attention. Bathsheba, on the other hand, is depicted in the visual and performing arts almost exclusively as a seductress.

BATHSHEBA, WIFE OF KING DAVID, MOTHER OF KING SOLOMON[*]

[*King David desires Bathsheba: he arranges to have her husband killed and then brings Bathsheba as one of his wives.*]

It happened, late one afternoon, when David rose from his couch and was walking about on the roof of the king's house that he saw from the roof a woman bathing; the woman was very beautiful. David sent someone to inquire about the woman. It was reported, "This is Bathsheba daughter of Eliam, the wife of Uriah the Hittite." So David sent messengers to get her, and she came to him, and he lay with her. (Now she was purifying herself after her period.) Then she returned to her house. The woman conceived; and she sent and told David, "I am pregnant."

David wrote a letter to Joab, and sent it by the hand of Uriah. In the letter he wrote, "Set Uriah in the forefront of the hardest fighting, and then draw back from him, so that he may be struck down and die."

When the wife of Uriah heard that her husband was dead, she made lamentation for him. When the mourning was over, David sent and brought her to his house, and she became his wife, and bore him a son. But, when David saw that his servants were whispering together, he perceived that the child was dead; and David said to his servants, "Is the child dead?" They said, "He is dead."

[*Bathsheba is the mother of Solomon.*]

Then David consoled his wife Bathsheba, and went to her, and lay with her; and she bore a son, and he named him Solomon. The Lord loved him, and sent a message by the prophet Nathan; so he named him Jedidiah, because of the Lord.

[*Many years later, at the end of King David's life Bathsheba secures the throne for Solomon.*]

Then Nathan said to Bathsheba, Solomon's mother, "Have you not heard that Adonijah son of Haggith has become king and our Lord David does not know it? Now therefore come, let me give you advice that you may save your own life and the life of your son Solomon." So Bathsheba went to the king in his room. The king was very old; Abi-shag the Shunammite was attending the king. Bathsheba bowed and did obeisance to the king, and the king said, "What do you wish?" She said to him, "My Lord, you swore to your servant by the Lord your God, saying: Your son Solomon shall succeed me as king, and he shall sit on my throne. But now suddenly Adonijah has become king, though you, my Lord the king, do not know it. He has sacrificed oxen, fatted cattle, and sheep in abundance, and has invited all the children of the king, the priest Abiathar, and Joab the commander of the army; but your servant Solomon he has not invited. But you, my Lord the king, the eyes of all Israel are on you to tell them who shall sit on the throne of my Lord the king after him. Otherwise it will come to pass, when my Lord the king sleeps with his ancestors, that my son Solomon and I will be counted offenders."

[*David assures Bathsheba that Solomon will be King.*]

The king swore, "As the Lord lives, who has saved my life from every adversity, as I swore to you by the Lord, the God of Israel, 'Your son Solomon shall succeed me as king, and he shall sit on my throne in my place,' so will I do this day." Then

---

*NRSV, 1991, 2 Samuel 11:2–4, 14–15, 26–27, 12:19, 24–25, 1 Kings 1:11–12, 15–21, 29–31, 32–34.

Bathsheba bowed with her face to the ground, and did obeisance to the king, and said, "May my Lord King David live forever!"

King David said, "Summon to me the priest Zadok, the prophet Nathan, and Benaiah son of Jehoiada." When they came before the king, the king said to them, "Take with you the servants of your Lord, and have my son Solomon ride on my own mule, and bring him down to Gihon. There let the priest Zadok and the prophet Nathan anoint him king over Israel; then blow the trumpet, and say, 'Long live King Solomon.' "

Although Solomon received the unconditional support of David, such was not the fate of Tamar, the daughter of King David who was raped by her brother Amnon. The story recounts her deep anguish and the failure of the king to punish Amnon because he was David's firstborn son and his favorite. Women's aristocratic social status becomes irrelevant in relation to their vulnerability to subjugation by the patriarch of the family. Her brother Absolom, who came to her defense, was exited by David, thus illustrating their vulnerability to censure of males who defend women who have been violated.

TAMAR, DAVID'S DAUGHTER, RAPED BY HER BROTHER AMNON[*]

... [Tamar's brother Absolom avenges his sister's rape.]

Her brother Absalom said to her, "Has Amnon your brother been with you? Be quiet for now, my sister; he is your brother; do not take this to heart." So Tamar remained, a desolate woman, in her brother Absalom's house. When King David heard of all these things, he became very angry, but he would not punish his son Amnon, because he loved him, for he was his firstborn. But Absalom spoke to Amnon neither good nor bad; for Absalom hated Amnon, because he had raped his sister Tamar. Two years later Absalom prepared a banquet to which he invited all the king's sons. He instructed his servants to slay Amnon. When this deed was accomplished Absalom, having vindicated the rape of his sister fled for his life. His father King David, who had taken Amnon's stand in the case with Tamar, had Absalom exiled from Israel.

This selection references a female ruler from outside Israel who not only possessed untold wealth, but also *autonomy* (self-governance), *agency* (self-determination), and sufficient assurance about her power and authority to put "hard questions" to a reigning male monarch. In the *Kebra Nagast,* an Ethiopian text about the great monarchs, the name of this queen is Makeda.

QUEEN OF SHEBA AND SOLOMON: MUTUAL ADMIRATION[**]

When the queen of Sheba heard of the fame of Solomon, (fame due to the name of the Lord), she came to test him with hard questions. She came to Jerusalem with a very great retinue, with camels bearing spices, and very much gold, and precious stones; and when she came to Solomon, she told him all that was on her mind. Solomon answered all her questions; there was nothing hidden from the king that he could not explain to her. When the queen of Sheba had observed all the wisdom of

*NRSV, 1991. 2 Samuel 13:1–2.
**NRSV, 1991. 1 Kings 10.

Solomon, the house that he had built, the food of his table, the seating of his officials, and the attendance of his servants, their clothing, his valets, and his burnt offerings that he offered at the house of the Lord, there was no more spirit in her. So she said to the king, "The report was true that I heard in my own land of your accomplishments and of your wisdom, but I did not believe the reports until I came and my own eyes had seen it. Not even half had been told me; your wisdom and prosperity far surpass the report that I had heard. Happy are your wives! Happy are these, your servants, who continually attend you and hear your wisdom! Blessed be the Lord your God, who has delighted in you and set you on the throne of Israel! Because the Lord loved Israel forever, he has made you king to execute justice and righteousness." Then she gave the king one hundred twenty talents of gold, a great quantity of spices, and precious stones; never again did spices come in such quantity as that which the queen of Sheba gave to King Solomon. Meanwhile King Solomon gave to the queen of Sheba every desire that she expressed, as well as what he gave her out of Solomon's royal bounty. Then returned to her own land, with her servants.

The name Jezebel, perhaps more than the name of any other woman in the biblical tradition, has echoed throughout the centuries as the epitome of the "wicked" woman. Tradition ascribes sin to Eve, but Jezebel is interpreted as bad. Among strategies developed to discredit powerful women who successfully challenge the status quo is to attribute to them sexual misconduct and "loose" morals. A woman whose sexual morality can be questioned has, for centuries, been referred to as a "Jezebel." In the present day, a woman so accused may or may not have power, but her sexual morality is being designated as questionable. Yet, thorough examination of biblical texts related to Queen Jezebel reveals an extremely devout and religious woman and nowhere is there any reference to or inference of "sexual sin." We do, however, find this queen to be a very powerful woman who successfully challenged the status quo. Jezebel, the daughter of a king, was given in marriage to King Ahab, who reigned in Israel for 22 years. When she left her homeland to marry Ahab, she brought as a part of her retinue 450 prophets of Ba'al and 400 prophets of the Goddess Asherah.

Jezebel, a Despised Foreign Queen of Israel; Devotee of Ba'al and Asherah[*]

Ahab son of Omri did evil in the sight of the Lord more than all who were before him. And as if it had been a light thing for him to walk in the sins of Jeroboam son of Nebat he took as his wife Jezebel daughter of King Ethbaal of the Sidonians, and went and served Baal, and worshiped him. He erected an altar for Baal in the house of Baal, which he built in Samaria. Ahab also made a sacred pole.
[Elijah challenges Jezebel's prophets.]
When Ahab saw Elijah, Ahab said to him, "Is it you, you troubler of Israel?" He answered, "I have not troubled Israel; but you have, and your father's house, because you have forsaken the commandments of the Lord and followed the Baals. Now therefore have all Israel assemble for me at Mount Carmel, with the four hundred fifty-prophets of Baal and the four hundred prophets of Asherah, who eat at Jezebel's table."

*NRSV, 1991. 1 Kings 16:31-33.

So Ahab sent to all the Israelites, and assembled the prophets at Mount Carmel. [*Elijah humiliated the prophets of Ba'al and had them slain.*]

Ahab told Jezebel all that Elijah had done, and how he had killed all the prophets with the sword. Then Jezebel sent a messenger to Elijah, saying, "So may the Gods do to me, and more also, if I do not make your life like the life of one of them by this time tomorrow." Then he was afraid; he got up and fled for his life, and came to Beersheba, which belongs to Judah. . . .

Queen Athaliah (2 Kings 11:1–3, 13–21) was a reigning monarch in Israel for six years. Her status as the daughter of Jezebel, however, and her indignation at the treatment of her mother and her son worked to her distinct disadvantage. Had Jezebel been a queen who was fervently devoted to Yahweh, instead of Ba'al, and Athaliah a queen who defended her mother's religion and insisted on the worship of Yahweh in a foreign court, both women would be considered heroes in Israel.

RELIGION

The Holy

In this selection of readings we discover several understandings of the female Principle of the Divine in Ancient Israel. In a culture where the principal deity is traditionally understood as male (with no female consort) prophetic admonitions against female deities such as Anat, Astarte, and Asherah from adjacent cultures are not surprising. Biblical traditions have not generally discussed biblical texts that affirm the presence of these same deities within the Jerusalem Temple, (though, as we shall see, they were indeed present). Beginning in the Post-Exilic period, images of the Female Principle of Divine Wisdom emerged in Israel's sacred literature. Expression of the Female Principle of God as Sophia (Wisdom) continued in the Hellenistic Period, in Early Christianity, the Middle Ages, and into the present.

The book of Proverbs is part of the body of Wisdom literature in Ancient Israel. Different sections of the book were composed during different periods and edited in their final form during the Post-Exilic period. Proverbs chapters 1-9, composed during the Post-Exilic period in Israel, included poems such as this selection in which Hockhmah, the female Principle of Divine Wisdom, speaks about her presence at creation.

THE FEMALE PRINCIPLE OF DIVINE WISDOM WAS PRESENT AT CREATION[*]

The Lord created me at the
beginning of his work,
the first of his acts of long ago-
Ages ago I was set up
at the first before the beginning
of the earth.
When there were no depths I was
   brought forth,
when there were no springs
abounding with water.
Before the mountains had been
shaped, I was brought forth
before the hills
when he had not yet made earth
and fields, or the world's first bits of soil
When he established the heavens, I
was there, when he drew a circle on the
face of the deep,

*NRSV 1991. Proverbs 8:22- 36.

when he made firm the skies above,
when he established the fountains of the
    deep
when he assigned to the sea its limit,
so that the waters might not
transgress his command, when he
    marked out the
foundations of the earth
then I was beside him, like an
expert helpmeet; and I was daily in his
    delight, rejoicing before him always.
Rejoicing in his inhabited world and de-
    lighting in the human race.

And now my children, listen to me
happy are those who keep my ways.
Hear instruction and be wise
and do not neglect it.
Happy is the one who listens to me,
watching daily at my gates
waiting beside my doors.
For whoever finds me finds life and ob-
    tains favor from the Lord
but those who miss me injure
    themselves
all who hate me love death.

Two very different accounts of the female at creation are found in the first two chapters of Gene-sis. The first version (Gen. 1:26-28) was written by scribes in the priestly class during the Post-Exilic period, ca. 540 B.C.E. In this creation story, the female created by God happens in the same manner and in the same moment as the male. She does not derive from the male. The female is created equally in the image of God as the male. Neither the male nor the female is named and no implication of evil is present. During the early Post-Exilic period, men and women who returned from captivity in Babylon were actively engaged together in rebuilding and restoring their lives in Israel. References to women in several texts from the Post-Exilic period suggest women's contribution in that process was valued equally with that of men.

The second version of the female at creation was written during the early monarchy in Israel, ca. 950 B.C.E when the nation was at its zenith. It was during the early monarchy in Israel that a formal, hi-erarchical social stratification was established throughout all social institutions. Among biblical texts the creation story in Genesis 2 has provoked profoundly negative consequences for historical women's lives. The Genesis 1 account, on the other hand, has implications to support gender equality and partnership.

IMAGES OF THE FEMALE AT CREATION: GENESIS 1 AND GENESIS 2[*]

THE LATER TEXT: GENESIS 1

Then God said, "Let us make humankind, in our image, according to our likeness; and let them have dominion over the fish of the sea, and over the birds of the air, and over the cattle, and over all the wild animals of the earth, and over every creep-ing thing that creeps upon the earth."

So God created humankind in his image, in the image of God he created them; male and female he created them. (Genesis 1:26–28)

God blessed them, and God said to them, "Be fruitful and multiply, and fill the earth and subdue it; and have dominion over the fish of the sea and the birds of the air and over every living thing that moves upon the earth."

*NRSV, 1991. Gen. 1:26–28; 2:4–7, 20b–23.

THE EARLY TEXT: GENESIS 2

These are the generations of the heavens and the earth when they were created.

In the day that the Lord God made the earth and the heavens, when no plant of the field was yet in the earth and no herb of the field had yet sprung up—for the Lord God had not caused it to rain upon the earth, and there was no one to till the ground; but a stream would rise from the earth, and water the whole face of the ground— then the Lord God formed man from the dust of the ground, and breathed into his nostrils the breath of life; and the man became a living being.

When the people of Israel occupied Canaan, religious traditions that incorporated the worship of female deities, such as those we discussed in Mesopotamia, had been established for thousands of years. It should therefore not be surprising to discover the presence of these deities among citizens of lands conquered by Israel. In addition, political marriages within the monarchy resulted in the presence of a variety of deities from other cultures within the court and in the Temple in Israel. The third king of Israel, King Solomon, is said to have had 700 wives and 300 concubines. It is considered that these were political marriages. The king would bring daughters of the rulers of small city-states and wealthy land owners as brides or concubines in the royal household in exchange for their fathers' loyalty to the court. Many of the women were not worshipers of Yahweh and required shrines to their own deities; some of these shrines were installed in the temple at Jerusalem. The Goddess Asherah was installed in the Jerusalem Temple by King Rehoboam, the son of Solomon, in or about 928 B.C.E. "It appears that of the 370 years during which the Solomonic Temple stood in Jerusalem, for no less than 236 years (or almost two-thirds of the time) the statue of Asherah was present and her worship was a part of the legitimate religion approved and led by the king, the court, and the priesthood. This practice was opposed by a few prophetic voices crying out against it at relatively long intervals" (Patai 1967, 50).

The Goddesses Asherah, Astarte, and Anath appear throughout biblical texts that reflect the life of Pre-Exilic Israel (1000-586 B.C.E.). The religious reform begun by Josiah was intensified following Huldah's prophetic interpretation of the mysterious scroll discovered in the Temple at Jerusalem. As a part of his reform, Josiah commanded that all of the Asherahs be removed from the temple. The Canaanite Goddess Asherah was "Lady Asherah of the Sea"; "Progenitress of all the Gods"; the wife of the chief God, El; and was venerated as a Mother Goddess. Asherah's fertility aspect may have been the source of her appeal among the Israelites. The following selection demonstrates a situation in which devotion to one of these three deities is described and interpreted. Israelites who have escaped the Babylonian exile by moving to Egypt make offerings to the Queen of Heaven. Jeremiah's censure of this practice is answered by the people's explanation of their continued commitment to Astarte.

ISRAELITES MAKE OFFERINGS TO THE QUEEN OF HEAVEN[*]

Then all the men who were aware that their wives had been making offerings to other Gods, and all the women who stood by, a great assembly, all the people who lived in Pathros in the land of Egypt, answered Jeremiah: "As for the word that you have spoken to us in the name of the Lord, we are not going to listen to you. Instead, we will do everything that we have vowed, make offerings to the Queen of Heaven and pour out libations to her, just as we and our ancestors, our kings and our

*NRSV 1991, Jeremiah 44:15–19

officials, used to do in the towns of Judah and in the streets of Jerusalem. We used to have plenty of food, and prospered, and saw no misfortune. But from the time we stopped making offerings to the Queen of Heaven and pouring out libations to her, we have lacked everything and have perished by the sword and by famine." And the women said, "Indeed we will go on making offerings to the Queen of Heaven and pouring out libations to her; do you think that we made cakes for her, marked with her image, and poured out libations to her without our husbands' being involved?"

The Holy/Ritual

There are few texts in the Hebrew Bible representing sacred rituals that are specifically related to women's contributions to culture. Recitation of Miriam's/Moses' Song of the Sea (Exodus 15) and Deborah's Victory Ode (Judges 5) are examples of women's heroic actions that were integrated into ritual contexts. The text we have selected also meets that specification and is clearly part of a ritual celebration in Israel.

This text is located at the close of the biblical book of Esther when Esther, a Jewess who was queen of the king of Persia, had bravely secured the freedom of the Jewish people. Esther remains a heroine in Judaism; and the feast described in the selection that follows continues to be celebrated. The contemporary Jewish women's organization, Hadassah (the Hebrew word for "Esther") is a formidable advocate for causes among Jewish people worldwide.

QUEEN ESTHER AND THE FEAST OF PURIM[*]

Now in the twelfth month, which is the month of Adar, on the thirteenth day, . . . the Jews gathered in their cities throughout all the provinces of King Ahasuerus to lay hands on those who had sought their ruin; and no one could withstand them.

[*The Jewish Feast of Purim is declared to celebrate Queen Esther's intervention and the victory of the Jews.*]

This was on the thirteenth day of the month of Adar, and on the fourteenth day they rested and made that a day of feasting and gladness.

But the Jews who were in Susa, gathered on the thirteenth day and on the fourteenth, and rested on the fifteenth day, making that a day of feasting and gladness. Therefore the Jews of the villages, who live in the open towns, hold the fourteenth day of the month of Adar as a day for gladness and feasting, a holiday on which they send gifts of food to one another.

Queen Esther daughter of Abihai, along with the Jew Mordecai, gave full written authority, confirming this second letter about Purim. Letters were sent wishing peace and security to all the Jews, to the one hundred twenty-seven provinces of the kingdom of Ahasuerus, and giving orders that these days of Purim should be observed at their appointed seasons, as the Jew Mordecai and Queen Esther enjoined on the Jews, just as they had laid down for themselves and for their descendants regulations concerning their fasts and their lamentations. The command of Queen Esther fixed these practices of Purim, and it was recorded in writing.

*NRSV 1991. Esther 9:1A, 2A, 17, 18–19, 29–32.

Female Religious Functionaries

In ancient Israel we have evidence of women's agency as wise women (Tekoa and Abel); judges (Deborah); prophets (Miriam, Deborah, Huldah, the wife of Isaiah, and the woman of Endor); and women warriors (Miriam, Deborah, Ja'el). Hierodules were the only female religious functionaries scholars identified associated within the temple until Anna the Prophet during the Hellenistic period. Women in the following selections possess spiritual authority that is validated within their particular communities. Each woman demonstrates agency and autonomy as a contributor to the dominant culture. It is important to consider to what extent the fact that they are included (and often even "named") in the sacred texts might be related to their apparent support of the status quo. Consider, however, the fate that befell Miriam when she challenged the authority of her younger brother Moses. We also consider that the author of Judges neglects to elaborate aspects of Deborah's "untold" story that made the great warrior Barak refuse to go into battle unless Deborah rode with him.

Miriam

The excerpts related to Miriam show her functioning in ancient Israel as a prophet, as an administrator of law, and as a leader of worship. The Exodus out of slavery in Egypt into the promised land which marks Miriam's leadership is among the most significant events in the history of Israel. Miriam is a prophet and one who proclaims the messages of Yahweh to the people. In pre-monarchic Israel the message of a prophet often included expression in music and dance. This passage, and its counterpart, the Song of Deborah, are among the oldest texts in the Hebrew bible.

THE PROPHET MIRIAM AT THE SEA OF REEDS[*]

> The Lord will reign forever and ever. When the horses of Pharaoh with his chariots and his chariot drivers went into the sea, the Lord brought back the waters of the sea upon them; but the Israelites walked through the sea on dry ground. Then the prophet Miriam, Aaron's sister, took a tambourine in her hand; and all the women went out after her with tambourines and with dancing. And Miriam sang to them: "Sing to the Lord, for he has triumphed gloriously; horse and rider he has thrown into the sea."

MIRIAM: ADMINISTRATOR OF LAW AT KADESH[**]

> [*Miriam is ratified by the people in her judgments against Moses.*]
> While they were at Hazeroth, Miriam and Aaron spoke against Moses because of the Cushite woman whom he had married (for he had indeed married a Cushite woman); and they said, "Has the Lord spoken only through Moses? Has he not spoken through us also?" And the Lord heard it. Now the man Moses was very humble, more so than anyone else on the face of the earth. Suddenly the Lord said to Moses, Aaron, and Miriam, "Come out, you three, to the tent of meeting." So the three of them came

*NRSV 1991. Exodus 15: 18–21.

**NRSV 1991. Numbers 12: 1–14, 15b–16.

out. Then the Lord came down in a pillar of cloud, and stood at the entrance of the tent, and called Aaron and Miriam; and they both came forward. And he said, "Hear my words: When there are prophets among you, I, the Lord, make myself known to them in visions; I speak to them in dreams. Not so, with my servant Moses; he is entrusted with all my house. With him I speak face to face. . . clearly, not in riddles, and he beholds the form of the Lord. Why then were you not afraid to speak against my servant Moses?" And the anger of the Lord was kindled against them, and he departed.

[*The male prophet finds favor with Yahweh and Miriam is punished for challenging her brother.*]

When the cloud went away from over the tent, Miriam had become leprous, as white as snow. And Aaron turned towards Miriam and saw that she was leprous. Then Aaron said to Moses, "Oh, my Lord, do not punish us for a sin that we have so foolishly committed. Do not let her be like one stillborn, whose flesh is half consumed when it comes out of its mother's womb." And Moses cried to the Lord, "O God, please heal her." But the Lord said to Moses, "If her father had but spit in her face, would she not bear her shame for seven days? Let her be shut out of the camp for seven days, and after that she may be brought in again." Miriam was shut out of the camp for seven days.

[*The people refused to leave until Miriam was restored to the community.*]

. . . and the people did not set out on the march until Miriam had been brought in again. After that the people set out from Hazeroth, and camped in the wilderness of Paran.

Exodus relates the story of the infant Moses which is told to Jewish, Christian, and Muslim children from the time they are very young. In the story a young Hebrew maiden helps her mother rescue her baby brother from being slain by Pharaoh's soldiers. However, none of the women in the passage are named. Religious tradition associates this sister of Moses with Miriam, the sister of Aaron and Moses. As we have seen, Miriam is identified by name in later passages as a prophet and an administrator of law and as one who, with Moses and Aaron, was chosen by Yahweh to bring Israel out of Egypt.

Deborah

Over the centuries the story of Deborah, Mother in Israel, has been revisited many times. With each retelling of her story, this remarkable woman is described in a manner that celebrates her valor, courage, and wisdom in the context of the period in which she is being acknowledged (e.g., *pseudepigraphical* texts [many texts written in Israel's late Second Temple period ca. 250 B.C.E.-70 C.E.] and *midrashim* [the rabbi's elaborations on the biblical accounts that make the narratives, and figures in the narratives, more relevant to the time in which the *midrashim* are written]). Unlike many women from sacred texts who are represented in the sacred literature and the arts, Deborah's character is never diminished, only enhanced.

DEBORAH: PROPHET, JUDGE, AND WARRIOR IN ISRAEL[*]

At that time Deborah, a prophetess, wife of Lappidoth was judging Israel. She used to sit under the palm of Deborah between Ramah and Bethel in the hill country of Ephraim; and the Israelites came up to her for judgment.

*NRSV 1991. Judges 4:4–16.

[Deborah summons the armies of Israel and prophecies Israel's Victory.]

She sent and summoned Barak son of Abinoam from Kedesh in Naphtali, and said to him "The Lord, the God of Israel, commands you, 'Go, take position at Mount Tabor, bringing ten thousand from the tribe of Naphtali and the tribe of Zebulun will draw out Sisera the general of Jabin's army, to meet you by the Wadi Kishon with his chariots and his troops; and I will give him into your hand.'"

Barak said to her, "If you will go with me, I will go; but if you will not go with me, I will not go." And she said, "I will surely go with you; nevertheless, the road on which you are going will not lead to your glory, for the Lord will sell Sisera into the hand of a woman." Then Deborah got up and went with Barak to Kedesh. Barak summoned Zebulun and Napthali to Kedesh; and ten thousand warriors went up behind him; and Deborah went up with him.

Now Heber the Kenite had separated from the other Kenites, that is, the descendants of Hobab the father-in-law of Moses, and had encamped as far away as Elon-bezananim, which is near Kedesh. When Sisera was told that Barak son of Abinoam had gone up to Mount Tabor, Sisera called out all his chariots, nine hundred chariots of iron, and all the troops who were with him, from Harosheth-ha-goilm to the Wadi Kishon.

[Deborah prophecies that the battle will be won by the hand of a woman.]

Then Deborah said to Barak, "Up! For this is the day on which the Lord has given Sisera into your hand. The Lord is indeed going out before you." So Barak went down from Mount Tabor with ten thousand warriors following him. And the Lord threw Sisera and all his chariots and all his army into a panic before Barak; Sisera got down from his chariot and fled away on foot, while Barak pursued the chariots and the army to Harosheth-ha-goilm. All the army of Sisera fell by the sword; no one was left.

Unlike Deborah, Ja'el, by whose "hand" the enemy general, Sisera, was actually slain, has often been depicted as a temptress and femme fatale.

We know very little about Huldah the prophetess. We are given the name of her husband, his "job description" at court, and their street address in Jerusalem. We do know that she was a prophet and that she could read. We also know that it was to this woman that the High Priest and the king's personal attendant were sent by the king to validate and authenticate a mysterious legal text that was discovered in the temple. The presence of an educated female prophet of the royal court suggests several questions. Where and under what conditions was Huldah educated? Given that many of the male prophets in Israel remain nameless, is it possible that Huldah was not an anomaly, but rather one of many or at least several female prophets? Such a discovery would, by analogy, be consistent with other societies in the region. Mention of and/or allusions to several "schools of prophets" in Ancient Israel are present in the scripture, and both the court and the temple would have had scribal schools. Whether or not there were instances of female prophets in Israel, such as those in the Mari texts from Chapters 2 and 3, and the extensive presence of female prophets in the Ishtar traditions, Huldah, at least in some way, continued the legacy of Miriam and Deborah. Anna, the prophetess in the New Testament Gospel of Luke, served as a prophet who lived in the Temple complex.

HULDAH, COURT PROPHET TO KING JOSIAH[*]

[*The king determines that Huldah the prophet will authenticate the Book of the Law that was discovered hidden in the Temple.*]

When the king heard the words of the book of the law, he tore his clothes. Then the king commanded the priest Hilkiah, Ahikam son of Shaphan, Ach-bor son of Micalah, Shaphan the secretary, and the king's servant Asaiah, saying, "Go, inquire of the Lord for me, for the people, and for all Judah, concerning the words of this book that has been found; for great is the wrath of the Lord that is kindled against us, because our ancestors did not obey the words of this book, to do according to all that is written concerning us."

[*The High Priest and Administrators go to Huldah.*]

So the priest Hilkiah, Ahikam, Achbor, Shaphan, and Asaiah went to the prophetess Huldah the wife of Shallum son of Tikvah, son of Harhas, keeper of the wardrobe; she resided in Jerusalem in the Second Quarter, where they consulted her.

WOMEN OUTSIDE THE NOBILITY

It is heartening to identify women's agency in the Hebrew Bible and to recognize that as such stories are emphasized they can be appropriated by women and men within religious traditions that have foundations in the Hebrew Bible. It is equally important to acknowledge that the Hebrew Bible recounts stories that validate the subjugation, exploitation, and sexual victimization of women. Women had to use their wits and wisdom and other resources in order to define their own experience and advance their causes. Tamar was a widow who disguised herself as a prostitute to assure that she would bear a child within her deceased husband's family, thus ensuring him an heir and a viable life for herself.

Levirite Law was developed to secure the properties of a deceased son (who dies without sons) in the estate of his father's family. The son's widow can marry her husband's brother. If the widow does wish to remarry within her deceased husband's family, it is the responsibility of the oldest brother to wed her. If they do not wish to marry, then each of her former husband's brothers is, in turn, by seniority, considered, and one of the brothers must marry her. If the widow does not wish to remain in this family, or, if there are no brothers, she is required to return to the home of her father. She can marry someone else, but of course the question of her eligibility (age, wealth, ability to bear children) may preclude her ever being asked.

The widow Tamar recognized the harsh rules within her patriarchal culture that treat the widow as property to be "dealt with" in order to maintain (or increase) the "private property" of her deceased husband's family. Fate took a bizarre turn in Tamar's life when each of two brothers that she married died shortly thereafter. The remaining brother was still a child. Tamar, who wanted children and a family, surveyed all possibilities, predicted the responses of Judah, her former father-in-law, summoned her courage, and devised a plan. Through the use of her wits and her wisdom Tamar secured a future for herself that preserved her dignity and guaranteed her survival.

Another story from the Book of Judges demonstrates lawlessness that existed during this period. This selection represents the most brutal treatment of a woman recorded in the Hebrew Bible. This woman, the concubine of a landowner, was betrayed, raped, tortured, and dismembered. The master of the concubine had gone to her father's home to bring her back to his own home. On the way back

*NRSV, 1991, 2 Kings 22: 11–14

an old man extended hospitality to them. When, however, men from the town came to the old man's home and demanded that the male visitor be given to them for sexual pleasure, the old man intervened and refused to permit his male guest to be violated. Instead he offers the strangers his own virgin daughter and the concubine of his guest. The men from the town took the concubine.

AN UNNAMED CONCUBINE IS SEXUALLY ABUSED IN THE NAME OF HOSPITALITY[*]

In those days when there was no king in Israel, a certain Levite residing in the remote parts of the hill country of Ephraim, took to himself a concubine from Bethlehem in Judah. But his concubine became angry with him, and she went away from him to her father's house at Bethlehem in Judah, and was there some four months. Then her husband set out after her, to speak tenderly to her and bring her back. He had with him his servant and a couple of donkeys. When he reached her father's house, the girl's father saw him and came with joy to meet him. His father-in law, the girl's father, made him stay, and he remained with him three days. . .

[*Two days later the man and his concubine left for home. On the way, the man decides to stop at Gibeah. He waits in the town square for an offer of hospitality.*]

Then at evening there was an old man coming from his work in the field. The man was from the hill country of Ephraim, and he was residing in Gibeah. (The people of the place were Benjaminites). When the old man looked up and saw the wayfarer in the open square of the city, he said, "Where are you going and where do you come from?" He answered him, "We are passing from Bethlehem in Judah to the remote parts of the hill country of Ephraim, from which I come. I went to Bethlehem in Judah; and I am going to my home. Nobody has offered to take me in. We your servants have straw and fodder for our donkeys, with bread and wine for me and the woman and the young man along with us. We need nothing more." The old man said, "Peace be to you. I will care for all your wants; only do not spend the night in the square." So he brought him into his house, and fed the donkeys; they washed their feet, and ate and drank.

While they were enjoying themselves, the men of the city, a perverse lot, surrounded the house, and started pounding on the door. They said to the old man, the master of the house, "Bring out the man who came into your house, so that we may have intercourse with him." And the man, the master of the house, went out to them and said to them, "No, my brothers, do not act so wickedly. Since this man is my guest, do not do this vile thing. Here are my virgin daughter and his concubine; let me bring them out now. Ravish them and do whatever you want to them; but against this man do not do such a vile thing." But the men would not listen to him. So the man seized his concubine, and put her out to them. They wantonly raped her, and abused her all through the night until the morning. And as the dawn began to break, they let her go. As morning appeared, the woman came and fell down at the door of the man's house where her master was, until it was light.

In the morning her master got up, opened the doors of the house, and when he went out to go on his way, there was his concubine lying at the door of the house, with her hands on the threshold. "Get up," he said to her, "we are going." But there

*NRSV 1991, Judges 19:1–30.

was no answer. Then he put her on the donkey; and the man set out for his home. When he had entered his house, he took a knife, and grasping his concubine he cut her into twelve pieces, limb by limb, and sent her throughout all the territory of Israel. Then he commanded the men whom he sent, saying, "Thus shall you say to all the Israelites, 'Has such a thing ever happened, since the day that the Israelites came up from the land of Egypt until this day? Consider it, take counsel, and speak out.'"

This reading is an important selection for validating women's sexual autonomy and agency. However, as with all biblical texts the crucial point is the interpretive framework in which the text is understood. Here we are interpreting The Song of Solomon as a dramatic dialogue that celebrates human sexual love. Both form and content are very similar to the love poems from ancient Egypt. Note as well the same literary convention from Mesopotamia and Egypt in which the lovers refer to one another as brother and sister. This similarity suggests an early dating for the poem, but scholars are reluctant to assign a specific date. As we saw in the selections from Inanna and Dumuzi, the female in this poem is comfortable in her own sexuality and in the sexuality of her beloved.

THE BELOVED LOVER IN THE SONG OF SONGS[*]

Let him kiss me with the kisses of his
    mouth!
For your love is better than wine, your
    anointing oils are fragrant,
your name is perfume poured out;
    therefore the maidens love you.
Draw me after you, let us make haste.
The king has brought me into his
    chambers.
We will exult and rejoice in you; we will
    extol your love more than wine;
    rightly do they
love you.
I am black and beautiful, O daughters of
    Jerusalem, like the tents of Kedar,
like the curtains of Solomon.
Do not gaze at me because I am dark,
    because the sun has gazed on me.
My mother's sons were angry with me;
    they made me keeper of the
vineyards, but my own vineyard I have
    not kept!
Tell me, you whom my soul loves, where
    you pasture your flock, where you
    make it lie

down at noon;
for why should I be like one who is
    veiled beside the flocks of your
    companions?
If you do not know,
O fairest among women, follow the
    tracks of the flock,
and pasture your kids beside the shep-
    herds' tents. . . .
He brought me to the banqueting house,
and his intention toward me was love.
Sustain me with raisins,
refresh me with apples; for I am faint
    with love. O that his left hand were
    under my head,
and that his right hand embraced me!
I adjure you, O daughters of
Jerusalem,
by the gazelles or the wild does:
do not stir up or awaken love
until it is ready!
The voice of my beloved! Look, he
    comes,
leaping upon the mountains, bounding
    over the hills.

*NRSV 1991, Song of Solomon, 1: 1–8, 2: 2–12, 2: 16a, 3: 11, 4: 9–16, 4: 16b.

My beloved is like a gazelle or a young
stag.
Look, there he stands behind our wall,
gazing in at the windows, looking
through the
lattice. My beloved speaks and says
to me:
"Arise, my love, my fair one, and come
away; for now the winter is past, the
rain is over
and gone.
The flowers appear on the earth; the
time of singing has come, and the
voice of the
turtledove is heard in our land.". . .
My beloved is mine and I am his; . . .
Daughters of Jerusalem, come out.
Look, O daughters of Zion,
at King Solomon, at the crown with
which his mother crowned him on
the day of his
wedding, on the day of the gladness of
his heart. . . .
You have ravaged my heart, my sister,
my bride,

You have ravaged my heart, with one
glance of your eyes,
with one jewel of your necklace
How sweet is your love, my sister, my
bride!
how much better is your love than wine,
and the fragrance of your oils than any
spice!
Your lips distill nectar, my bride;
honey and milk are under your tongue;
the scent of your garments is like the
scent of Lebanon.
A garden locked is my sister, my bride, a
garden locked, a fountain sealed.
Your channel is an orchard of
pomegranates
with all choicest fruits, henna with nard,
nard and saffron, calamus and
cinnamon,
with all trees of frankincense myrrh and
aloes, with all chief spices-
a garden fountain, a well of living water,
and flowing streams from Lebanon. . . .
Let my beloved come to his garden and
eat its choicest fruits.

SUGGESTED READINGS

Burns, Rita J. "Has the Lord Spoken Only Through Moses?" SBL Dissertation Series 84. Atlanta: Scholars Press, 1987.

Diamant, Anita. *The Red Tent.* New York: Picador USA, 1997.

A Feminist Companion to the Old Testament. Edited by Athalyah Brenner. Sheffield, UK: Sheffield Academic Press, 1988.

Frankel, Ellen. *The Five Books of Miriam.* New York: Grosset/Putnam, 1996.

Olyan, Saul M. *Asherah and the Cult of Yahweh in Israel.* Society of Biblical Literature Monograph Series. Atlanta: Scholars Press, 1988.

Sheres, Ita. *Dinah's Rebellion.* New York: Crossroad, 1990.

Teubal, Savina J. *Sarah the Priestess: The First Matriarch of Genesis.* Athens, Ohio: Swallow Press, 1984.

Trible, Phyllis. *Texts of Terror.* Philadelphia: Fortress Press, 1984.

The Women's Bible Commentary. Edited by Carol A. Newsom and Sharon H. Ringe. Louisville, KY: Westminster John Knox Press, 1992.

Women in the Hebrew Bible. Edited by Alice Bach. New York: Routledge Press, 1999.

Sources Cited

Sarah and Hagar, Mothers of Two Nations. *The New Oxford Annotated Bible.* Edited by Bruce M. Metzger and Roland E. Murphy. New Revised Standard Edition, New York: Oxford University Press, 1991. Genesis 16.

Bathsheba, Wife of King David, Mother of King Solomon. *The New Oxford Annotated Bible.* Edited by Bruce M. Metzger and Roland E. Murphy. New Revised Standard Edition, New York: Oxford University Press, 1991. 1 Samuel 11:2–4, 14–15, 26–27, 12:19, 12:24–25. 1 Kings 1:11–12, 15–21, 29–31, 32–34.

Queen of Sheba and Solomon: Mutual Admiration. *The New Oxford Annotated Bible.* Edited by Bruce M. Metzger and Roland E. Murphy. New Revised Standard Edition, New York: Oxford University Press, 1991. 1 Kings 10.

Jezebel, A Despised Foreign Queen of Israel; Devotee of Ba'al and Asherah. *The New Oxford Annotated Bible.* Edited by Bruce M. Metzger and Roland E. Murphy. New Revised Standard Edition, New York: Oxford University Press, 1991. 1 Kings 16:31–33.

The Female Principle of Divine Wisdom Was Present at Creation. *The New Oxford Annotated Bible.* Edited by Bruce M. Metzger and Roland E. Murphy. New Revised Standard Edition, New York: Oxford University Press, 1991. Proverbs 8:22–36.

Images of the Female at Creation: Genesis 1 and Genesis 2. *The New Oxford Annotated Bible.* Edited by Bruce M. Metzger and Roland E. Murphy. New Revised Standard Edition, New York: Oxford University Press, 1991. Genesis 1:26–28; 2:4–7, 20b–23.

Israelites Bake Breads for the Queen of Heaven. *The New Oxford Annotated Bible.* Edited by Bruce M. Metzger and Roland E. Murphy. New Revised Standard Edition, New York: Oxford University Press, 1991. Jeremiah 44:15–19.

Queen Esther and the Feast of Purim. *The New Oxford Annotated Bible.* Edited by Bruce M. Metzger and Roland E. Murphy. New Revised Standard Edition, New York: Oxford University Press, 1991. Esther 9:1A, 2A, 17–19, 29–32.

The Prophet Miriam at the Sea of Reeds. *The New Oxford Annotated Bible.* Edited by Bruce M. Metzger and Roland E. Murphy. New Revised Standard Edition, New York: Oxford University Press, 1991. Exodus 15:18–21.

Miriam: Administrator of Law at Kadesh. *The New Oxford Annotated Bible.* Edited by Bruce M. Metzger and Roland E. Murphy. New Revised Standard Edition, New York: Oxford University Press, 1991. Numbers 12:1–14, 15b–16.

Deborah: Prophet, Judge, and Female Warrior in Israel. *The New Oxford Annotated Bible.* Edited by Bruce M. Metzger and Roland E. Murphy. New Revised Standard Edition, New York: Oxford University Press, 1991. Judges 4:4–16.

Huldah, Court Prophet to King Josiah. *The New Oxford Annotated Bible.* Edited by Bruce M. Metzger and Roland E. Murphy. New Revised Standard Edition, New York: Oxford University Press, 1991. 2 Kings 22:11–14.

An Unnamed Concubine Is Sexually Abused in the Name of Hospitality. *The New Oxford Annotated Bible.* Edited by Bruce M. Metzger and Roland E. Murphy. New Revised Standard Edition, New York: Oxford University Press, 1991. Judges 19:1–30.

The Beloved Lover in the Song of Songs. *The New Oxford Annotated Bible.* Edited by Bruce M. Metzger and Roland E. Murphy. New Revised Standard Edition, New York: Oxford University Press, 1991. Song of Solomon 1:1–18, 2:2–12, 2:16a, 3:11, 4:9–16, 4:16b.

PART II

WOMEN IN THE MEDITERRANEAN AND THE GRECO-ROMAN WORLD

Part II of Volume One treats women's participation in culture from the Bronze Age in Minoan Crete to Ancient Greece, Etruria, the Roman Republic, the Hellenistic world, and culminates with texts from Hellenistic Judaism. In Part II there emerges yet another element of the *expansive vs. intensive* dilemma discussed in the introduction to this volume. Geographically Part II is more contained than Part I. By far the majority of texts proceeds from regions that are either in the Mediterranean Basin or are in close proximity to it; yet our time line spans from circa 1800 B.C.E. at Crete to the first century C.E. Selections of texts continue to be more expansive in scope than intensive. We include selections from a broad spectrum of several categories yet find very few texts penned by women. Traditions represented in this section continue to be written predominately by males from the point of view of male experience. There is far less biographical information available on the women represented in this part of the volume than will be found in some selections in Part III and all the way through Volume Two. By far the greater part of available biographical information for the selections continues to be contextualized by the agenda of the males who wrote the texts and/or the male historians who preserved them.

Chapter 6, "Women at Crete and Greek Women beyond Athens," provides a pleasant yet sometimes perplexing quest to consider what can be learned about women's contributions to culture on the island of Crete. This tiny island was first inhabited circa 6100 B.C.E. (Neolithic) and first excavated in 1900 C.E. Its unique culture was destroyed by 1100 B.C.E. Archaeologists and scholars who study Crete have discovered two text groups: Linear B (dated from 1400–1100 B.C.E.), the texts of Myceanean (martial, pre-Greek) invaders of Crete, and Linear A (predates Linear B), the texts of preMycenean culture. Linear B texts closely resemble Greek and were promptly translated. Linear A texts, which represent a preGreek culture, were first published in 1985 and are, at last, being deciphered and translated. Because there are no translated texts available for the major culture periods at Crete, the first section of Chapter 6, like Chapter 1, "Paleolithic, Neolithic, and Proto-History Culture," relies on "image as text." The prominent female presence at Crete in public and private spheres is stunning and extensive.

A variety of types of texts by and/or about Greek women at Sparta and other city-states on the Greek mainland, as well as the islands and Crotona in Southern Italy, affirms women's agency as contributors to culture. It is apparent that culture not only at Crete but throughout the Mediterranean was influenced to a considerable degree by Ancient Near Eastern civilizations.

Texts about *Athenian* women in Greek literature introduced in Chapter 7, "Athens," demonstrate that restraints of patriarchal culture in restricting women's agency introduced in the Homeric epics were legislated by Solon in fifth-century Athens. In the Athenian *polis* (city-state) as transitions to a patriarchal social organization were accomplished. Philosophical, political, educational, economic, and religious ideologies of patriarchal perspectives were formally institutionalized. Patterns that took root and flourished at Athens, in particular, set precedents that have been adopted by the patriarchal hierarchy throughout Western civilization.

Legitimation of political institutions and political ideologies based on male dominance significantly influenced women's experience. At Athens and during the Roman Republic the delineation of public and private spheres according to gender had a similarly profound impact upon women's *autonomy* (self governance and freedom to define their own experience). Marriage for females at puberty (14 years was the median age at Athens) and the relegation of women to the private sphere determined that the physical and psychological boundaries within which women lived their lives severely restricted their experience of the world. Women were defined in terms of their relationships to the men in their lives and distinctions are noted in lifestyles among wives and daughters of male citizens, non-citizen (or foreign) women, and female slaves. *Misogynistic* (contempt of women) literature presenting a negative interpretation of women that appears during the fifth century B.C.E. at Athens is contrasted by a meager but significant legacy of letters, inscriptions, legal tractates, archives, and literature in which women's own experience is recorded.

Vivid contrasts are noted between the apparent freedom and social equality of Etruscan women introduced in Chapter 8, "Etruria and the Roman Republic," and the life of the Roman matron during the Republic. During the Hellenistic period (Chapter 9, "The Hellenistic World"), in certain regions there was little change in women's public role. In areas like Hellenistic Egypt, however, urbanization, cosmopolitanism, beginnings of institutional education that included female students, and, for reasons that will be elaborated, the proliferation of mystery religions provided both aristocratic women and women from the working classes opportunities to experience new economic, legal, and social roles. Chapter 10, "Women in Hellenistic Judaism," introduces data from Hellenistic Judaism that are seldom, if ever, included in traditional textbooks or readers for the nonspecialist. The reading selections in Chapter 10 provide provocative insights concerning women in Early Judaism and create a foundation for understanding the religious and economic agency of Jewish/Christian women in Christian origins.

Throughout Part II the sources consulted for clarification of women's experience include archival, epigraphical, and inscriptive evidence as well as historical, philosophical, narrative, and religious documents.

Texts that are recognized as the *canons* (texts that are most highly esteemed by the dominant culture) of the so-called Classical periods in Greece and Rome are countered by cultural patterns at less prominent sites such as Lesbos, Miletus, Croton, Gortyn, Sparta, and Etruria, where societal norms about gender differed considerably. We begin Part II with representations of female iconography on the island of Crete just off the coast of Greece.

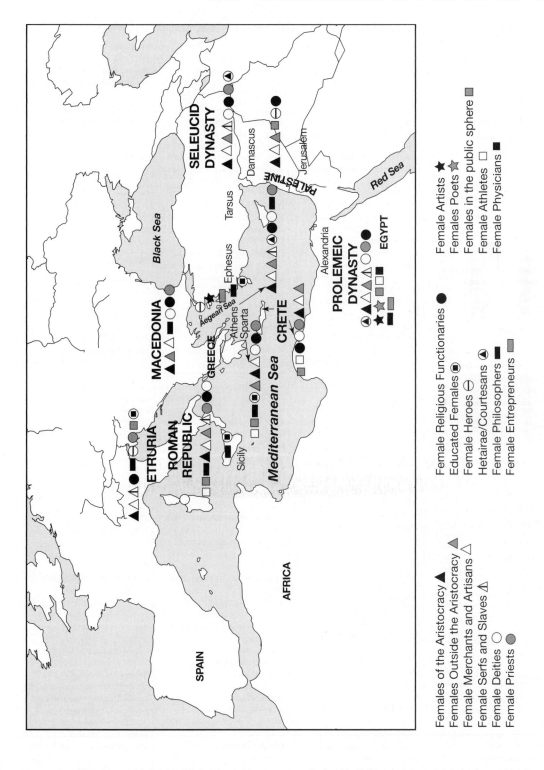

Females of the Aristocracy ▲
Females Outside the Aristocracy ▲
Female Merchants and Artisans △
Female Serfs and Slaves ⧍
Female Deities ○
Female Priests ●

Female Religious Functionaries ●
Educated Females ▣
Female Heroes ⊖
Hetairae/Courtesans ◑
Female Philosophers ■
Female Entrepreneurs ▪

Female Artists ★
Females Poets ★
Females in the public sphere ▪
Female Athletes □
Female Physicians ■

Time Lines and Constituents of Culture

This chart covers a time period that begins at Crete, and the islands and Greek cities beyond Athens from the seventh to the fourth centuries B.C.E., to Athens in the Classical period (fifth century B.C.E.), the Etruscans (ninth century B.C.E.), and the Roman Republic (eighth century B.C.E.). The tradition for patriarchal societies among the Greeks in Athens and in the Roman Republic became paradigmatic for Western Civilization. Note however, in societies that coexist with these two models for the West, there are societies that honored the female in which women had greater autonomy.

Crete 1800-1100 B.C.E.

Social Organization
There was a preponderance of female images.
Technology
Archeitecture, hydraulic systems, gold jewelry, exquisite ceramics, products from the sea.
***Goddesses**
Early Hera, Athena, The Serpent Deities
Symbol Systems
Life, Death, Rebirth, and Fertility Themes: Labyris, Bucrania, Butterflies
Female Functionaries
Priestesses in public and private spheres
*All Cultures in the West become Patriarchal and socially stratified.
Sparta and Greek Women beyond Athens:
Sparta
Greek men attest to the freedoms, activities, education, and wealth among Spartan women.
Lesbos
Sappho sixth century B.C.E., poet, head of an academy for young women.
Telos
Erinna fourth century B.C.E., poet
Crotona (Southern Italy)
Female Pythagoreans
Theano and Myia of Crotona sixth century B.C.E.
Female Heroes
Queen Thargalia of Thessaly fifth century B.C.E.,
Marpessa of Tarea seventh century B.C.E.,
Telesilla of Argos fifth century B.C.E.,
Artemisia of Helicarnasus fifth century B.C.E.

Athens 600-350 B.C.E.

Wives of Citizens
Men dictated and defined women's experience and wrote about it. These women relegated to the private sphere. Girls marry at 14 years of age to husbands 28 or 30.

No formal education. No women writers among wives of citizens.
Hetairae/Courtesans
Many hetairae at Athens were non-Athenians, educated, and politically astute; couldn't marry citizen males; and became mistresses. Most famous were Aspasia of Miletus fifth century B.C.E.
Philosophers
Aspasia from Miletus, also a philosopher, wrote speeches for Pericles, *Menexenus.Students of Plato fourth century B.C.E., Lasthenia of Mantinea, Axiotha of Phlius*
Religion
The Holy Olympian Goddesses: Athena, Aphrodite, Hera, Demeter, Hestia, and Artemis.
Female Religious Functionaries
Priestesses of each deity
The Pythia (prophetess) at Delphi.
The bacchae-female followers of Dionysius

Etruria 800–500 B.C.E.

Women in the Aristocracy
Women present in the public sphere with or without males, Queen Larthia ninth or eight century B.C.E., Queen Tannaquil, seventh century B.C.E., Ramtha sixth century B.C.E.
Women Outside the Aristocracy
Women present in the public sphere with or without males.
Produced textiles, jewelry, and amber
Religion
The Holy Female Deities
Uni, Mnrva, and Turan
Female Religious Functionaries
The Prophetess
Vegoia fourth to the third century B.C.E.

Roman Republic
753 Traditional date.

Social Organization
Republican government begins in the sixth century B.C.E.

Patrician Women
Lucretia sixth century B.C.E. (paradigm of noble Roman matron)
Tertia Aemilia. Sulpicia, second to the first century B.C.E. Amymone first century B.C.E. Claudia second century B.C.E.
Principal Female deities
Minerva, Juno, Vesta, Venus, Ceres, and Diana
Myth/Ritual Functionaries
Priestesses for all Goddesses
Vestal Virgins Taracia, Quinta, and Claudia second century B.C.E.

Hellenistic World
323 –27 B.C.E.

(Focus on the Seleucid and Ptolemaic Dynasties)
Women in the Aristocracy
Hellenistic Queens
Dynastic Names include: Euridice, Olympias, Arsinoe Berenice, Miriamne, and Cleopatra. Focus on Olympias mother of Cleopatra I and Alexander the Great fourth century B.C.E., Arsinoe II Phiadelphus third century B.C.E., Cleopatra VII, first century B.C.E. These queens were educated and literate. Administered, government-commanded armies patronized artists, architects, and musicians
Women Outside the Aristocracy
Education
Education for many women and girls in the public and private spheres
Female Philosophers
Hipparchia the Cynic third century B.C.E.,
Female Pythagoreans:
third to the first century B.C.E.
Aesara, Perictione I, Theano II, and Perictione II
Female Physicians
Agnodice and Philistia studied, practiced, and taught medicine second century B.C.E.
Female Poets
Anyte third century B.C.E. Nossis third century B.C.E. Sulpicia first century B.C.E.
Female Politicians
Hortensia first century B.C.E.

Female Painters and Musicians
Polygnata (harpist) 86 B.C.E. Painters Timarete, Irene, Aristarete, Iaia of Cyzicus, and Olympias.
Religion
Mystery religions emerge.
Goddesses from the East re-emerge.
Isis, Cybele, and The Great Mother.
Priestesses and female religious functionaries for all deities except the male God, Mithras.

Hellenistic Judaism 323–27 B.C.E.

Israel under foreign rule by Seleucids and Ptolemies until the Hasmonean Dynasty 135 B.C.E.
Hellenistic culture impacted Judaism.
Women in the Aristocracy
Salome Alexandra, Queen of Israel 76-67 B.C.E., was first of the Jewish Hellenistic Queens. Dynastic names: Alexandra, Berenice, and Miriamne
Women Outside the Aristocracy
Education
Evidence for educated women among Essenes. Female Theraputae, Mishnaic tractates.
Religion
The Holy
Female Principle of Divine Wisdom, Sophia
Myth
Textual Retelling of Deborah, Hannah, and Seila as Mothers of Israel. Vindication of Susanna
Ritual in texts
Judith's victory ode and Seila's pilgrimage
Historical Women
Female Theraputae first century B.C.E. to the first century C.E. Wrote hymns and prayers, sang and danced in ritual celebration. Venerable female Essenes are honored and esteemed second (?) to the first century B.C.E.
Female Religious Functionaries
Jewish female ascetics in Egypt
Jewish Female Ascetics at Qumran.
Female Entrepreneur
Mibtahiahof Elaphantine third century B.C.E.

Chapter 6

Women at Crete and
Greek Women beyond Athens

Chapter 6 presents selections from the Western Mediterranean region that either precede or are synchronous with Greek culture in Athenian society. The selections are indicative of a variety of women's experiences that differ radically from the gender norms at Athens and Rome that became paradigmatic for women throughout the Western world.

BRIEF OVERVIEW OF ARCHAEOLOGICAL EXCAVATIONS AT CRETE

The island of Crete is in the Aegean Sea just off the coast of Greece. Civilization at Crete has origins (ca. 6100 B.C.E.) in the Neolithic period and shares significant correspondences with late Neolithic culture, including the prominence of female imagery throughout. There are several ways in which an examination of culture at Crete in the ancient world serves as a cultural linkage with Neolithic culture, the Ancient Near East, and the early Greeks. Yet, even a brief overview of this highly sophisticated and vital culture highlights the vivid contrasts between representations of women at Crete and other cultures in the Mediterranean world that ultimately evolve into the "classical civilizations" of the West.

The earliest language at Crete, which is referenced as Linear A, was discovered at the dawn of the twentieth century, but has only recently begun to be translated. The organizational pattern for the first part of this chapter is, therefore, similar to that followed for Anatolia and also features "image as text" as did Chapter 1 on Paleolithic and Neolithic cultures.

British archaeologist Sir Arthur Evans initiated the first archaeological excavations at Crete. Many archaeological teams have continued reconstructions and interpretations of this perplexing but compelling Neolithic/Bronze Age site. At several junctures in its history, Crete has been the subject of debate concerning the status of women. We suggest the principal point in question resides in archaeologists' androcentric analysis of female imagery at Crete. A male centered world view continues to make it difficult for many archaeologists to imagine female authority, leadership, equity, and creativity suggested by the evidence. Scholars in the field also inhibit beginning archaeologists who would challenge the history of interpretation.

Much of the published research about Crete is based on data from the Mycenean period (1300–1100 B.C.E.) just before the Palace culture was destroyed. The Myceneans were a patriarchal, martial people who worshiped a sky god and whose artifacts lack the lyrical expression of the Minoan culture.

SOCIAL ORGANIZATION

When Sir Arthur Evans discovered the large Palace at Knossos on Crete he decided that this must have been the island home of the *mythical* King Minos from Greek mythology. Based upon his feeling about this connection, Evans designated all of culture at Crete, beginning around 3000 B.C.E., as "Minoan."

For most of the twentieth century only a handful of classicists and archaeologists who continued to work at Crete challenged Evans' assumptions. Over time, however, greater numbers of specialists evaluated the data and challenged the history of interpretation. Their assessment of an overwhelming preponderance of female imagery, female iconography and female deities, and the nominal representations of males, among other factors, provoked significant challenges to interpretations of pre-Mycenean social organization at Crete. Theories for patriarchy, matriarchy, egalitarian matrifocal and nonegalitarian matrifocal culture have been debated without resolution. Perspectives that marginalize (treat as having questionable validity) interpretive models that challenge Evans' "King Minos" hypothesis need to be questioned. Interpretive approaches that continue to discuss Minoan culture (3000 B.C.E.-1100 B.C.E.) predominantly in terms of evidence from the Mycenean occupation 1400-1100 B.C.E. also need to be addressed.

As we have noted, representations of women in the public sphere at Crete are normative. Several women are represented on large frescoes and are seated prominently among an assembly at Knossos (Figure 6.1). Iconography at Crete that represents women in the public sphere also includes women in

Figure 6–1   Women and men in the courtyard at Knossos. *The Bridgeman Art Library International Ltd.*

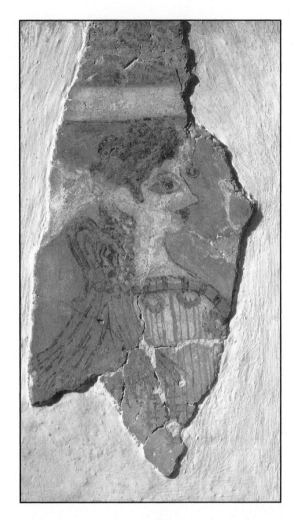

Figure 6–2   Minoan fresco entitled "La Parisienne." *Nimatallah, Art Resource, N.Y.*

the bull leaping fresco in the public arena, and women driving their own chariots. The Parisienne, was seated among a group of young people sitting on benches and having something to drink (Figure 6.2 and Figure 6.3). The Dancer whose image was originally in the so-called Queen's *megaron* (chamber) at Knossos, is dancing so exuberantly that her hair is depicted as flying out to the sides.

SUBSISTENCE

Subsistence at Crete included agriculture, fishing, maritime industry, metallurgy, the production of jewelry, especially work in gold with particular expertise in the technique called repousse, seal stones, and the production of several notable styles of pottery over the generations. Extensive trade and commerce abroad included the Cycladic Islands, Egypt, Anatolia, and the Ancient Near East.

The visual art and architecture at Crete are unique in the ancient world. Evidence of syncretism notwithstanding, the elegance and the "joy of life" that characterize art and artifacts from Minoan civilization are without parallel. Historian Marymay Downing suggests that at Crete we see four principal

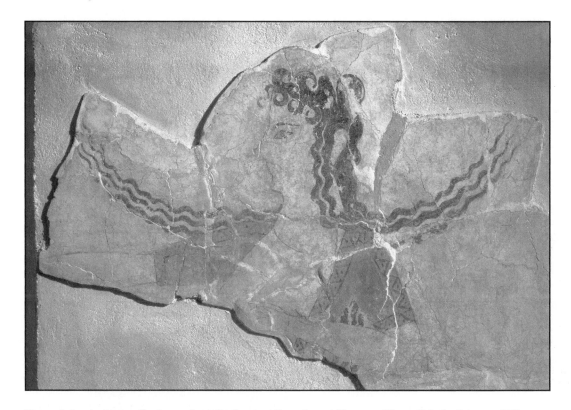

Figure 6–3   An image of a dancer from the fresco at the palace at Knossos. *Nimatallah, Art Resource, N.Y.*

motifs in culture related to Goddess worship at Crete: protection, technology, nature, and themes related to the sea. All of these themes are present in the art and architecture at Crete. (Downing, *Journal of Feminist Studies in Religion* 1, no. 1 1984)

TECHNOLOGY

Architecture

At the palace at Knossos, sophisticated technological advances include complex architectural structures, and creative and imaginative use of light that permits shafts of light to flood into the multistoried palaces. Advanced hydraulic engineering is evidenced by strategically situated lustral basins (pools) and even a bathtub in the so called "Queen's megaron" (chamber, literally space) at Knossos.

Nature

Astonishing beauty marked by spontaneity, whimsicality, and vibrant colors characterize visual art, artifacts, and iconography celebrating nature at Crete as shown in the Partridge Frescoes (Figure 6.4) in the Throne Room at Knossos. There is a reverence for plant, animal, and human life represented in frescoes and pottery. The Octopus Jug (Figure 6.5) and the Bee Fibula are excellent examples (Figure 6.6).

Figure 6–4 A partridge fresco. *Bibliotheque des Arts Decoratifs Paris/Dagli Orti, Picture Desk, Inc./Kobal Collection*

Figure 6–5 Octopus flask. *D.A. Harissiadis, Archaeological Museum of Herakleion*

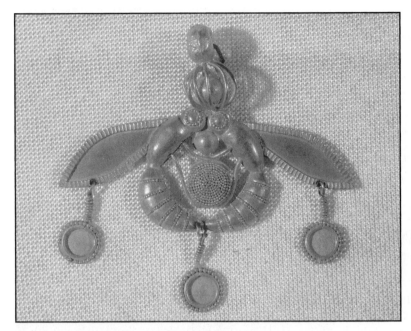

Figure 6–6   A bee fibula. *Erich Lessing, Art Resource, N.Y.*

Maritime Motif

Frescoes and pottery provide especially vivid examples of maritime motifs at Crete. The dolphins are depicted on a fresco; their lyric movement is characteristic of the representation of nature themes in Minoan art (Figure 6.7).

Figure 6–7   A dolphin frescoe. *Knossos, Crete/Kurt Scholz/Superstock*

Figure 6–8   A serpent deity. *Erich Lessing, Art Resource, N.Y.*

Protection Motif

Images of the Serpent Deity were discovered not only in palaces and villas but also in habitation and work sites throughout the island and have been interpreted by some scholars as a Divine Protectress. This Serpent Deity has an owl atop her headdress. Given that iconography and statuary for Athena, patron deity at Athens, include a serpent and an owl, and that Athena is attested at Crete in Linear B texts, the Serpent Deity at Crete may indeed be a precursor to Athena as a "patron" deity and protectress (Figure 6.8). (Nilsson, 1927, 189)

RELIGION

The Holy

Matrifocal/Gynocentric religious orientation at Crete is indisputable. Anthropomorphic representations of The Holy at Crete are almost exclusively female, and are found in varieties of settings throughout the island. Bucrania also abound at Crete. Bucrania can be interpreted as symbolic of male fertility, and/or as symbolic of both female and male fertility (see Figure 1.13). The following illustrations indicate the variety of expressions of the Goddess at Crete and attest as well to a number of worship sites where they were discovered.

Archaeologists have found images of the Goddess at Mountain Shrines (Figure 6.9), a large grouping of Golden Labyris (votive double-axes) discovered in a sacred cave (Figure 6.10), and the Goddess and her Priestesses in Sacred Groves (Figure 6.11). Bucrania are also dominant in both art and architecture (Figure 6.12) and from the Mycenean period, the Haigya Triada Sarcophagus (Figure 6.13) depicts priestesses presiding over the sacrifice of a bull.

Myth

Greek Literature from the Archaic and Classical periods propose origins for the Greek Goddesses Hera, Eileithiya, Athena, and Artemis at Crete. Linear B translations from the Mycenean occupation at Crete associate Athena as a protectress of maritime industry at Crete (Nilsson 1927, 210). Some scholars also suggest that the earliest versions of the Demeter/Persephone life/death/rebirth myth that is central to the Elusynian Mysteries had roots at Anatolia and later at Crete. (Harrison 1955, 54 and Nilsson 1927, 200)

Ritual

Numerous art, artifacts and iconography at Crete are interpreted as examples of religious ritual. These include Priestesses Dancing in Sacred Groves (Figure 6.14) and Votive Offerings in Sacred Caves made by male and female worshipers (Figure 6.14).

Figure 6–9   A stone seal and plaster cast. *Heraklion Museum/Dagli Orti, Picture Desk, Inc./Kobal Collection*

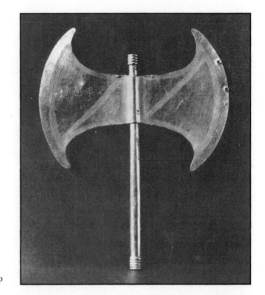

Figure 6–10   Minoan gold votive axe. *"Votive double ax,"*
Early Aegean, Minoan, Bronze age, Late Minoan I A Period,
about 1550-1500 B.C.E., Arkalokhori, Crete, Greece. Gold, 9 x
8.3 cm (3-9/16 x 3-1/4 in). Museum of Fine Arts, Boston.
Theodora Wilbour Fund in Memory of Zoe Wilbour, 58.1009. P

Figure 6–11   Seal stone rings picturing the Goddess and her priestesses. *Hellenic Republic*
Ministry of Culture

Figure 6–12   A vase in the shape of a bull's head.
Hellenic Republic Ministry of Culture

The Bull Leaping ritual included an activity in which female and male athletes assisted one another in leaping onto the back of the bull. The athlete then catapulted over the bull's head and landed upright on the ground where another athlete was poised to "catch" the leaping athlete. Scholars speculate that this activity may have indeed had sacred ritual significance Figure 6.15.

The sacrifice of a bull (shown in the Haigya Triada Sarcophagus) that is represented on a sarcophagus (tomb) from the villa by the same name is a complex ritual that was administered by priestesses and included the assistance of female and male attendants. The ritual included the slaying of a bull by the two priestesses represented in the upper part of the sarcophagus, the male and female attendants on the lower part of the sarcophagus transported gifts and sacrifices to the burial site.

Symbol Systems

Included among the sacred symbols that are pervasive at Crete are images of the *labyris* (ceremonial double axes), the *bucrania*, bees, butterflies as images of regeneration, images of the Serpent Goddess, as well as two symbol systems, Linear A and Linear B, which represent archaic stages of formal language. Linear B, the later of the two, bears striking similarities to early Greek languages, and is associated with the Myceneans whose social organization was patriarchal. Texts and artifacts that were written in Linear B were translated early on, and most scholars projected information in Linear B from

Figure 6–13   Haigya Triada Sarcophagus. *Nimatallah, Art Resource, N.Y.*

the Mycenean period back onto preMycenean culture at Crete. Publication in 1985 of the Linear A script marked renewed enthusiasm and a revisiting of numerous questions about Crete.

Female Religious Functionaries

We are fortunate to have artifacts and iconography to substantiate women's sacramental vocations at Crete. Religious functionaries are engaged in liturgical practices (worship work) that are not dissimilar to the activities of women in Neolithic Anatolia and Old Europe. There are also traces of cultural diffusion among artifacts from the Ancient Near East at Crete.

In Figure 6.16, we find a priestess carrying an incense brazier and in Figure 6.17, large palace frescoes featuring sacred processions. One such fresco at Knossos includes a procession with a High Priestess and male attendants who are carrying sacred vessels. Seal stone rings like the one in Figure 6.11 represent consecrated women celebrating an epiphany of the Goddess. Continuities from Goddess worshiping cultures in Old Europe and Anatolia, discovered also in Egypt and the Ancient Near East, appear to be inherent in religious practice on Crete. The interpretive framework in which we have elected to discuss Crete suggests that Minoan culture is, among other things, a final expression of matrifocal culture in the West. Discussions of Athenian democracy in Greece move us directly into

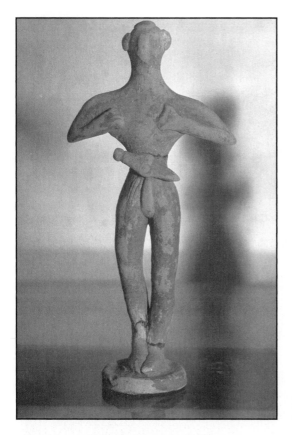

Figure 6–14   Votive offerings made by male worshiper. *Borromeo, Art Resource, N.Y.*

models of social organization that, together with androcentric interpretations of the biblical tradition, anticipate the specific patriarchal cultural norms of Western Civilization. Before entering Athenian culture, however, we introduce selections that highlight Greek women in the ancient world beyond Athens.

Figure 6–15   Fresco painting of acrobats leaping over a charging bull. *Gianni Dagli Orti, Corbis/Bettmann*

Figure 6–16   An image of a priestess carrying an incense brazier. *National Archaeological Museum, Athens, Greece, The Bridgeman Art Library International Ltd.*

GREEK WOMEN'S EXPERIENCE BEYOND ATHENS

The following selections are by and about Greek women from the Archaic and Classical periods who had agency and autonomy as poets, philosophers, musicians, and entrepreneurs. The women in the selections lived during the sixth to third centuries B.C.E. It is clear that in their homelands at Sparta, Lesbos, Telos, Miletus, and Croton they were afforded far greater opportunities for creatively and productively contributing to their societies in both public and private spheres than were Athenian women of the period.

SPARTA

Texts about women at Sparta demonstrate that the subjugation of women that became normative at Athens was not the only model of women's experience that flourished in Ancient Greece. Unlike Crete, for which we do not find notable martial imagery until the Mycenean period, Spartan society was blatantly militaristic. Yet, the centrality of a military focus, and its requirement that males live

Figure 6–17   Large palace frescoes of Knossos, Crete. *Heraklion Museum/Dagli Orti, Picture Desk, Inc./Kobal Collection*

communally in barracks after the age of six, functioned in an interesting and surprisingly liberating manner for female citizens.

Our information for this assertion proceeds from several sources that emerge among Greek historians, philosophers, and figures in philosophical dialogues. The earliest examples refer to writers in the fifth century B.C.E., including the legendary law giver Lycurgus at Sparta, Xenephon in the fourth century B.C.E., and Plutarch in the second century C.E. We find at Sparta that males from age 6 to 60 were almost exclusively devoted to maintaining and expanding Spartan military hegemony. Women were essentially responsible for maintaining and administering innumerable aspects of life in Spartan society.

REGULATIONS OF LYCURGUS CONCERNING SPARTAN WOMEN[*]

> In the matter of education, which he regarded as the greatest and noblest task of the lawgiver, he [Lycurgus] began at the very source, by carefully regulating marriages and births. For it is not true that, as Aristotle says, he tried to bring the women under proper restraint, but desisted, because he could not overcome the great license

[*]Excerpts from Plutarch, Lycurgus, Women at Sparta, translated by Bernadete Perrin. In *Plutarch's Lives.* Loeb Classical Library, Cambridge, MA and London: Harvard University Press, 1914. 1.XV-XVI.

and power which the women enjoyed on account of the many expeditions in which their husbands were engaged. During these the men were indeed obliged to leave their wives in sole control at home, and for this reason paid them greater deference than was their due, and gave them the title of Mistress. But even to the women Lycurgus paid all possible attention. He made the maidens exercise their bodies in running, wrestling, casting the discus, and hurling the javelin, in order that the fruit of their wombs might have vigorous root in vigorous bodies and come to better maturity, and that they themselves might come with vigour to the fullness of their times and struggle successfully and easily with the pangs of child-birth. He freed them from softness and delicacy and all effeminacy by accustoming the maidens no less than the youths to wear tunics only in processions, and at certain festivals to dance and sing when the young men were present as spectators. There they sometimes even mocked and railed good naturedly at any youth who had misbehaved himself; and again they would sing the praises of those who had shown themselves worthy, and so inspire the young men with great ambition and ardour. For he, who was thus extolled for his valour, and held in honour among the maidens, went away exalted by their praises; while the sting of their playful raillery was no less sharp than that of serious admonitions, especially as the kings and senators, together with the rest of the citizens, were all present at the spectacle.

Nor was there anything disgraceful in this scant clothing of the maidens, for modesty attended them, and wantonness was banished; nay, rather, it produced in them habits of simplicity and an ardent desire for health and beauty of body. It gave also to woman-kind a taste of lofty sentiment, for they felt that they too had a place in the arena of bravery and ambition. Wherefore they were led to think and speak as Gorgo, the wife of Leonidas, is said to have done. When some foreign woman, as it would seem, said to her: "You Spartan women are the only ones who rule their men," she answered: "Yes, we are the only ones that give birth to men." . . .

XENOPHON ON THE EDUCATION OF SPARTAN WOMEN[*]

It was not by imitating the customs of other states, but by knowing, and doing the opposite to most of them, that Lycurgus made his fatherland preeminently successful.

To begin at the beginning, here is his legislation about the procreation of children. Other people raise the girls who will bear their children and who are supposed to have a good upbringing with the limited portions of food and the smallest possible amount of delicacies. They make sure they abstain from wine completely or give it to them mixed with water. The other Greeks think that girls ought to sit in isolation doing women's work, leading a sedentary existence like many craftsmen. How could they expect that girls raised in this way could produce significant offspring. By contrast, Lycurgus thought that slave women could ask (sufficient quantity of clothing.)

But as far as free women were concerned, because the male childbearing was their most important function, he decreed that female sex ought to take bodily

[*]Xenophon, "Constitutions of the Lacedaemonians," LCL, 1931, 1.2–9.

exercise no less than the male. He established competitions of running and of strength for women with another, just as he did for the men, because he thought that strong offspring would be born if both parents were strong.

As for a wife's sexual relations with her husband, Lycurgus saw that men in other cultures during the first part of the time had unlimited intercourse with their wives, but he knew that the opposite was right. He made it a disgrace for the husband to be seen approaching or leaving his wife. As a result it was inevitable that their desire for intercourse increased, and that as a result the offspring (if there were any) that were born were stronger than if the couple were tired of each other.

In addition, he stopped men from taking a wife whenever they chose and decreed that they marry when they were in their prime, because he thought that this was better for their offspring. He saw that in cases where it happened that an old man had a young wife, the men were particularly protective of their wives, and he knew that the opposite was right. He required that the older man bring in a man whose body and mind he admired and have him beget the children. But in case a man did not want to cohabit with his wife, but wanted worthy children, he made a law that he could beget children from a woman who was noble and had borne good children, if he could persuade her husband. He agreed to allow many such arrangements, for the wives who wanted to have two households and husbands who wanted to acquire brothers for their children, who had blood and powers in common, but did not inherit their property.

Thus Lycurgus had different ideas about the begetting of children, and anyone who wishes to may judge whether or not he succeeded in producing in Sparta men who were superior in height and strength from the men in other states!

Spartans were the only Greek girls for whom the state prescribed a public education. This education included a significant physical component. In the Partheneion, Spartan girls are praised for swiftness in the comparisons with racehorses. Spartan women were the only Greek women we know of who stripped for athletics, as Greek men did, and engaged in athletics on a regular basis. Some sources report that total nudity, even in public in the presence of men, was not unthinkable for Spartans, as it was for other respectable Greek women. Thus in Plato's Republic, the proposal that women exercise in the nude is considered not only radical, but laughable. When Spartan women participated in footraces at Olympia in honor of Hera, goddess of marriage, they wore a short chiton like those worn by the legendary Amazons.

PLUTARCH ON THE PRIDE AND ASSURANCE OF SPARTAN WOMEN[*]

Being asked by a woman from Attica, "Why is it that you Spartan women are the only women that lord it over your men?" [one woman] said, "Because we are the only women that are mothers of men." . . .

Another was burying her son, when a commonplace old woman came up to her and said, "Ah the bad luck of it, you poor woman." "No, by heaven," said she, "but good luck, for I bore him that he might die for Sparta, and this is the very thing that has come to pass for me." . . .

[*]Plutarch, *Aforailia*, LCL, 1931, 249, 240–42.

A Spartan woman who was being sold as a slave, . . . asked by a man if she would be good if he bought her, said, "Yes, and if you do not buy me."

Another who was being sold as a slave, when the crier inquired of her what she knew how to do, said, "To be free." And when the purchaser ordered her to do something not fitting for a free woman, she said, "You will be sorry that your meanness has cost you such a possession", and committed suicide.

The following selection, from Aristotle's *Politics* is insightful for both its elaboration on women's agency at Sparta and the Athenian's adamant resistance to this. Flaws in the living out of democratic principles across lines of gender and class in the ancient world and in the present day have their origins in the perpetuation of documents such as this.

ARISTOTLE ON WOMEN AT SPARTA[*]

Again, the freedom in regard to women is detrimental both in regard to the purpose of the constitution and undue regard to the happiness of the state . . . the inevitable result is that in a state thus constituted wealth is held in honour, especially if it is the case that the people are under the sway of their women, as most of the military and warlike races are, except the Celts and such other races as have openly held in honour attachments between males. . . . Hence this characteristic existed among the Spartans, and in the time of their empire many things were controlled by the women; yet what difference does it make whether the women rule or the rulers are ruled by the women? The result is the same. . . .

But, as was also said before, errors as regards "the status of women" seem not only to cause a certain unseemliness in the actual conduct of the state but to contribute in some degree to undue love of money. For next to the things just spoken of one might censure the Spartan institutions with respect to the unequal distribution of wealth. It has come about that some of the Spartans own too much property and some extremely little. And also nearly two-fifths of the whole area of the country is owned by women, because of the number of women who inherit estates and the practice of giving large dowries; yet it would have been better if dowries had been prohibited by law or limited to a small or moderate amount. . . .

LESBOS

Sappho

Over the centuries this enigmatic female poet has captured the imagination of her readers, especially among scholars. A standard introduction to Sappho includes mention that she was born into a wealthy family who traveled widely because her father was culpable in political machinations. Although we now know that the High Priestess Enheduanna in the eighteenth century B.C.E. was the first female poet, Sappho is customarily referred to as the first female poet. She was indeed a poet and was also head of an academy for young women on the island of Lesbos. The poems and fragments of her poems

[*]Aristotle, excerpts from the *Politics*, LCL, 1932, II vi 4–6.

that remain have provided numerous allusions to and hints about the curriculum of the academy that included dance, music, and poetry.

SELECTIONS FROM SAPPHO'S POEMS*

8

I took my lyre and said—

Come now, my heavenly tortoise shell:
become a speaking instrument

9

Although they are
Only breath, words which I command
    are immortal

40

Yes, Atthis you may be sure
Even in Sardis Anactoria will think often
    of us
of the life we shared here, when you
    seemed
the Goddess incarnate to her
and your singing pleased her best

Now among Lydian women she in her
    turn stands first
as the red fingered moon rising
at sunset takes precedence over stars
    around her;

her light spreads equally on the salt sea
    and fields thick with bloom
Delicious dew pours down to freshen
    roses,
delicate thyme and blossoming sweet
    clover; she wanders aimlessly, think-
    ing of
gentle Atthis her heart hanging heavy
    with longing in her little breast
She shouts aloud, Come! we know if
    thousand-eared night repeats that cry
    across the
sea shining between us

64

Tonight I've watched
The moon and then the Pleiades go
    down

The night is now half-gone; youth goes;
    I am
in bed alone.

*Sappho, Poems, translated by Mary Barnard. Berkeley, Los Angeles, and London: University of California Press, 1958, 8, 9, 40, 64.

TELOS

Selections from Erinna's Poems

We know little about Erinna except that which we find in her poetry. Like Sappho, she resided on an island in the Mediterranean and wrote, among other things, about her close friendship with women. These fragments, from the poet Erinna's corpus (fourth century B.C.E.) capture poignant memories of sentiments for her now deceased friend from childhood.

TWO EPIGRAMS FOR BAUCIS[*]

A.

I am the tomb of Baucis the bride.
This stone has heard much lamentation.
As you pass by, tell this to Death be-
    neath the ground:
'You are jealous Death As you look, the
    fine inscription on the tomb
tells you of Baucis' savage fate:
how her husbands father lighted her fu-
    neral pyre
with the torches they carried while they
    sang to Hymenaeus, the marriage
    God.
And you Hymenaeus transformed the wed-
    ding dances into cries of lamentation

B.

Column and my sirens, and mourning
    urn, you hold my death,
These few ashes.
Tell all who pass by my tomb to greet
    me,
Be they from, this city or another coun-
    try: The tomb holds a bride,
my father called me Baucis, I came from
    Tenos,
so they will know.
And, tell them my friend Erinna in-
    scribed this epigram on my tomb.

CROTONA (ITALY)

Early Female Pythagoreans

Pythagoreanism represented an active and popular school of philosophy from the end of the sixth century B.C.E. through the second and third centuries C.E. Female followers of Pythagoras among the "Early" school (sixth through fifth B.C.E) included Pythagoras' wife Theano and their daughters Arignote, Myia, and Damo. Themistoclea, who was a Pythia (High Priestess) at Delphi would also be counted among the Early Pythagoreans who disseminated his teachings in Italy and in Greece. (Waithe, 1987, 11–18.)

Central to philosophical thought among Early Pythagoreans was the concept of *harmonia,* this principle obtained in the macrocosm and the microcosm. Topics discussed in the selections that follow range from the principles of *harmonia* and *sophrosyne* (balance) as they are cultivated in theory, to application of these principles in the rearing of children.

*Erinna, Two Epigrams, WLGR, 1998,5

Theano of Crotona, Excerpts

Theano, was from an aristocratic family in Crotona (Italy). She was bright, inquisitive, and, not unlike other female philosophers, she left a life of elegance and luxury to adopt the simple lifestyle of the community of "seekers" who lived and studied with Pythagoras.

Theano's essays confirm the Pythagorean interests in "divine justice," the afterlife, and the transmigration of souls.

On the Immortality of the Soul[*]

> "If the soul is not immortal, then life is truly a feast for evil-doers who die after having lived their lives so iniquitously."

According to Theano, if the soul is not immortal, then people who create disorder in the universe and do so without consequence would be violating principles of justice. Theano contends that the very principle of justice and moral law forbids this. The following saying by Theano reveals Pythagorean attitudes toward women.

Advice to Women[*]

> A wife's sexual activity is to be restricted to pleasing her husband—she is not to have other lovers. In the context of marriage, chastity and virtue are not identified with abstinence. When Theano was asked how many days following sexual intercourse are required for a woman to once again be considered "pure," her reply was that "if the activity was with the woman's own husband, she remains pure, but if it was with someone else, she can never again become pure." When asked what duties are incumbent upon a married woman, her response is "to please her husband.". . .
> "Better to be on a runaway horse than to be a woman who does not reflect."

Myia, Daughter of Theano and Pythagoras

Myia's husband came from her mother's native Crotona and was a professional athlete. Myia's writings are concerned with *sosphrosyne* (balance) and with *harmonia* in every sphere. When she writes to a woman who has just had an infant her concern was that the baby be nurtured in a world in which utmost care is given to achieve and maintain moderation in every aspect of the child's environment. All of this care is to assist the child in "embodying" a moderation that has roots in Pythagorian philosophy.

Myia's Letter to Phyllis[*]

> Myia to Phyllis: Greetings. Because you have become a mother, I offer you this advice. Choose a nurse that is well-disposed and clean, one that is modest and not given to excessive sleep or drink. Such a woman will be best able to judge how to bring up your children in a manner appropriate to their freeborn station . . . A nurse

---

[*]Theano, *AHWP,* 1987, 13.

[*]Theano *AHWP,* 1987, 13–15.

[*]Myia, *AHWP,* 1987, Vol. I, 15–16.

has a great part in this which is first and prefatory to a child's whole life, i.e., nurturing with a view to raising the child well. . . . Let her not be irascible or loquacious or indiscriminate in the taking of food, but orderly and temperate and—if at all possible—not foreign but Greek. It is best to put the newborn to sleep when it has been suitably filled with milk, for then rest is sweet to the young, and such nourishment is easy to digest. If there is any other nourishment, one must give food that is as plain as possible. . . . Don't continually give the child baths. A practice of in-frequent baths, at a mild temperature, is better. In addition, the air should have a suitable balance of heat and cold, and the house should not be too drafty or too closed in. The water should be neither hard nor soft, and the bed-clothes should be not rough but falling agreeably on the skin. In all these things nature yearns for what is fitting, not what is extravagant. These are the things it seems useful to write to you for the present: my hopes based on nursing according to plan. With the help of god, we shall provide feasible and fitting re-minders concerning the child's upbringing again at a later time.

FEMALE HEROES

Each of the following stories about a female hero seems to tell itself. The women in these stories have a fiercely independent character, and agency to sustain themselves, their integrity, and their values despite great costs. These stories about brave women who defied patriarchal norms were entered into the literature with legendary status. We do not know to what extent they may have been transmitted among women and girls over the millenia. We know only that they have survived and have been translated and transmitted in the present and can be appropriated as exemplars for people who aspire to greatness.

TELESILLA[*]

No action taken by women for the common good is more famous than the conflict against Cleomenes by the Argive women, which they fought at the instigation of the poetess Telesilla. They say that she was the daughter of a distinguished family but, because she was sickly in body, inquired about her health at Delphi; the oracle said to cultivate the Muses. In obedience to the god she applied herself to song and harmony and was quickly cured of her suffering and admired by the women for her poetry.

But when Cleomenes king of Sparta had killed many Argives (but not, as some have imagined, 7,777) and marched against the city, an impulsive courage, divinely inspired, impelled the younger women to defend their country against the enemy. With Telesilla as general, they took up arms and made their defence by manning the walls around the city, and the enemy was amazed. They drove Cleomenes off after inflicting many losses. They also repulsed the other Spartan king, Demaratus, who (according to Socrates) managed to get inside and seize the Pamphylacium. After the city was saved, they buried the women who had fallen in battle by the Argive road, and as a memorial to the, achievements of the women who were spared they dedicated a temple to Ares Enyalius. Up to the present day they celebrate the Festival of

[*]Plutarch, *Moralia* III, LCL, 1931, 245.

Impudence (Hybristika) on the anniversary [of the battle], putting the women into men's tunics and cloaks and the men in women's dresses and head coverings.

The following selection is a local legend from Halicarnassus, a city in Asia Minor and Herodotus' home. Halicarnassus was an ally of Persia in the second war with Greece, at the battle of Salamis in 480.

ARTEMISIA[*]

I cannot offer a precise account of how anyone else fought, either on the Greek or the Persian side, but as far as Artemisia is concerned, this is what happened, and as a result of it she rose in King Xerxes' estimation.

The king's forces had been thrown into great confusion, and at this point Artemisia's ship was being chased by an Athenian ship. She wasn't able to get away (three friendly ships were in her way, and her own ship happened to be closest to the enemy). So she decided to act as follows, and the plan worked out well for her.

As she was being pursued by the Athenian ship, she attacked at full speed a friendly ship, manned by Calyndians and the king of Calynda himself, Damasithymus. Whether she had been involved in a dispute with him while they were at the Hellespont, I can't say; nor whether her action was premeditated or whether the Calyndian ship had the bad luck to get in her way. In any case, she attacked it and sank it, and used her good luck to get herself a double advantage. When the captain of the Athenian ship saw that she was attacking a Persian ship, he thought that Artemisia's ship either was Greek or had defected from the Persians and was fighting on the Athenian side, so he turned away and took off after other ships.

That was the first benefit, to be able to get away and not be killed. The second was that by doing damage she rose higher as a result in Xerxes' estimation. The story goes that when the king was watching the battle and saw her ship making its attack, one of the bystanders said: "Master, do you see how well Artemisia is fighting and that she has sunk an enemy ship?" The king asked if this were truly Artemisia's achievement, and they confirmed that it was, because they recognised her ship's insignia; they believed that the ship she had destroyed was the enemy's. In addition to everything else, she had the good luck that there were no survivors from the Calyndian ship to accuse her. Xerxes is said to have remarked on what he had been told: "My men have turned into women, and my women into men."

SUGGESTED READINGS

Marinatos, N. "The Minoan Harem: The Role of Eminent Women and the Knossos Frescoes." *Dialogues d'Histoire Ancienne [Hommage a Ettore Lepore]* 15.2 (1989): 33–50.
———"Formalism and Gender Roles. A Comparison of Minoan and Egyptian Art." In *Politeia. Society and State in the Aegean Bronze Age. Proceedings of the 5th International Aegean Conference / 5e Rencontre Egeenne Internationale, University of Heidelberg, Archaeologisches Institut,* edited by Robert

[*]Herodotus. "Artemisia, the Sea Captain." In *Histories 8.87–8.* No. 164, *Women's Life in Greece and Rome.* Mary R. Lefkowitz and Maureen B. Fant, editors. Baltimore: Johns Hopkins University Press. 130.

Laffineur and Wolf-Dietrich Niemeier, 577–85. Aegaem 12, vol. II. University of Texas at Austin, Program in Aegean Scripts and Prehistory, 10–13 April 1994.

Rehak, R. "New Observations on the Mycenaean 'Warrior Goddess.'" In *Archaologischer Anzeiger,* 535–45, 1984.

Vermeule, Emily. *Greece in the Bronze Age.* Chicago; London: University of Chicago Press, 1972.

Sources Cites

"Regulations of Lycurgus Concerning Spartan Women," translated by B. Perrin. In *Plutarch's Lives.* Loeb Classical Library, Cambridge, MA and London: Harvard University Press, 1914. 1.XV–XVI.

Xenophon. "The Education of Spartan Mothers." In *Constitution of the Lacedaemonians.* Translated by C. L. Brownson, Loeb Classical Library, Cambridge, MA and London: Harvard University Press, 1918. 1.2–9.

Pausanias. "On the Education of Spartan Women," translated by Segal. In *Partheneion 2, Frag. 3., Women in the Classical World.,* edited by E. Fantham, et al, New York and Oxford: Oxford University Press, 1994. 59.

Plutarch. "Plutarch on the Pride and Assurance of Spartan Women," In *Aforalia,* translated by F.C. Babbitt. Loeb Classical Library, Cambridge, MA and London: Harvard University Press, 1931. 240–42.

"Aristotle on Women at Sparta," translated by H. Rackham. In *Politics II.* Loeb Classical Library, Cambridge, MA and London: Harvard University Press, 1932. vi. 4–6

Sappho. Poems 8, 9, 40, 64. translated by Mary Barnard. Berkeley, Los Angeles, and London: University of California Press, 1958.

"Two Epigrams for Baucis." In *Palantine Anthology VII.712, 710.* No. 11, *Women's Life in Greece and Rome,* edited by Mary R. Lefkowitz and Maureen B. Fant, Baltimore: Johns Hopkins University Press, 1992.

Waithe, Mary Ellen. "Early Pythagoreans: Themistoclea, Theano, Arignote, Myia, and Damo." In *Ancient Women Philosophers 600 B.C.-500 A.D.,* edited by Mary Ellen Waithe, *A History of Women Philosophers,* vol. 1. Dordrecht, The Netherlands: Kluwer Academic Publishers, 1987. 11–18.

Theano. "On Piety" translated by Vicki Lynn Harper. In *Ancient Women Philosophers 600 B.C.-500 A.D.,* edited by Mary Ellen Waithe, *A History of Women Philosophers,* Vol. 1, Dordrecht, The Netherlands: Kluwer Academic Publishers, 1987. 12–13.

"Myia's Letter to Phyllis." In *Ancient Women Philosophers 600 B.C.-500 A.D.,* edited by Mary Ellen Waithe. A History of Women Philosophers, vol. I. Dordrecht, The Netherlands: Kluwer Academic Publishers, 1987.

Plutarch. "Telesilla." In *Moralia.* translated by, Frank C. Babbit, Loeb Classical Library Cambridge, MA and London: Harvard University Press, LCL., 1931. 240–42, 245.

Herodotus. "Artemisia, the Sea Captain." In *Histories 8.87–8.* No. 164, *Women's Life in Greece and Rome.* edited by Mary R. Lefkowitz and Maureen B. Fant, Baltimore: Johns Hopkins University Press. 130

Chapter 7

Athens

Among the several cultures discussed from pre-history to the present, texts from the biblical traditions from ca. 1000 B.C.E. and Classical Athenian society from ca. 490 B.C.E., have been most widely appropriated to legitimate and justify the subjugation of women in Western culture. In this chapter therefore, we explore several aspects of culture that shaped Athenian attitudes and customs concerning women.

SOCIAL ORGANIZATION

As we enter the world of Classical Greece it is important to be attentive to social and cultural patterns that were advanced to justify the subjugation of women. Because the process of legitimating women's subjugation took place over time, selections in this chapter are taken both from the Archaic and the Classical periods. It is significant that religion ceased to be a principal ordering factor in society at this time. Political reforms that paved the way for Athenian democracy instituted in the fifth century were initiated in the Archaic period by Draco (621 B.C.E.), Solon (640–558 B.C.E.), Pisistratus (605–527 B.C.E.), and Cleisthenes (d.508 B.C.E.). Cleisthenes declared Demes (neighborhoods) to define the ten tribes of Athens. Each tribe was allotted fifty seats on the Council of 500. Present scholarship does not attest to the presence of female representation from the Demes, although in the Archaic period this may have been a more feasible possibility than it would have been at a later time. The council elected 10 generals each year to run the city; at the head of the generals one was elected Archon (head or "commander-in-chief").

Ironically, these (idealistically) more inclusive forms of social organization in the move away from monarchy, increasingly diminished possibilities for women's autonomy and conferred power upon male citizens who were land and property owners. Men of privilege were responsible for establishing and defining social institutions, public policy, and law.

In a remarkable response to major military victories, jubilation following the defeat of the Persians at Marathon in 490 B.C.E. is marked by historians as the genesis of a flourishing of the arts and humanities at Athens. Under the archonship (rule) of Pericles a cultural explosion erupted among males in Athenian society that has been advanced as rivaling any subsequent outburst of excellence in the West. Architecture, sculpture, theater, poetry, science, and philosophy achieved new heights and set standards of distinction that persist. Throughout this "golden age," while citizen males relished their monumental accomplishments, female citizens of Athens were relegated to the private/domestic sphere. (See Chart 7.1)

The playwright Aeschylus (525–456 B.C.E.) experienced the glories of victory when the Greeks defeated the Persians in 480 B.C.E., and the exuberance that characterized the subsequent establishment of a "new world order" in Athenian society. His was a time of great intellectual, scientific, and artistic ferment. His was also a time when old political traditions were undergoing radical change. There were revolutions and transitions in religion, law, government, and social structures. It is these transitions that are Aeschylus's concern as a playwright in his trilogy, *The Orestia*. In the final play, *Eumenides* (458 B.C.E.) he reveals the internal processes within society that these transitions required. The play posits the old social order in conflict with the new, brings that conflict to a climax, and suggests a resolution that permits an honorable incorporation of the old justice as a working principle into the new justice of social law.

The "Eumenides" is essentially a conflict between the female, *chthonic* deities from the underworld who are called the *Erinyes* or Furies, and the God Apollo, that is, the deity of one social order versus the deities of the other. This conflict will be resolved, in Aeschylus' play, among human beings at Athens. The *Erinyes* represent the ancient world order with which we are, by now, becoming familiar. They appeal to a gynocentric and matrifocal spirit in which social relationships are determined by blood relationships. In this ancient social order the rights of the mother are honored above those of others. When a criminal's hands are stained with the blood of a kin person, the *Erinyes* are bound by ancient law to hunt the criminal down. Apollo, on the other hand, represents a younger order in society. This order is patriarchal; it honors the marriage relationship and considers the father as superior. The younger order maintains that there may be circumstances where homicide is justified; the offender could receive absolution after certain rituals were performed,

---

Chart 7–1 Social Stratification of Women in Athenian Democracy

1. Wives, mothers, daughters, and sisters of wealthy, land owning citizen males
   (Citizen males from this class comprise the generals from whom the Archon is selected.)
2. Priestesses
3. Merchants, artisans, or wives, mothers, daughters, and sisters of merchants and artisans
   (Citizen males from this class could sit on the Council of 500.)
4. Hetaira, "foreign" women were prohibited from marriage to citizen males. Some of the women who came to Athens from other parts of Greece and the Islands were educated, skilled in the musical arts, dance, and the arts of conversation. Because male citizens of Athens in the fifth century were restricted by law from marrying women who were not from the family of an Athenian citizen, many women who came to Athens from elsewhere elected to become *hetairae*. This term can be translated simply "companion." To distinguish hetaira from their less fortunate sisters who would, without reservation be defined as prostitutes, a more common understanding of the term in the period under discussion is concubine or mistress.
5. Female Serfs
6. Female Slaves

EUMENIDES*

The Eumenides *commences at Delphi, The* Pythia *(who despite very ancient origins is now the High Priestess of Apollo) is terrified by the sight of a blood-stained, sword bearing Orestes who is surrounded by sleeping* Erinyes *and by the ghost of his mother Clytemnestra. Clytemnestra insists that the* Erinyes *continue in their duty to punish Orestes for his crime of matricide. Apollo appears and states that Orestes has been absolved from all guilt, that he has been purified at Apollo's own altar and that he should suffer no further punishment. At this point the conflict between Clytemnestra and Orestes which dominated the second play of the trilogy and the beginning of the third, becomes, in effect, a conflict between the* Erinyes *and Apollo, thus shifting the focus for resolution of the conflict for human beings from the human sphere to the sphere of the deities.*

The scene changes from Delphi to Athens. Orestes has completed the rituals required for absolution yet he continues to be hunted by the Erinyes. *Apollo directs Orestes to seek sanctuary at the temple of Athena where must beseech her to decide his fate;* **Apollo [to Orestes]** *You must fly before them [the Furies (Erinyes)] . . . until you find sanctuary in Athena's citadel, And there, embracing her primeval image, you shall stand trial, and after healing words from me, who commanded you to kill your mother, you shall be free and win your salvation.*

The Erinyes *pursued him there. Athena requests both Orestes and the* Erinyes *to present their defenses. Athena recognizes the gravity of the situation and decides to establish a court of judges composed of noble Athenian males that will decide such cases in the future. They shall swear to make no judgement that is not just and to make clear in this action where the truth resides. As the court convenes Apollo appears and testifies for Orestes and states that he bears responsibility for Orestes' matricide. The trial begins and the* Erinyes *question Orestes. He responds by stating clearly that he did indeed slay his mother, but he did so, at the order of Apollo, that he has no fear, and that he has no doubt but that his father will help him from the grave.*

As the Erinyes *persist with more intense questioning it becomes clear that the most significant issue is to which parent Orestes owes prior duty, (just as the* Erinyes *defend the rights of the mother, so Apollo makes his position clear by championing the father).*

Erinyes: Now the world shall see the fall of old commandments made long ago, if the accursed matricide should win his case. Many a bitter blow awaits parents from their own children in times to come . . . Crimes shall spread from house to house like a plague, and whole cities shall be desolate . . . Choose a life despot free, yet restrained by rule of law . . . So, we say men must bow down before the shrine of right. Those who defy it shall fall, for the ancient commandments stand, to respect parents and honor the stranger. Only the righteous shall prosper.

Apollo: The mother is not a parent, only the nurse of the seed which the true parent, the father, commits to her as a stranger to keep it with God's help, safe from harm. And I have proof of this. There can be a father without a mother. We have a witness here, This daughter of Olympian Zeus, who sprang, armed from her father's head, a goddess whom no goddess could have brought to birth. Therefore out of good will

---

*Aeschylus, *Eumenides,* Translated by G. Thompson, The Laurel Classical Drama Series, New York: Dell, 1965. 5 brief excerpts, lines:102, 113, 117, 118, 119.

to your country and your people I sent this suppliant to seek refuge with you, that you, Athena, may find in him and his a faithful ally in times to come.

When the evidence has been presented Athena addresses the judges: She warns them not to ignore the value of the *Erinyes* function in society (according to this interpretation they function to inspire fear), she formally establishes the tribunal, and she expounds the nobility of their juridical task for the future of Athenian society,

Athena: Citizens of Athens, hear my declaration. This first trial in the history of man, this great tribunal shall remain in power meeting in session on this hill, where long ago the Amazons encamped . . . I warn you not to banish from your lives all terror but to seek the mean between autocracy and anarchy; and in this way you shall possess in ages yet unborn an impregnable fortress of liberty. Such as no people has throughout the world. With these words I establish this tribunal . . . let the judges now rise and cast their votes.

[At the most crucial moment of the drama Athena declares that if the votes of the Judges are even, she will cast her vote for Orestes.]

Athena: . . . the final judgment rests with me, and I announce that my vote shall be given to Orestes. No mother gave me birth, and in all things, save marriage, I commend with all my heart, the masculine, my father's child indeed. Therefore I cannot hold in higher esteem a woman killed because she killed her husband. If the votes are equal, Orestes wins . . .

The votes were even and thus Orestes was acquitted.

When Athena recognized that the *Erinyes* did not accept this verdict she was determined to persuade them to change their minds. This attempt was successful (as Aeschylus determined it would be) and the *Erinyes* (Furies) became "The Eumenides" (Gracious Goddesses) who would function as patrons of the court. They are incorporated into the new social order. The play concludes with a hymn of praise to the new deities as they process to the underworld. Thus a new order is established by Athena in which the conflicts of the old order are reconciled through the "fusion of opposites in the mean" which we recognize as the democratic process.

WIVES, DAUGHTERS, AND MOTHERS OF CITIZENS

Numerous implications of relegating citizens' women to the private sphere continue in Western civilization to the present day. The most detrimental implication is that the home is considered to be the single appropriate location within which women are to express their aspirations, needs, desires, and creativity. Athenian citizens' wives and daughters and their servants/slaves were confined to dark, isolated, often unsanitary separate quarters designated as the areas in which they would live their entire lives. Citizens' wives and daughters were married on average at age 14, to men who were at least 30. The average life span for men during the classical period was ca. 48 years and the average age for women ca.36 years.

Whereas young male citizens lived at the home of their parents until they were educated young adults, daughters of citizens at Athens were, by age 15, often mistresses of their own homes and mothers of young children. A woman's husband might indeed entertain in their home, but a dutiful wife would be excluded from the festivities, so that she could fulfill her duties as homemaker and mother. Education for Athenian girls (from childhood until they married) was confined to developing skills in weaving and other domestic arts. There is evidence to suggest that some citizens' women received additional education, and one text tells us that certain citizen males took their wives to study with the female philosopher Aspasia. Aspasia, who came from a highly regarded family on the island of Miletus, became a *hetaira* at Athens and was the beloved companion of Pericles until his death.

It was in the women's quarters that mothers, sisters, and nurses transmitted, via oral tradition, small children's initial exposure to the myths, customs, protocol, values, and traditions that constituted Greek culture. It is in this traditioning process that women would have had opportunities to convey stories about legendary and historical female heroes.

Considerable literature from Classical Athens is misogynistic and displays a contempt for women. The first set of selections in this section are representative of numerous misogynistic poems, essays, fables, and plays written by male citizens about the women who were their wives, mothers, sisters, and daughters. In contrast, the second section includes a text that is representative of strong, autonomous female protagonists in dramas and comedies written by male citizen playwrights.

The following selection represents the place of women in Aristotle's rationale for a systemic ordering of society. Note that it is common for theologians in the Middle Ages of the common era to refer to Aristotle's philosophy to legitimate the sublimation of women.

ARISTOTLE, EXCERPTS FROM *POLITICS*[*]

> The three divisions of household management include: the relation of master to slave; the paternal relation and the conjugal . . . for it is a part of the household science to rule over wife and children (over both as over freemen, yet not with the same mode of governments but over the wife to exercise republican government and over the children monarchical); for the male is by nature better fitted to command than the female (except in some cases where their union has been formed contrary to nature) and the older and fully developed person than the younger and immature.
>
> It is true that in most cases of republican government the ruler and the ruled interchange in turn (for they tend to be on an equal level in their nature and to have no difference at all), although nevertheless during the period when one is ruler and the other ruled, they seek to have a distinction by means of insignia and titles and honours, . . . but the male stands in this relationship to the female continuously. The rule of the father over the children on the other hand is that of a king; for the male parent is the ruler in virtue both of affection and of seniority, which is characteristic of royal government . . . .
>
> . . . hence there are by nature three classes of rulers and ruled. For the free rules the slave, the male the female and the man the child in a different way . . . .

Women Represented in Greek Tragedy and Comedy

There remains considerable debate among classicists about representations of powerful women in Greek tragedy. One scholarly position holds that representations of women reflect the lives of at least some women in the cultural ambient of the author. The student of drama will soon become familiar with Clytemnestra, Helen, Antigone, the Trojan Women, and others. The selections included here relate specifically to women whose dignity as a person has been so deeply violated that they move beyond acceptable civilized behavior to avenge their own honor.

*Aristotle, *Politics,* LCL, 1932, XXI 1.V. 1–3.

In addition to the famous descriptions of women's lives in surviving plays, such as Euripides' *Medea* or *Andromache*, fragments of lost plays testify to male poets' understanding of the social forces that compelled women to violence. Medea, who passionately loved her husband Jason, is so distraught and overwhelmed by his unfaithfulness, that she slays their two children as a recompense for his cruelty.

EURIPEDES, *MEDEA*, MEDEA'S ASSESSMENT OF HUSBANDS[*]

Of all creatures who live and have intelligence, we women are the most miserable. First of all, we must buy a husband by vast expenditure of wealth, in order to obtain a master for our body. This is a greater misery than the dowry, because everything depends on whether we get a bad husband or a good one. Being divorced harms a woman's reputation, and she cannot refuse her husband. She must be a prophet when she arrives among new habits and customs, which she did not learn at home, to deal with the sort of husband she has acquired. And if when we manage all this well our husbands live with us not bearing the yoke (of marriage) unwillingly, our lives are enviable. But if not, it's best to die: a man, when he becomes unhappy with the people inside his home, goes out and puts an end to the ache in his heart . . . but we must look to that one man alone. People say that we women lead a life without danger inside our homes, while men fight in war; but they are wrong. I would rather serve three times as in battle than give birth once.

LEGAL STATUS OF WOMEN

Types of Laws at Athens concerning women illustrate the extent to which women are represented as the property of men. Laws selected for this chapter address issues related to marriage, divorce, inheritance, acquisition, and distribution of property as well as proscriptions concerning women's sexuality and their access to the public sphere.

ISAEUS, ON PROPERTY LAWS FOR WOMEN AND CHILDREN[**]

A child is not permitted to make a will. For the law expressly forbids children and women from being able to make a contract [about anything worth] more than a bushel of barley.

INHERITANCE LAWS FOR ATHENIAN WOMEN[†]

The dowry system ensured that daughters would inherit some portion of their father's estate, but if there were no sons, laws of succession ensured that so far as possible the money would stay in the father's family through marriage.

---

[*]Euripedes "Medea's Complaint," *WLGR,* 1992, No. 28 10

[**]Isaeus, Property Laws, *WLGR* 1992, No. 83. 64.

[†]*WLGR,* 1992 no.80 61. Introduction.

PROVISIONS FOR FEMALE CHILDREN[*]

> If a man dies intestate and leaves female children, the estate goes with them; if not, his male heirs inherit his property, as follows: if he has brothers from the same father, and if there are legitimate sons of the brothers, they are to inherit the father's share. But if there are no brothers or sons of brothers, their descendants shall inherit as follows. The males shall have precedence and the descendants of the males, if they have any, even though their relationship be more remote. But if there are on the father's side no relations closer than the children of cousins, the male relatives on the mother's side shall inherit according to the same principles. If there are no relatives on either side within those limits, then the next of kin of the father shall inherit. But no illegitimate son or daughter is to have the right of inheritance either to religious or civic privileges, since the time of Euclides' Archonship (403 BC).

RELIGION

In Athenian culture of the classical period, the function of religion as an ordering process in society diminished among male citizenry as politics, government, and military supremacy assumed increasing importance. This transformation, however, did not obtain for women in the same way. Rather, for women in Athens, most of whom were confined within grim domestic quarters beginning in their adolescence, activities connected with religious rituals and the calendar of sacred festivals provided a central focus for social interaction outside the home.

Women were responsible for keeping religious shrines within their homes; they participated in ritual activities related to rites of passage including birth, young girlhood, adolescence, marriage, and death as a part of maintaining the heritage of their particular *oikosl* family. Priestesses continued to have prestige and privilege within the framework of patriarchal culture. Religious themes of Life, Death, and Regeneration persisted in the myths and rituals of Orphic, Dionysian, and Elusynian Mystery traditions, as did festivals associated with Hera, Artemis, and Athena. Women served as priestesses at Temples to major deities of the Greek Pantheon; women and girls also served as "temporary" priestesses for a particular festival, sometimes for an entire year. Permanent female religious functionaries included the famous *Pythia,* High Priestess/Prophetess/oracle at Delphi, and priestesses at Eleusis, who officiated at the Eleusyinian Mysteries and all rites associated with Demeter and Persephone. Worship and rituals associated with the god Dionysius were especially meaningful for women. Euripedes' *The Bacchae* attests to women's participation in Dionysian rituals.

Whether or not they were literate and educated in the same manner as male priests, female religious functionaries would have been educated in the myths, customs, history, lore, and liturgical/ritual practices of the deities they served. Women's participation in festivals and burials and in transmitting myth and tradition constituted a major element of their contribution to culture. Selections in this section are representative of an extensive body of texts attesting to women's participation in religious traditions within Greek culture.

The Holy

The sacred story of Demeter and Persephone is an ancient version of a dying and rising deity that incorporates life, death, and rebirth themes related to fertility and immortality. The earliest written version of such a myth is found in ancient Sumer as was noted in Chapter 2. The story of the Goddess

*Diosthenes "Provisions for Female Children" *WLGR* 1992, no. 80 61–62

Chart 7–2   Chart of Olympian Deities

Zeus, the son of Cronus and Rhea, is the *Chief God* of the Greek Pantheon
Zeus' Brothers and Sisters: Hestia, Goddess of the Hearth; *Hades,* God of the Underworld; *Poseidon,* God of the
   Sea; and *Hera,* originally a Mother Goddess, here is the model of Wife and Mother
Zeus and his sister *Hera* produce:
   Eleithyia: Goddess of Childbirth
   Hebe: Goddess; Cupbearer for the Deities
   Ares: God of War
   Hephaestus: God of Creative Fire and a divine smith
Zeus and *Metis* produce *Athena:* Goddess of Wisdom, War, Patroness of Arts and Crafts, Virgin Goddess
Zeus and *Leto* produce:
   Apollo: God of the Hunt, and later of Wisdom
   Artemis: Goddess of the Hunt, Virgin Goddess
Zeus and *Semele* produce *Dionysus:* God of Wine, Revelry, and Bacchic Rites
Zeus and *Maia* produce *Hermes:* The Messenger God
Zeus and *Dione* produce *Aphrodite:* Goddess of Love, Beauty, and Marriage

The study of Greek mythology involves journeys into varieties of literary genres that span several centuries and extend far beyond the borders of Hellas. Numerous myths exist in Greek literature associated with Zeus and the mortals and deities mentioned here. There are also numerous myths involving their connections and intrigues with deities and mortals not mentioned here.

Demeter, however, differs significantly because the deity who dies and rises is not a male consort or son of a Goddess, but Demeter's daughter, Persephone. The prevalence of life, death, and regeneration themes in the Neolithic period in Old Europe and Anatolia might suggest to scholars that, just as the *Pythia* has ancient roots as a prophet at Delphi, the Demeter/Persephone mythos is the legacy of a very early version of the tale that reflects matrilineal lines of descent and matrifocal culture.

The Homeric Hymn to Demeter describes in detail how Hades, God of the Underworld, stole Persephone, how her mother searched for her and hid the seed within the earth until she got her daughter back again. This excerpt describes how Persephone returns, but only for part of the year, because she ate seeds in the underworld and must now forever return to spend four months of the year with her husband, Aidoneus.

HOMERIC HYMN TO DEMETER[*]

> So Aidoneus spoke, and wise Persephone was delighted, and swiftly rose up from the bed; but Aidoneus gave her to eat the sweet seed of a pomegranate, furtively, looking out for himself to keep her from spending all of her days here on earth with revered black-robed Demeter. And before them Aidoneus, ruler of many, got ready his immortal horse, in his golden chariot. Persephone got into the chariot, and beside her strong Hermes took the reins and whip in his hands and drove out of the palace. The two horses flew on eagerly; they easily completed the journey—neither the sea nor the water of rivers nor grassy valleys nor mountain peaks held back the horses' speed, but as they went they cut the steep air beneath them. Hermes stopped them and brought her where fair-crowned Demeter was waiting beside her fragrant temple [at Eleusis].

[*]Hesiod, *Homeric Hymn to Demeter,* LCL, 1914. 11. 45. 105

And when Demeter saw Persephone, she rushed like a maenad along the mountain shaded in forest; and Persephone opposite . . . leaped down . . . [Demeter asked . . .] "Child . . . ? You have not tasted food in the Underworld? Tell me! Because if you refused it, you could live with me and your father, Zeus of the black clouds, honoured by all the immortals But if you have tasted food, you must reside in the Underworld for a third part of the seasons and for two parts with me and the other immortals. When the earth blooms with all kinds of fragrant spring flowers, then from the murky darkness you will come up once again and be a great wonder to gods and to mortal men. And with what trick did the strong Receiver deceive you"?

Then beautiful Persephone addressed her in return: "Then, Mother, I will tell you everything truthfully. When Hermes came as a messenger from my father Zeus and the other gods of Heaven to say I was to come from the Underworld, so you could see me with your own eyes and end your anger and cruel rage against the immortals, then in my joy I got up from the bed and he furtively put into me the seed of a pomegranate, sweet food; he compelled me to taste it by force, against my will. And I will tell you how Aidoneous carried me off because of my father's clever plan, and went and took me beneath the depths of the earth; I will relate everything in detail, as you request" . . . .

So then with their hearts in agreement they cheered their souls and hearts by embracing each other, and their hearts had respite from their sorrows. They took and gave joyousness to one another. And Hecate with her bright headband came near them, and embraced many times the daughter of holy Demeter; since then she has been her guardian and attendant queen. And then far-seeing Zeus of the loud thunder sent them a messenger, fair-haired Rhea, to bring black-robed Demeter back to the family of the gods, and he promised to give her honours that she could choose for herself among the immortals. He agreed that her daughter should spend the third part of the circling year beneath the murky darkness, but two parts with her mother and the other immortals . . . .

Ritual

Women celebrated the annual festival of Demeter Thesmophoria (Lawgiver) to ensure the continued fertility of the earth. In this hymn the poet Callimachus tells how Demeter punished young Erysichthon when he cut down her sacred tree by giving him an insatiable appetite. The hymn concludes with a prescription for appropriate tribute to the goddess.

CALLIMACHUS, *THESMOPHORIA* HYMN 6[*]

Sing, virgins, and mothers join the chorus: "Demeter, all hail, nurse of many, giver of full measure." And as four white horses pull the basket, so will the great goddess, the wide-ruler, come to us bringing white spring, and white summer, and winter and the season of withering. She will protect us through another year. As we walk through

---

[*]Callimachus, *Thesmophoria,* translated by A, W, Mair, LCL, 1914. Hymn 6.

the city without sandals and with our hair unbound, so we shall have our feet and hands unharmed forever. And as the basket-bearers bring baskets full of gold, so may we taste boundless gold. The uninitiated women may process as far as the city hall; the initiated right to the goddess's temple—all who are younger than sixty. But women who are heavy, who stretch their hands to Eileithuia goddess of childbirth, or who are in pain—it's enough that they go as far as their legs can carry them. For these Deo (Demeter) will give all things full to the brim and let them come to her temple. Hail goddess, and keep this city safe in harmony and in prosperity. Bring all things from the fields in abundance. Nourish the cattle, bring us sheep, bring us grain, bring in the harvest, nourish peace also, so that he who sows may reap. Have mercy on me, thrice-prayed to, great queen among Goddesses.

Female Functionaries

The list of priestesses at Argos was the oldest chronological record available to fifth-century historians. In other cities, dates for records were reckoned by the (male) holders of public office. Here we have particulars for a chronology of several events in the professional career of Chrysis, a priestess dedicated to the Goddess Hera.

THUCYDIDES, CHRYSIS, PRIESTESS OF HERA[*]

In the fifteenth year of the 30 years' truce, when Chrysis had been priestess in Argos 48 years, Aenesias was Ephor in Sparta and Pythodorus had two months more as archon in Athens (431 B.C.E.). During the same summer, 431 B.C.E., the temple of Argos was destroyed by fire, when Chrysis the priestess placed a lighted torch near the garlands and fell asleep, so that she did not notice that everything had caught fire and had been burned. Then Chrysis fled immediately to Phlious in the middle of the night because she was afraid of the Argives. The Argives appointed another priestess according to their established custom, whose name was Phaeinis. Chrysis had been priestess for 8 years of the war and half of the ninth, when she went into exile.

This selection describes a delightful example of what might be "expected" of a proper young female.

THE RELIGIOUS DUTIES OF ARISTOCRATIC YOUNG GIRLS[**]

We are setting out, all you citizens, to say something useful for the city, as we well may, because it reared me in splendid affluence. From the moment I was seven I served as arrhephoros; then at ten I was a baker for Athena Archegetis; then I had my saffron robe (krokotos) and was a [little] bear [for Artemis] at the Brauronia; and then I was once basket-carrier (kanephoros), a lovely girl with a bunch of figs.

---

[*]Thucydides, *History,* LCL 1919, 2.2.1, 4., 133. 2–3.

[**]Aristophanes, *Lysistrata, WLGR,* 1992, No. 399, 282

WOMEN OUTSIDE THE ARISTOCRACY

Hetairae

Because it was imperative to citizen males that their prospective wives be virgins, and thus unschooled in the arts of lovemaking, males found sexual pleasure with male and female prostitutes, with other males (as described in historical accounts of male mentoring among citizen males), or with *hetairae*. *Hetairae* were "courtesans," women who were skilled in the arts of music, poetry and dance, and lovemaking. Many *hetairae* were "foreign" women from outside Athens among whom some were educated. Among educated citizen males at Athens many were trained in rhetoric and were vitally engaged in political discourse. *Hetairae,* who socialized with these men were also well informed about political matters. Although *hetairae* were dependent upon the favor of their patrons to support themselves, they enjoyed greater autonomy and opportunities for personal accomplishment than wives of Athenian citizens at either end of the economic ladder.

Aspasia of Miletus

Perhaps the most famous *hetaira,* Aspasia of Miletus, (died ca. 401 B.C.E.), is recognized as a rhetorician, as a member of Pericles' philosophic circle and as his mistress. Aspasia's composition titled the *Epitaphia* was the subject of Socrates' conversation in the *Menexenus.*

To question the existence of Socrates, who, as far as we know, wrote nothing, would be scandalous, yet despite a variety of ancient references to Aspasia as a learned woman there have, for centuries, been heated arguments about the authenticity of her writings. We include the excerpt from the *Menexenus* specifically because in it there are several references to her writings. The reader is also invited to read Waithe's discussion of arguments about the authenticity of Aspasia's writings (Waithe, 1987, 75–80). We look first at Plutarch's on *Pericles on Aspasia* and then at the *Menexenus.*

PLUTARCH ON ASPASIA[*]

> Now, since it is thought that he proceeded thus against the Samians to gratify Aspasia, this may be a fitting place to raise the query what great art or power this woman had, that she managed as she pleased the foremost men of the state, and afforded the philosophers occasion to discuss her in exalted terms and at great length. That she was a Milesian by birth, daughter of one Axiochus, is generally agreed; and they say that it was in emulation of Thargelia, an Ionian woman of ancient times, that she made her onslaughts upon the most influential men. This Thargelia came to be a great beauty and was endowed with grace of manners as well as clever wits. Inasmuch as she lived on terms of intimacy with numberless Greeks, and attached all her comforts to the king of Persia, she stealthily sowed the seeds of Persian sympathy in the cities of Greece by means of these lovers of hers, who were men of the greatest power and influence. And so Aspasia, as some say, was held in high favour by Pericles because of her rare political wisdom. Socrates sometimes came to see her with his disciples, and his intimate friends brought their wives to her to hear her discourse, although she presided over a business that was anything but honest or even reputable, since she kept a house of young courtesans. And Aeschines says that Lysicles the sheep-dealer, a man of low birth and nature, came to be the first man at Athens

*Plutarch, *Pericles* LCL, 1916, XXIV.

by living with Aspasia after the death of Pericles. And in the "Menexenus" of Plato, even though the first part of it be written in a sportive vein, there is, at any rate, thus much of fact, that the woman had the reputation of associating with many Athenians as a teacher of rhetoric. However, the affection which Pericles had for Aspasia seems to have been rather of an amatory sort. For his own wife was near of kin to him, and had been wedded first to Hipponicus, to whom she bore Callias, surnamed the Rich; she bore also, as the wife of Pericles, Xanthippus and Paralus. Afterwards, since their married life was not agreeable, he legally bestowed her upon another man, with her own consent, and himself took Aspasia, and loved her exceedingly. Twice a day, as they say, on going out and on coming in from the marketplace, he would salute her with a loving kiss. . . .

So renowned and celebrated did Aspasia become, they say, that even Cyrus, the one who went to war with the Great King for the sovereignty of the Persians, gave the name of Aspasia to that one of his concubines whom he loved best, who before was called Milto. She was a Phocaean by birth, daughter of one Hermotimus, and, after Cyrus had fallen in battle, was carried captive to the King, and acquired the greatest influence with him. These things coming to my recollection as I write, it were perhaps unnatural to reject and pass them by. . . .

MENEXENUS[*]

Menexenus: Do you think that you could speak yourself if there should be a necessity, and if the Council were to choose you?

Socrates: That I should be able to speak is no great wonder. Menexenus, considering that I have an excellent mistress in the art of rhetoric—she who has made so many good speakers, and one who was the best among all the Hellenes, Pericles, the son of Xanthippus.

Menexenus: And who is she? I suppose that you mean Aspasia.

Socrates: Yes, I do, and besides her I had Connus, the son of Metrobius, as a master, and he was my master in music, as she was in rhetoric. No wonder that a man who has received such an education should be a finished speaker.

Menexenus: And what would you be able to say if you had to speak?

Socrates: Of my own wit, most likely nothing, but yesterday I heard Aspasia composing a funeral oration about these very dead. For she had been told, as you were saying, that the Athenians were going to choose a speaker, and she repeated to me the sort of speech which he should deliver—partly improvising and partly from previous thought, putting together fragments of the funeral oration which Pericles spoke, but which, as I believe, she composed.

Menexenus: And can you remember what Aspasia said?

Socrates: I ought to be able, for she taught me, and she was ready to strike me because I was always forgetting.

*HAMILTON, Edith; PLATO ©1961 Princeton University Press, 1989 renewed, reprinted by permission of Princeton University Press.

Menexenus: Then why will you not rehearse what she said?

Socrates: Because I am afraid that my mistress may be angry with me if I publish her speech.

Menexenus: Nay, Socrates, let us have the speech, whether Aspasia's or anyone else's, no matter. I hope that you will oblige me.

Socrates: But I am afraid that you will laugh at me if I continue the games of youth in old age.

Menexenus: Far otherwise, Socrates. Let us by all means have the speech.

Socrates: Truly I have such a disposition to oblige you that if you bid me dance naked I should not like to refuse, since we are alone. Listen then. If I remember rightly, she began as follows, with the mention of the dead.

There is a tribute of deeds and of words. The departed have already had the first, when going forth on their destined journey they were attended on their way by the state and by their friends; the tribute of words remains to be given to them, as is meet and by law ordained. For noble words are a memorial and a crown of noble actions, which are given to the doers of them by the hearers. A word is needed which will duly praise the dead and gently admonish the living, exhorting the brethren and descendants of the departed to imitate their virtue, and consoling their fathers and mothers and the survivors, if any, who may chance to be alive of the previous generation. What sort of a word will this be, and how shall we rightly begin the praises of these brave men? In their life they rejoiced their own friends with their valor, and their death they gave in exchange for the salvation of the living. And I think that we should praise them in the order in which nature made them good, for they were good because they were sprung from good fathers. Wherefore let us first of all praise the goodness of their birth, secondly, their nurture and education, and then let us set forth how noble their actions were, and how worthy of the education which they had received. . . . soonest forget their misfortunes, and live in a better and nobler way, and be dearer to us.

This is all that we have to say to our families, and to the state we would say, Take care of our parents and of our sons—let her worthily cherish the old age of our parents, and bring up our sons in the right way. But we know that she will of her own accord take care of them, and does not need any exhortation of ours.

This, O ye children and parents of the dead, is the message which they bid us deliver to you, and which I do deliver with the utmost seriousness. And in their name I beseech you, the children, to imitate your fathers, and you, parents, to be of good cheer about yourselves, for we will nourish your age, and take care of you both publicly and privately in any place in which one of us may meet one of you who are the parents of the dead. And the care of you which the city shows, you know yourselves, for she has made provision by law concerning the parents and children of those who die in war; the highest authority is specially entrusted with the duty of watching over them above all other citizens, and they will see that the fathers and mothers have no wrong done to them. The city herself shares in the education of the children, desiring as far as it is possible that their orphanhood may not be felt by them. While they are children she is a parent to them, and when they have arrived at man's estate she sends them to their several duties, in full armor clad; and bringing freshly to their minds the ways of their fathers, she places in their hands the instruments of their fathers' virtues. For the sake of the omen, she would have them from the first begin to rule over their own houses arrayed in the strength and arms of their fathers. And as for the dead, she never ceases honoring them, celebrating, in common for all, rites which become the property of each, and in addition to this, holding gymnastic and equestrian contests, and musical festivals of every sort. She is to the dead in the place of a son and heir, and to their sons in the place of a father, and to their parents and elder kindred in the place of a guardian—ever and always caring for them. Considering this, you ought to bear your calamity the more gently, for thus you will be most endeared to the dead and to the living, and your sorrows will heal and be healed. And now do you and all, having lamented the dead in common according to the law, go your ways.

    You have heard, Menexenus, the oration of Aspasia the Milesian.

Socrates: Well, and do you not admire her, and are you not grateful for her speech?

Menexenus: Yes, Socrates, I am very grateful to her or to him who told you, and still more to you who have told me.

Socrates: Very good. But you must take care not to tell of me, and then at some future time I will repeat to you many other excellent political speeches of hers.

Menexenus: Fear not. Only let me hear them, and I will keep the secret.

Socrates: Then I will keep my promise.

PLATO'S FEMALE PUPILS[*]

Diogenes names seventeen of Plato's many male pupils, he also includes two women: Lasthenia of Mantinea and Axiothea of Phlius; she dressed like a man, according to Dicaearchus. Themistius uses the case of Axiothea as an illustration of the powerful attractions of Plato's philosophy: For Axiothea, when she had read some of Plato's Republic left her home in Arcadia and went to Athens. She attended Plato's lectures without anyone noticing that she was a woman. . .after Plato's death [Lasthenia?] also studied with Speusippus, according to Hippobotus, and then with Menedemus the Eretrian. Again Hieronymus of Rhodes writes about her in his treatise on Physics. Aristophanes the Peripatetic similarly tells the story in his treatise on Painlessness that the girl was pretty and full of unaffected charm.

WOMEN AT WORK

The excerpts included about working women's occupations in classical Athens are not a feature in the text traditions of the period. Some data are available in inscriptions, lists of workers, and can be inferred from vase paintings.

[*]Diogenes Laertius, *WLGR*, 1992, 167

Chart 7–3   Occupations of Freedwomen I

(A.221) Onesime, sesame seed-seller . . . (255) Lampris, wet-nurse
(259) Eupeithe, her child, wet-nurse . . .
(328) Lyde, woolworker . . . (468) Rhodia, woolworker . . .
(472) Cordype, her child, woolworker
(493) Thraitta, grocer . . . (497) Itame, woolworker . . . (505) Demetria, harpist . . .
(518) Olympias, woolworker . . . (B.91) . . . one, horsetender . . . (112) Atta, vendor (114) Malthace, wool-
    worker (with her three children) . . . 212 . . . rityra, aulos player, 214 . . . Echo . . . woolworker

WLGR, 1992, No. 329,221

Chart 7–4   Occupations of Freedwomen.II

(49.4-5) Elpis, 30 aulos-player . . . (50.34) Habrosyne, perfume vendor. Hesperia, 37 [1968 8 1368 8]
WLGR, 1992, No.330, 221.

Chart 7–5   Occupations of Freedwomen III

(11561.22-77) Midas sesame seed-seller and Soteris sesame seed-seller (from the same household) . . .
    (1570.73) Piloumene, honeyseller . . . (1576.15.) Melitta, frankincense seller . . . (1578.5.) shoe-seller . . .

WLGR, 1992, No.331,221

Occupations

Inscriptions from Athens contain specific information about women in retail trade. These inscriptions, and others like them, represent the written information available about women whose occupations demanded that they be in the public sphere. These women's names are included in this reader specifically to honor women who otherwise would not be acknowledged. We see as well that types of occupations open to females were quite limited. Men dominated lucrative trades (armaments, books, animals); women handled only relatively small sums. Prostitution may have been an exception, but we lack data about prices and fees paid to owners or employers.

SUGGESTED READINGS

Fairweather, Janet A. "Biographies of Ancient Writers." *Ancient Society* 5 (1974): 231–75.
Foley, Helen P. "The Conception of Women in Athenian Drama." In *Reflections of Women in Antiquity*, edited by Helen P. Foley. New York: (np), 1981.

Gould, John. "Law, Custom and Myth: Aspects of the Social Position of Women in Classical Athens." *Journal of Hellenistic Studies* 100: 38–59.

Peradotto, John and J.P. Sullivan Editors, *Women in the Ancient World: The Araethusa Papers.* Albany: State University of New York Press, 1984.

Snyder, Jane. "The Web of Song: Weaving Imagery in Homer and the Lyric Poets." *Classical Journal* 76 (1981): 193–96.

Zeitlin, Froma. "Playing the Other: Theater, Theatricality and the Feminine in Greek Drama." *Representations,* 11:63–94.

Sources Cited

Aeschylus. "Eumenides," translated by G. Thomson. In *Aeschylus,* Short excerpts. The Laurel Classical Drama Series. New York: Dell, 1965. lines: 102, 113, 117, 118, 119.

Aristotle. *Politics.* Translated by H. Rackham, Loeb Classical Library, London and Cambridge, MA: Harvard University Press, 1932. 1.v.1–3.

Euripedes. "Medea's Complaint," *Women's Life in Greece and Rome.* Mary R. Lefkowitz and Maureen B. Fant, editors, Baltimore: Johns Hopkins University Press, 1992. No. 28, 10.

Isaeus. "Property." 10.10. No. 83, translated by M.R. Lefkowitz, *Women's Life in Greece and Rome.* Mary R. Lefkowitz and Maureen B. Fant, editors. Baltimore: Johns Hopkins University Pres, 1992. 64.

Diosthenes. "Provisions for Female Children." In *Demosthenes, Or. 43, Against Macartatus 51, 54.* No. 80, *Women's Life in Greece and Rome.* Mary R. Lefkowitz and Maureen B. Fant,editors. Baltimore: Johns Hopkins University Pres, 1992. 61.

Hesiod. "Homeric Hymn to Demeter," translated by Hugh G. Evelyn-White. *The Homeric Hymns and the Homerica,* Loeb Classical Library, Cambridge, MA and London: Harvard University Press, William Heinmann Ltd., 1914.

Thucydides." Chrysis, Priestess of Hera." In *History* translated by C. F. Smith, Loeb Classical Library, Cambridge, MA and London: Harvard University Press, William Heinmann Ltd., 1919, 2.2 1, 4; 133.2–3.

Aristophanes. "The Religious Duties of Aristocratic Young Girls," translated by H. Lloyd-Jones. In *Lysistrata 638–47, Women's Life in Greece and Rome.* Mary R. Lefkowitz and Maureen B. Fant, editors. Baltimore: Johns Hopkins University Pres, 1992. No. 399–282.

"Aspasia of Miletus." In *Ancient Women Philosophers 600 B.C.-500 A.D.,* edited by Mary Ellen Waithe. *A History of Women Philosophers,* vol. 1. Dordrecht, The Netherlands: Kluwer Academic Publishers, 1987. 75–81.

Plutarch. "The Courtesan Aspasia, Mistress of Pericles." In *Life of Pericles 24.1–6, 32.1–2.* translated by B. Perrin, Loeb Classical Library, Cambridge, MA and London: Harvard University Press, William Heinmann Ltd., 1916 XXIV.

HAMILTON, Edith; PLATO ©1961 Princeton University Press, 1989 renewed, reprinted with permission of Princeton University Press.

Laertius, Diogenes. "Plato's Female Pupils." In *Themistius, Orations 295e; OxyrhynchusPapyrus 3656. Women's Life in Greece and Rome.* Mary R. Lefkowitz and Maureen B. Fant, editors. Baltimore: Johns Hopkins University Pres, 1992, No. 216, 167.

"Occupations of Freedwomen I." In *Lewis, Hesperia 28 [1959] 208–38. Women's Life in Greece and Rome,* Mary R. Lefkowitz and Maureen B. Fant, editors. Baltimore: Johns Hopkins University Pres, 1992, No. 329. 221.

"Occupations of Freedwomen II." In *Lewis, Hesperia 37 [1968] 368–80. Women's Life in Greece and Rome,* Mary R. Lefkowitz and Maureen B. Fant, editors. Baltimore: Johns Hopkins University Pres, 1992, No. 330 221.

"Occupations of Freedwomen III." In *IGII(2). 1561.22-7, 1570.73, 1576.15 Ff., 1578.5 Ff. Women's Life in Greece and Rome,* Mary R. Lefkowitz and Maureen B. Fant, editors. Baltimore: Johns Hopkins University Pres, 1992, No. 331, 221.

Chapter 8

Etruria and the Roman Republic

ETRURIA

The Etruscans were a distinct ethnic group who settled on the western coast of Italy whose origins remain a mystery. They were a non-Indo-European people who survived in the Mediterranean Basin. Despite the relatively limited amount of information available about the Etruscans, analysis of data from archaeological excavations of Etruscan sites, and from surviving inscriptions, has revealed evidence that attests to a prominence of women in Etruscan culture.

The brief selections presented here are included to familiarize readers with yet another culture in which, despite patriarchal social organization, women enjoyed an elevated status. Women's presence in the public sphere contrasts dramatically with the status of women at Athens in Greece, and women in the Roman Republic.

SOCIAL ORGANIZATION

The Etruscans shared a common language, religion, and culture and lived in a loosely structured collection of city-states from ca. 750–100 B.C.E. The differences among the cities were notable and in many ways speak to the independent spirit of their citizens. Each city apparently was recognized for excellence in its creation of particular products (products made of bronze and iron, sculpture, jewelry, textiles, etc.). They enjoyed a healthy competitive engagement in the economic markets. Cities did aspire to ascendancy yet the competitions among the cities did not, like those among the Greeks, result in a warfare that eventually decimated many of their fellow city-states. When the Etruscans emerged into history as a notable culture in about 750 B.C.E. they functioned as a monarchy; yet it is clear that this model of governance did not require the subjugation of women among the aristocracy.

The principal sources for information about the Etruscans are archaeological. There is ample evidence to suggest that women had prestige in society and that they had political power. Etruscan women acquired wealth and could own property in their own right. Like the Spanish custom, women's surnames were given to children as well as men's, and there is evidence for the education of women in the upper classes.

Figure 8–1   A drawing depicting an early wrestling contest. *Don Bolognese*

The Romans who wrote about Etruscan women were appalled by female assertiveness and by Etruscan women's comfort level within the public sphere (see Figure 8.1). The status of women throughout Etruria contrasts markedly with the status of women in Athens where misogyny prevailed and in the Roman Republic where, as we shall see, the virtuous noble matron exemplified republican ideals.

WOMEN IN THE ARISTOCRACY

The Textual Evidence

We know from the Romans who wrote about the Etruscans that from ca. 700 B.C.E. the Etruscans produced numerous writings including histories and a great number of religious writings. The script of their language was influenced by both Greek and Phoenician language systems and was usually written from right to left. At present, artifacts excavated from Etruscan sites have yielded thousands of short inscriptions, but we do not have lengthy narratives.

Ancient sources attesting to women's participation in culture among the Etruscans include the Roman writer Livy, who provides accounts of Tarquin and his Etruscan wife Tanaquil who became king and queen at Rome in the seventh century B.C.E.

Tanaquil was a woman of the aristocratic class. Her husband, a man of mixed birth (Etruscan and Greek), was referred to as Lucius Tarquinius by the Romans, and was unpopular among the Etruscan nobility. Tanaquil was accustomed to social favor and prestige and soon became dissatisfied with their life in Tarquinia. She convinced Tarquin to move to Rome which she described to him as an up and coming city and one that should be more open to "foreigners" than Tarquinia.

As queen of Rome, Tanaquil was Tarquin's counselor and constant advisor concerning the will of the gods; she played a major role in the government. Through her prophetic gifts Tanaquil also chose Tarquin's successor to the throne. In a prophetic vision she saw Servius Tullius, the child of a slave woman, in a crib, with a flame encircling his head. Tanaquil appeared and said it was an omen that the child would become king of Rome, and the fire went out.

Years after this prophetic vision Tarquin was murdered. Tanaquil kept the fact of Tarquin's death from the people and told them instead that he had been seriously wounded. In this manner, by convincing the Roman public that Tarquin was recuperating, she was able to subtly install Servius Tullius as his successor. Tanaquil's reputation as a kingmaker was further ratified when, once Servius Tullius's power base was firmly established, they announced Tarquin's death and Servius Tullius was installed as king.

QUEEN TANAQUIL: KINGMAKER*

... It was now about thirty-eight years since Tarquinius had begun to reign, and not only the king, but the Fathers and the commons too, held Servius Tullius in the very highest honour. ...

[It happened that Tarquinius was attacked and severely wounded.]

The dying Tarquinius had hardly been caught up in the arms of the bystanders when the fugitives were seized by the lictors. ... In the midst of the tumult Tanaquil gave orders to close the palace, and ejected all witnesses. ... Having hastily summoned Servius, she showed him her husband's nearly lifeless body, and grasping his right hand, besought him not to suffer the death of his father-in-law to go unpunished, nor his mother-in-law to become a jest to her enemies. "To you, Servius," she cried, "if you are a man, belongs this kingdom, not to those who by the hands of others have committed a dastardly crime. Arouse yourself and follow the guidance of the gods, who once declared by the token of divine fire poured out upon this head that you should be a famous man. Now is the time for that heaven-sent flame to quicken you! Now wake in earnest! ... If your own counsels are benumbed in this sudden crisis, at least use mine." When the shouting and pushing of the crowd could hardly be withstood, Tanaquil went up into the upper storey of the house, and through a window ... addressed the populace. She bade them be of good cheer: the king had been stunned by a sudden blow; the steel had not sunk deep into his body; he had already recovered consciousness; the blood had been wiped away and the wound examined; all the symptoms were favourable; she trusted that they would soon see Tarquinius himself; meanwhile she commanded that the people should obey Servius Tullius, who would dispense justice and perform the other duties of the king. ... In this way for several days after Tarquinius had breathed his last he concealed his death, ... Servius surrounded himself with a strong guard, and ruled at first without the authorization of the people, but with the consent of the Fathers. ...

Archaeological Evidence

According to archaeologists, the wealthy Etruscans painted the interiors of their tombs with scenes that emulated their daily lives. Correspondences in the vitality and opulence portrayed in these wall paintings are reminiscent of interior images at the Palace of Knossos on Crete. Here, however, we have

*Livy, *History of Rome*, LCL, 1926, 139, 141, 143, 145, 147.

considerably more detail. There is much evidence to suggest that Etruscan women's lives were substantially more unconfined than women who were their contemporaries at Athens or in the Roman Republic which follows. The image of Etruscan women attending a wrestling contest (Figure 8.1) with husbands and/or male companions and children would be unheard of in Athens or Rome. The gentle exchange of affection in this image speaks to a mutual valuing between the sexes. Art, iconography, and artifacts suggest that Etruscan women were integrated into both public and private life.

Queen Larthia and the Regolini-Galassi Tomb

The principal evidence for women's status comes from the excavation of Etruscan tombs. Once again we employ "images as texts" as we focus on the Regolini-Galassi tomb from the cemetery of the city of Cerveteri in southern Etruria, dating ca. 650 B.C.E. to 625 B.C.E. This tomb was built originally for a powerful woman, probably a queen of Cerveteri, a counterpart of the Etruscan queen Tanaquil at Rome. This woman's name was Larthia.

The stone roof of this burial chamber indicates a costly burial. The first burial chamber beyond the entry is that of Larthia, the other two burials are probably those of Larthia's husband and son. The Etruscans often cremated their dead in order to set their spirits free. If, however, archaeologists who interpret an ornate conveyance found in the tomb as the hearse upon which Larthia's son was brought into the tomb are correct, we can assume that Larthia's husband and son were inhumed (buried in the earth). Among funeral goods discovered in Larthia's burial chamber are between 400 to 500 items, including several pair of dice for gaming or for magical numerology. There is a silver vessel 3 inches high upon which Larthia's name is written from right to left in Greek letters (see Figure 8.2). Also associated with the Regolini-Galassi tomb is a pottery vessel 8 inches high, assumed to be an inkwell with letters inscribed around the base of the vessel. The body of the vase has a number of syllables suggesting it may have been used for practicing or studying the alphabet and learning to write. Larthia's name is inscribed on her cup; this inscription and other evidence indicates it is likely that Larthia was indeed literate.

Larthia's personal effects from her burial chamber include a magnificent gold bib (see Figure 8.3) found on her body. It is 16 inches long and went to her waist. A *fibula,* or type of safety pin 14 inches long, found in Larthia's tomb is the largest such pin found in any Greek, Roman, or Etruscan grave. It is intricately decorated with gold granules and has three-dimensional ducks and lions hammered into it. It is important to note that Etruscans were in touch with people in eastern Asia Minor as is evidenced by a bracelet, 3 inches in diameter, representing female figures holding palms, a motif that is common in the East. Amber jewelry, such as Larthia's amber necklace, was prized by the Etruscans, especially by women, and was thought to have magical qualities. Amber can generate electricity, and it was assumed that women could control its magic.

Images of men and women, husbands and wives partying together were scandalous to the Romans; and, at Athens only a *hetaira* would have appeared in public with a man. The Etruscan tomb painting in Figure 8.4 shows life in the setting of an aristocratic lifestyle. The "keg" of wine in the center of the image and a vivacious atmosphere attest not only that Etruscan women imbibed in public but also that they danced with male partners and apparently enjoyed themselves heartily (see Figure 8.5). This is a vivid contrast to women in the Roman Republic who, as we shall see, were not allowed to drink at all, under punishment of death.

Note that the couple dancing are nearly nude and are not dancing in a group, according to gender, as did the Greeks. Women in Etruria also danced solo (see Figure 8.6). The Romans would likely assume that the solo dancer was a prostitute. Etruscan women went to the theater as spectators and were also accepted as entertainers, jugglers, and dancers.

Figure 8–2   Larthia's bowl. *Musei Vaticani, Vatican Museums, Rome, Italy*

Figure 8–3   A golden bib. *Musei Vaticani, Vatican Museums, Rome, Italy*

Figure 8–4   Paintings on the front wall of Giacomo Leopardi's tomb in Tarquinia, Italy, depicting men and women banqueting together. *Fratelli Alinari, Art Resource, N.Y.*

Figure 8–5   Figures dancing together. © *Archivo Iconografico, S.A./CORBIS*

Etruscan women liked fashions that were bold, definitive costumes. Etruscan styles, however, were considered bizarre by the Romans, especially when they were compared with the demure and simple clothing of Greek and Roman women.

Ramtha, Immortalized on the "Banquet of Eternity" Sarcophagus

Another prominent and wealthy Etruscan woman, Ramtha, is shown on a sarcophagas with her husband embracing and reclining under a mantle or cloak. The theme of the couple reclining and conversing together in eternity shows the equal status of women. The male is represented with his attendant carrying emblems of his office as magistrate; the woman's retinue also bears symbols of her status (see Figure 8.7).

Figure 8–6 Detail of a mural painting from the Tomb of the Jugglers depicting a female dancing alone. *Etruscan necropolis/Tarquinia/Digli, Picture Desk, Inc./ Kobal Collection*

RELIGION

The Holy

Although most of what has been discovered about Etruscan religion in the present state of research attests to a male sky God, Tinia, female images of deities persist as an influential presence in Etruscan religion. Another interesting feature of the religion is that the chief characteristics of three principal goddesses, Uni, Menrva, and Turan, are equated by scholars to their Greek and Roman counterparts: Uni/Hera/Juno, Turan/Aphrodite/Venus, and Minrva/Athena/Minerva, respectively. Images of these

Figure 8–7   Sarcophagus from Cervetri. *Fratelli Alinari, Art Resource, N.Y.*

three goddesses appear together on the back of a well-known Etruscan mirror (see Figure 8.8). The etched image on the back of the mirror portrays the theme of the "divine beauty pageant" in which the three goddesses compete for the compliment of Elcsentre/Alexander/Paris. Professor Nancy Thompson de Grummond continues extensive research on Etruscan mirrors and finds connections between the mirrors, spirituality, sacred myth, and prophecy.

Myth

Turan is not unlike Aphrodite, the Goddess of Love and Uni is very similar to Hera, but is more like Hera in Sparta and Corinth and cities other than Athens, where she is depicted as the shrewish wife of Zeus. The Goddess Menrva was, like Athena at Athens, said to have been born from the head of Apollo, and yet she was the goddess of marriage and childbirth. Interestingly, in the Greek hinterlands of Athens and in smaller poleis (cities), Athena retained, and was also celebrated in, her fertility attribute.

Etruscan mirrors are among the greatest treasures from the tombs. They are made of bronze, are highly polished, and are found in graves of both women and men. Many had the names of their owners

Figure 8–8   Etruscan inscription on a bronze mirror depicting the Judgement of Paris. © *Indiana University Art Museum. Photograph by: Michael Cavanagh/Kevin Montague*

inscribed on the back. The backs are also engraved with scenes from Greek religion and mythology, and scenes from daily life. Many scholars argue that the mirrors, which portray scenes from mythology, reveal widespread literacy among women.

Ritual

The Romans comment on Etruscan religion with some admiration, especially for their priests who were experts at divination. According to Etruscan tradition, the gods and goddesses in Etruria occupied the macrocosm and the microcosm of the universe, including the livers of sheep! It was believed that each of the principal deities inhabited an area in the liver. After being boiled the livers were examined for their shape, texture, and the location of various lumps and bumps. From this "information" priests foretold the future (De Grummond 1992. 2).

Female Religious Functionaries

The following excerpt explores the social location of the prophetess Vegoia, her prophecies, and a mirror that depicts her as a messenger (see Figure 8–9).

Figure 8–9   Figure of Vegoia. *Nancy De Grummond, Florida State University*

VEGOIA, ETRUSCAN PROPHETESS[*]

A highly important figure in Etruscan divination is the prophetess called "Nymph Begoe" (or "Vegoia") in Latin texts. She is mentioned as the author or source of books on lightning that were kept in the Temple of Apollo (presumably on the Palatine Hill in Rome), and especially as a source for an account about the creation of the world. Her books are referred to as *libri Vegontici*. A thunder calendar attributed to the Roman savant Nigidius Figulus, surviving in a Greek translation, may be derived from her prophecies. A Roman expert on Etruscan lore, Tarquitius Priscus, a contemporary of Cicero, translated her books into Latin. A precious scrap of her prophecy exists in Latin, perhaps from the translations made by Tarquitius Priscus; the text pertains to the sanctity of boundaries and thus is preserved in the ancient

[*]N. T. De Grummond, "Vegoia," from a forthcoming book, to be published by the University of Texas Press.

collections on field surveys (*Gromatici Latini*, Lachmann I. 348–350). "Vegoia" delivered her prophecy to a certain Arruns Veltymnus, sometimes equated with Arruns, an early prince of the Etruscan city of Clusium, though with little firm evidence. The prophecy in Latin makes specific reference to Jupiter, the equivalent of the Etruscan sky god Tinia. It begins with the origin of the sea and sky, and relates how Jupiter had worked out boundaries in Etruria; for those who violated these boundaries, disastrous consequences were predicted, including storms, whirlwinds, drought, hail and mildew.

"(Prophecy) of Vegoia, to Arruns Veltymnus: 'Know that the sea was separated from the sky. But when Juppiter claimed the land of Aetruia for himself, he established and ordered that the fields be measured and the croplands delimited. Knowing the greed of men and their lust for land, he wanted everything proper concerning boundaries. And at some time, around the end of the eighth *saeculum,* someone will violate them on account of greed by means of evil trickery and will touch them and move them[....]. But whoever shall have touched and moved them, increasing his own property and diminishing that of another, on account of this crime he will be damned by the gods. If slaves should do it, there will be a change for the worse in status. But if the deed is done with the master's consent, very quickly the master will be uprooted and all of his family will perish. The ones who move [the boundaries] will be afflicted by the worst diseases and wounds and they will feel a weakness in their limbs. Then also the earth will be moved by storms and whirlwinds with frequent destruction, crops often will be injured and will be knocked down by rain and hail, they will perish in the summer heat, they will be felled by mildew. There will be much dissension among people. Know that these things will be done when such crimes are committed. Wherefore be not false or double-tongued. Keep this teaching in your heart.'"

The writing down of the prophecy of "Vegoia" has been thought to date from the first century B.C.E. (some 500 years later than Arruns of Clusium), because it refers to the eighth *saeculum* of Etruscan history. The Etruscan doctrine of the *saeculum* is only dimly known and understood, but the eighth *saeculum* may be convincingly related to the last century of Etruscan civilization, when the Etruscans were being overrun by the Romans and a prophecy on boundaries might seem especially pertinent.

It is generally agreed that the "Nymph Begoe" may be found in Etruscan art, twice on engraved bronze Etruscan mirrors and once on a gold ring bezel. On a mirror from Vetulonia (ca. 300–275 B.C.E.) appears a winged female figure labeled *Lasa Vecuvi(a)*, from which the translation to Latin of "Nymph Begoe" or "Vegoia" might easily have been made. (The word "Lasa" in Etruscan means "spirit.") The figure appears in the bottom of the mirror, underneath an image of Tinia holding the thunderbolt, thus suggesting a connection between the two. On a mirror of unknown provenance in the Villa Giulia, of similar date, appears a winged figure in short chiton labeled *Lasa Vecu.* This time, however, the Lasa appears with Menrva. She seems to stand and listen, holding in her hand an object that is sometimes identified as a small lightning bolt, though more often as a plant. Either attribute would be acceptable for the prophetess who left a book on lightning but also had concern for boundaries, a matter of agrarian significance.

Finally, on the ring bezel, from Todi in Umbria (dated around the same time as the two preceding examples), the goddess is called Lasa Vecuvia, and is represented as a nude, nymph-like figure holding a mirror. From the fact that numerous scenes of prophecy are represented on Etruscan mirrors, it may be conjectured that the mirror itself was an instrument of prophecy, as in the attested examples of *katoptromanteia* (conjuring with mirrors) attested in Greek and Roman ritual. Rather like making predictions by gazing in a crystal ball or a vessel filled with liquid (*lekanomanteia*), one could discern the future by looking at a reflected, but somewhat mysterious image in the shiny surface of the mirror. There are several Etruscan mirrors that show a female figure gazing intently into a mirror, seemingly not in the act of grooming, but rather as a part of *katoptromanteia*. It may be hypothesized that Lasa Vecuvia prophesied on occasion by means of a mirror.

WOMEN OUTSIDE THE ARISTOCRACY

For many years archaeological excavation of Etruscan sites consisted almost exclusively of tombs such as those already described. In recent years, however, excavations that reveal more about the daily life of the Etruscans have started to come to light. Evidence of women's involvement in making textiles dates to the earliest Neolithic periods. Woven textiles were produced for the family and were also a significant contribution to the economy through trade and commerce. This is also the case in Etruria and is virtually our most important insight into women's production in society. Etruscan women were indeed involved in the making of textiles, and, unlike their contemporaries at Athens, their industrious accomplishments were not relegated to the private sphere. Loom weights along with spindles and spools were found not only in women's tombs and houses, but also in workshops/studios in the public sphere.

As we proceed to discuss women of the Roman Republic, it becomes clear that despite shared history in the political sphere, stark contrasts characterize the lifestyles and self-understanding of the women in these two neighboring societies.

THE ROMAN REPUBLIC

Trade, commerce, and political relations between the Etruscans and Romans were quite common, as was depicted in the story of Tanaquil and Tarquin. As texts about the Etruscan kings revealed, monarchy preceded the establishment of the republic at Rome and was indeed at least among the earliest forms of governance in that city. Our narrative in this section of the chapter addresses texts that describe events traditionally associated with the beginning of the Republic.

The Republic at Rome was patriarchal and was ordered hierarchically. The government provided the principal organizing and ordering framework in society. Reverence for the Goddess Vesta (Greek Hestia), Goddess of the hearth, was pervasive during the Republic and had symbolic significance in both politics and domestic life. Vesta was represented in the perpetual fire kept aflame by consecrated virgins in her temple. In sharp contrast to their Etruscan sisters, women at Rome were relegated to life within the home, where they, like the Vestals, "kept the home fires burning."

The texts selected for this section clarify both the high esteem in which a "proper" Roman matron, such as Lucretia, was held by her countrymen and the numerous restraints that were imposed upon women to so shape their experience that the matronly "ideal" became more attractive than other alternatives.

SOCIAL ORGANIZATION

A republic is defined as a state or nation in which supreme power resides in all of the citizens entitled to vote (the electorate) and is exercised by representatives elected by them and responsible to them. Chart 8.1 provides a general description.

PATRICIAN WOMEN

The status of women in the Roman Republic was determined by their relationship to the men in their lives whether as wives, mothers, mothers-in-law, sisters, or daughters. All women were part of the social class into which they were born and they married within that class. Women were not represented nor were they active participants in the central government or its bureaucracy. Roman women were, nonetheless, used to secure marriages that solidified power relations among Patrician families, and eventually among upwardly mobile Equestrian and Plebian families that constituted the power elite.

Women of the nobility were relegated exclusively to the domestic sphere. They were responsible for having children, raising children, managing the household and any servants or slaves, and for the producing of textiles for their families. Women made the fabric and the clothing for members of their households. Male children were educated beginning around age seven. Female children were educated to become good mothers and good household managers. They assumed these "careers" in adolescence and were, from that point relegated to the domestic sphere. Women were not formally educated in the humanities, mathematics, or the sciences. Some females learned to play musical instruments and although women were not customarily literate, women and men among the nobility sometimes had slaves who served as tutors to instruct female children in reading and writing.

Female educators of small children transmitted via oral tradition their initial exposure to myths, customs, protocol, values, and traditions that constituted Roman culture. It is in this traditioning process that women would also have had opportunities to convey stories about legendary and historical female heroes.

Men Writing about Patrician Women

The story of Lucretia is one of several about Patrician women in the earliest history of Rome who became paradigmatic legends in defining the virtue of the Roman matron. Themes of honor, integrity, self-denial for husband and children, pride, humility, long-suffering, diligence, and purity are just a few

---

Chart 8–1   Social Stratification in the Roman Republic

Patricians
> **Two Consuls** (with power of Imperium; wore the purple, led the army, had religious duties [served for one year], and two to eight Quaestors served as financial officials)
> **Senate** (retired consuls become senators, senators served for life)
> **Priestly Class**

Equestrian/Praetors, The Military Class

Plebians
> Plebians were barred from public office, and initially, from priesthood and other public religious offices. They could not serve as judges and because there was no published legal code, could not even know the law. The Struggle of the orders results in Plebian success in 287 B.C.E. by which time certain Plebians could serve in the priesthood, marry Patricians, have access to laws, and have the right to be one of the two consuls and members of the dictatorship (a martial post) and the censorship (took census)

among the many virtuous characteristics attributed to, and expected of, the Patrician female. Patrician women were expected to exemplify behavior and set an example for women across lines of social status. Distinctions are noticeable between descriptions of the Roman matron and the citizen wife who was her Athenian counterpart. The virtuous Roman woman was admired and set forth as an exemplary model of piety and virtue. If she breached the requirements of propriety, however, she forfeited her honor. A critique of the behavioral demands on a Roman female suggest that such demands functioned as a form of social control. The Athenian matron was not given this option. Roman males clearly disapproved of the freedom and assertiveness of Etruscan women. The story that follows presents a discussion about the virtue of their wives among several young princes on furlough from a slowly advancing war.

LIVY'S ACCOUNT OF LUCRETIA[*]

It chanced, as they were drinking in the quarters of Sextus Tarquinius, where Tarquinius Collatinus, son of Egerius, was also a guest, that the subject of wives came up. Every man fell to praising his own wife with enthusiasm, and, as their rivalry grew hot, Collatinus said that there was no need to talk about it, for it was in their power to know, in a few hours' time, how far the rest were excelled by his own Lucretia. "Come! If the vigour of youth is in us let us mount our horses and see for ourselves the disposition of our wives. Let every man regard as the surest test what meets his eyes when the woman's husband enters unexpected." They were heated with wine. "Agreed!" they all cried, and clapping spurs to their horses were off for Rome. Arriving there at early dusk, they thence proceeded to Collatia, where Lucretia was discovered very differently employed from the daughters-in-law of the king. These they had seen at a luxurious banquet, whiling away the time with their young friends; but Lucretia, though it was late at night, was busily engaged upon her wool, while her maidens toiled about her in the lamplight as she sat in the hall of her house. The prize of this contest in womanly virtues fell to Lucretia. As Collatinus and the Tarquinii approached, they were graciously received, and the victorious husband courteously invited the young princes to his table. It was there that Sextus Tarquinius was seized with a wicked desire to debauch Lucretia by force; not only her beauty, but her proved chastity as well, provoked him. However, for the present they ended the boyish prank of the night and returned to the camp.

LVIII. When a few days had gone by, Sextus Tarquinius, without letting Collatinus know, took a single attendant and went to Collatia. Being kindly welcomed, for no one suspected his purpose, he was brought after dinner to a guest-chamber. Burning with passion, he waited till it seemed to him that all about him was secure and everybody fast asleep; then, drawing his sword, he came to the sleeping Lucretia. Holding the woman down with his left hand on her breast, he said, "Be still, Lucretia! I am Sextus Tarquinius. My sword is in my hand. Utter a sound, and you die!" In affright the woman started out of her sleep. No help was in sight, but only imminent death. Then Tarquinius began to declare his love, to plead, to mingle threats with prayers, to bring every resource to bear upon her woman's heart. When he found her obdurate and not to be moved even by fear of death, he went farther and threatened

[*]From Livy, *History of Rome*, LCL, 1926, 1.57.6–58.

her with disgrace, saying that when she was dead he would kill his slave and lay him naked by her side, that she might be said to have been put to death in adultery with a man of base condition. At this dreadful prospect her resolute modesty was overcome, as if with force, by his victorious lust; and Tarquinius departed, exulting in his conquest of a woman's honour. Lucretia, grieving at her great disaster, dispatched the same message to her father in Rome and to her husband at Ardea: that they should each take a trusty friend and come; that they must do this and do it quickly, for a frightful thing had happened. Spurius Lucretius came with Publius Valerius, Volesus' son. Collatinus brought Lucius Junius Brutus, with whom he chanced to be returning to Rome when he was met by the messenger from his wife. Lucretia they found sitting sadly in her chamber. The entrance of her friends brought the tears to her eyes, and to her husband's question, "Is all well?" she replied, "Far from it; for what can be well with a woman when she has lost her honour? The print of a strange man, Collatinus, is in your bed. Yet my body only has been violated; my heart is guiltless, as death shall be my witness. But pledge your right hands and your words that the adulterer shall not go unpunished. Sextus Tarquinius is he that last night returned hostility for hospitality, and armed with force brought ruin on me, and on himself no less—if you are men—when he worked his pleasure with me." They give their pledges, every man in turn. They seek to comfort her, sick at heart as she is, by diverting the blame from her who was forced to the doer of the wrong. They tell her it is the mind that sins, not the body; and that where purpose has been wanting there is no guilt. "It is for you to determine," she answers, "what is due to him; for my own part, though I acquit myself of the sin, I do not absolve myself from punishment; not in time to come shall ever unchaste woman live through the example of Lucretia." Taking a knife which she had concealed beneath her dress, she plunged it into her heart, and sinking forward upon the wound, died as she fell. The wail for the dead was raised by her husband and her father.

VALERIUS MAXIMUS PRAISES THREE VIRTUOUS FEMALES[*]

Tertia Aemilia, the wife of Scipio Africanus and the mother of Cornelia, was a woman of such kindness and patience that, although she knew that her husband was carrying on with a little serving girl, she looked the other way, [as she thought it unseemly for] a woman to prosecute her great husband, Africanus, a conqueror of the world, for a dalliance. So little was she interested in revenge that, after Scipio's death, she freed the girl and gave her in marriage to one of her own freedmen. When Quintus Lucretius Vespillol was proscribed by the triumvirs, his wife Turia hid him in her bedroom above the rafters. A single maidservant knew the secret. At great risk to herself, she kept him safe from imminent death. So rare was her loyalty that, while the other men who had been proscribed found themselves in foreign, hostile places, barely managing to escape the worst tortures of body and soul, Lucretius was safe in that bedroom in the arms of his wife.

*Valerius Maximus, *Memorable Deeds and Sayings,* LCL, 1927. 6.7.1–3.

Sulpicia, despite the very close watch her mother Julia was keeping on her so that she would not follow her husband to Sicily (he was Lentulus Crusadllio, proscribed by the triumvirs), nevertheless put on slave's clothing and, taking two maids and the same number of menservants, fled secretly and went to him. She was not afraid to risk proscription herself, and her fidelity to her proscribed spouse was firm.

LEGAL STATUS OF WOMEN

The study of the Laws at Rome viewed in general, and from the perspective of women's experience, is a compelling enterprise. We discover that the laws function for the economic, social, and political benefit of male Patricians, and eventually, an upper strata of male Equestrians. For centuries multitudinous legal codes, arbitrarily applied at Rome, were the sole province of wealthy, landed Patricians to which people of lesser status did not have access. Codification of laws concerning women represents women's position as property of the man to whom they belong. Marriage, inheritance, and proscriptions on women's behavior are among the topics addressed.

The Laws of the Kings, Rome

Many of the laws and customs of Rome have their roots in the legends and myths of a distant past. The Laws of the Kings and the Twelve Tables represent laws that are said to have proceeded from early kings of Rome. Excerpts that follow pertain to laws that affect women's experience.

LAWS ATTRIBUTED TO ROMULUS*

6. By the enactment of a single law Romulus brought the women, -to great prudence and orderly conduct. . . The law was as follows: woman united with her husband by a sacred marriage' shall share in his possessions and in his sacred rites.

7. The cognates sitting in judgment with the husband . . . were given power to pass sentence in cases of adultery and if any wife was found drinking wine Romulus allowed the death penalty for both crimes.

9. He also made certain laws, one of which is severe, namely that which does not permit a wife to divorce her husband, but gives him power to divorce her for the use of drugs or magic on account of children or for counterfeiting the keys or for adultery. The law ordered that if he should divorce her for any other cause, part of his estate should go to the wife and that part should be dedicated to Ceres. Anyone who sold his wife was sacrificed to the gods of the underworld.

10. It is strange when he established no penalty against patricides, that he called all homicide patricide.

11. If a daughter-in-law strikes her father-in-law she shall be dedicated as a sacrifice to his ancestral deities. Traditional dates, 753–716 B.C.E.

---

*Excerpts from "The Twelve Tables." FIRA, Vol. 1, 3–4 in A.C. Johnson, P.R. Coleman-Norton, and F.C. Burns, tr. and eds., *Ancient Roman Statutes,* Austin TX: University of Texas Press, 1961.

LAWS ATTRIBUTED TO NUMA POMPILIUS*

On the Vestal Virgins he conferred high honours, among which was the right of making a will while their fathers lived and of doing all other juristic acts without a guardian.

13. A royal law forbids the burial of a pregnant woman before the child is extracted from the womb. Whoever violates this law is deemed to have destroyed the child's expectancy of life along with the mother.

14. A concubine shall not touch the altar of Juno. If she touches it, she shall sacrifice, with her hair unbound, a ewe lamb to Juno.

The Twelve Tables form the foundation of Roman civil law and their public presentation on twelve bronze tablets in the Roman Forum represented a victory for the Plebeian class. Previous to their publication, traditionally understood to have transpired in 450 B.C.E., laws were interpreted and administered by patricians in ways that privileged their own agendas.

EXCERPTS FROM *THE TWELVE TABLES***

TABLE IV. PATERNAL POWER

1. A notably deformed child shall be killed immediately.
3. To repudiate his wife, her husband shall order her to have her own property for herself, shall take the keys, shall expel her.
A child born within ten months of the father's death shall enter into the inheritance. . . .

TABLE V. INHERITANCE AND GUARDIANSHIP

1. Women, even though they are of full age, because of their levity of mind shall be under guardianship except Vestal Virgins, who shall be free from guardianship.

TABLE VI. OWNERSHIP AND POSSESSION

5. If any woman is unwilling to be subjected in this manner to her husband's marital control, she shall absent herself for three successive nights in every year and by this means shall interrupt his prescriptive right of each year.

TABLE X. SACRED LAW

4. Women shall not tear their cheeks or shall not make a sorrowful outcry on account of a funeral.

*From *FIRA*, Vol. 1, 4, ARS 1961.

**ARS, 1961, FIRA, 13–18.

Husbands' Punishment of Wives in Early Rome[*]

Egnatius Metellus . . . took a cudgel and beat his wife to death because she had drunk some wine. Not only did no one charge him with a crime, but no one even blamed him. Everyone considered this an excellent example of one who had justly paid the penalty for violating the laws of sobriety. Indeed, any woman who immoderately seeks the use of wine closes the door on all virtues and opens it to vices.

There was also the harsh marital severity of Gaius Sulpicius Gallus. He divorced his wife because he had caught her outdoors with her head uncovered: a stiff penalty, but not without a certain logic. "The law," he said, "prescribes for you my eyes alone to which you may prove your beauty. For these eyes you should provide the ornaments of beauty, for these be lovely: entrust yourself to their more certain knowledge. If you with needless provocation, invite the look of anyone else, you must be suspected of wrongdoing."

Quintus Antistius Vetus felt no differently when he divorced his wife because he had seen her in public having a private conversation with a common freedwoman. For, moved not by an actual crime but, so to speak, by the birth and nourishment of one, he punished her before the crime could be committed, so that he might prevent the deed's being done rather than punish it afterwards.

To these we should add the case of Publius Sempronius Sophus who, disgraced his wife with divorce merely because she dared attend the games without his knowledge. And so, long ago, when the misdeeds of women were thus forestalled, their minds stayed far from wrongdoing.

The Roman Jurists

The Roman jurists were legal specialists and interpreters of private law during Rome's classical period (50 B.C.E.–250 A.D.). Among the numerous sources of laws at Rome over the centuries the jurists were most concerned with developing and cultivating laws that Roman citizens used in suing one another.

RELIGION

The Holy

Principal Roman deities (see Chart 8–2) were patterned on the Greek pantheon.

Note, however, that unlike Hestia, who was a relatively insignificant member of the Greek pantheon, Vesta, Goddess of the Hearth was accorded great prominence at Rome. The eternal flame of the city of Rome was maintained by sacred Vestal Virgins. This fire was also a metaphor for the hearth in each individual home in the Republic. It is in this context that generations of the ideal of the Roman matron took root with such tenacity.

Veneration of the deity of the hearth/home is an example of the religious legitimization of a political/social philosophy for the subjugation of women. Virtuous women were elevated in the society and "placed on a pedestal." This theme of honoring women while denying them access to educational, civil, economic, social, and political freedom runs throughout Western civilization and civilizations colonized by Western peoples.

[*]Valerius Maximus, *Memorable Deeds and Sayings* LCL, 1927, 6.3.9–12

Chart 8–2   Chart of Roman Deities and Their Greek And Etruscan Counterparts

Chief God Jove (Greek-Zeus)

Juno (Greek-Hera; Etruscan-Uni)

Minerva (Greek-Athena; Etruscan-Menrva)

Vesta (Greek-Hestia)

Venus (Greek-Aphrodite; Etruscan-Turan)

Ceres (Greek-Demeter)

Diana (Greek-Artemis)

Mars (Greek-Ares)

Neptunis (Greek-Poseidon)

Vulcanus (Greek-Hephaestus)

Mercury (Greek-Hermes)

Apollo

Benn

Myth

Themes of life, death, and rebirth, introduced in the Paleolithic and Neolithic periods, persist in the Roman Republic. Myths of Venus and Adonis parallel Inanna and Damuzi, Ishtar and Tammuz, Isis and Osiris. Myths of Vesta, Minerva, Juno, and Diana often parallel those of their Greek foresisters. We will see, however, as noted earlier, that the Roman Goddess Vesta became an archetypal figure for the Roman matron. Her purity and her responsibilities at the hearth to keep the sacred/civil fire of Rome aflame perpetually were foundational elements in defining the social norms and expectations for the ideal Roman woman in the Republic.

Rituals

Participation in religious rituals may have afforded women some degree of authentic expression of spirituality and religious self-understanding that had meaning in their lives. In the Republic temples continued to be consecrated to female deities. Rituals performed in these temples, celebrations of religious festivals, and caring for the dead may have reflected more closely women's own experience than Roman mythology would suggest.

Female Religious Functionaries

Female Priestesses, Vestal Virgins, and Prophetesses in the Roman Republic, were, with few exceptions, represented by Patrician families. Women who were religious functionaries, whether or not they were literate, would have been educated in the myths, customs, history, lore, and liturgical/ritual practices of the deities they served.

AULUS GELLIUS' ACCOUNT OF THE VESTAL VIRGINS[*]

> The Vestal Virgin, at what age and from what sort of family and by what ritual and ceremonies and rites and under what title she is taken by the Pontifex Maximus, and

[*]From Aulus Gellius, *Attic Nights*, LCL, 1927 1.12.

what rights she has as soon as she is taken; and that, as Labeo says, by law she cannot be heir of an intestate person nor can anyone be her heir if she dies intestate.

Those who have written about the taking of a Virgin, of whom the most diligent was Labeo Antistius, say that it is unlawful to take a girl younger than six or older than ten, or to take a girl whose father and mother are not living, or who has a speech or hearing defect, or any other bodily imperfection. She must not have been freed from her father's power, even if her father is alive and she is in the power of her grandfather; likewise, neither of her parents must ever have been slaves nor held lowly occupations. But they say that she is exempt if her sister was elected to the priesthood; likewise if her father is a *flamen* or augur or one of the Fifteen in charge of the Sibylline Books, one of the Seven of the banquets, or a Salian priest (of Mars). Also exempt are girls who are betrothed to a *pontifex* [a Roman guild of Priests] or daughters of priests of the *tubilustrium* [feast of trumpets]. Moreover, Ateius Capito writes that the daughter of a man who does not have a residence in Italy cannot be chosen, and the daughter of a man who has three children is to be excused.

As soon as a Vestal Virgin is taken and brought to the atrium of Vesta and handed over to the pontifices, from that moment she leaves her father's power without being emancipated and without diminution of her rights and gains the right to make a will.

As to the custom and ritual of taking a Virgin, we do not possess ancient writings, except that the first one was taken by Numa when he was king. But, we find the Papian law, according to which under the direction of that Pontifex Maximus twenty girls are to be chosen from among the people and one of these chosen by lot in an assembly and the Pontifex Maximus takes the winner who now belongs to Vesta. But the lottery of the Papian law is usually not needed nowadays. For if a man of respectable birth goes to the Pontifex Maximus and offers his daughter for the priesthood, insofar as it can be done in keeping with the religious observations, he is given exemption from the Papian law by the senate.

The word "taken" is used, so it seems, because the Pontifex Maximus literally takes her by the hand and leads her away from the parent in whose power she is, as though she had been captured in war. In his book, Fabius Pictor gives the words the Pontifex Maximus must say when he takes a Virgin. They are: "I take you, Amata, to be a Vestal priestess who will carry out sacred rites which it is the law for a Vestal priestess to, perform on behalf of the Roman people, on the same terms as her who was a Vestal on the best terms." Many think that the term "taken" should apply only to Vestal Virgins but also the *flamines Diales,* and *pontiff* and augurs were said to be "taken". Lucius Sulla wrote in book two of his autobiography: Publi Cornelius, who was the first to receive the cognomen Sulla, was taken flamen Dialis. Marcus Cato, writing on the Lusitanians, accused Servi Galba: "Nevertheless they say he wanted to revolt. I now want to know pontifical law as well as possible; does that mean I am to be 'taken' pontiff? If I want to know augury, should I be 'taken' for an augur?" Moreover, in Labeo's Commentaries on the Twelve Tables, he wrote: "Vestal Virgin is neither heir to an intestate person nor is anyone her heir if she dies intestate, but her estate passes to the public treasury. It is uncertain what the law meant."

The Pontifex Maximus calls the girl "Amata" when he takes her because that is the traditional name of the first Vestal Virgin to be taken.

PLUTARCH ON NUMA POMPILIUS AND THE VESTAL VIRGINS*

The goddess of the hearth, Vesta, was served by six Virgins, whose duty it was to keep the sacred fire which took the place of a cult statue. Vesta's temple was a round building in the Roman Forum. Its institution was attributed to Numa Pompilius, the pious second king of Rome (715–673 B.C.E.), who succeeded the warlike Romulus. At first they say that Gegania and Verenia were made priestesses by Numa, and next Canuleia and Tarpeia. Later Servius added two more, to bring the number up to what it has been since that time. The king set the term of service for the holy Virgins at thirty years; in the first decade they learn their duties, in the middle decade they do what they have learned, and in the third they teach others. After that a Virgin is free to marry if she wishes to or to adopt another style of life, once her term of service has been completed. But few are said to have welcomed this opportunity, and matters did not go well for those who did, but rather because they were afflicted by regret and depression for the rest of their lives they inspired pious reverenced in the others, so that they remained constant in their virginity until old age and death.

Numa gave them significant honours, one of which is the right to make a will during their father's lifetime and to conduct their other business affairs without a guardian, like the mothers of three children. When they go out they are preceded by lictors with the fasces, and if they accidentally happen to meet a criminal being led to execution, his life is spared. The Virgin must swear that the meeting was involuntary and accidental and not planned. Anyone who goes underneath a Vestal's litter when she is being carried is put to death.

The Virgins' minor offences are punished by beating, which is administered by the Pontifex, with the offender naked, and in a dark place with a curtain set up between them. A Virgin who is seduced is buried alive near what is known as the Colline gate. At this place in the city there is a little ridge of land that extends for some distance, which is called a mound in the Latin language. Here they prepare a small room, with an entrance from above. In it there is a bed with a cover, a lighted lamp, and some of the basic necessities of life, such as bread, water in a bucket, milk, oil, because they consider it impious to allow a body that is consecrated to the most holy rites to die of starvation. They put the woman who is being punished on a litter, which they cover over from outside and bind down with straps, so that not even her voice can be heard, and they take her through the Forum. Everyone there stands aside silently and follows the litter without a word, in serious dejection. There is no other sight so terrifying, and the city finds no day more distasteful than that day. When the litter is borne to the special place, the attendants unfasten her chains and the chief priest says certain secret prayers and lifts his hands to the gods in prayer because he is required to carry out the execution, and he leads the victim out veiled and settles her on the ladder that carries her down to the room. Then he, along with the other priests, turns away. The ladder is removed from the entrance and a great pile of earth is placed over

*Excerpts from Plutarch, *Life of Numa Pompilius*, LCL, 1916, 9.5–10.7.

the room to hide it, so that the place is on a level with the rest of the mound. That is how those who abandon their sacred virginity are punished.

PLEBIAN WOMEN

Until laws were established during the Republic that permitted Plebians to participate in determining policy, upward social mobility for Plebian women was extremely unusual. Women in the lower classes worked in the fields and vineyards, in shops, in the marketplaces and taverns, and in producing textiles, managing their households, and rearing their children.

Slave women in households among the nobility fulfilled many types of labor. Some women did gardening, cleaning, and food preparation; others were wet nurses, engaged in childcare, or were hairdressers and personal attendants to their mistresses. Women in domestic service also assisted with carding, spinning, and weaving fabric.

Some women were prostitutes. Prostitutes, pimps, and their customers are the mainstays of the comedies of Plautus and Terence which should be enjoyed in their entirety. In this brief extract from one of Plautus's plays, the character Syra, a madam, suggests that what the prostitutes need is a little organization, as the matrons have already learned.

SHOULD WE ORGANIZE?*

> It certainly seems right to me, Selenium dear, that our class should be kind to each other and stick together, when you see those highborn women, those top matrons, how they cultivate their friendship and how tight they are with one another. If we were to do the same thing, if we imitate them, even then we can hardly live, they hate us so much. They want us poor women to need their wealth. They want for us to be able to do nothing on our own but to have to ask them all the time for favours. If you go to them, you prefer to leave than go inside, the way they publicly flatter women of our rank, but in private, if they get the chance they pour cold water on us - they're so crafty. They claim we always go with their men, they say we are their concubines, and try to squelch us. Because we are freedwomen, both your mother and I became prostitutes. She brought you up, and I brought up this one [Gymnasium], your fathers being from various quarters. I didn't make my girl become a prostitute because of pride but so that I shouldn't starve.

The historian Livy retells the legend of the Sabine women: how they were snatched from their families at a religious festival to help Roman men to populate Rome. Livy's telling of the tale avoids any acknowledgement of the horror of rape. Rather, Livy's rendition contends that the women's hearts and minds were won over by violence followed by sweet words and childbearing.

THE RAPE OF THE SABINE WOMEN**

> When the time came for the show, and people's thoughts and eyes were busy with it, the preconcerted attack began. At a given signal the young Romans darted this way and that, to seize and carry off the maidens. In most cases these were taken by the

*From *The Casket/Cistellaria, LCL,* 1917, Vol. 2.
**From Livy, *History of Rome,* LCL 1919, 1.9.

men in whose path they chanced to be. Some, of exceptional beauty, had been marked out for the chief senators, and were carried off to their houses by plebeians to whom the office had been entrusted. One, who far excelled the rest in mien and loveliness, was seized, the story relates, by the gang of a certain Thalassius. Being repeatedly asked for whom they were bearing her off, they kept shouting that no one should touch her, for they were taking her to Thalassius, and this was the origin of the wedding-cry. The sports broke up in a panic, and the parents of the maidens fled sorrowing. They charged the Romans with the crime of violating hospitality, and invoked the gods to whose solemn games they had come, deceived in violation of religion and honour. The stolen maidens were no more hopeful of their plight, nor less indignant. But Romulus himself went amongst them and explained that the pride of their parents had caused this deed, when they had refused their neighbours the right to intermarry; nevertheless the daughters should be wedded and become co-partners in all the possessions of the Romans, in their citizenship and, dearest privilege of all to the human race, in their children; only let them moderate their anger, and give their hearts to those to whom fortune had given their persons. A sense of injury had often given place to affection, and they would find their husbands the kinder for this reason, that every man would earnestly endeavour not only to be a good husband, but also to console his wife for the home and parents she had lost. His arguments were seconded by the wooing of the men, who excused their act on the score of passion and love, the most moving of all pleas to a woman's heart.

SUGGESTED READINGS

Dyczek, Piotr. "The Status of Women in Aegean Culture. Some Considerations," in *Studia Aegaea et Balcanica in honorem Lodovicae Press,* Wydawnictwa Uniwersytetu Warszawskiego, edited by Anna Lipska, Ewa Niezgoda, and Maria Zabecka, Warszawa (1992) 81–91.

Flory, Marlene B. "The Deification of Roman Women." *The Ancient History Bulletin* 9.3–4 (1995): 127–34.

Gardner, J. *Women in Roman Law and Society.* London: Croom Helm, 1986.

I Claudia, Women in Ancient Rome. Edited by D. Kleiner and S. Matheson. Austin: University of Texas Press, 1996.

Marinatos, N. "The Minoan Harem. The Role of Eminent Women and the Knossos Frescoes," in *Dialogues d'histoire ancienne [Hommage à Ettore Lepore]* 15.2 (1989) 33–50.

——— "Formalism and Gender Roles. A Comparison of Minoan and Egyptian Art," in *Politeia. Society and State in the Aegean Bronze Age. Proceedings of the 5th International Aegean Conference/ 5e Rencontre égéenne internationale,* University of Heidelberg, Archäologisches Institut, 10–13 April 1994, Vol II., *Aegaeum* 12, edited by Robert Laffineur and Wolf-Dietrich Niemeier.

McDougall, Lain. "Livy and Etruscan Women." *The Ancient History Bulletin* 4.2 (1990): 24–30.

McGinn, Thomas A. J. *Prostitution, Sexuality and the Law in Ancient Rome.* Oxford: Oxford University Press, 1998.

Rabinowitz N.S. and A. Richlin, eds. *Feminist Theory and the Classics.* New York: Routledge Press, 1993.

Rehak, P. "New Observations on the Mycenaean 'Warrior Goddess,'" *Archaeologischer Anzeiger* (1984): 535–545.

"Rescuing Creusa: New Methodological Approaches to Women in Antiquity." *Helios* 13 (2) (1986): 69–84.

Treggiari, S. *Roman Marriage.* Oxford: Clarendon Press, 1991.

Uchitel, Alexander. "Women at Work. Pylos and Knossos, Lagash and Ur." *Historia* 33.3 (1984) 257–282.

Warren, Larissa Bonfante. "Etruscan Women: A Question of Interpretation." *Archaeology* 26, no. 4 (October 1975): 242–249.

Warren, Larissa Bonfante. "The Women of Etruria," in *Women in the Ancient World: The Arethusa Papers,* edited by J. Peradato and J.P. Sullivan. Albany: State University of New York Press, 1984.

Audio-Visual Source

Etruria and the Etruscan Woman. 1998. Princeton, NJ: Films for the Humanities & Sciences, 1998. CD-ROM. BVL10009.

Sources Cited

De Grummond, Nancy Thompson, "Vegoia" from a forthcoming book on prophecy in Etruscan religion.

Livy. Livy's Account of Lucretia. *History of Rome,* translated by B.O. Foster. Loeb Classical Library. Cambridge, MA and London: Harvard University Press, 1926. 1.57.6–58.

Valerius Maximus. Valerius Maximus Praises Three Virtuous Females. *Memorable Deeds and Sayings,* Loeb Classical Library. Cambridge, MA and London: Harvard University Press, 1927, 6.7.1–3.

Livy. Cloelia the Hostage. *History of Rome,* translated by B.O. Foster. Loeb Classical Library, Cambridge, MA and London: Harvard University Press, 1926. 2.13.6–11.

Laws Attributed to Romulus from "The Twelve Tables," from *FIRA,* Vol. 1, 3–4, in A.C. Johnson, P.R. Coleman-Norton, and F.C. Burns, trans. and eds. *Ancient Roman Statutes,* Austin TX: University of Texas Press, 1961.

Laws Attributed to Numa Pompilius from *FIRA,* Vol. 1, 4 in A.C. Johnson, P.R. Coleman-Norton and F.C. Burns, trans. and eds. *Ancient Roman Statutes,* Austin TX: University of Texas Press, 1961

"The Twelve Tables," *FIRA,* Vol. 1, 13–18, in A.C. Johnson, P.R. Coleman-Norton, and F.C. Burns, trans. and eds. *Ancient Roman Statutes,* Austin TX: University of Texas Press, 1961.

Valerius Maximus. Husbands' Punishment of Wives. *Memorable Deeds and Sayings.* Loeb Classical Library, Cambridge, MA and London: Harvard University Press, 1927. 6.3.9–12.

Aulus Gellius. Aulus Gellius' Account of the Vestal Virgins. *Attic Nights,* translated by John C. Rolfe, Loeb Classical Library, Cambridge, MA and London: Harvard University Press, 1927. 7.12.

Plutarch. Plutarch on Numa Pompilius and the Vestal Virgins. *Life of Numa Pompilius,* translated by B. Perrin. Loeb Classical Library, Cambridge, MA and London: Harvard University Press, 1916. 9.5–10.7.

Plautus. Should We Organize? *Cistellaria 22–41.* No. 181. *Women's Life in Greece and Rome.* Loeb Classical Library. Cambridge, MA and London: Harvard University Press, 1917, Vol.2, 1.22–41.

Livy. "The Rape of Sabine Women," *History of Rome,* translated by B.O. Foster. Loeb Classical Library. Cambridge, MA and London: Harvard University Press, 1.9.11–9.16.

Chapter 9

The Hellenistic World

Cultural changes in the Hellenistic period extending from the life and death of Alexander the Great (d. 323 B.C.E.) to the beginnings of the Roman Empire in the late first century B.C.E. are significant for the record of women's contributions to culture. Most undergraduate textbooks discuss Alexander's military campaigns and then move on to discuss the Roman Empire. In the present chapter we will speculate briefly about why this is so and then move on to discuss aspects of Hellenistic culture that were particularly relevant for women in Western civilization, namely: urbanization and *paideia* (Greek education).

Notions of what constitutes history are often limited and ideologically selective. Many of the restrictions on what historians report and transmit are governed by limitations imposed by what is available, or by what has survived. There are, however, also instances in which voluminous amounts of data are available concerning a particular time period that would fall outside the "canon" and boundaries of "traditional" patterns, of what is expected to be transmitted. We suggest that this is the case concerning women in the Hellenistic period. The selections that follow indicate that, although for the majority of women in this period the status quo prevailed, for others there were numerous opportunities for creative and liberating experiences in the Hellenistic period.

An example of such a woman is Olympias of Macedonia (died ca. 305 B.C.E.). The first of the Hellenistic Queens, and wife of Philip of Macedonia, she devoted special care and concern to the education of her son Alexander and her daughter Cleopatra I. They were taught music, gymnastics, falconry, and how to ride and to hunt (Macurdy, 1932).

Scholarly studies for Alexander and his sister Cleopatra incorporated a rigorous curriculum that was administered by the finest scholars available, including tutorials with Aristotle who resided in Macedonia for a time. We are told that the young Alexander found inspiration in the teachings of Aristotle that shaped his own philosophy and his vision for the future of the world.

Following the death of Philip, Alexander succeeded his father as king and expanded his military initiatives. Military campaigns that extended throughout the Mediterranean basin, Asia Minor, up to the Black Sea region and south into India secured for Alexander the most extensive empire in history up to that point. The traditional interpretation of Alexander's empire holds that he intended to "make Greek the world," and create a world civilization founded on many of the principles of Athenian culture. Alexander's death in 323 B.C.E. meant that the grand plan was aborted. What did in fact transpire in the next two centuries, however, functioned in many ways as foundational for the prolif-eration of the Roman Empire.

A principal reason that the Hellenistic period is seldom taught extensively in an undergraduate setting is that it is particularly difficult to find unifying themes that facilitate clarity about the period. What is clear is that it was a period of transition from the world as it had been experienced and under-stood in the preceding 2000 years in the Assyrian, Babylonian, and Persian empires, as well as Greece, the Roman Republic, and Celtic societies in Europe and the British Isles. The disruption that is an inte-gral aspect of any substantive cultural change, was disorderly, erratic, variable, and theoretically incon-sistent. After Alexander's death, prominent Generals in his army (referred to as the *Diadochi*) divided the empire and appointed themselves as leaders of the major territorial domains. According to tradi-tion, it was their intention to bring into being Alexander's dream of a world culture. We do not know to what extent or even whether each leader was committed to this end. We do know that for the next two hundred years among the most powerful surviving *Diadochi* and their heirs, ambitions for politi-cal supremacy, territorial expansion, and the accumulation of wealth and power characterized political and military reality.

SOCIAL ORGANIZATION

A brief discussion of social organization throughout the entire territory will be superficial at best, but is worthwhile because it provides insight concerning the syncretism and diversity that prevailed in the Hellenistic period. Suffice to say that the *Diadochi* who prevailed were autocrats. The Hellenistic dy-nasties were comprised of hundreds of thousands of inhabitants and created a very different sense of what constituted a state for the Greeks. The *polis* and the petty kingdom as they had previously been understood were not appropriate to the new situation. The Hellenistic dynasties relied heavily upon the administrative systems put in place by the Persian Empire or by the Egyptians.

The transfer of power was, however, accompanied by access to a highly developed Greek economy that could stimulate local economies. Expeditions to India and to the Sudan further expanded eco-nomic horizons.

Urbanization and *Colonization* by the Greeks throughout the regions conquered by Alexander, and later ruled by the surviving *Diadochi,* are among the principal defining characteristics of the Hellenis-tic world. The concepts of the cosmopolis (world-city) and *Cosmopolitanism* are also defining charac-teristic of the Hellenistic period. There were enormous migrations to a vast number of newly built Greek cities, and to old established cities that were reconstructed by colonizers and transformed by new values and cultural changes. *Individualism* expressed in art, literature, and culture is also charac-teristic of Hellenistic culture.

Greek language became the language of intellectual and cultural discourse, as well as the language for *trade and commerce* throughout the cities in the various Hellenistic dynasties. Greek education (*paideia),* discussed as we proceed, was the model for public and private education. *Mystery religions,* which will be examined in some detail were "universal religions" in the sense that adherents under-stood that the deities worshiped were not bound to particular locations, and worshipers throughout the Hellenistic world were connected by the common experience of secret initiation rituals. *Voluntary associations* functioned to strengthen the cosmopolis by providing a mechanism for networking among residents and settings in which mutual interests were shared and cultivated among diverse members of communities. Mystery Religions and Voluntary Associations are social institutions and or-ganizations, respectively, that have increasing relevance for women's autonomy as history proceeds into the Roman Empire, and are two further characteristics that defined Hellenistic culture.

As is apparent when we consider common themes that do emerge in the Hellenistic period, many of Alexander's objectives for a world culture did in fact come to fruition.

Among the *Diadochi,* in the late fourth century B.C.E., the two most prominent survivors were the general Seleusis, who established an empire in Syria and surrounding regions and the general Ptolemy, who became Pharoah of Egypt and governed Egypt as well as territories that extended into the Mediterranean Basin.

Particular windows of opportunity that occurred during periods of cultural transition and the shifting of cultural paradigms of the Hellenistic world often afforded women more participation as agents who were determining the course of their own lives. Some of these women were engaged in the shaping of the culture to which they contributed as monarchs, artists, philosophers, athletes, physicians, religious functionaries, and entrepreneurs. Texts from the Hellenistic period and Hellenistic Judaism that are incorporated in Part II, Volume One of this anthology provide surprising and provocative insights concerning women's participation in culture.

WOMEN IN THE ARISTOCRACY

Women in the aristocracy, in the Hellenistic world, consist of female representatives of the Court and a wealthy, landed elite whose profiles varied widely. The lives of some women in the aristocracy, in Greece, for example, did not change radically while the lives of women in the late Roman Republic became rather less restrictive. It is in Egypt, however, and in the Near East that the greatest changes in women's lives occurred. Beginning in the fourth century B.C.E., an impressive and distinctive array of female leaders emerged who are referred to as the "Hellenistic Queens." The queens bearing dynastic names of Euridyce, Arsinoe, Bernice, Mariamne, and Cleopatra were indeed exceptional women. They were literate, educated, skilled in social protocol, and capable of making and carrying out military strategies and administering governments. Several Hellenistic queens also patronized the arts, hiring skilled artisans and artists as architects, builders, and decorators of monumental buildings, temples, and tombs as well as their elaborate villas and estates. They also patronized persons engaged in the theater, musicians, dancers, poets, and philosophers. It is clear from the selections about the Hellenistic Queens and the dynasties they ruled and co-ruled that many, if not most, female leaders in this period can be described in terms very similar to those of their male counterparts. Many were ambitious, exploitive, manipulative, and driven by a will to power. These queens were, as we have noted, renown not only for their diplomatic expertise and political sagacity but for their commitment to learning and to patronage of the arts and religion. It is impossible to assess the effect of legends about these regal figures upon the lives of historical women in the Hellenistic period. It is not difficult to imagine, however, that, especially for aristocratic women who aspired to attain what we might refer to as *self-fulfillment,* their influence was considerable.

Despite their influence within their times, our sources of information about the Hellenistic queens are found in a sentence here, a paragraph there, and almost without exception the information is embedded in texts about male leaders. In the early part of the twentieth century Grace H. Macurdy produced a remarkable work in which she gathered these multiple sources and then wove into a fascinating narrative the stories of each queen with quotations by and about most of the women under discussion. Many of the narratives in the present reader that contain quotations by and about the queens are shaped with reference to Macurdy's work. In order to provide a meaningful context for quotes about Olympias and Arsinoe we will sometimes quote Macurdy and then highlight the quotation. (Grace H. Macurdy, *The Hellenistic Queens: A Study of Woman-Power in Macedonia, Seleucid Syria, and Ptolemaic Egypt.* Chicago: Ares Publishers, 1932. 2nd edition 1985)

Olympias

Olympias was born ca. 370 B.C.E. She met her husband on the island of Samothrace when they were both still children. Both she and Philip had been brought by their parents to take part in sacred initiation "Mysteries" and they were betrothed during this visit. When he and Olympias wed, she became his chief wife, much as Sibtu was the chief wife of Zimri-Lim (Chapter 3, "Ancient Near Eastern Mesopotamia: The Social Context").

OLYMPIAS, QUEEN OF MACEDONIA[*]

> Olympias bore Alexander in 356 B.C.E. and Cleopatra I in 354 B.C.E. Early in the marriage, when Philip was away on campaigns, he entrusted Olympias with great political power and responsibility. Plutarch (*Life of Alexander*, LCL, 1919, LXXVII) mentions Olympias' love of power as well as her obstinacy and desire to get her own way as principal characteristics of her personality throughout her life. Her clever wit indicated not only her intelligence but also her ability to make light, at least verbally, of events that might otherwise have been hurtful or grossly misunderstood. To stories that Alexander was the son of Zeus, Plutarch notes that she customarily retorted with great wit, asking for example, "Will Alexander never stop getting me into trouble with Hera?"

When Philip died, Olympias was in a good position politically. Her daughter was queen of Molossia, her son, Alexander, was king of Macedonia. Olympias was mistress of the Macedonian court while Alexander was on campaign. Arrian (VII, 12. 6) tells us that throughout Alexander's campaigns he and Olympias maintained a rigorous correspondence that was superceded only by the correspondence to Alexander of Olympias' political opponents. Plutarch quotes Alexander as saying that his mother's political rivals were unaware of the extent to which he would go to please his mother.

OLYMPIAS' TEARS[**]

> "One of his mother's tears would wash out the complaints of a thousand letters" . . .

After Alexander's death Olympias' life was in constant jeopardy. She lived in various forms of exile, and constantly conspired to re-establish herself and her power. Finally one of her councilors plotted to get her restored to the throne in Macedonia. To accomplish this feat it was necessary for her to ride into battle against the "pretenders" (Eurydice and Phillip Arhidaeus) who had taken the throne with the support of the Macedonian Army, but without the consent of the nobility.

THE AGED OLYMPIAS RIDES INTO BATTLE[†]

> Olympias entered battle like a bacchanal (Maenad, follower of Dionysius) with the beat of the Dionysiac drums, . . . And a miracle was wrought for her, for when the Macedonian soldiers saw their old queen advancing, they were so struck by her

---

[*]Plutarch, *Life of Alexander*, LCL, 1918, III.

[**]Plutarch, *Life of Alexander*, LCL, 1919, XXXIX.

[†]Diodorus, LCL, 1946, IX, 11, 107.

majesty and her noble air, so like that of her glorious son, that they remembered that she was the wife of their great Philip and mother of their great Alexander and came over to her side—a proud moment for the old queen. In this way Olympias captured the king and queen without risk to herself and secured the royal power.

Hellenistic Queens in Ptolemaic Egypt: Arsinoe II Philadelphus

Perhaps the most intriguing of the queens was Arsinoe II Philadelphus, the Ptolemaic queen who ruled Egypt and vast holdings outside Egypt. A Macedonian by birth, she was very beautiful, was well educated, and endowed with intelligence as well as common sense. Arsinoe II was the most politically astute of all the Hellenistic queens. Much of her power is attributed to her ambition and her organizational skills. Arsinoe's first marriage was to Lysimachus king of Thrace who was killed in battle at Ephesus. Arsinoe recognized that, as a young queen, alone in alien territory, she was quite vulnerable.

Disguised as a beggar, Arsione secured passage on a ship and returned safely to Macedonia. Once there she promptly hired a mercenary army to insure her continued safety. A half brother, Cerannus, sought a marital alliance with Arsinoe who was eager to be legitimated again as queen. Immediately following the marriage to Cerannus, he killed two of Arsinoe's children and made her forever painfully aware of the potential cost of political alliances over which she had no control. Cerranus was murdered by Gauls the following year. Arsinoe fled to Egypt and set about convincing her younger half brother Ptolemy (II Philadelphus) to marry her. It is from her position as queen of Egypt that Arsinoe most clearly distinguished herself.

[*]In Egypt Osiris and Isis set the precedent for brother/sister marriage and it was no doubt no surprise to Arsinoe that Egyptians would respond enthusiastically. Arsinoe's brother, who was far more interested in his own sensual appetites than in affairs of state was, apparently not only content that Arsinoe directed the power of government but also that she was a superb military strategist. Arsinoe was bestowed with many honors during her lifetime and surrounded herself with circles of scholars and artists whom she patronized. Cities, towns, temples, buildings, and streets were named for her, magnificent sculpture captured her likeness, she was honored as a goddess, and was the first of the Ptolemies to be raised to the status of a divinity when she died in 270 B.C.E.

ARSINOE II PHILADELPHUS[**]

> *Pliny tells of splendid yellow topaz brought from the Topaz Island in the Red Sea for Berenice, mother of Ptolemy, which so pleased the king that,*
>
> . . . he had a statue of Arsinoe, six feet in height, carved from it and set up in the Arsinoeum in Alexandria which he had built in her honor. He had an obelisk one hundred and twenty feet high brought with great labor and expense to place in her precinct. Statuary depicting the beautiful queen adorned Temples, shrines, and palaces. She was worshipped in elegant Temples and in humble places of worship throughout Egypt. Hymns, odes, and prayers were written to sing her praises. . . .

Yet, Macurdy sums up Arsinoe by saying, "In her energy, political foresight, and utter unscrupulousness, the Gods made her to match the men of her time."[***]

*(Memnon, translated by C. Muller. In *Fragmentum Historicum Graecorum III,* 530. *Hellenistic Queens.* Chicago: Ares Press, 1932.)

**Pliny, *Natural History,* LCL 1962, X. 36

***Macurdy, 1932, 129

Cleopatra VII

Cleopatra VII, the last of the great Hellenistic queens, was mistress to two of the greatest Romans of her time and was an active queen from the beginning of her reign. Early on she set her sights on establishing and maintaining good terms with Rome. She first met Caesar when she was 19 and he was 52 and she had just returned from exile with a mercenary army, intent on regaining her crown. Caesar insisted that she marry her younger brother, and then proceeded to take her as his mistress. During their liaison, Cleopatra bore Caesar two sons. In 46 B.C.E. she joined Caesar in Rome. Cleopatra was politically astute enough to recognize that her aspirations to retain the throne of Egypt required that she have the backing of Caesar.

After Caesar's death Cleopatra waited to see who would emerge as his successor and correctly surmised that it would be the Roman general Marc Antony. Cleopatra pursued Marc Antony who succumbed to her charm. When their relationship was favored with children, Antony and Cleopatra declared themselves Emperor and Empress of the East and their children were to be the heirs of their glory. When Octavian and Roman legions defeated Antony and the Egyptian armies in 30 C.E., Antony took his life; Cleopatra waited. When it became evident that Octavian would demand that she process through Rome as a vanquished and defeated queen of Egypt, Cleopatra elected to end her life. Cleopatra VII was queen of Egypt from 51 B.C.E. to 30 B.C.E.. She manipulated political maneuvers not so much with armies as with the charm and ingenuity of her own personality. Because of Cleopatra's history with Julius Caesar and with Marc Antony, most of what is written about her by contemporaries from Rome, is quite negatively disposed toward her. The following selection is an exception and is included for that reason and also because it paints such an intriguing portrait of this Hellenistic queen.

A SYMPATHETIC PORTRAIT OF CLEOPATRA VII[*]

> For her beauty, as we are told, was in itself not altogether incomparable, nor such as to strike those who saw her; but converse with her had an irresistible charm, and her presence, combined with the persuasiveness of her discourse and the character which was somehow diffused about her behaviour towards others, had something stimulating about it. There was sweetness also in the tones of her voice; and her tongue, like an instrument of many strings, she could readily turn to whatever language she pleased, so that in her interviews with Barbarians she very seldom had need of an interpreter, but made her replies to most of them herself and unassisted, whether they were Ethiopians, Troglodytes, Hebrews, Arabians, Syrians, Medes or Parthians. Nay, it is said that she knew the speech of many other peoples also, although the kings of Egypt before her had not even made an effort to learn the native language, and some actually gave up their Macedonian dialect.

We cannot know with certainty how, and to what extent women outside the aristocracy were influenced by living in societies in which women were acknowledged as unmistakably powerful and viable in leadership. Because education was a common factor among the women cited and/or quoted in this chapter an examination of what constituted Greek education (*paideia*) seems in order.

---

*Plutarch, *Life of Antony,* B.Perrin, trans. LCL, 1919. Vol.IX, XXVI.2 to end of XXVI.

EDUCATION

In "Ancient Education in the time of the Early Roman Empire" John T. Townsend criticizes a tendency of classical scholars to discuss education in the ancient world in terms of Classical Athens and Rome without a thorough discussion of Hellenistic education. Pedagogical and curricular paradigms integral to Hellenistic education were integral as well to education throughout the Imperial period and continued to the end of Byzantine history (Townsend, 1984). Henri Marrou's classic study, *A History of Education in Antiquity* (1956), points to the age of Hellenism as the age of *paideia,* and argues that Hellenistic education provided a unifying concept of culture.

The following general overview indicates that Greek education proceeded according to three stages: Primary, Secondary, and Advanced. Students began schooling at about seven years of age, completed secondary school in their mid to late teens, and those few who received advanced training, called *ephebetes,* usually completed it within two years' time (18–20 years old). In some areas schools (*gymnasia*) were supported by endowed foundations, commonly, however, they were privately funded; the practice of hiring tutors in the home continued. (Townsend, 1984, 155–156)

Physical education at the *gymnasium* was presided over by the *gymnisarch* and included exercises and competitions in running, jumping, discus throwing, javelin throwing, wrestling, and boxing. This training continued throughout each stage in the educational program. Curriculum for the *didaskaleion* (reading school) at the Primary level consisted of reading and writing, some mathematics, music, and sometimes painting.

Education at the secondary level was presided over by the *grammatikos* and consisted predominately in study of the classics (Homer, Euripides, Menander, Demosthenes, Plato, Sophocles, and others). Grammar, rhetoric, music, and geometry traditionally constituted the *encyclios paideia* or liberal arts curriculum at the secondary level. (Townsend, 1984, 156–157)

Advanced education could take various forms. Most common perhaps was the *ephebeia,* which was the original locus for military training but which by the second century B.C.E. served essentially as a "finishing school" for young men. Here for approximately two years students of the aristocracy attended lectures in philosophy and classics, devoted considerable attention to physical education, and emerged as "truly Greek in culture and outlook." Other students engaged in advanced studies in specific disciplines such as rhetoric, philosophy, medicine, and law.

Education for Women

Amid transitions in culture, women encountered challenges, opportunities and developed self-understandings that differed considerably from former patterns of socialization. Among changes significant to this conversation were the opportunities for education at primary and secondary levels which were made available to young girls. Although it is known that females were not educated as extensively as males, substantial textual evidence and inscriptions for women in the professions indicate that for at least some women advanced education was also a reality.

From the fourth century B.C.E., evidence for "widespread literacy among women" became apparent. Although there were some "girls' schools," boys and girls generally studied together, and with few exceptions, the curriculum for male and female students was the same. Marrou mentions a flourishing system of secondary education for girls in a number of cities in the Aegean and Asia Minor and notes sources which indicate that curriculum for girls included physical education, sometimes on the same sports-ground with boys.

WOMEN OUTSIDE THE ARISTOCRACY

Female Philosophers

Within various professions in the Greco-Roman world little evidence exists for educated female rhetoricians. The historical record consistently indicates a number of female philosophers who are attached to one or the other of the principal philosophical movements. Although we have little information about the lives of most of these female philosophers, women are discovered not only among Pythagoreans and Neo-Pythagoreans, but also as disciples of individual sages at the Platonic Academies and in the Epicurean garden.

Hipparchia the Cynic[*]

Hipparchia fell in love with both Crates' discourses and his way of life. Hipparchia paid no attention to any of her suitors, their money, their high birth or their good looks. To her Crates was everything. And in fact she told her parents that she would kill herself, if they didn't let her follow him. Her parents begged Crates to dissuade her. He did everything true but finally when he couldn't persuade her, he stood up and took off his clothes in front of her and said: "This is your bridegroom; these are his possessions, plan accordingly!" He didn't think she would be able to unless she could share in the same pursuits. But the girl chose him. She adopted the same dress and went about with him; she made love to him in public; she went to dinner parties with him. Once, when she went to a dinner party at Lysimachus' house, she put down Theodorus, called the Atheist, by using the following trick of logic, if an action could not be called wrong when done by Theodorus it could not be called wrong when done by Hipparchia. Therefore, if Theodorus does nothing wrong when he hits himself, Hipparchia does nothing wrong if she hits Theodorus. He had no defence against her logic, and started to pull off her cloak. But Hipparchia did not get upset or excited as other women would. Then when he said to her: "Here I am, Agave, who left behind my shuttle beside my loom "Indeed it is I," said Hipparchia; "Theodorus—you don't think that I have arranged my life so badly, do you, if I have used the time I would have wasted on weaving for my education?" These and many other stories are told about the woman philosopher.

Female Pythagoreans

The *apothgems* (terse sayings) of Theano and the writings of Aesara of Lucania, Theano II, Phintys, and Perictione I all suggest the advantages to a woman of being a philosopher. A woman who understands and can appreciate the ways in which her actions satisfy the principle of *harmonia* is better able to act virtuously. The suggestion of both Phintys and Perictione I is that when women live in a society that severely limits the ways in which women can fulfill this principle, there is a special need for women to be philosophers.

*Diogenes Laertius, LCL, 1925, 6.96–98.

On Human Nature[*]

Human nature seems to me to provide a standard of law and justice both for the home and for the city. By following the tracks within . . . whoever seeks will make a discovery: law is in [that person] and justice, which is the orderly arrangement of the soul. . . . it is organized in accordance with triple functions: that which effects judgment and thoughtful-ness is [the mind], that which effects strength and ability is [high spirit], and that which effects love and kindliness is desire. . . .

By virtue of these things the best life for man seems to me to be whenever the pleasant should be mixed with the earnest, and pleasure with virtue. Mind is able to fit these things to itself, becoming lovely through systematic education and virtue.

Late Pythagoreans

M.E. Waithe follows Prudence Allen in identifying the author of *On the Harmony of Women* as Perictione I, the mother of Plato, and refers to the author of *On Wisdom* as Perictione II. Perictione I seems to encourage philosophizing by women. She encourages women to exercise wisdom and self-control as a means to embodying justice and courage. The *telos*, or goal is to achieve happiness and harmony for herself and her family.

Perictione I: On the Harmony of Women[**]

One must deem the harmonious woman to be full of wisdom and self-control; a soul must be exceedingly conscious of goodness to be just and courageous and wise, embellished with self-sufficiency and hating empty opinion. Worthwhile things come to a woman from these—for herself, her husband, her children and household, perhaps even for a city—if, at any rate, such a woman should govern cities and tribes, as we see in the case of a royal city. . . .

But let her not think that nobility of birth, and wealth, and coming from a great city altogether are necessities, nor the good opinion and friendship of eminent and kingly men. If these should be the case, it does not hurt. But, if not, wishing does not make them so. Even if these should be allotted to her, let her soul not pursue the grand and wonderful. Let her walk also apart from them. They harm more than they help, dragging one into misfortune. Treachery and envy and malice abide with them; such a woman would not be serene.

Perictione I shows no interest in an ideal theory, or in an examination of what society ought to be like. Her ethic is grounded in pragmatism. Given that society is the way it is, and given that women's roles are severely limited, how might a woman satisfy the normative principle of *harmonia*?

This wonderful letter from Theano II to her friend Rhodope permits rare insight into the intimate sharing from one intellectual to another. It is not until several centuries later that we begin to find any substantial number of such letters among female intellectuals.

---

[*]Aesara, "On Human Nature," *AHWP*, 1987, Vol. 1 20–21.

[**]Perictione I, "On the Harmony of Women," *AHWP*, 1987 Vol. I, 38.

LETTER FROM THEANO II TO RHODOPE[*]

Are You dispirited? I myself am dispirited. Are you distressed because I have not yet sent you Plato's book, the one entitled "Ideas on Parmenides"? But I myself am grieved to the greatest extent, because no one has yet met with me to discuss Kleon. I will not send you the book until someone arrives to clarify matters concerning this man. So exceedingly do I love the soul of the man - on the grounds that it is the soul of a philosopher, of one zealous to do good, of one who fears the gods beneath the earth? And do not think the story is otherwise than it has been told.

For I am half mortal, and cannot bear to look directly on the star that makes day manifest [the sun].

The selection that follows is Perictione II's brilliant treatise on Wisdom. Note that her cosmology is not shaped by a Platonic dualistic model, but is rather shaped by a remarkable inclusivity that honors the natural world. This is a feature that is not uncommon among female theologians.

PERICTIONE II: SOPHIAS (WISDOM)[**]

Mankind came into being and exists in order to contemplate the principle of the nature of the whole. The function of wisdom is to gain possession of this very thing, and to contemplate the purpose of the things that are. . . . Wisdom is concerned with all that is, just as sight is concerned with all that is visible and hearing with all that is audible.

Therefore, whoever is able to analyze all the kinds of being by reference to one and the same basic principle, and, in turn, from this principle to synthesize and enumerate the different kinds, this person seems to be the wisest and most true and, moreover, to have discovered a noble height from which he will be able to catch sight of god and all the things separated from him [god] in seried rank and order.

Female Physicians

While women have practiced the healing arts for thousands of years, in the Hellenistic period they also were educated as medical professionals. Although for the most part women's training at this point was usually restricted to obstetrics and gynecology, women who studied at the Medical Academy at Cnidos studied the full curriculum. In his *Natural History*, Pliny names several women physicians. Two of the more notable female physicians in the Hellenistic period include Agnodice, a student of Hierophilus and Elephantis (sometimes identified as Philistia) who wrote medical books and was a professor at Rome.

---

[*]Theano II, "Letter to Rhodope," *AHWP,* 1987, 53.

[**]Perictione II, "Sophias," *AHWP,* 1987, Vol. I 55–56.

Female Poets

A notable characteristic of women's poetry in the Hellenistic period is a quality of introspection, and its composition in a loosely structured style. Named women poets in the Hellenistic period include Erinna of Telos, Anyte of Tegra, Nossis, Philaneus, and Hedyle, whose mother and son were also poets. Moero who wrote epic poetry was the daughter of a tragic actor. Selections presented below are representative of the rather vast array of poems that are now available in translation.

Anyte: Epigrams
MILETUS*

> We leave you, Miletus, dear homeland, because we rejected the lawless insolence of impious Gauls. We were three maidens, your citizens. The violent aggression of the Celts brought us to this fate. We did not wait for unholy union or marriage, but we found ourselves a protector in Death.

THERSIS**

> Instead of a bridal bed and holy rites of marriage, your mother set here on your marble tomb a maiden, like you in size and in beauty, Thersis. So now we can speak to you although you are dead.

Nossis Epigrams
TO HERA†

> Sacred Hera—since you often come down from heaven to see Lacinion with its fragrant incense—take this linen cloth. Theophilis, daughter of Cleocha, and her noble daughter Nossis, wove it for you.

TO THAUMARETE††

> This picture captures Thaumarete's form—how well he painted her pride and her beauty, her gentle eyes. If your little watch-dog saw you, she would wag her tail, and think that she saw the mistress of her house.

Musicians and Painters

References in classical sources for female musicians and painters attest not only to their education but also to tensions inherent in acceptance of these women as established professionals in their own right. Iaia of Cyzicus, probably the most respected artist of the Hellenistic period, known especially for her portraits of women, is said by Pliny to have received higher fees than the two most popular male painters.

---

*Miletus, WLGR, 1992, 6
**Thersis, WLGR, 1992, 6–7
†To Hera, WLGR, 1992. 7
††To Thaumarete, WLGR, 1992, 9

WOMEN PAINTERS[*]

There have also been women artists—Timarete the daughter of Micon who painted the extremely archaic panel picture of Artemis at Ephesus; Irene daughter and pupil of the painter Cratinus who did the Maiden at Eleusis, a Calypso, an Old Man and Theodorus the Juggler, and painted also Alcisthenes the Dancer; Aristarete the daughter and pupil of Nearchus, who painted an Asclepius. When Marcus Varro was a young man, Iaia of Cyzicus, who never married, painted pictures with the brush at Rome (and also drew with the *cestrum* or graver on ivory), chiefly portraits of women, as well as a large picture on wood of an Old Woman at Naples, and also a portrait of herself, done with a looking-glass. No one else had a quicker hand in painting, while her artistic skill was such that in the prices she obtained she far out-did the most celebrated portrait painters of the same period, Sopolis and Dionysius, whose pictures fill the galleries. A certain Olympias also painted; the only fact recorded about her is that Autobulus was her pupil.

The next excerpt attests to the successful career of Polygnota, a female harpist in Hellenistic Greece. Here she is honored for her musical expertise and her dedication.

POLYGNOTA THE HARPIST[**]

. . . The city of Delphi has decreed: whereas Polygnota, daughter of Socrates, a Theban harpist having come to Delphi, at the appointed time of the Pythian games, which could not be held on account of the present war, began on that very day and gave a day's time and performed at the request of the archons and the citizens for three days, and won the highest degree of respect, deserving the praise of Apollo and of the Theban people and of our city—she is awarded a crown and 500 drachmas. With good fortune.

Voted: to commend Polygnota, daughter of Socrates, the Theban, for her piety and reverence towards the god and for her dedication to her profession; to bestow on her and on her descendants the guest-friendship of the city, the right to consult the oracle, the privileges of being heard first, of safety, of exemption from taxes, and of front seating at the games held by the city, the right of owning land and a house and all the other honours ordinarily awarded to other benefactors of the city; to invite her to the town hall to the public hearth, and provide her with a victim to sacrifice to Apollo. To the god. With good fortune.

Occupations

Women who worked in the public sphere during the Hellenistic period were entrepreneurs, land owners, shopkeepers, dyers, barkeepers, serving maids, fishmongers, hairdressers, weavers, seamstresses, bakers, alemakers . . . the list goes on at length. The abbreviated selection for this section is from the second century B.C.E. in the Egyptian Fayum. Archival documents record Eirene's entrepreneurial transactions.

*Pliny, Natural History, LCL, 1952. XXXV.40 xi.146–xiii 151.
**Pleket 6 WLGR, 1992, 216.

EIRENE, AGRICULTURAL ENTREPRENEUR[*]

Eirene, a Macedonian, daughter of Orphis and wife of Agamemnon, exploited land in the Fayum. Both Eirene and Agamemnon were descended from important families. . . . It seems more natural to assume that—like Apollonia, wife of Dryton—Eirene personally supervised her business. . . .

Eirene's holdings were unusually extensive for a woman. It was also uncommon for a woman to rent crown and gift lands, although she did so. Eirene was also an exception to the rule that most cultivators of royal land were Egyptians, not Greeks. Her high status must have rendered her fearless in dealing with the bureaucracy in charge of state-owned land. However, in the variety of the crops she cultivated, in her management of cash and produce, and in her business relationships with men, her activities were typical of women landholders—though on a larger scale. . . .

Like the other women landholders, . . . she held orchards and vineyards but had a particular affinity for the latter. She did not subcontract for the vineyard, but managed it herself. Her agricultural accounts of 181/180 B.C. are extant. She seems to have been able to sign her own name (*P. Mich.* III 183). Perhaps she kept her own accounts, too. Her accounts give day-by-day entries for the expenses incurred in hiring laborers for the vintage. . . .

RELIGION

Mystery Religions

Mystery religions became a defining characteristic of the Hellenistic world. From the last two centuries B.C.E. to the second century C.E., these "new" religions were a response to felt needs for the familiar that emerged on the tumultuous transitioning demanded by vast migrations, urbanization, and colonization. When the Hellenistic period began, each municipality had firmly established religions of the state, city, or people. But with the vast migrations, people transported their deities to the new, Greek cities. Religions of female and male deities from the East were introduced into the new culture by sailors, seamen, traders, slaves, and merchants. These religions usually kept their rituals and cultic practices intact but when their myths and legends were translated into Greek, Greek ideas and concepts shaped new interpretations. (Adapted from Helmut Koester, *History, Culture and Religion of the Hellenistic Age, Introduction to the New Testament,* Vol. I, Philadelphia: Fortress Press, 1982, 166.)

The following descriptors in Chart 9–1 of mystery religions are paraphrased from Koester (Koester, 1982, 166) and provide an excellent background for discussions of the mystery religions.

Before Christianity became the state religion of the Roman Empire, the two most widespread mystery religions were Mithraism and the Isis tradition that had roots in the Isis mythos from at least 3000 B.C.E. In the Hellenistic period, the Isis tradition first emerged as a component of a "new" religion. Koester suggests that religious syncretism that occurred in the Hellenistic world is not a result of artificial manipulations but that it emerges out of historical situations. It is a response to two opposing historical forces: first, the constraints that arise from inherited traditions, dignified by a long history

> **Chart 9–1   Characteristics of Mystery Religions**
>
> 1. Mystery religions are religions of symbolism in which the mythology, allegory, iconography, relics, liturgies, and sacraments function to provoke in the initiate a sense of regeneration.
> 2. Mystery religions are religions of redemption. They reduce the sense of separation of the person from the deity and provide a sense of forgiveness. They provide a means of purification; formulae for access to the deity; acclamations of confidence and victory and the promise of salvation in this life and the next.
> 3. Mystery religions also provide a system of secret knowledge that fulfills the desire for a knowledge of God and gives a new outlook on the world, the self, the deity, and a sense of security and belonging that is denied to the uninitiated.
> 4. The Mysteries consisted of a sacramental or holy drama in which the privileged observer sees a ritual acting out of the suffering, struggle, and conflict in the life of the deity and Her/His victory over death. An eschatalogical component addresses concerns of life and death, guarantees protection by the deity in this life and the next.
> 5. Membership in a mystery religion was not an accident of birth nor did one inherit membership. One entered a mystery tradition as a matter of individual, personal choice and must be initiated into a mystery religion to receive individual, personal salvation. These mystery religions were also cosmic religions, and functioned as a necessary complement to a personal religion. They reflect the need for order, both within the self as a person and without, that is, in the exterior reality in which we live, move, and have our being.
> 6. Further characteristics include a firm organization in each congregation to which all members are subject, rites of initiation, regular meetings with sacramental rituals (including sacred meals), obligations to adhere to certain moral codes and ascetic practices, mutual support of all members, and obedience to the leader of the community. (Koester, 1982, 198)

and second, the need to enter into discourse with a new culture and its spirit. The artificial creation of a new religion is the attempt to harmonize these opposing forces.

THE HOLY/MYTH

Isis and Osiris

There are myriad versions and incarnations of the central myth about Isis. A brief summary of the story notes four principal characters: the Goddess Isis, her sister Nepthys, her brother Osiris who became the mythical embodiment of its fertile lands which flooded every year and thus were restored to new life, and her brother Seth.

The most popular aspect of their story was appropriated as a fertility myth that was similar to the Demeter/Persephone story and stories about Inanna/Damuzi, Ishtar/Tammuz, Venus/Adonis, Cybele/Attis, and others.

In this tale, Seth is envious of Osiris and seeks to kill him. He succeeds and dismembers Osiris and scatters his body parts into the Nile. Isis and Nepthys come to their brother's rescue. They search the world over, retrieve the body parts of their brother, reassemble him, add a golden phallus to replace the phallus that could not be found. Isis then mates with her brother and brings forth a son, Horus. According to legend Horus (the fifth principal character) was the mythical representation of the living Pharoah.

During the early Ptolemaic period in Egypt a syncretistic version of Apis, the sacred bull, and the soul of the dying Osiris emerged as Oserapis. This new cultic figure was given many Greek features and over time, came to combine features of Egyptian, Greek, and Roman Gods, namely Osiris, Zeus-Jupiter, Hades-Pluto, Asclepius, Helios, and Dionysus.

At the inception of this new religion, Isis was "imported" as the consort of Serapis. Over the next 100 years, however, it is Isis who became the dominant figure and Serapis was interpreted as her consort. And, "If ever any deity of that time was on the way to becoming the central divine figure of a world religion, it was Isis. . . . The syncretistic Isis was the goddess of heaven and mother of the All, who united in her person everything that was significant to religious expectations of the time." (Koester, 1982, 188). The impact of the Isis tradition on the lives of women is explored in Chapter 11, "The Roman Empire."

SELECTED READINGS

Fantham, Elaine, et al. *Women in the Classical World.* Oxford: Oxford University Press, 1994.

Kampen, Natalie. "Hellenistic Artists: Female." *Archaeology Classics* 27 (1975): 9–17.

Pomeroy, Sarah B. "Technikai Kai Musikai: The Education of Women in the Fourth Century and in the Hellenistic Period." *AJAH* 2 (1977): 51–68.

_____. "Macedonian Queens and the Feminization of Greek Culture." Presented at the The George Rude Inaugural Lecture. Concordia University, Montreal, 1980.

Thompson, Dorothy Burr. "More Hellenistic Queens." *AK* 12 (1980): 181–84.

Sources Cited

Macurdy, Grace H. *The Hellenistic Queens: A Study of Woman-Power in Macedonia, Seleucid Syria, and Ptolemaic Egypt.* Chicago: Ares Publishers, 1932.

Tarn, W.W. *Antigonos Gonatos.* Oxford: Oxford University Press, 1913.

Plutarch. "Olympias, Queen of Macedonia, Wife of Philip of Macedonia, Mother of Alexander," translated by B. Perrin. In *Lives,* Alexander. The Parallel Lives, Loeb Classical Library. Cambridge and London: Harvard University Press 1919. vol. II, III, VII, XXXIX, LXXVIII.

——— "On Olympias' Wit," translated by B. Perrin. In *Life of Alexander.* The Parallel Lives, Loeb Classical Library, Cambridge and London: Harvard University Press 1919. vol. III, VII.

——— "On Olympias' Tears," translated by B. Perrin. In *Lives,* Alexander. XXXIX. The Parallel Lives, Loeb Classical Library. Cambridge and London: Harvard University Press, 1919, vol. VII.

Diodorus Siculus. "The Aged Olympias Rides Into Battle," translated by Russel M. Geer. Library of History. Loeb Classical Library, Cambridge and London: Harvard University Press, 1933.

Memnon. "Concerning Arsinoe," translated by C. Muller. In *Fragmentum Historicum Graecorum III,* 530. *Hellenistic Queens.* Chicago: Ares Press, 1932.

Pliny. "Images of Arsinoe II Philadelphus," translated by D.E. Eicholz, 68. Natural History, Loeb Classical Library, Cambridge and London: Harvard University Press 1962. vol. X, Book 36.

——— Translated by D.E. Eicholz. Natural History, Loeb Classical Library, Cambridge and London: Harvard University Press, 1962. vol. X, Book 37.

Plutarch. "A Sympathetic Portrait of Cleopatra VII," translated by B. Perrin. In *Life of Mark Antony.* The Parallel Lives, Loeb Classical Library, Cambridge and London: Harvard University Press, 1919. vol. IX, 25.5–28.1, 29.

Diogenes Laertius. "Hipparchia," translated by R.D. Hicks. Lives of Eminent Philosophers, Cambridge and London: Harvard University Press, Loeb Classical Library, 1925. vol. II, 6.96–98.

Aesara, Pythagorean of Lucania. "On Human Nature." In *Ancient Women Philosophers 600 B.C.-500 A.D.,* edited by Mary Ellen Waithe, *A History of Women Philosophers,* vol. 1. Dordrecht, The Netherlands: Kluwer Academic Publishers, 1987. 20–21.

Perictione I. "On the Harmony of Women." In *Ancient Women Philosophers 600 B.C.-500 A.D.*, edited by Mary Ellen Waithe, *A History of Women Philosophers,* vol. 1. Dordrecht, The Netherlands: Kluwer Academic Publishers, 1987. 38–39.

Theano II. "Text of Letter to Rhodope." In *Ancient Women Philosophers 600 B.C.-500 A.D.*, edited by Mary Ellen Waithe, *A History of Women Philosophers,* vol. 1. Dordrecht, The Netherlands: Kluwer Academic Publishers, 1987. 53.

Perictione II. "Text of Sophias (On Wisdom)." In *Ancient Women Philosophers 600 B.C.-500 A.D.*, edited by Mary Ellen Waithe, *A History of Women Philosophers,* vol. 1. Dordrecht, The Netherlands: Kluwer Academic Publishers, 1987. 55–56.

Anyte. "Thersis." In *Palantine Anthology VII.649.* No. 14, Johns Hopkins, Lefkowitz, Mary R., and Maureen B. Fant, Eds. *Women's Life in Greece and Rome:* A Source Book in Translation, p. 216 ©1992 (Copyright Holder Reprinted with the permission of The Johns Hopkins University Press.

———. "Miletus." In *Palantine Anthology VII.492.* No. 12, Johns Hopkins, Lefkowitz, Mary R., and Maureen B. Fant, Eds. *Women's Life in Greece and Rome.* A Source Book in Translation, p. 216 ©1992 (Copyright Holder Reprinted with the permission of The Johns Hopkins University Press.

"Nossis of Locri, Epigrams: Epigram II." In *Greek Anthology, Hellenistic Epigrams,* edited by A.S.F. Gow and D.L. Page. Cambridge, MA: Harvard University Press, 1968. 7 and 9.

Koester, Helmut. *Introduction to the New Testament, History, Culture and Religion of the Hellenistic Age,* vol. I. Philadelphia: Fortress Press, 1982. 166.

"Polygnota the Harpist." In *Corpus Papyrorum Raineri,* edited by C. Wesseley. Inscription, vol. XIII, 1895, Johns Hopkins, Lefkowitz, Mary R., and Maureen B. Fant, Eds. *Women's Life in Greece and Rome.* A Source Book in Translation, p. 216 ©1992 (Copyright Holder Reprinted with the permission of The Johns Hopkins University Press.

Pomeroy, Sarah B. "Eirene, Agricultural Entrepreneur." In *Women in Hellenistic Egypt,* New York: Schoken Books, 1984. 158–59.

Chapter 10

Hellenistic Judaism

The Jewish texts selected for the present chapter were written within the chronological periods addressed in the chapters on women in the Hellenistic, Roman, and Early Christian periods (Chapter 9, "The Hellenistic World," Chapter 11, "The Roman Empire," and Chapter 12 "Christian Origins"). Selections in this chapter are significant in the development of Western civilization to the extent that they represent world views that were a part of Jewish culture throughout the Hellenistic period. The canon of Classical literature has privileged texts from Greece and Rome as the foundation of Western civilization and has neglected to acknowledge and reference the myriad texts that were generated in Early Judaism (200 B.C.E.–200 C.E.). Among these texts exists a literature that is especially rich in representations of Jewish women in various expressions of social, economic, political, and religious culture. These representations of women are significant, not only for the history of women in Early Judaism, but also because they help to set the stage for women in Christian origins.

Judaism is one of the oldest living religions on the earth. It has withstood thousands and thousands of years of social, cultural, and historical change. A look at the map illustrates clearly, however, the vulnerability of Israel's position, situated as it was between the Seleucid Dynasty in Syria and the Ptolemaic Dynasty in Egypt during the Hellenistic period. This geographic coincidence becomes a significant factor in determining a wide variety of religious expression in Judaism, especially during the last two centuries before the common era (B.C.E.) and the first two centuries of the common era (C.E.). There were, during these four centuries in particular, numerous responses to the potential influences of *paideia* (Greek education) and Greek culture on Jewish education, Jewish culture, and Jewish self-understanding. All of the elements of Hellenistic culture referenced in Chapter 9 influenced Early Judaism in a variety of ways. Early Judaism wrestled with urbanization, paideia, mystery religions, individualism, cosmopolitanism, voluntary associations, and other characteristics of Hellenistic culture that impacted the known world during the period from approximately the second century B.C.E., to the second century C.E. In addition, Israel was particularly vulnerable, not only because of the tensions that arose between Hellenistic culture and Jewish religious identity, but also because, situated geographically as it was exactly between the Seleucids in Syria and the Ptolemies in Egypt, Israel was frequently a political and economic pawn as the two dynasties strategized and battled for political ascendancy. Nevertheless Judaism emerged from this period intact and firmly grounded in the foundations of the Rabbinic Judaism we know today.

SOCIAL ORGANIZATION

When the Hellenistic period began in 323 B.C.E., Israel had been under the rule of the Persian govern-ment for at least a century. As the Seleucids and the Ptolemies established their governments, they in turn vied for rule of Israel. Israel had been under foreign domination since the Babylonians destroyed the Temple in Jerusalem in 586 B.C.E. and took all influential and wealthy Jews into exile in Babylon. The Judean monarchy ended during the exile. Upon return from exile, wealthy, and not so wealthy, Is-raelites were successfully engaged in commerce and trade with Syria and Egypt as well as other Hel-lenistic societies. Many Israelites spoke Greek and in 175 B.C.E. a Greek *gymnasium* (academy of learning) was established in Jerusalem where a Greek (and Jewish) curriculum was administered to the male children of Israelites who enrolled their sons. Many aspects of Hellenistic culture found their way into Jewish culture in Israel.

A number of religious sectarian movements emerged in Judaism during this period as a response to Hellenistic culture, including *Hasidim* (holy men), who traveled throughout Israel teaching with deep concern to preserve Judaism in the face of an encroaching Hellenistic culture. They sought to convince all Jews of the importance of learning, knowing, teaching, and following the *Torah* (Law).

Essenes took exception to many consequences of Hellenization and withdrew from the main-stream of society. Evidence suggests that they formed communities where they lived together, in cities and towns of Palestine and Syria, as well as in the desert community of Qumran on the banks of the Dead Sea. They formed communities of single individuals and families as they awaited expectantly two *Messiahs* (Savior figures), a priest and a king.

Essenes lived their lives based on the *Manual of Discipline* (and many other documents discovered among what are now known as the Dead Sea Scrolls). Texts generated among the Essenes included bibli-cal, legal, and ritual texts and a rule of life for members of the communities. *Pharisees* followed the writ-ten and *Oral Torah* and were less apocalyptic (interested in the end of the age and the advent of the Messiah) than the *Essenes*. They believed in angels and the resurrection of the dead. Pharisees, who are the historic forebears of contemporary Judaism, were committed to keeping the 613 *mitzvot* (obligations) that are set out in the *Oral Torah* (verbally transmitted commentaries and interpretations of the Law).

From the period of the post-exilic return to Israel ca. 533 B.C.E., the *Sadducees* had constituted the political party of power. The Sadducees perceived the economic and political advantages to be derived from going along with the wishes of the particular government (Seleucid or Ptolemaic) to which Israel was subject. Sadducees were aristocratic Jews associated with the Jerusalem Temple. Sadducees, who were well established politically and economically, cooperated with policies and programs of their captors. They rejected the Oral Torah, did not await a Messiah, and did not believe in the resurrection of the dead.

Jewish *Gnostics* were Jewish intellectuals who sought secret, sacred *gnosis* (knowledge) that would answer questions such as, Where do we come from? Why are we here? And, how do we find our way back? They anticipated a sacred messenger who would impart this knowledge. Jewish *Hekhalot* mystics entered an altered state of consciousness and sought prophetic visions at the throne of God. Wisdom scholars and sages spoke and wrote of the Divine *Sophia*, the Wisdom of God in female form.

Theraputae in Egypt, like Essenes in Palestine, withdrew from society to pursue a spiritual life. They were male and female Jewish ascetics who lived together in monastic-type communities. Their energies were devoted to composing hymns, interpreting scriptures, and living a life of prayer and fast-ing. The reading selections in this chapter reflect this very rich period in the history of Judaism and provide insights into women's experience during this time.

A major political shift occurred in Israel in 168 B.C.E. when a man named Judas Maccabeus and his sons decided to strike out against the military force of the Seleucid emperor, Antiochus IV. This im-petuous ruler had imposed severe sanctions and persecutions against Jews for refusing to worship his statue in the Jerusalem Temple. Antiochus IV polluted the Temple by placing swine in the Temple precincts. He forbade the keeping of the Sabbath, forbade the circumcision of male children, and made a variety of humiliating restrictions that outraged pious Jews. This uprising, called the *Maccabean Revolt*, used guerilla forces to eventually defeat the Seleucids. A new Jewish dynasty, called the Hasmonean Dynasty, was established by the sons of Judas Maccabeus in 135 B.C.E. following the defeat of the Seleucids, and the cleansing and rededication of the Temple in 142 B.C.E. (The dedication event marks the origin of the Jewish feast of Chanukah.) John Hyrcanus was the first Hasmonean king in the revived monarchy that survived until 63 B.C.E.

Israel was, during this period, once again an independent monarchy. The first selection representative of women in the aristocracy depicts Salome Alexandra who ruled as queen of Israel from 76-67 B.C.E.

WOMEN IN THE ARISTOCRACY

Salome Alexandra

Among the aristocratic Jewish women presented in this section, the Hasmonean queen, Salome Alexandra, is the most prominent. Female descendants of Salome Alexandra were part of the drama of the Herodian dynasty during the Roman occupation of Israel.

There was among these Jewish queens and wives of princes in the Hellenistic period a heritage of Alexandras, Berenices, and Miriamnes who are counterparts to the Eurydices, Cleopatras, and Arsinoes among Ptolemaic and Macedonian queens. Talmudic sources from the fifth and seventh centuries C.E. look back upon the time of Salome Alexandra as one of great prosperity in Israel. It is told that in the days of Simeon ben Shetah (thought to be her brother) and Salome Alexandra rain fell on the Sabbath nights until wheat grew to the size of kidneys, barley to that of olive berries, and lentils to that of gold denarii. Some scholars suggest that if it were not for the abundant wealth accumulated under Salome Alexandra and her late husband, Israel would not have been able to endure the taxes and exploitation by the Romans from the time of Pompey's conquest.

While Salome Alexandra did continue diplomatic relations following some of the policies of her deceased husband, under her leadership the spiritual direction of the country was completely reversed. In opposition to the Sadducees who had constituted her husband's principal support, Salome Alexandra supported and empowered the Pharisees and their conventions. Whether or not the great Pharisaic leader Simeon ben Shetah was in fact Salome Alexandra's brother, theirs was a powerful alliance. She was committed to him and to the reforms which he instituted. Interestingly, Simeon ben Shetah is known not only for educational reforms introduced during Salome Alexandra's reign but also for reforms that improved the position of Jewish women.

SALOME ALEXANDRA PORTRAYED BY JOSEPHUS[*]

> [King Alexander] had left his throne to his wife Alexandra, confident that the Jews would most readily submit to her, since by her freedom from any trace of his brutality and her constant opposition to his excesses she had gained the good-will of

[*]Excerpts from Josephus, *Antiquities*, translated by L. H. Feldman. Loeb Classical Library, Cambridge, MA: Harvard University Press, 1969. XV 43–49.

the people. And he was right in his expectations; woman though she was, she established her authority by her reputation for piety. She was most particular in her observance of the national customs, and offenders against the Holy Law she turned out of office. Of the two sons she had borne Alexander she appointed the elder, Hyrcanus, high priest, in view of his age and his natural disinclination to interfere with state affairs; the younger, Aristobulus, who was an impulsive character, she kept out of the public eye.

Alongside her was the growing power of the Pharisees, a Jewish sect that appeared more pious than the rest and stricter in the interpretation of the Law. Alexandra, being devoted to religion, paid too great heed to them and they, availing themselves more and more of the simplicity of the woman, ended by becoming the effective rulers of the state, ... short, the privileges of royal authority were theirs, the expenses and vexations Alexandra's. She was very shrewd, however, in making major decisions, and by regular recruiting doubled the size of her army, collecting also a large mercenary force, so that beside making her own country strong she inspired a healthy respect in foreign potentates. But while she ruled others, the Pharisees ruled her. Thus Diogenes, an eminent man who had been a friend of Alexander, was put to death by them on the charge of having abetted the king in his crucifixion of eight hundred citizens. Then they pressed Alexandra to execute the rest of those who had incited Alexander against them: her superstitious nature made her give way, and they killed whom they would. The most prominent of the threatened citizens sought the aid of Aristobulus, and he persuaded his mother to spare them in view of their station, expelling them from the City if not sure of their innocence. Thus granted impunity, they scattered over the country.

Alexandra dispatched an army to Damascus on the ground that Ptolemy was regularly meddling there; but the army returned with no particular success to its credit. However, while Tigranes the Armenian king was encamped before Ptolemais besieging Cleopatra, she won him over by bargaining and bribery. But he had to withdraw in hot haste to deal with troubles at home, Lucullus having invaded Armenia. Meanwhile Alexandra sickened; the younger son Aristobulus seized his chance, and with his numerous servants—all devoted to him because of his impulsive character—got all the strongholds into his power, and with the money found there raised a force of mercenaries and proclaimed himself king. This so upset Hyrcanus that his mother felt very sorry for him, and locked up the wife and children of Aristobulus in Antonia. This was a fortress adjoining the Temple on the north side; as stated already, it was first called Baris and later renamed when Antony was supreme, just as the cities of Sebaste and Agrippias were named after Sebastos (Augustus) and Agrippa. But before Alexandra could proceed against Aristobulus for the unseating of his brother, she died, after ruling the country for nine years.

Herodian Queens: Alexandra, Berenice, Miriamne

In early Roman Palestine, Alexandra, who was the granddaughter of Salome Alexandra, was the wife of Alexander. Alexander, the son of Aristobulus, was one of the *dramatis personae* in the intrigues at Herod's court. Alexandra's daughter Miriamne was Herod's second wife and she fancied her son

Aristobulus as a legitimate contender for the throne. Josephus's report of Alexandra's correspondence with Cleopatra VII and their consequent plan to protect Aristobulus with temporary exile in Egypt attests to her literate participation in diplomatic relations.

EDUCATION

Influence of Greek Education in Palestine

John Townsend (1971, 154–57) has suggested that in Palestine and the Jewish diaspora, methods of teaching, organizational structure, and the format for presenting curriculum that became normative for Jewish education had a strong Hellenistic influence. The Greek orientation of some aspects of the curriculum directly influenced dissemination of Greek culture among the Jews. This enhanced the abilities of certain Jews to participate in a cosmopolitan environment.

The advent of formal elementary schools for Jewish children meant that a *bet sopher* or primary school was presided over by a *sopher* or scribe. Curricula included the study of scripture and instruction in Jewish liturgies. By the time of the rabbis, Jewish students moved from a *bet sopher* to a *bet midrash* or secondary school for study of the Oral Torah. This practice had its genesis in the Hellenistic period. During this time (ca. 180 B.C.E.) Sirach, a teacher in the Wisdom tradition in Israel had founded an *oikia paideia* (literally, house of education) (Sirach 51:23). This school functioned as a secondary school in pre-Maccabean Jerusalem.

Among the earliest evidence for a formal school for Jewish children in Palestine is Du Pont Sommer's reference to the "children's class" among the Essene community at Qumran (1QSA 1.8), in the second half of the first century B.C.E. (DuPont Sommer 1962.1QSA 1.4–12). Considering the immense number of texts discovered at Qumran it is reasonable to assume that "Secondary" and "Advanced" training among the community who generated this large body of writings consisted in the knowledge of and meditation upon a variety of types of texts.

Some scholars find evidence to suggest that within the immense Jewish community in Alexandria (Egypt) the education of Philo (author of several texts in this volume) the Jewish philosopher, mystic, and theologian, (20 B.C.E. to 50 C.E.), included elements of *Hellenistic encyclios paideia* (Conley 1975, 24). Philo was, of course, also required to have knowledge of the Law and the Prophets of Israel. During the Hellenistic period anyone who belonged to the people of God, even the proselyte, was invited to study Wisdom (Sophia), and provided that person had the application and the aptitude, the person had the possibility to become a great teacher of the Law.

Jewish Women's Education in the Hellenistic Period

In recent years there has been greater recognition among scholars that Jewish women attained some prominence in public life during the Hasmonean Dynasty. Significant studies by H. I. Marrou and S.B. Pomeroy, (Marrou 1956, 95–101; Pomeroy 1984; *AJAH* 1977, 51–68) attest to the education of female children and adults in Greece, Rome, and Hellenistic Egypt. The education of Jewish females in Israel's Second Temple period has only in recent times received attention in scholarly discourse. It should, however, be apparent that in the context of the emphasis on education in Hellenistic culture in general, and the longstanding interest in the education of children in Judaism in particular, some Jewish women in the Second Temple period were educated. Despite the number of texts in *Mishnaic* tractates that represent ambivalence and resistance to the prospect of educated Jewish women, in other texts where women's education is implied, women have an elevated status and access to culture. Within the chronological margins of the Late Second Temple period (142 B.C.E.-70 C.E.) we are most likely to find educated Jewish women among female members of the aristocracy, female Essenes, female Theraputae, and female leaders of the synagogues. Selections of readings that follow also include references in *Mishnaic* texts (the written version of the Oral Torah) that relate to educated females.

This selection from the Dead Sea Scrolls refers to the educational responsibilities of young male and female Essenes from the time they are in the children's class (v.8). While the focus is on the young male, the young woman would have also been in the children's class, and by age 20 she was expected to be fully skilled in the knowledge of Good and Evil as interpreted by the writings of the Essene community, and schooled in the law of the community. A wife was responsible to know the law, and to be so committed to the law as a member of the community that she must be prepared to invoke the Ordinances of the Law against her husband, if necessary. This invocation would take place in the public forum that included female members of the community.

THE RULE ANNEXE, 1QSA*

> On their arrival, they shall gather them all together, including the children and the women, and shall read into [their ears] all the precepts of the Covenant and shall instruct them in all their ordinances lest they stray in [their] st[raying], And this is the rule for all the hosts of the Congregation, concerning every native in Israel. From [his] you[th] he shall be instructed in the Book of Meditation and shall be taught the precepts of the Covenant in accordance with his age, and I [shall receive] his education in their ordinances for ten years from the time of entry into the children's class. Then at the age of twenty (he shall be subject) [to] the census: he shall enter into the lot in the midst of his clan (to live) in community in the holy Congregation. And he shall not [approach] a woman to know her sexually unless he is twenty years old when [she] I knows [good] and evil; and this being so, she shall be admitted to invoke the ordinances of the Law against him, and to take her place at the hearing of the ordinances and among the crowd which is there.

The *Mishnah* is the first written version of the Oral Law of the Torah. It is followed in the fifth century C.E. by the Jerusalem *Talmud* and then in the seventh century C.E. by the Babylonian *Talmud*. The Talmuds are *commentaries* on the texts that comprise the Mishnah. Although the *Mishnah* was not completed until the second century of the Common Era, its teachings are believed to reflect practices from earlier times that would include the Late Second Temple Judaism that is the subject of this chapter. *Tractates* (formal groupings of texts such as those found in the Dead Sea Scrolls and the *Mishnah*) and their later interpretation by Rabbinic scholars in the Talmud reflect the experience of some Jewish women. Interestingly however, they are not representative of all Jewish women's experience. Mishnaic Tractates and later Talmudic discussions which point back to the Hellenistic Age include both implicit and explicit references to the education of women and both affirm and deny the wisdom of this practice.

*From *The Rule Annexe*, translated by A. DuPont Sommer. In *The Essene Writings From Qumran*, Cleveland and New York: The World Publishing Company, 1962. 1QSA 1.4–12.

Mishnaic Tractates

In the Tractate entitled *Sotah* (3.4), Ben Azzai states that a man is under obligation to instruct his daughter in Torah. Another text that attests to a female Pharisee (*Sotah* 21b-22a) associates her with destruction, "a foolish pietist, a cunning rogue, a female Pharisee and the plagues of the Pharisees bring destruction upon the world." The rabbis attest to women's knowledge of the Law in a Mishnaic text from Sanhedrin 94b that reads

> *from Dan to Beersheba . . . from Gabbath to Antipris no boy or girl or man or woman was found who was not thoroughly versed in the laws of cleanliness and uncleanliness . . .*

That women were capable and qualified to read from Torah is affirmed in Mishnaic tractate *Magilla* 2.4. Women's presence at synagogue on weekdays as well as Sabbath and festivals is attested in tractate Abodah Zarah 33-38b. Some scholars of Hellenistic Judaism also point to the presence of women in synagogues recounted in the Christian testament as for example in the Acts of the Apostles and in the Pauline Epistles. (*The Mishnah* 1988)

LEGAL STATUS OF WOMEN

Mishnaic Tractates Concerning Marriage and Inheritance

In laws of the Greco-Roman world, in almost all cases, women are understood not as individuals but in the context of their relationship to a male (e.g. father, husband, brother, brother-in-law, cousin). Within this context, and in addition to cultural obligations placed upon them, Hellenistic Jewish women were guaranteed certain rights. The Mishnaic tractates were written from the first to second centuries C.E. thus extending beyond the time period covered in this chapter. Nevertheless, some of these often perplexing texts, from The Third Division of the Mishnah on Women (*Ketubot*), lists interesting texts relating to marriage and inheritance that were likely in effect in the Hellenistic period.

KETUBOT[*]

KETUBOT 4:12 VI

A. [if he did not write for her] "you will dwell in my house and derive support from my property as long as you are a widow in my house."
B. His estate is nonetheless liable to support his widow.

KETUBOT I 1:1

D. A widow's heirs who inherit her marriage contract are liable to bury her.

The following passages related to Marriage and Inheritance are also recorded in a section of the Mishnah titled Ketubot.

The Mishnah. Edited and translated by Jacob Neusner, New Haven, CT: Yale University Press, 1988. *Ketubot* 4:12 VI; I 1:1; 4:4; 5:5; 12:3; 3:4.

KETUBOT 4:4

A.   The father retains control of his daughter [younger than twelve and a half] and affecting any of the tokens of betrothal: money, document, or sexual intercourse.

B.   And he retains control of what she finds, of the fruit of her labor, and of abrogating her vows.

C.   And he receives her writ of divorce [from a betrothal].

D.   But he does not dispose of the return [on property received by the girl from her mother] during her lifetime.

E.   [When] she is married, the husband exceeds the father, for he disposes of the return [on property received by the girl from her mother] during her lifetime.

F.   But he is liable to maintain her, and to ransom her, and to bury her.

G.   R[abbi] Judah says, "Even the poorest man in Israel should not hire fewer than two flutes and one professional wailing woman."

KETUBOT 5:5

A.   These are the kinds of labor which a woman performs for her husband,

B.   she (1) grinds flour, (2) bakes bread, (3) does laundry, (4) prepares meals, (5) feeds her child, (6) makes the beds, (7) works in wool.

C.   [If] she brought with her a single slave girl, she does not (1) grind, (2) bake bread, or (3) do laundry.

D.   [If she brought] two, she does not (4) prepare meals and does not (5) feed her child.

E.   [If she brought] three, she does not (6) make the bed for him and does not (7) work in wool.

F.   If she brought four, she sits on a throne.

G.   R[abbi] Eliezer says, "Even if she brought him a hundred slave girls, he forces her to work in wool,"

H.   "for idleness leads to unchastity."

I.   R[abbi] Simeon b. Gamaliel says, "Also: He who prohibits his wife by a vow from performing any labor puts her away and pays off her marriage contract.

J.   "For idleness leads to boredom."

KETUBOT 12:3

A.   A widow who said, "I don't want to move from my husband's house,"

B.   the heirs cannot say to her, "Go to your father's house and we'll take care of you [there]."

C.   But they provide for her in her husband's house,

D.   giving her a dwelling in accord with her station in life.

E.   [If] she said, "I don't want to move from my father's house,"

F.   the heirs can say to her, "If you are with us, you will have support. But you are not with us, you will not have support."

G.   If she claimed that it is because she is a girl and they are boys, they do provide for her while she is in her father's house.

KETUBOT 3:4

A.   The one who seduces a girl pays on three counts, and the one who rapes a girl pays on four:

B.   the one who seduces a girl pays for (1) the shame, (2) the damage, and (3) a fine,

C.   and the one who rapes a girl adds to these,

D.   for he in addition pays for (4) the pain [which he has inflicted].

RELIGION

The Holy

Men and women in the present day recognize that even religions in which the principal deity is male, and in which the social organization of the religion is a patriarchal hierarchy, the Female Principle of the Divine is expressed and honored. Just as the first chapter in the Book of Genesis in the Hebrew Bible states, "and God created humankind in God's own image, male and female God created them," both the Male and the Female Principle of the Divine find expression within the sacred texts. For both Judaism and Christianity the Wisdom of God has been represented in the Female Principle. This practice began in Judaism in the period following Israel's exile in Babylon (late sixth to early fifth centuries B.C.E.) in the Book of Proverbs and continued in the Hellenistic period and beyond. The *Shekhinah Matronit* is another female representation that flourished in Jewish mystical literature in the Middle Ages. Wisdom (*Sophia*) is present in many Christian texts from the first two centuries in Christianity; her traditions persisted in the Middle Ages and also find expression in the present day. Both *Hockhmah* (Wisdom, in Hebrew) and *Sophia* (Wisdom, in Greek) are feminine nouns and are represented in the texts as female.

The texts that follow are from a body of Hellenistic Jewish texts written in the Greek language, referred to as the Apocrypha, that were not included in the canon of the Hebrew Bible. Apocryphal texts are considered deutero-canonical (a second canon) texts and are part of the Bible used by Orthodox Roman Catholic and Anglican Christians.

This excerpt from the Wisdom of Solomon in the Apocrypha is an *aretology* derived from the Greek word for virtue, *arete*, that praises the virtues of Sophia, the Wisdom of God. Texts that value highly the Female Principle of the Divine, by implication, associate the stated virtues with females as well as males. What might be the implications for female children and female adults if such texts were regularly included in services of worship? There are distinct similarities in literary form of aretologies enumerating the virtues of Isis during the time when she was the most popular deity in the Greco-Roman world. The Wisdom of Solomon, Sirach, and Baruch are Wisdom texts included in the Apocryphal writings.

Sophia in the Wisdom of Solomon*

I loved her [Sophia] more than health
    and beauty,
and I chose to have her rather than life
    because her radiance never ceases.
All good things came to me along with
    her, and in her hands uncounted
    wealth.
I rejoiced in them all, because wisdom
    leads them; but I did not know that
she was their mother. I learned both
    what is secret and
    what is manifest,
    for wisdom, the fashioner of all
    things, taught me.
There is in her a spirit that is
    intelligent, holy,
    unique, manifold,
    subtle mobile, clear, unpolluted,
    distinct, invulnerable, loving the
      good, keen,
    irresistible, beneficent, humane,
      steadfast, sure,
    free from anxiety, all-powerful, over-
      seeing all,
    and penetrating through all spirits
      that are intelligent,
    pure, and altogether subtle.
For wisdom is more mobile than any
    motion;

because of her pureness she
    pervades and penetrates all manner
      of things.
For she is a breath of the power of God
    and a pure emanation of the glory of
      the Almighty;
    therefore nothing defiled gains en-
      trance into her.
For she is a reflection of eternal light
    a spotless image of the working of
      God
    and an image of His goodness.
Although she is one she can do all things;
    in every generation she passes into
      holy souls
    and makes them friends of God and
      prophets.
For God loves nothing so much as the
    person who lives with wisdom,
She is more beautiful than the sun,
    and excels the constellations of the
      stars
Compared to night she is seen to be
    superior
    for it is succeeded by night but
    against wisdom, evil does not prevail.
She reaches mightily from one end of
    the earth to the other
    and she orders all things well.

SIRACH CHAPTER 24

Sophia in Sirach**

Wisdom praises herself,
    and tells of her glory in the midst
      of her people.
In the assembly of the Most High
    she opens her mouth,
    and in the presence of his hosts
      she tells of her glory:

"I came forth from the mouth of
    the Most High,
    and covered the earth like a mist.
I dwelt in the highest heavens,
    and my throne was in a pillar of cloud.
Alone I compassed the vault of heaven
    and traversed the depths of the abyss.

*Excerpts from Wisdom of Solomon, *The New Oxford Annotated Bible*. Edited by Bruce M. Metzger and Roland E. Murphy. New Revised Standard Edition, (New York: Oxford University Press, 1991). 7–8.

**Sirach, NRSV, 1991. 24:1–17, 19–23, 25–34.

Over waves of the sea, over all the earth,
   and over every people and nation I
      have held sway.
Among all these I sought a resting place;
   in whose territory should I abide?

"Then the Creator of all things gave me
   a command,
   and my Creator chose the place for
      my tent.
He said, 'Make your dwelling in Jacob,
   and in Israel receive your inheritance.'
Before the ages, in the beginning, he created me,
   and for all the ages I shall not cease to
      be.
In the holy tent I ministered before him,
   and so I was established in Zion.
Thus in the beloved city he gave me a
   resting place,
   and in Jerusalem was my domain.
I took root in an honored people,
   in the portion of the Lord, his heritage."

"I grew tall like a cedar in Lebanon,
   and like a cypress on the heights of
      Hermon.
I grew tall like a palm tree in En-gedi,
   and like rosebushes in Jericho;
like a fair olive tree in the field,
   and like a plane tree beside water I
      grew tall.
Like cassia and camel's thorn I gave
   forth perfume,
   and like choice myrrh I spread my
      fragrance,
like galbanum, onycha, and stacte,
   and like the odor of incense in the tent.
Like a terebinth I spread out my branches,
   and my branches are glorious and
      graceful.
Like the vine I bud forth delights,
   and my blossoms become glorious
      and abundant fruit."

"Come to me, you who desire me,
   and eat your fill of my fruits.
For the memory of me is sweeter than
   honey,

and the possession of me sweeter
   than the honeycomb.
Those who eat of me will hunger for
   more,
   and those who drink of me will thirst
      for more.
Whoever obeys me will not be put to
   shame,
   and those who work with me will not
      sin."

All this is the book of the covenant of
   the Most High God,
   the law that Moses commanded us
   as an inheritance for the congrega-
      tions of Jacob.
It overflows, like the Pishon, with wisdom,
   and like the Tigris at the time of the
      first fruits.
It runs over, like the Euphrates, with understanding,
   and like the Jordan at harvest time.
It pours forth instruction like the Nile,
   like the Gihon at the time of vintage.
The first man did not know wisdom fully,
   nor will the last one fathom her.
For her thoughts are more abundant
   than the sea,
   and her counsel deeper than the great
      abyss.

As for me, I was like a canal from a river,
   like a water channel into a garden.
I said, "I will water my garden and
   drench my flower-beds."
And lo, my canal became a river, and my
   river a sea.
I will again make instruction shine forth
   like the dawn,
   and I will make it clear from far away.
I will again pour out teaching like
   prophecy,
   and leave it to all future generations.
Observe that I have not labored for myself alone,
   but for all who seek wisdom.

The Holy/Myth

Judith was written in the Hellenistic period by a Palestinian Jew, probably some time between the end of the Macabbean War and the beginning of the Roman occupation of Jerusalem. This fictional story is set in the period of Nebuchadnezzar and recounts the story of Judith's victory over the Assyrian General, Holofernes. Judith is hailed as a hero and her story became a part of both Jewish and Christian mythology celebrating women's valor. Although Judith has been represented in visual arts, dramatic literature, opera, and oratorio as well as dance for over a thousand years, she is not included in the canon of the Hebrew bible. What is the potential significance for historical women of such a powerful and holy female heroine? What is the significance for powerful men of such a figure?

JUDITH'S VICTORY ODE[*]

All the women of Israel gathered to see her, and blessed her, and some of them performed a dance in her honor. She took ivy-wreathed wands in her hands and distributed them to the women who were with her; and she and those who were with her crowned themselves with olive wreaths. She went before all the people in the dance, leading all the women, while all the men of Israel followed, bearing their arms and wearing garlands and singing hymns.

Judith began this thanksgiving before all
    Israel, and all the people loudly
  sang this song of praise. And Judith
  said,
Begin a song to my God with
    tambourines,
  sing to my Lord with cymbals.
Raise to him a new psalm;
  exalt him, and call upon his name.
For the Lord is a God who crushes wars;
  he sets up his camp among his
    people;
  he delivered me from the hands of my
  pursuers.
The Assyrian came down from the
    mountains of the north;
  he came with myriads of his warriors;
their numbers blocked up the wadis,
  and their cavalry covered the hills.
He boasted that he would burn up my
    territory,
  and kill my young men with the
    sword,
and dash my infants to the ground,
  and seize my children as booty,
  and take my virgins as spoil.

But the Lord Almighty has foiled them
  by the hand of a woman.
For their mighty one did not fall by the
    hands of the young men,
  nor did the sons of the Titans strike
    him down,
  nor did tall giants set upon him;
but Judith daughter of Merari
with the beauty of her countenance
    undid him.

For she put away her widow's clothing
  to exalt the oppressed in Israel.
She anointed her face with perfume;
  she fastened her hair with a tiara
  and put on a linen gown to beguile
    him.
Her sandal ravished his eyes,
  her beauty captivated his mind,
  and the sword severed his neck!
The Persians trembled at her boldness,
  the Medes were daunted at her
    daring.

Then my oppressed people shouted;
  my weak people cried out, and the
    enemy trembled;

*Judith, NRSV, 1991. Chapter 15: 12–16: 17.

they lifted up their voices, and the
enemy were turned back.
Sons of slave-girls pierced them through
and wounded them like the children
of fugitives;
they perished before the army of my
Lord.

I will sing to my God a new song:
O Lord, you are great and glorious,
wonderful in strength, invincible.
Let all your creatures serve you,
for you spoke, and they were made.
You sent forth your spirit, and it formed
them;
there is none that can resist your
voice.
For the mountains shall be shaken to
their foundations with the waters;

before your glance the rocks shall
melt like wax.
But to those who fear you
you show mercy.
For every sacrifice as a fragrant offering
is a small thing,
and the fat of all whole burnt offerings to you is a very little thing;
but whoever fears the Lord is great
forever.

Woe to the nations that rise up against
my people!
The Lord Almighty will take
vengeance on them in the day of
judgment;
he will send fire and worms into their
flesh;
they shall weep in pain forever.

The Holy Ritual

This version of the story of Jepthah's daughter, Seila, was written in the Hellenistic period, the daughter is named, and unlike the story in the Book of Judges 17, is told from her point of view. Several aspects of these verses are pertinent to Jewish women in the Late Second Temple period. Seila is a
psychological heroine. She is willing to die to save her father's honor, but she does not mince words in
communicating to him how she feels about her situation. The Sages (wise ones) of the community
recognize Seila's wisdom and state not only that she is wiser than her father, but also that they have
no deeper wisdom about this situation than Seila herself. Seila also values deeply her friendships with
young women her own age. She, in fact, requests that she be given time alone with her friends to wander in nature and to ponder the severity of all that she will never be able to experience. In a poignant
lament Seila reflects on her forfeiture of her womanhood, marriage, and children in order to fulfill
the vow of her ambitious father. The text tells us that Seila's female friends instituted a ritual every
year to commemorate the death of this wise and courageous young woman. The recognition of Seila's
wisdom suggests a recognition that women are capable of Wisdom, and its attendant virtues, that
may indeed exceed that of males.

JEWISH MAIDENS RE-ENACT SEILA'S PILGRIMAGE[*]

And when the daughter of Jephthah came to Mount Stelac, she began to weep, and
this is her lamentation that she lamented and wept over herself before she departed.
And she said,

*Psuedo-Philo 40. "Jewish Maidens Re-Enact Seila's Pilgrimage," translated by D.J. Harrington. In *Old Testament Pseudepigrapha*. Vol. II of *Biblical Antiquities*, edited by James Charlesworth. Garden City, NY: Doubleday and Co., 1985. 354.

"Hear, you mountains, my lamentation;
and pay attention, you hills, to the tears
  of my eyes;
and be witnesses, you rocks, of the
  weeping of my soul.
Behold how I am put to the test!
But not in vain will my life be taken
  away.
May my words go forth in the heavens,
and my tears be written in the firmament!
That a father did not refuse the daughter whom he had sworn to sacrifice,
that a ruler granted that his only daughter be promised for sacrifice.
But I have not made good on my marriage chamber,
and I have not retrieved my wedding
  garlands.
For I have not been clothed in splendor
  while sitting in my woman's chamber,
And I have not used the sweet-smelling
  ointment,
And my soul has not rejoiced in the oil
  of anointing that has been prepared
  for me.
O Mother, in vain have you borne your
  only daughter,

because Sheol has become my bridal
  chamber,
and on earth there is only my woman's
  chamber.
And may all the blend of oil that you
  have prepared for me be poured
  out,
and the white robe that my mother has
  woven, the moth will eat it.
And the crown of flowers that my nurse
  plaited for me for the festival, may it
  wither up;
and the coverlet that she wove of hy-
  acinth and purple in my woman's
  chamber, may the worm devour it.
And may my virgin companions tell of
  me in sorrow and weep for me
  through the days.
You trees, bow down your branches and
  weep over my youth,
You beasts of the forests, come and be-
  wail my virginity,
for my years have been cut off
and the time of my life grown old in
  darkness."

And on saying these things Seila *returned to her father, and he did everything that he had vowed* and offered the holocausts. Then all the virgins of Israel gathered together and buried the daughter of Jephthah and wept for her. And the children of Israel made a great lamentation and established that in that month on the four-teenth day of the month they should come together every year and weep for Jeph-thah's daughter for four days. And they named her tomb in keeping with her name: Seila. *And Jephthah judged* the sons of *Israel* ten *years, and he died and was buried* with his fathers.

Theraputae are male and female *ascetics* (people who practice self denial toward a spiritual goal). A highlight of their life in community is the celebration of a feast that is described in the texts that follow. Note that it is not the food, consisting of bread, water, and hyssop, that is the center of the fes-tivities. Rather, hymns and prayers created for the occasion as well as celebratory dances are the high-lights of this feast.

FEMALE THERAPUTAE CELEBRATE IN HYMNS AND DANCES[*]

This common sanctuary in which they meet every seventh day is a double enclosure, one portion set apart for the use of the men, the other for the women. For women too regularly make part of the audience with the same ardour and the same sense of their calling. The wall between the two chambers rises up from the ground to three or four cubits built in the form of a breast work, while the space above up to the roof is left open. This arrangement serves two purposes; the modesty becoming to the female sex is preserved, while the women sitting within ear-shot can easily follow what is said since there is nothing to obstruct the voice of the speaker.

The feast is shared by women also, most of them aged virgins, who have kept their chastity not under compulsion, like some of the Greek priestesses, but of their own free will in their ardent yearning for wisdom. Eager to have her for their life mate they have spurned the pleasures of the body and desire no mortal offspring but those immortal children which only the soul that is dear to God can bring to the birth unaided, because the Father has sown in her spiritual rays enabling her to behold the verities of wisdom.

After the meal they hold the sacred vigil, which is celebrated in the following manner. They all rise up in a body and at the center of the refectory they first form two choirs, one of men, the other of women, the leader and precentor chosen for each being the most highly esteemed among them and the most musical. They then sing hymns to God composed in many meters and melodies, now chanting together, now moving hands and feet in concordant harmony, and full of inspiration they sometimes chant processional odes, and sometimes the lyrics of a chorus in standing position as well as executing the strophe and antistrophe of the choral dance.

Then when each choir has completed for itself its own part in the feasting, having drunk as in Bacchic revelries of the strong wine of god's love, they mix, and the two choirs become one, a copy of the choir organized at the Red Sea on the occasion of the wonders there wrought. For at the divine command, the sea became a cause of salvation to the one side and of utter destruction to the other. For as the sea was rent asunder, drawn downward by the violent recoil of its waves, and on either side, facing each other, the waters virtually walled up in solid form, the intervening space thus opened up broadened into a highway fully dry, through which the people marched to the opposite mainland, safely escorted to higher ground. But when the waters came rushing in with the returning tide, and from either side poured over the dried sea floor, the pursuing enemy were overwhelmed and perished. After witnessing and experiencing this act, which went beyond word, thought, and hope, men and women alike were filled with divine ecstasy, formed a single choir, sang hymns of thanksgiving to God their Savior, the men led by the prophet Moses and the women by the prophetess Miriam.

Modeled above all on this, the choir of the Therapeutae, both male and female, singing in harmony, the soprano of the women blending with the bass of the men, produces true musical concord.

Exceedingly beautiful are the thoughts, exceedingly beautiful are the words, and august the choristers, and the end goal of thought, words, and choristers alike is piety.

---

*Philo, *On the Contemplative Life*, translated by F. H. Colson, LCL, 1941. III. 32–33; VIII. 68–69.

Philo, *On the Contemplative Life (Vita Contemplativa)*, translated by David Winston. The Classics of Western Spirituality Series. New York, Ramsey, Toronto: Paulist Press, 1981. X. 83–90.

Thus they continue till dawn intoxicated with this exquisite intoxication and then, not with heavy head or drowsy eyes, but more alert than when they came to the banquet, they stand with their faces and whole body turned to the east, and when they behold the rising sun, with hands stretched heavenward they pray for a joyous day, truth, and acuity of thought. And after the prayers they retire each to his own sanctuary once more to ply the trade and cultivate the field of their wonted philosophy.

Conclusion
     So much then for the Therapeutae who have embraced the contemplation of nature and its constituent parts, and have lived in the soul alone, citizens of Heaven and the universe, truly commended to the Father and Creator of all by virtue, which has secured for them God's friendship in addition to the most fitting prize of nobility, which excels all good fortune and attains to the very summit of joy.

Among females mentioned in Dead Sea Scroll texts found at Qumran, it can be argued that Daughters of Truth and the Venerable Women referenced in scroll 4Q502 from Cave Four are educated women.

In a scholarly article, "4Q502: Marriage or Golden Age Ritual," Joseph Baumgarten challenges the first translator of the text, Maurice Baillet, and proposes that 4Q502 is a fixed feast to celebrate venerable men and women of the community at Qumran (Baumgarten 1987, 266–69). Baumgarten later established the presence and primacy of the older members of the community who comprise an Order of Sisters of the Community and Brothers of the Community. In the present context we are interested in the wide variety of females who participate in this feast at Qumran. Translated fragments from the scroll that survived are presented below.

Venerable Female Essenes Are Honored and Esteemed[*]

the man and his wife (F[ragment]
     1. L[ine.3)
his female/beloved (F-1 L.7)
the Daughter of Truth (F.2 L.3)
their venerable ones and some young
     people (F.9 L.4)
sons and daughters (F.14 L.6)
The man and his female companion
seated in the assembly of the Righteous
     Ones . . . (F 19. L.1)
. . . old men and old women and young
     people (F. 19 L.2)

and virgins, boys and girls (E19 L.3)
her husband, the man who gives bless-
     ing to his wife/the woman (F.24 L.2)
[the woman's] numerous lineage,
     Daughters of Eve . . . among eternal
     people (F.24 L.3)
the woman who gives blessing to her
     husband/ the man . . . while standing
     in the assembly
of the venerable men and the venerable
     women . . .

Female Religious Functionaries

Female Leaders Featured in Texts   The following three texts are found among collections of texts referred to as *Pseudepigraphical* writings. This designation relates to the fact that these writings, most of which were penned in the Late Second Temple period, ca. 200 B.C.E.–70 C.E., are ascribed to authors who pre-date the actual authors of these texts. The intention of such ascription is not subterfuge, but

*Maurice Baillet, "Qumran Grotte 4Q 502 Rituel de Mirage," in *Discoveries in the Judean Desert* 7, Fragment 17. Oxford, 1982. (English translation by L. Bennett Elder.)

rather an intention to pay homage to the original authors of these texts. Some of the original authors include, for example, Enoch, Moses, and other such biblical figures.

Contemporary Biblical scholar Daniel Harrington does an analysis of one such collection of pseudepigraphical texts, titled *Pseudo-Philo* (also referred to as *Biblical Antiquities*) that was probably written between 135 B.C.E. and 70 C.E. (Harrington OTPS, 1985).

Harrington situates these texts in the context of the synagogue and notes concerning the treatment of women "interesting plays on Old Testament [sic] cliches from what would now be described as a feminist perspective." Following an analysis of texts about Hannah in *Pseudo-Philo,* Joan E. Cook concludes that if the *Pseudo-Philo* corpus was written to be read in the synagogues, "the listening congregation acknowledged and respected women as wise teachers in the community" (Cook, *Hannah's Desire, God's Design,* 1999). The figures of Deborah (*Pseudo-Philo* 30–33) and Seila, daughter of Jephthah (*Pseudo-Philo* 40:1–9) as they are depicted in *Pseudo-Philo* also affirm Cook's hypothesis.

The reader can refer back to the introduction to Seila's story in the section on The Holy/Ritual in the present chapter. In the passages that precede Seila's Lament, the Sages refer explicitly to Seila's wisdom, noting that her wisdom exceeds their own. Because these texts were read in the synagogue we can surmise their appreciation of wisdom that emerges from a woman, who happens also to be young and unmarried.

THE SAGES RECOGNIZE SEILA'S WISDOM[*]

> *And Jephthah came and attacked the sons of Ammon, and the Lord delivered them into his hands, and he struck down* sixty of their *cities. And Jephthah returned in peace,* and women came out *to meet him in song and dance. And it was his only daughter who came out* of the house first in the dance *to meet her father. And* when *Jephthah saw her, he grew faint and said,* "Rightly was your name called Seila, that you might be offered in sacrifice. And now who will put my heart in the balance and my soul on the scale? And I will stand by and see which will win out, whether it is the rejoicing that has occurred or the sadness that befalls me. And because *I opened my mouth to* my *Lord* in song with vows, *I cannot* call that back again." *And* Seila *his daughter said to him,* "And who is there who would be sad in death, seeing the people freed? Or do you not remember what happened in the days of our fathers when the father placed the son as a holocaust, and he did not refuse him but gladly gave consent to him, and the one being offered was ready and the one who was offering was rejoicing? And now do not annul everything you have vowed, but carry it out. Yet one request I ask of you before I die, a small demand I seek before I give back my soul: that *I may go into the mountains and stay* in the hills and walk among the rocks, *I and my virgin companions,* and I will pour out my tears there and tell of the sadness of my youth. And the trees of the field will weep for me, and the beasts of the field will lament over me. For I am not sad because I am to die nor does it pain me to give back my soul, but because my father was caught up in the snare of his vow; and if I did not offer myself willingly for sacrifice, I fear that my death would not be acceptable or I would lose my life in vain. These things I will tell the mountains, and afterward I will return." *And* her father *said,* "Go." And Seila the daughter of Jephthah, she and her virgin companions, *went out* and came and told it to the wise men of the people, and no one could respond to her word. And afterward she came to Mount

[*]*Pseudo-Philo 40.* Translated by D. J. Harrington. In *Old Testament Pseudepigrapha.* Vol. II of *Biblical Antiquities,* edited by James Charlesworth, Garden City, NY: Doubleday and Co., 1985. 353–54.

Stelac, and the LORD thought of her by night and said, "Behold now I have shut up the tongue of the wise men of my people for this generation so that they cannot respond to the daughter of Jephthah, to her word, in order that my word be fulfilled and my plan that I thought out not be foiled. And I have seen that the virgin is wise in contrast to her father and perceptive in contrast to all the wise men who are here. And now let her life be given at his request, and her *death* will be *precious before* me always, and she will go away and fall into the bosom of her mothers."

And when the daughter of Jephthah came to Mount Stelac, she began to weep, and this is her lamentation that she lamented and wept over herself before she departed.

WOMEN OUTSIDE THE ARISTOCRACY

Jewish Women in Alexandrian Public Life

We have seen how Philo praises the virtues of the ascetic, sequestered female Theraputae. But, he takes issue with women's self-assertion in the public sphere. Philo's misogyny is highlighted in the following explication of a dualistic world view concerning the sexes. His proscriptions against assertive actions by a female are diametrically opposed to the assertion of her autonomy that is implicit in his praise of a Theraputae's choice to give herself to God in the desert life of an ascetic community that is comprised of both females and males.

PHILO ON THE SPECIAL LAWS[*]

Market-places and council-halls and law-courts and gatherings and meetings where a large number of people are assembled, and open-air life with full scope for discussion and action, these are suitable to men both in war and peace. The women are best suited to the indoor life which never strays from the house, within which the middle door is taken by the maidens as their boundary, and the outer door by those who have reached full womanhood. Organized communities are of two sorts, the greater which we call cities and the smaller which we call households. Both of these have their governors; the government of the greater is assigned to men under the name of statesmanship, that of the lesser, known as household management, to women. A woman, then, should not be a busybody, meddling with matters outside her household concerns, but should seek a life of seclusion. She should not shew herself off like a vagrant in the streets before the eyes of other men, except when she has to go to the temple, and even then she should take pains to go, not when the market is full, but when most people have gone home, and so like a free-born lady worthy of the name, with everything quiet around her, make her oblations and offer her prayers to avert the evil and gain the good. . . .

*Philo, "On the Special Laws." *Moses and the Law*, edited and translated by F. H. Colson, Loeb Classical Library, Vol. VII, Book III, Lines 169–171.

FEMALE ENTREPRENEURS

The most substantive evidence for female entrepreneurs in early Judaism is found in documents concerning inheritance. In Judaism the Greek term for dowry (*pherne*) appeared as early as the reign of Ptolemy II Philadelphus (283–246 B.C.E.) in the *Septuagint* (Greek version of the Hebrew Bible). It is suggested that the dowry was first introduced into a Jewish marriage contract (*ketuvah*) by scribes in the diaspora. Bickerman proposes that

> In Hellenistic Jerusalem, the desire to imitate Greek ways must have provided the stimulus for the introduction of the institution of the dowry into the Jewish system of marriage payments, so that the contribution of the wife made to the husband for the household was in addition to the settlement made upon the bride by the groom (Bickerman 1988, 92).

It is suggested that in the interest of the wife, scribes "evaded the principle of inheritance by males only established by the Mosaic Law".

In these instances the scribes employed the device of private agreement. By explicitly articulating the rights pertaining to a wife in the marriage contract itself, which were not expressed and therefore were unprotected in biblical law, the scribes raised the status of married women in Jerusalem. Some of the texts from the Second Temple period that attest to women's inheritance include archival records from the Jewish settlement at Elephantine in Egypt.

FEMALE ENTREPRENEURS AT ELEPHANTINE[*]

From two private archives of Jewish families at Elephantine come texts which show women as inheritors of their father's and their husband's properties, respectively. Mibtahiah was a daughter in the most prominent family in the Jewish community; Tamut, the mother of Jehoishma, was an Egyptian handmaid, a status held by her daughter as well until their manumission on June 12, 427 B.C.E. The father of Jehoishma was a Temple official. These documents thus provide an opportunity for insights into the life and social status of one woman who began at the top of the social scale and one who began at the bottom.

The archives record the inheritance stipulated for Tamut from the time of her marriage contract in 449 B.C.E. and include in the final draft gifts of property which are given to her gratis "from this day, forever, [to you] and your children whom you bore me." Her daughter Jehoishma was well provided for by her father, the husband of Tamut. In addition to the ketuvah, at the time of her marriage she received gifts of property from her father, and later she received gifts willed to her by him, on three subsequent occasions. The final gift (which was to be transferred to her upon the death of the donor) was given to her with provisions for complete power and with no clauses restricting her rights of alienation (K9:3; K9:16; K9:21). 60.

The Archives also record her husband Ananiah's instructions that his wife, Jehoishma, was to succeed to his possessions if she were left a childless widow, for as

*B. Porten, *The Archives at Elephantine*, Berkeley and Los Angeles: University of California Press, 1968. 217, 225, 229, 237–39, 254–55.

long as she remained a widow (K:28). Similarly, if there were no heirs and she predeceased him, he was to succeed to her possessions.

Mibtahiah, thrice married and a prominent property holder in her own right was the daughter of the prestigious Mahseiah. There are seven documents in the archives pertaining to Mibtahiah: four concerning property given to her by her father (C:5, 61, 81, 9); a fifth concerning a house given to her by her father in exchange for goods (C:13); a sixth document on a settlement arising from the divorce of her second husband (C: 14); and a seventh (C: 16), the marriage contract from her third husband, Ashor the builder. As a woman of quite considerable means, Mibtahiah secured a formidable marriage contract. Mibtahiah secured recognition as Ashor's sole heir for her future children, and assured for herself full access to his property during his lifetime and after his death if they had no children (C:15–17). As long as Ashor chose to maintain the union he could in no way diminish Mibtahiah's full support, limit her legitimate rights to his property, disinherit her should she die childless or share patrimony with other children should they have offspring of their own.

SUGGESTED READINGS

Arthur, Rose Horman. *The Wisdom Goddess, Feminine Motifs in Eight Nag Hammadi Documents*. Lanham, New York, and London: University Press of America, 1984.

Darr, Katheryn Pfisterer. *Far More Precious Than Jewels, Perspectives on Biblical Women*. Louisville, KY: The Westminster/John Knox Press, 1991.

Women Like This: New Perspectives on Women in the Greco-Roman World. In *SBL, Early Judaism and Its Literature*. Edited by Amy Jill Levine. Atlanta, GA: Scholars Press, 1991.

No One Spoke Ill of Her: Essays on Judith. In *SBL Early Judaism and Its Literature*. Edited by James C. Vander. Atlanta, GA: Scholars Press, 1992.

Elder, Linda Bennett. "The Woman Question and Female Ascetics Among Essenes." *Biblical Archaeologist* 57:4 (1994).

Sources Cited

Josephus. Salome Alexandra. *Antiquities*. Translated by L. H. Feldman. Loeb Classical Library. Cambridge, MA: Harvard University Press, 1969. XV 43–49.

"The Rule Annexe." Translated by A. DuPont Sommer. In *The Essene Writings from Qumran*, Cleveland and New York: The World Publishing Company, 1962. 1QSA 1.4–12.

Ketubot. *The Mishnah*. Edited and translated by Jacob Neusner, New Haven, CT: Yale University Press, 1988. Ketubot 4:12 VI; I 1:1; 4:4; 5:5; 12:3; 3:4.

Sophia in the Wisdom of Solomon. *The New Oxford Annotated Bible*. Edited by Bruce M. Metzger and Roland E. Murphy. New Revised Standard Edition, New York: Oxford University Press, 1991. 7:10–12, 21–30, 8:1.

Sophia in Sirach. *The New Oxford Annotated Bible*. Edited by Bruce M. Metzger and Roland E. Murphy. New Revised Standard Edition, New York: Oxford University Press, 1991. 24: 1–17, 19–23, 25–34.

Judith. *The New Oxford Annotated Bible*. Edited by Bruce M. Metzger and Roland E. Murphy. New Revised Standard Edition, New York: Oxford University Press, 1991. 16:1–25.

Jewish Maidens Re-Enact Seila's Pilgrimage. *Psuedo-Philo 40.* Translated by D.J. Harrington. In *Old Testament Pseudepigrapha.* Vol. II of *Biblical Antiquities,* edited by James Charlesworth, No. 40. Garden City, NY: Doubleday and Co., 1985. 354.

Philo. *On the Contemplative Life,* translated by F. H. Colson, 1941. III. 32–33; VIII. 68–69. Loeb Classical Library.

Philo. Female Theraputae Celebrate in Hymns and Dances. *On the Contemplative Life (Vita Contemplativa).* Translated by David Winston. The Classics of Western Spirituality, New York, Ramsey, Toronto: Paulist Press. 1981. X. 83–90.

Baillet, Maurice. Venerable Female Essenes Are Honored and Esteemed. "Qumran Grotte 4Q, 502 Rituel de Mirage," *Discoveries in the Judean Desert 7,* Fragment 17. Oxford, 1982. English translation by L. Bennett Elder.

Sages Recognize Seila's Wistom. *Pseudo-Philo 40.* Translated by D. J. Harrington. In *Old Testament Pseudepigrapha.* Vol. II of *Biblical Antiquities,* edited by James Charlesworth, Garden City, NY: Doubleday and Co., 1985, 353–54.

Philo on the Special Laws. From *Moses and the Law.* Edited and translated by F. H. Colson, Loeb Classical Library, Vol. VII, Book III, Lines 169–171.

Porten, B. Female Entrepreneurs at Elephantine. *The Archives at Elephantine,* Berkeley and Los Angeles: University of California Press, 1968. 217, 225, 229, 237–39, 254–55.

PART III

ROMAN EMPIRE, EARLY CHRISTIANITY, LATE ANTIQUITY, AND THE MIDDLE AGES

In Part III, Roman Empire, Christian Origins, Late Antiquity, and the Middle Ages, we examine women's experiences and cultural contributions from ca. 30 B.C.E.–1500 C.E. in the following, principal areas of concentration. We consider the Roman Empire, the dissemination of Christianity, the Byzantine world, and the subsequent divisions between contextual perspectives in the East (Byzantine) and West (Roman). Part III concludes with the emergence of Europe and its distinctive culture during the Middle Ages. This part of the book is divided into five chapters. Chapter 11 addresses the Roman Empire, Chapter 12 focuses on Women in Christian Origins (first through third centuries), Chapter 13 on Late Antiquity (fourth through eighth centuries), and Chapters 14 and 15 describe women in religious and secular Medieval Europe from the fifth through the fifteenth centuries.

THE EARLY EMPIRE

The transition at Rome from Republic to Empire marked the beginnings of transformations in culture that have shaped and influenced women's experience from that time to the present in both favorable and detrimental ways. The self-understanding at Rome during the Republic tended to be conservative, more insular than expansive and steeped in political and philosophical ideologies that were considered inviolable, especially among the elite. However, as the Empire spread throughout the Mediterranean Basin and into the Near East and Europe, the power of Republican Roman ideological foundations to control and determine cultural norms that were less than superficial was eroded despite even the most noble efforts to sustain them. Military expansion, unprecedented colonization, and occupation of foreign territories to the East and to the North; institutional, organizational, and bureaucratic differences among these societies; and cultural, linguistic, and religious diversity were some of the significant factors that challenged Rome's hegemony. Considering the challenges, the long-term success of Roman influence on institutional systems is remarkable.

The variety of women in the Roman Empire that are represented in Chapter 11 provides a sense of the diversity that emerged in the cultural transformations of the early Empire.

CHRISTIAN ORIGINS

Foundations for contextualizing Chapter 12 on Christian Origins are articulated in Chapters 9, and 10 in Part II of this volume and in Chapter 11 on women in the Roman Empire. The various opportunities for women that began to appear in the Hellenistic period and that continued into the early Empire at the beginning of the Common Era are significant factors among women in the Jesus movement in Palestine. This holds true as well in Palestine, Syria, and the Mediterranean Basin as the Apostolic Church spread throughout the Roman Empire. Women who were status inconsistent emerged as elders, teachers, preachers, missionaries, deacons, presbyters, prophets, priests, and bishops.

LATE ANTIQUITY AND THE BYZANTINE EMPIRE

By the end of the third century, the vast and unwieldy Roman Empire was disintegrating in the face of internal strife, economic troubles, weak leadership, and invasions by tribes from Europe to the North and by Persians from the East. Emperor Constantine temporarily reversed that process during his reign (324–337 C.E.) when he restored imperial control, but he also inadvertently paved the way for the permanent East-West division of the Empire. When Constantine built a new capital, Constantinople, on the site of the ancient city of Byzantium, he shifted the center of the old Roman Empire to the East. The new capital was a vibrant intellectual and artistic center that blended classical culture with Christian beliefs and iconography, Roman law, and artistic influences from the East. Byzantine culture, as it quickly became known, enjoyed a golden age between 324 and 632, particularly under the leadership of Constantine and, later, Emperor Justinian (527–565 C.E.) and his wife, the Empress Theodora. Constantinople remained the greatest city in the Christian world and a flourishing cultural center until it was conquered by the Turks in 1453. Meanwhile, the West disintegrated and in 476, a Germanic chieftain deposed the last Roman emperor. Although Emperor Justinian temporarily restored Byzantine control over Italy and other parts of the West, his effort to reunite the Empire ultimately failed, and the East-West division became permanent.

Political developments had important consequences for Christianity. Throughout this period there were many competing religions, sects, and movements, and among Christians themselves, a number of different sects. Christians continued periodically to experience persecution, by secular officials and religious rivals, and Christian leaders themselves all too frequently persecuted or condemned non-believers and minority Christian sects with whom they disagreed. Nevertheless, through a series of imperial edicts, Christianity became the official religion of the Roman Empire by the end of the fourth century.

As Christianity spread and enjoyed governmental support, the Patriarchs or church leaders began to perfect its organization, define its core beliefs, and standardize religious practices and church rules. The loosely structured early Jesus movement and diverse forms of worship of the early churches in the Apostolic period gave way to a formal religion governed by male bishops located throughout the empire. The highest offices in the hierarchy were held by five Patriarchs whose constituencies were in Constantinople, Antioch, Jerusalem, Alexandria, and Rome. In the fifth century a schism began in the Church that would be resolved in the emergence of the Eastern (Byzantine) Church and the Western (Roman Catholic) Church. This schism, that became final by the tenth century C.E., reflected sharp cultural, linguistic, political, doctrinal, and structural differences between the East and West.

Meanwhile, male and female converts to Christianity continued to spread the new religion and explore diverse ways of living out their faith. They created new communities (monasteries) where they could work, live, and pray together as they defined what it meant to be a Christian, and developed rituals and iconography that enhanced the meaningfulness of their spirituality. Women were important participants and leaders in each of these endeavors, despite the increasingly patriarchal character of the official Church. Inevitably, female leaders also sometimes found themselves at odds with official dogma and male leaders.

As we leave Late Antiquity and enter the Middle Ages, we shift our attention from the Mediterranean world and return to the region where we began our exploration of women and culture, Western Europe.

MEDIEVAL EUROPE

For centuries, Western Europe remained a peripheral region, largely untouched by important developments in Western civilization. Although Rome had extended her empire across Europe, west into Spain and north to England by the fourth century, she took little interest in the region, focusing instead on the richer Mediterranean territories. In the context of what had become the "high culture" of the Greco-Roman world at its zenith, Europe remained a frontier. Muslim scholars, especially in Spain, were largely responsible for the transmission of texts and the intellectual heritage of the Greco-Roman world among Europeans who came to Spain to study in their universities. The rich culture of Celtic peoples flourished in Western Europe, and was both challenged by and integrated into Christianity as Europe was increasingly populated by Roman troops, a few bureaucrats, and Christian missionaries.

Beneath the surface, however, Western Europe was beginning its metamorphosis. By 700 C.E. the old Mediterranean world of the Roman Empire had changed drastically. It now consisted of three different societies: the Byzantine Empire, heirs of the Greeks and early Christianity; the Arabic world, which stretched from the Middle East, across North Africa, and through Spain to the Pyrenees; and the West or Europe, which was, by far, the weakest of the three. By the end of the Middle Ages, it would be an important civilization in its own right.

WOMEN AND CULTURE IN MEDIEVAL EUROPE

Chapters 14 and 15 are organized thematically to reflect the different contexts in which female creativity emerged during the Middle Ages. Chapter 14 documents women's experiences and contributions within a religious context, revealing in particular how monastic life fostered female leadership (cultural, religious, and political) and women's artistic, musical, literary, and intellectual talents. It also examines women's participation in new religious movements that emerged during the ferment of the late Middle Ages from the twelfth to the fifteenth centuries, their creation of alternative religious institutions and forms of religious expression, and their innovative contributions to theology, spirituality, and religious thought.

Chapter 15 focuses on female creativity in the secular arena during the Middle Ages. In this chapter, most of the selections come from the twelfth through the fifteenth centuries. During this period strong kingdoms and duchies emerged, trade revived, and towns and cities grew rapidly. As a result, new secular institutions such as banks, commercial establishments, guilds (trade or labor organizations), and universities as well as the royal and ducal courts began to replace monasteries as the centers of culture, learning, and artistic training and as producers and disseminators of art, manuscripts, and music. These developments to some extent broadened women's opportunities for education, training, and work, offered another alternative to marriage or monastic life, and provided some new venues in which women's creative talents could be nurtured and expressed. Such secular options became increasingly important as the Church restricted the autonomy and the educational and creative activities of female monasteries.

This chart addresses women's participation in four stages of development in Western Culture: the Roman Empire: first century B.C.E.—fourth century C.E., Early Christianity: first century C.E.—third century C.E.: Late Antiquity: third century C.E.—the late sixth century C.E., and the Middle Ages: eight century—fifteenth century C.E.

The Roman Empire first century B.C.E. to the third century C.E.

Social Organization

Patriarchal and built upon many aspects of Hellenistic culture. The model of the Noble Roman matron continued but was mostly mythic. Women were present and active in the public sphere. Many had great wealth and property.

Women in the Aristocracy

Empress Livia Augusta first century B.C.E.—first century C.E.; Julia daughter of Augustus first century B.C.E. —first century C.E.; Caenis, concubine of Vespasian, 71-75 C.E.; Flavia Publica Nicomachus second century C.E.; Modia Quinta second century to the third century C.E.; Aurelia Liete fourth century C.E.; Pamphile first century C.E.

Women Outside the Aristocracy

Phile, female magistrate; Junia Theodora, public benefactor, first century C.E.; Eumachis first century C.E.; Aufria, woman of letters, second century C.E.; Tarracina, a benefactress, second century C.E.

Female Physicians

Primilla first and second centuries C.E., Terenitia first and second centuries C.E.

Female Poets

Claudia Tropheme first century C.E., Caecilia Trebulla first century C.E., Balbila second century C.E.

Female Philosophers

Appolonia Mysia, Euphrosyne, first century C.E.

Female Priests

Served all female and some male deities. Isis was prominent in Mystery Religions as was Cybele. Vestal virgins were also prominent. Mamia first century C.E., the Leucippides second century C.E., Flavia Ammon first century C.E., Lalla first century C.E.

Female Religious Functionaries

Isis tradition, all female deities, religions of the state; musicians, singers, mourners, rituals, and prayers.

Christian Origins first century C.E.—third century C.E.

From its beginnings in the first century C.E. to the fourth century C.E., Christianity had first advanced in the merchant and artisan strata of society and was one of countless religious traditions in the Greco-Roman world. By the fourth century, the aristocracy had embraced the Christian tradition sufficiently so that in 386 C.E., it became the state religion of the Empire.

Early followers of Jesus and female ministers in Christian Origins

Mary, the mother of Jesus, first century B.C.E.—first century C.E.; Mary of Magdala, Apostle, first century C.E.; Martha and Mary of Bethany first century C.E.; Joanna first century C.E.

Female Prophets

Anna the Prophet first century B.C.E.—first century C.E.

Teacher, Missionary

Priscilla

Deacon, Prostasis

Phoebe

Apostle

Junia

Workers in the Early Church

Julia, Olympias, Tryphosa, Tryphena: All first century C.E.; Thecla, missionary first century C.E.; Maximilla and Priscilla were founders of a Montanist community which had female bishops, presbyters, and prophets second century C.E.; Order of Deaconesses third century—fourth century C.E.; Order of Widows third century C.E.

Late Antiquity fourth century—eighth century c.e.

During these centuries, after the fall of Rome, especially in the West, there is little recorded evidence for women's contributions in culture outside the aristocracy.

Women in Roman Aristocracy

Empress Julia Domna third century C.E., Ummidia Quadratilla third century—fourth century C.E.

Female Philosopher

Asclepigenia of Athens

Jewish Women Women in the Aristocracy

Queen Helena of Adiabbene first century C.E.

Female Entrepreneur

Babata fourth century C.E.

Female Religious Functionaries first century C.E.—sixth century C.E.

Heads of Synagogues

Sophia and Theopempte, Female Priest Maria Gaudentia

Rabbinic Judaism

Female Rabbi Beruriah

Women in the Aristocracy

Helen, Mother of Constantine, fourth century C.E.

Female Philosopher

Hypatia of Alexandria fifth century C.E., Empress Theodora sixth century C.E.

Female Religious Functionaries

The Desert Mothers: Amma Syncletica fifth century C.E., Amma Sarah fifth century C.E., Thaiis fifth century C.E., Pelagia fifth century C.E.

Eastern Monasticism

St. Macrina fifth century C.E.

Western Monasticism

Marcella fifth century C.E., St. Paula fifth century C.E., Egeria fifth century C.E.

The Celts

Queen Boudicca first century C.E., Queen Maeb fifth century C.E., Rhiannon, the Horse Goddess, early oral history written in 1325 C.E.

(continued)

Celtic Saints
St. Anna, St. Non, St. Melangell, St. Brede, fifth—sixth centuries C.E.

Medieval Culture: The Religious Context
The most pervasive and influential social institution in the Middle Ages was the Church. Education and the arts flourished despite an increasingly powerful clerical bureaucracy. Many women who entered monastic orders became well educated and found creative fullfilment. Many acquired superb adminis-trative skills and were recognized as great spiritual leaders.

Holy Women sixth—fourteenth century C.E.

Radegund of Poitiers sixth century C.E., Hrotswitha of Gandersheim tenth century C.E., Hildegard of Bingen twelfth century C.E., Clare of Assisi thirteenth century C.E., Mechtilde of Magdeburg thirteenth century C.E., Margurite Porete thirteenth to the fourteenth centuries C.E., Julian of Norwich fourteenth century C.E.

Medieval Culture the Secular Context
Despite the pervasive influence of the church, some women created careers for themselves as artists, writers, poets, and even traveling minstrels.

Female Troubadors
Castelloza thirteenth century C.E., La Comtessa de Dia twelfth century C.E., Bieris de Romans.

Female Writers
Marie de France twelfth century C.E., Christine de Pizan fourteenth century C.E.

Chapter 11

The Roman Empire

The transition at Rome from Republic to Empire ranks among the most significant events in the development of what we refer to today as Western Civilization. In many ways the Roman Empire represents a culmination of *cultural* development that began with Alexander's intention to "make Greek" the world. Following the demise of the Republic, Roman *political* and *military* hegemony and its attendant *ideologies* became a paradigm of a *world power* that would be modeled throughout the West. Some of the advances for women that transpired in the Hellenistic period did continue during the Empire and beyond. Implications, however, of restrictive customs, policies, traditions, and laws concerning women that became normative characteristics of Roman culture also persisted as normative. Future chapters reveal that many of these cultural norms have affected the quality of life for women in Western Civilization to the present day.

SOCIAL ORGANIZATION

Essential elements of social organization at the close of the Republic are clarified in Chart 11–1 and Chart 11–2.

It is also instructive to look at a very general sketch of the two principal governing bodies.

Before the end of the Republic several initiatives sought to institute a governmental structure that included a broader spectrum of the total population. The power of the oligarchy however, and agendas designed to perpetuate their authority and power, militated against such initiatives. Nevertheless, all was not well. Rome was engaged in numerous military conflicts that would indeed change the concentration of political power.

Military successes among Sulla, Pompey, Crassus, and Caesar, in the last half of the first century B.C.E. functioned for their political advantage at Rome. Political alliances among Pompey, Caesar, and Crassus, the First Triumvirate, were also, however, characterized by rivalries and betrayals. Caesar and Pompey both served as Consuls at Rome and both continued to return to their military conquests. Julius Caesar's not-so-subtle political reforms at Rome, as he moved toward instituting what was in fact a monarchy, permanently alienated the Roman Senate and resulted in his untimely assassination. Caesar's nephew and heir, Gaius Octavius, who, along with Caesar's other generals Antony and Lepidus

---

Chart 11–1   Social Organization During the Late Roman Republic

Patricians
Upper-class males, leaders of clans and patrons of many clients, conducted religious ceremonies, served as judges, sat in the Senate, had access to the written and unwritten laws by which they governed Rome. By the end of the Republic, the Senate was no longer a closed caste.

Plebians
Initially lower "classes." In government the Plebians were organized into Assemblies. As Rome expanded many Plebians became very wealthy. Access to privilege among Plebians was minimal and took an inordinate amount of time as is demonstrated by the following list:

450 B.C.E. - Gained access to Laws
445 B.C.E. - Gained right to marry Patricians
367 B.C.E. - At least one Plebian could be a Consul
300 B.C.E. - Plebians admitted to Priesthood
287 B.C.E. - Decisions made by the Roman Assembly bound all Romans
127 B.C.E. - Equestrians became a class
 83 B.C.E. - Sulla brings Equestrians into the Senate

Nobiles = Patricians and Plebians who were wealthy and powerful
Populares = Citizenry outside the Nobility
Metoikoi = Non-citizen residents
Slaves

Chart 11–2   Governing Bodies

The Senate
Initially, the Senate consisted of prominent Patricians. By the end of the Republic, Equestrians were included as well. (Numbers fluctuated from 300 to 900 at one point.)
    2 Consuls = Led the Senate, one year appointment, had Imperium, led the army, served as judges
    2–8 Quaestors = Financial officials
    Lictors = Minor officials who served the Consuls

The Assemblies
Assemblies elected the Consuls and several magistrates, voted on bills, made decisions of war and peace, and were the court of appeal. The Assemblies were hierarchically ranked based upon wealth and prestige. The Centuriate Assembly, for example, was the Roman Army acting in a political capacity. Over time, members of the Equestrian (Cavalry) Assembly came to include a large number of very wealthy businessmen and entrepreneurs. By the end of the Republic, the Equestrians were institutionalized as a functioning political "party" and as a social "class." Equestrians sometimes were members of the Senate.

---

formed the Second Triumvirate. This alliance was also undermined by personal ambition and ended finally with Octavian's defeat of Antony in 30 B.C.E. and marked the beginning of his status as Emperor Caesar Augustus, founder of an Empire that lasted from 27 B.C.E. to the second half of the fifth century C.E.

Urbanization, individualism, increased access to opportunities, and the rise in trade and commerce that were characteristic of Hellenization generated an appetite for economic security and prosperity among the populous. Yet the quest for wealth and power remained inextricably bound with an *ideology* that valued and aspired to preserve an elite, hierarchically determined status, prestige, and privilege based upon wealth and power. The Romans retained the internal legalistic ethos that characterized the Republic where laws had been developed to protect the nobility and both to protect and to exploit the *populares.* Commitment to values that shaped Roman culture in the Republic persisted, despite radical inconsistencies, and, as the Empire advanced this value system took root in the West.

Family as it facilitated the acquisition, increase, maintenance, and inheritance of wealth was integral to the value system of the Roman *nobiles.* Republican ideologies remained intact but social realities concerning marriage, adultery, sexuality, and a reduction in the "production" of progeny contrasted radically with those doctrines. Divisive factions and the growing number of families with newly acquired wealth who now also enjoyed the prosperity of the old ruling class indicated disrespect for traditional social structures.

Octavian Becomes Caesar Augustus

From the outset of his formal political career as emperor, Octavian (Emperor 27 B.C.E. to 14 C.E.) referred to himself as Caesar, but unlike his uncle he determined to achieve both personal and political objectives by accommodating the Senate's need for at least the appearance of status and power. Octavian maintained the appearances of a functioning "Republic," but he appropriated for himself the civil and military power of the state and functioned as a monarch. When he resigned his power in the Senate and took the title of *Princeps* or First Citizen, he was given power to conduct public business in the Assemblies and the Senate, power to veto, and immunity from arrest and punishment. Octavian's relationship with the Senate "concealed the novel, un-Republican nature of the regime and the naked power on which it rested" (Nagle 2002, 334).

Octavian's reforms reduced inefficiency and corruption and ended the danger to peace from those whose ambitions were unbridled. He established a stable government that saw a significant rise in colonization and the revitalization of Greek cities in the East. An increase in industry and commerce, public works, a system of roads and highways, and major building projects are also a part of his legacy.

The mythos of the Roman Empire proclaimed a social order founded on peace and prosperity in which marriage and stability within the family were central features. The *Ara Pacis Augustus* (Altar of Augustan Peace), a monumental tribute to this effort, includes all of the members of Octavian's family, priests and priestesses of the state religions, and children, signifying that peace is found in unity and conformity in religion and family. Laws to minimize adultery and divorce, and to encourage early marriages and the procreation and legitimization of children were created. The success of the Empire relied substantially upon women's compliance with these laws concerning marriage and bearing of children.

Social Organization at the Beginning of the Roman Empire

Among categories that are important to our understanding of social organization and stratification at the beginning of the Imperial period (see Chart 11–3), ***ordo*** and ***status*** are the most helpful.

The generalized status of a person is a composite of his or her ranks in all the relevant dimensions (Meeks 1988, 54). Distinctions of status provide the most helpful tools for determining women's experience. There were women inside and outside the nobility who secured for themselves vast estates, and slaves who were skilled professionals as scribes, physicians, and attorneys. Freedwomen (who had been manumitted from slavery) and female *metoikoi* were counted among these numbers. We begin our discussion in the household of Caesar.

Chart 11–3   Social Organization

The "orders" in Imperial Roman society were legally established categories. The two most important and enduring ones, who constituted less than one percent of the population were the

Senators and the Equestrians (discussed at length above) and **Cursus Honorum** (families whose members had served in the councils or senates of the provincial cities constituted a local order)

Plebs (in Rome) and the **ordo libertinorum** (referred, essentially, to everyone else) **Status** is perhaps the most helpful key for understanding the way that social stratification actually worked in the ancient world. And for this to be relevant we must consider how an individual ranked along each of several relevant dimensions: **Power** (how well an individual achieved goals within the social system)

Occupational prestige   **Family and ethnic group position**
Income or wealth   **Local community status** (Evaluation within some sub-group)
Education and knowledge
Religious and ritual purity

(Meeks, *The First Urban Christians*, 1983, 54.)

WOMEN IN THE ARISTOCRACY

The following selections reveal discrepancies in life experience within the household of Caesar Augustus. From Livy we include an account of Octavian's second wife, Livia, and her prominence in Octavian's life as mate, friend, political consultant, and his model of the ideal Roman woman for the Empire. In contrast, Caesar's daughter Julia who was also an accomplished woman, was blatantly used by her father as a political pawn to insure his own political objectives.

Livia, Empress of Augustus

The Empress Livia Augusta enjoys undisputed renown as a commanding figure in Roman history. Her public persona epitomized the noble Roman matron, and in the public performance of her duties as well as her social activities her presentation of herself was irreproachable. Octavian and Livia strategized together, met their individual obligations, and, despite situations that threatened their many successes, they worked as a team for over 50 years.

This enduring relationship, however, had rather dubious beginnings. Born Livia Drusilla in 58 B.C.E., Livia was the daughter of Marcus Livius Drusus Claudius and was known for her imposing presence. When Octavian met her, she was married to Tiberius Claudius Nero, a rival of Octavian, was the mother of one child, and pregnant with her second. As Octavian's interest in Livia intensified, she returned his affection, divorced her husband, and before the child in her womb was delivered she wed Octavian on January 17, 38 B.C.E.

Whereas the marriage created a minor scandal that subsided readily enough, the prestige that accompanied this marriage was integral to Octavian's successful quest to control the Senate. Octavian relied on Livia's innate political savvy for counsel in his own undertakings. As their political position became permanently ratified, he was also careful to promote her best image in public statues, coins, and in the dedication of public buildings and projects. Livia's image was customarily associated with traditional morals and values of the Roman nobility, especially as it pertained to marriage and family.

The excerpts below from Dio Cassius's *History of Rome* relate events that took place following Octavian's death.* He records the unprecedented inheritance that Livia received from Octavian and her political activities in relationship to her son, the Emperor Tiberius. Livy, *History of Rome*, LCL 1926, IV. CXXXVII.

---

*Dio Cassius, *Roman History*, LCL, 1925. VII, LVI.32.1-4; 42, 1-4; 46.1-47.1.

OCTAVIAN'S GENEROSITY TO LIVIA

. . . his will Drusus took from the Vestal Virgins, with whom it had been deposited, and carried it into the senate. Those who had witnessed the document examined the seals, and then it was read in the hearing of the senate.

It showed that two-thirds of the inheritance had been left to Tiberius and the remainder to Livia; at least this is one report. For, in order that she, too, should have some enjoyment of his estate, he had asked the senate for permission to leave her so much, which was more than the amount allowed by law . . . he did not restore his own daughter from exile, though he did hold her worthy to receive gifts; and he commanded that she should not be buried in his own tomb. So much was made clear by the will.

TIBERIUS'S RESENTMENT OF LIVIA

. . . Livia occupied a very exalted station, far above all women of former days, so that she could at any time receive the senate and such of the people as wished to greet her in her house; and this fact was entered in the public records. The letters of Tiberius bore for a time her name, also, and communications were addressed to both alike. Except that she never ventured to enter the senate-chamber or the camps or the public assemblies, she undertook to manage everything as if she were sole ruler. For in the time of Augustus she had possessed the greatest influence and she always declared that it was she who had made Tiberius emperor; consequently she was not satisfied to rule on equal terms with him, but wished to take precedence over him. As a result, various extraordinary measures were proposed, many persons expressing the opinion that she should be called Mother of her Country, and many that she should be called Parent. Still others proposed that Tiberius should be named after her, so that, just as the Greeks were called by their father's name, he should be called by that of his mother. All this vexed him, and he would neither sanction the honours voted her, with a very few exceptions, nor otherwise allow her any extravagance of conduct. For instance, she had once dedicated in her house an image to Augustus, and in honour of the event wished to give a banquet to the senate and the knights together with their wives, but he would not permit her to carry out any part of this programme.

LIVIA'S LEGACY IS INFLUENCED BY TIBERIUS

. . . Livia passed away at the age of eighty-six. Tiberius neither paid her any visits during her illness nor did he himself lay out her body; . . . The senate, however, did not content itself with voting merely the measures that he had commanded, but ordered mourning for her during the whole year on the part of the women, . . . They furthermore voted an arch in her honour—a distinction conferred upon no other woman—because she had saved the lives of not a few of them, had reared the children of many, and had helped many to pay their daughters' dowries, in consequence of all which some were calling her Mother of her Country. She was buried in the mausoleum of Augustus.

Tiberius did not pay to anybody a single one of her bequests.

Among the many excellent utterances of hers that are reported are the following. . . . When someone asked her how and by what course of action she had obtained such a commanding influence over Augustus, she answered that it was by being scrupulously chaste herself, doing gladly whatever pleased him, not meddling with any of his affairs, and, in particular, by pretending neither to hear of nor to notice the favourites that were the objects of his passion. Such was the character of Livia. . . .

Julia, Daughter of Augustus

One of the unhappiest father-daughter relationships of antiquity (for which we have documentation) was that of the Emperor Augustus and his daughter Julia. Most references about Julia neglect to point out the extent to which Octavian had arranged marriages for her that served his own political purposes. Julia retaliated by asserting her own independence and by engaging in social and sexual liaisons that suited her pleasure. When, finally, her father discovered his daughter's sexual behavior, he had her exiled from Rome. Macrobius' references to Julia point up the dramatic differences in the life experiences of Julia and Livia, both prominent members of the household of Caesar.

JULIA'S WIT[*]

Avienus the narrator of this section, . . . began talking about Julia saying something like this: "She was in her thirty-eighth year [and] she abused the indulgence of fortune no less than that of her father. Of course her love of literature and considerable culture, a thing easy to come by in that household, and also her kindness and gentleness and utter freedom from vindictiveness had won her immense popularity, and people who knew about her faults were amazed that she combined them with qualities so much their opposite.

"Her father had more than once, speaking in a manner indulgent but serious, advised her to moderate her luxurious mode of life and her choice of conspicuous associates. But when he considered the number of his grandchildren and their likeness to Agrippa, he was ashamed to entertain doubts about his daughter's chastity. So Augustus persuaded himself that his daughter was light-hearted almost to the point of indiscretion, but above reproach, and was encouraged to believe that his ancestress Claudia had also been such a person. He used to tell his friends that he had two somewhat wayward daughters whom he had to put up with, the Roman republic and Julia.

"One day she came into his presence in a somewhat risque costume, and though he said nothing, he was offended. The next day she changed her style and embraced her father, who was delighted by the respectability which she was affecting. Augustus, who the day before had concealed his distress, was now unable to conceal his pleasure. 'How much more suitable,' he remarked, 'for a daughter of Augustus in this costume!' 'Today,' she said, 'I dressed to be looked at by my father, yesterday to be looked at by my husband.'"

*Excerpt from Macrobius, *Saturnalia,* translated by H. Lloyd-Jones, 2.5.1–10, No. 266, in *WLGR,* 1992. 195.

. . . At a gladiatorial show Livia and Julia drew the attention of the people by the dissimilarity of their companions; Livia was surrounded by respectable men, Julia by men who were not only youthful but extravagant. Her father wrote that she ought to notice the difference between the two princesses, but Julia wittily wrote back, "These men will be old when I am old." When people who knew about her shocking behaviour said they were surprised that she who distributed her favours so widely gave birth to sons who were so like Agrippa, she said, "I never take on a passenger unless the ship is full."

CAENIS, CONCUBINE OF THE EMPEROR VESPASIAN[*]

At this time also Vespasian's concubine Caenis passed away. I mention her because she was extraordinarily faithful and because she had an excellent memory. Once, when Claudius' mother Antonia ordered her to write a secret letter to Tiberius about Sejanus, and then to erase it immediately, so that no trace of it remained Caenis replied, "Mistress, your orders are meaningless. For I carry everything that you have written, and anything else you tell me in my mind and no one can ever erase them." I think that she was remarkable for this response, and also because Vespasian got so much pleasure from her company; because of this she became very powerful, and acquired untold capital, so that the emperor was thought to have made money because of her efforts. For she received large sums from many sources, selling government offices to some, and to others procuratorships, generalships and priesthoods, and sometimes even imperial decisions. Vespasian never executed anyone for money, but he granted pardons to many who paid for them. And it was Caenis who took the money, though it was suspected that Vespasian was happy to delegate to her the job of taking money from the others.

NOBLE ROMAN WOMEN OUTSIDE OF ROME

The excerpts that follow in this section provide examples of the manner in which Roman women in the nobility who lived outside of Rome were able to achieve status in the "provinces." Great *virtue* among noble Roman matrons persisted as a characteristic that determined whether or not a matron was perceived favorably by males.

FLAVIA PUBLICIA NICOMACHIS. PHOCAEA, ASIA MINOR, SECOND CENTURY C.E.[**]

The council and the people, to Flavia Publicia Nicomachis, daughter of Dinomachus and Procle . . . their benefactor, and benefactor through her ancestors, founder of our city, president for life, in recognition of her complete virtue.

---

[*]Dio Cassius, *Roman History,* LCL, 1925, VIII, 65.14.1–5.

[**]From *Pleket 19,* No. 198, WLGR, 1992. 160.

Modia Quintia. Africa Proconsularis, Second–Third Centuries c.e.[*]

The town council decreed a statue of Modia Quintia, daughter of Quintus Modius Felix, perpetual priestess, who, on account of the honour of the priesthood, adorned the portico with marble paving, coffered ceilings and columns, exceeding in cost her original estimate with an additional contribution and quite apart from the statutory entry fee [for the priesthood] and also [built] an aqueduct. By decree of the town council, [erected] with public funds.

Aurelia Leite, Female Benefactor, Paros, 300 c.e.[**]

A monument to record the honours given her by her city, set up by the husband of a benefactress.

To the most renowned and in all respects excellent Aurelia Leite, daughter of Theodotus, wife of the foremost man in the city, Marcus Aurelius Faustus, hereditary high priest for life of the cult of Diocletian and his co-rulers, priest of Demeter and gymnasarch. She was gymnasarch (magistrate) of the gymnasium (school) which she repaired and renewed when it had been dilapidated for many years. The glorious city of the Parians, her native city, in return for her many great benefactions, receiving honour rather than giving it, in accordance with many decrees, has set up a marble statue of her. She loved wisdom, her husband, her children, her native city: (in verse) this woman, with her wisdom, best of mothers, his wife, Leite, renowned Faustus glorifies.

Pamphile, A Learned Woman, First Century c.e.[†]

Pamphile was an Epidaurian, a learned woman, the daughter of Soterides, who is also said to have been an author of books, according to Dionysius in the thirteenth book of his History of Learning; or, as others have written, it was Socratides her husband. She wrote historical memoirs in 33 books, an epitome of Ctesias history is three books, many epitomes of histories and other books, about controversies, sex, and many other things.

LEGAL STATUS OF WOMEN

Laws in the Roman Empire, 30 b.c.e.–250 c.e.

The selections below draw from a number of different types of legal writings. The Jurists, many of whom were teachers of the law, served in an advisory capacity to those who were administering the legal system. Gaius was a jurist and a teacher of law in the second century c.e. (150–180). By the time Gaius was writing, guardianship of women was a mere form, and by the reign of Constantine (306–337), it had vanished altogether.

---

[*]From *CIL VIII*.23888, No. 199, WLGR, 1992, 160.

[**]From *Pleket 31*, No. 200. WLGR, 1992. 160.

[†]*The Suda 23*, 3.520, *Fragmenta Historicorum Graecorum*, 1841–1870.

GAIUS ON THE GUARDIANSHIP OF WOMEN[*]

Where the head of a family has children in his power he is allowed to appoint guardians for them by will. That is, for males while under puberty but for females however old they are, even when they are married. For it was the wish of the old lawyers that women, even those of full age, should be in guardianship as being scatterbrained . . .

It is only under the Julian and Papian-Poppaean Acts that women are released from guardianship by the privilege of children. We speak, however, with the exception of the Vestal Virgins, whom even the old lawyers wished to be free of restraint in recognition of their priesthood; this is also provided in the Twelve Tables.

The ideal of the Roman family was seriously endangered in the late Republic and the early Empire. Among members of the upper classes moral and sexual dissipation was rampant. Of particular significance for perpetuating the empire was the fact that many couples did not marry and many couples elected not to have children. Augustus considered it a necessity to elevate moral standards at Rome, . . . to appease the sensibilities of the conservative members of the Senate and to increase the numbers of Roman citizens. Laws were enacted both to reward the begetting of children and to seriously punish anyone caught in adultery.

The first text that follows gives background for the passing of the laws. The remaining texts are from legal works interpreting the provisions of this legislation by a number of jurists.

Quintus Caecilius Metellus Macedonicus delivered this speech proclaiming legislation that required men to marry and procreate. Livy attributes this speech to Augustus as well, suggesting that it was in keeping with his own reform efforts to emphasize the importance of the family. In our next selection Dio Cassius echos this theme in Augustus.

A LAW REQUIRING MEN TO MARRY[**]

If we could survive without a wife, citizens of Rome, all of us would do without that nuisance; but since nature has so decreed that we cannot manage comfortably with them, nor live in any way without them we must plan for our lasting preservation rather than for our temporary pleasure.

REWARDS FOR MARRYING AND PRODUCING CHILDREN[†]

[Augustus] assessed heavier taxes on unmarried men and women without husbands, and by contrast offered awards for marriage and childbearing. And since there were more males than females among the nobility, he permitted anyone who wished (except for senators) to marry freedwomen, and decreed that children of such marriages be legitimate.

---

[*]Reprinted from *Institutes of Gaius,* by Gaius. ©1988 by Cornell University. Used by permission of the publisher Cornell University Press.

[**]Latin Fragment 6 Malcovati, WLGR, 1992, 103.

[†]Dio Cassius, *Roman History,* LCL, 1917, VI, 54–16.1–2.

THE CONSEQUENCES OF ADULTERY[*]

(1) In the second chapter of the Lex Julia concerning adultery, either an adoptive or a natural father is permitted to kill with his own hands an adulterer caught in the act with his daughter in his own house or in that of his son-in-law, no matter what his rank may be.

(4) A husband cannot kill anyone taken in adultery except persons who are infamous, and those who sell their bodies for gain, as well as slaves his wife, however, is excepted, and he is forbidden to kill her.

(8) It has been decided that a husband who does not at once dismiss his wife whom he has taken in adultery can be prosecuted as a pimp.

(11) It has been decided that adultery cannot be committed with women who have charge of any business or shop.

(12) Anyone who has sexual relations with a free male without his consent shall be punished with death.

(14) It has been held that women convicted of adultery shall be punished with the loss of half of their dowry and a third of their goods, and by relegation to an island. The adulterer, however, shall be deprived of half his property, and shall also be punished by relegation to an island; provided the parties are exiled to different islands.

(16) Sexual intercourse with female slaves, unless they have deteriorated in value or an attempt is made against their mistress through them, is not considered an injury.

Women with three or more children were legally authorized to function as agents in their own right in the purchase of property and other legal transactions. This significant legal right was the reward for bearing three children.

LOLLIANE, MOTHER OF THREE, REQUESTS LEGAL AUTONOMY[**]

Petition addressed to the most eminent prefect from Aurelia Thaisus also called Lolliane. [Laws exist] that grant authority to women who are honoured with the right of three children and that enable them to transact business without a kyrios in all household business they transact, and in particular women who are literate. Therefore, since I have been blessed with the honour of children, being literate and able to write with proficiency, in full confidence I petition your eminence with this application for the right to transact business without hindrance in all household affairs. I beg you to retain this application, without prejudice to my rights, in your eminence's office, and offer my eternal gratitude to you for your assistance. Farewell. Aurelia Thaisus also known as Lolliane has sent this petition for presentation. In the year 10 (emperor's name omitted), Epeiph 21. (added) Your application shall be kept in the office.

[*]Julius Paulus, *Civil Law, Opinions,* AMS Press, 1932. 1, 4, 8, 11, 12, 14, 16.
[**]From *Oxyrhynchus Papyrus,* 1896.1467.

RELIGION

A discussion of religious traditions in the Roman Empire takes into account the variety of religious institutions and new religious movements that emerged in the midst of radical social change. Civil religions were a part of Roman life having ancient roots in the conviction that ritual devotion to the Goddesses and Gods was integrally related to prosperity and peace in the state. For example, consider the indispensable connection between the worship of Vesta and the "home fires/hearths" of Roman families as well the negative implications for women's autonomy when the Vestal Virgins and their attention to the "home fires" serve as models for the Roman matron. Augustus revived many cults and ancient practices; he also restored numerous temples and from 12 B.C.E., he declared himself the religious head of the state (Nagle 2002, 337).

In addition to the traditional religious pantheon, religions dedicated to worship of the Emperor also emerged. As the Empire established colonies Rome adopted and adapted religious traditions from the various cultures that it incorporated. Many of the Gods and Goddesses from cultures conquered by Rome came to have great appeal among women in the Empire. Great religious festivals, holidays, and athletic tournaments to celebrate these deities highlighted each season of the Roman year. The Mystery traditions introduced previously held the most appeal of all. They were religions of redemption that provided a sense of forgiveness from sins. They provided a means of purification, formulae of access to the deity, and a promise of salvation in this life and the next. They provided a system of knowledge of the deity (*Gnosis*), a sacramental drama that included a ritual acting out of the suffering, struggles, and conflict in the life and death of the deity and her or his victory of faith. Mystery religions were also cosmic religions that reflected a human need for order both within and without that was characteristic of Hellenistic thought.

The Holy

Two mystery religions of the ancient female deities, Cybele and Isis, illustrate the importance of the Female Principle of the Divine in the Roman Empire.

During the threat of Hannibal's army, the Romans consulted the Sibyline Prophecies and found an oracle stating that an invading army could be defeated if the Mother Goddess were brought to Rome. The priestess who was Pythia at Delphi confirmed this and Cybele (whose precursor emerged in Anatolia ca. 7000 B.C.E.) was brought to Rome as a salvific deity in 204 B.C.E. Hannibal's retreat from Italy was credited to this deity. Worship of Cybele continued in the Empire for another 500 years.

By 200 C.E. Isis was the predominant deity in all of the Roman Empire. And no tradition provided as many opportunities for women's participation in capacities of leadership as did the Isis tradition.

The Mysteries in these religions were kept and remain mysteries. Lucius Apuleius, an Isaic priest and an attorney wrote his *Transformations,* better known as *The Golden Ass,* during the second century C.E. Embedded in this story of a zestful young man's quest for intrigue and adventure is his account of his *rescue* by the Goddess Isis, his subsequent initiation into her mysteries, and later his initiation into the Isaic priesthood.

Our excerpt begins when he is faced with an experience that would be so humiliating to Lucius that he would prefer death to such great "dishonor." It is at this very moment that the Goddess Isis intervenes.

THE TRANSFORMATION OF LUCIUS[*]

... All the perfumes of Arabia floated into my nostrils as the Goddess deigned to address me: "You see me here, Lucius, in answer to your prayer. I am Nature, the universal Mother, mistress of all the elements, primordial child of time, sovereign of all things spiritual, queen of the dead, queen also of the immortals, the single manifestation of all gods and goddesses that are. My nod governs the shining heights of Heaven, the wholesome sea-breezes, the lamentable silences of the world below. Though I am worshipped in many aspects, known by countless names, and propitiated with all manner of different rites, yet the whole round earth venerates me. ... Some know me as Juno, some as Bellona of the Battles; others as Hecate, others again as Rhamnubia, but both races of Aethiopians, whose lands the morning sun first shines upon, and the Egyptians who excel in ancient learning and worship me with ceremonies proper to my godhead, call me by my true name, namely, Queen Isis. I have come in pity of your plight, I have come to favour and aid you. Weep no more, lament no longer; the hour of deliverance, shone over by my watchful light, is at hand.

"Listen attentively to my orders. ...

"Tomorrow my priests offer me the first-fruits of the new sailing season by dedicating a ship to me. You must wait for this sacred ceremony, with a mind that is neither anxious for the future nor clouded with profane thoughts; and I shall order the High Priest to carry a garland of roses in my procession, ... Do not hesitate, push the crowd aside, join the procession with confidence in my grace. Then come close up to the High Priest as if you wished to kiss his hand, gently pluck the roses with your mouth and you will immediately slough off the hide of what has always been for me the most hateful beast in the universe.

"Above all, have faith ... "

Myth/Ritual

Lucius' account of initiation into the Isis tradition is the most detailed primary source text of its kind and is highly recommended to the reader. Lucius notes that he cannot tell us exactly what transpired during the most crucial part of his experience. But in the novel he provides a detailed treatise about his initiation including a vision from the Goddess, extended fasting, worshiping with the priests in the temple, the acquisition of special gifts and accessories, a purification ritual, and private instruction from ancient documents. In this brief excerpt Lucius brings us into the temple just before the mystery begins and greets us immediately as he emerges from the experience.

RITUALS OF INITIATION[**]

As evening approached a crowd of priests came flocking to me from all directions, each one giving me congratulatory gifts, as the ancient custom is. Then the High Priest ordered all uninitiated persons to depart, invested me in a new linen garment and led me by the hand into the inner recesses of the sanctuary itself.

---

[*]Excerpts from "The Goddess Intervenes" and "The Golden Ass is Transformed" *THE GOLDEN ASS* by Apuleius, translated by Robert Graves. © 1951 by Robert Graves. Reprinted by permission of Farrar, Straus, and Girous, LLC.
[**]Apeleius 1982, 277–280 excerpts.

I have no doubt, curious reader, that you are eager to know what happened when I entered. If I were allowed to tell you, and you were allowed to be told, you would soon hear everything; but, as it is, my tongue would suffer for its indiscretion and your ears for their inquisitiveness.

However, not wishing to leave you, if you are religiously inclined, in a state of tortured suspense, I will record as much as I may lawfully record for the uninitiated, but only on condition that you believe it. I approached the very gates of death and set one foot on Proserpine's threshold, yet was permitted to return, rapt through all the elements. At midnight I saw the sun shining as if the presence of the gods of the underworld and the gods of the upper-world stood near and worshipped them . . .

Well, now you have heard what happened, but I fear you are still none the wiser. The solemn rites ended at dawn and I emerged from the sanctuary wearing twelve different stoles. . . . The curtains were pulled aside and I was suddenly exposed to the gaze of the crowd, as when a statue is unveiled, dressed like the sun. That day was the happiest of my initiation, and I celebrated it as my birthday with a cheerful banquet at which all my friends were present. Further rites and ceremonies were performed on the third day, including a sacred breakfast, and these ended the proceedings. However, I remained for some days longer in the temple, enjoying the ineffable pleasure of contemplating the Goddess's statue, because I was bound to her by a debt of gratitude so large that I could never hope to pay it.

The following excerpt is from the *Fasti* (vi. 249–334), a poetical calendar of the Roman year written by Ovid (43 B.C.E.–17 C.E.). Ovid explains the origins of Vesta's temple, why it is round rather than the usual four-sided construction of Roman temples, why the Vestals are virgins, and why Vesta is not represented in anthropomorphic form.

OVID ON THE WORSHIP OF THE GODDESS VESTA[*]

O Vesta, grant me thy favour! In thy service now I open my lips, if it is lawful for me to come to thy sacred rites. I was wrapt up in prayer; I felt the heavenly deity, and the glad ground gleamed with a purple light. Not indeed that I saw thee, O goddess (far from me be the lies of poets!), nor was it meet that a man should look upon thee; but my ignorance was enlightened and my errors corrected without the help of an instructor.

The shape of the temple, as it now exists, is said to have been its shape of old, and it is based on a sound reason. Vesta is the same as the Earth; under both of them is a perpetual fire; the earth and the hearth are symbols of the home.

. . . Long did I foolishly think that there were images of Vesta: afterwards I learned that there are none under her curved dome. An undying fire is hidden in that temple; but there is no effigy of Vesta nor of the fire . . .

*From Ovid, *Fasti*, LCL, 1914. 5,339–43.

Female Functionaries

Among female priests of Isis there were a number of levels of authority in the hierarchy of ministers for which the priestess served on a temporary basis; often these terms were a one-year commitment. There were also permanent female priests of Isis who were committed for a lifetime of service. These women would have received training in the history of the Isis tradition, medicine and healing arts, astronomy, mathematics, rituals and myths of the Isis tradition, mysteries of the faith, baptisms, rituals to assure the rebirth of souls, and prayers and supplications for all of the feasts and fasts. This type of intensive training would also have applied to female priests in any tradition. In the Isis tradition, however, because the Egyptian priesthood had such a formidable history and legacy of highly specialized training, an Isaic priest was especially well trained (Witt, *Isis,* 1971; Heyob, *Cult of Isis,* 1979). Archaeological evidence suggests that most of the female priests for whom we have evidence were in smaller temples. Note that we will find similarities in the present day among female priests who are as equally well trained as male priests but who are assigned positions in smaller congregations or as assistant staff members at cathedrals and larger churches. Chart 11–4 lists the priestly titles held by female priests and a description of some of their duties.

Among the followers of Isis, as Chart 11–5 demonstrates, there were many roles and duties for women who were not in the priesthood. Thousands of women throughout the Empire filled these roles.

Chart 11–4   Priest's Titles in the Isis Tradition

Canephorai: Carried the sacrificial firstlings in processions.
Stolists: Unveiled the Sacred image of Isis, responsible for wardrobe of the Deities image; prepared her for veneration, at eventide disrobed her, familiar with all details for priestly ministry rituals, sacrifices, first fruits, prayers, processions, and festivals. Stolists rank right after the Chief Priest/ess.
Interpreter of Dreams
Pastophors: Carried small image of Isis in procession, less exacting, less ascetic than some priestesses. Practiced healing arts, studied medical treatises, understood anatomy, gynecology.
Prophets: Probably the Chief Priest/ess. There is evidence for female priests carrying the *sistula,* carried by the prophet. This woman knew philosophy, medicine, astronomy and was the protector of the Temple. The Prophet was also the collector of revenues.

(Heyob, The Cult of Isis, *1979)*

Chart 11–5   Female Religious Functionaries in the Isis Tradition

Melanephori: Honored Isis as the Black-robed queen. They lamented, chanted dirges, and celebrated the passion of Osiris. They were active as formal mourners at deaths and burials. Their lamentations were expressed in chanting and moaning for the deceased and for the grieving family.
Sacred Guilds
Theraputae: These were more practical servers who helped, for instance, with work on improvements at the Temple.
Isiaci: These followers of Isis were engaged in practical works.
Latria: Handmaids.
Decadistria: A cultic association that met on the 10th of every month.

(Heyob, Cult of Isis, *1979)*

WOMEN OUTSIDE THE NOBILITY

Musonius Rufus (30–101 C.E.), was a stoic philosopher, whose philosophical wisdom informed his decisions, his relationships, and his actions. Among writers at Rome who supported the education of women, Musonius penned a treatise that is exemplary in its pragmatic arguments for the "common sense" of this position. This selection provides the reader with excerpts from an extensive document that speaks to interconnections of philosophy and living life nobly and well, for females as well as males. He speaks eloquently about the quality of male/female relationships, specifically in marriages between partners who are equally well educated in philosophical discourse and commitment to the practice of virtue.

MUSONIUS RUFUS, ON THE EDUCATION OF WOMEN[*]

When he was asked whether women ought to study philosophy, he began to answer the question approximately as follows. Women have received from the gods the same ability to reason that men have. . . . It is reasonable, then, for me to think that women ought to be educated similarly to men in respect of virtue, and they must be taught starting when they are children, that this is good, and that bad, and that they are the same for both, and that this is beneficial and that harmful, and that one must do this, and not that. From these lessons reasoning is developed in both girls and boys, and there is no distinction between them. Then they must be told to avoid all base action. When these qualities have been developed both men and women will inevitably be sensible, and the well educated person, whether male or female, must be able to endure hardship, accustomed not to fear death, and accustomed not to be humbled by any disaster. . . . If someone asks me, which doctrine requires such an education, I would answer him that without philosophy no man and no woman either can be well educated. My point is that women ought to be good and noble in their characters, and that philosophy is nothing other than the training for that nobility.

He said that a husband and wife come together in order to lead their lives in common and to produce children, and that they should consider all their property to be common, and nothing private, not even their bodies. For the birth of a human being that such a union produces is a significant event, but it is not sufficient for the husband, because it could have come about without marriage, from some other conjunction, as in the case of animals. In marriage there must be complete companionship and concern for each other on the part of both husband and wife, in health and in sickness and at all times, because they entered upon the marriage for this reason as well as to produce offspring. When such caring for one another is perfect, and the married couple provide it for one another, and each strives to outdo the other, then this is marriage as it ought to be and deserving of emulation, since it is a noble union. But when one partner looks to his own interests alone and neglects the other's, or (by Zeus) the other is so minded that he lives in the same house, but keeps his mind on what is outside it, and does not wish to pull together with his partner or to cooperate, then inevitably the union is destroyed, and although they live together their common interests fare badly, and either they finally get divorced from one another or they continue on in an existence that is worse than loneliness.

*Musonius Rufus, *WLGR*, 1992. 50-54.

WOMEN'S OCCUPATIONS

Plebian Women, Freedwomen, and Female Slaves

The final section of this chapter is devoted to women who are remembered for posterity primarily in epigraphs, inscriptions, papyri, and lists. The selections are representative (not exhaustive) of the categories under which they appear. The bibliography for this chapter lists both primary and secondary sources for further research.

APOLLONIA, A PHILOSOPHER FROM MYSIA[*]

> For Magnilla, the philosopher, daughter of Magnus the of Menius, the philosopher.

A FEMALE COMMENTATOR ON RELIGIOUS RITUAL, DELPHI[**]

> With good fortune. The city of Delphi has decreed that Aufria of . . . is a citizen of Delphi, since she was present at the festival of the god, and demonstrated the entire range of her education, and delivered many excellent and enjoyable lectures at the assembly of Greeks at the Pythian games.

PHILE, FEMALE MAGISTRATE AND CIVIC BENEFACTOR, PRIENE[†]

> Phile, daughter of Apollonius wife of Thessalus son of Polydeuces; as the first woman stephanephoru she dedicated at her own expense a cistern and the water pipes in the city

Some of the women innkeepers, waitresses, and barmaids worked as prostitutes as well. Roman jurists addressed the situation of such women with liability. Apparently, considering the esteem in which she is held by her husband, Amemone was content with her work as a waitress.

AMEMONE, A BAR-MAID[††]

> . . . sweet . . . in this tomb lies Amemone, a bar-maid known [beyond the boundaries] of her own country, [on account of whom] many people used to frequent Tibur. [Now the supreme] god has taken [fragile life] from her, and a kindly light receives her spirit [in the aether]. I, . . . nus, [put up this inscription] to my holy wife. [It is right that her name] remain forever.

---

[*]*Epigraphica II, Pleket* 30, *WLGR,* 1992, 169.

[**]Fouilles de Delphes 4 79. *WLGR,* 1992. 158.

[†]*Pleket* 5, *WLGR,* 1992. 158.

[††]*WLGR,* 1992. 220.

Fine actors and actresses were greatly appreciated and admired by their public. In the social hierarchy, however, their lower status was maintained by laws that kept them marginalized, as illustrated in the following readings.[*]

An Actress from the Theatre at Aquileia

In the past she won resounding fame in many towns and many cities for her various accomplishments in plays, mimes, and choruses, and (often) dances. But she did not die on the stage, this tenth Muse.

To Bassilla, an Actress

To Bassilla the actress Heracleides, the skilled speaker and biographer, set up this stone. Even though she is dead, she will have the same honour she had in life, when she made her body "die" on the floor of the stage. This is what her fellow actors are saying to her: "Bassilla farewell, no one lives forever."

A Woman Who Practiced Medicine

This inscriptions for Primilla is one of numerous existing inscriptions about women who practiced medicine. Their designations as physicians distinguish them from midwives, although their medical expertise would undoubtedly have included gynecology and obstetrics.

Primilla, a Physician at Rome[**]

To my holy goddess. To Primilla, a physician, daughter of Lucius Vibius Melito. She lived 44 years, of which 30 she spent with Lucius Cocceius Apthorus without a quarrel. Apthorus built this monument for his chaste wife and for himself.

Women in the Service of the Imperial Household, Rome

The funerary inscriptions in Chart 11–6 are presented to acknowledge, by name, women, both slave and free who served the famous and the infamous in the imperial household.

Chart 11–6   Women in the Service of the Imperial Household

(8947) [The tomb] of Antonia Thallusa, freedwoman of the emperor, a midwife.

(8958) To Juno. [The tomb] of Dorcas, hairdresser of Julia Augusta, born a slave on Capri [in the imperial house].

(8949) To Julia . . . sia, freedwoman of the deified empress a midwife.

(5201) Gaius Papius Asclepiades, Papia, freedwoman of Eros, Julia Jucunda, nurse of Drusus and Drusilla.

(8959) Lycastus, polling-clerk, her fellow freedman, [put this up] for his dearest wife and for himself.

(4352) Prima, freedwoman of the emperor [Tiberius] and empress [Livia], nurse of Julia [Livilla, daughter of Germanicus.

(8957) To the gods of the dead. Claudia Parata, freedwoman of the emperor, hairdresser. She lived 27 years. Tiberius Julius Romanus, Tiberius Claudius Priscus, and Nedimus, slave of the emperor, her husbands, put up [this altar] at their own expense.

(9037) Extricata, seamstress of Octavia, daughter of [Claudius] Augustus, lived 20 years.

Data adapted from WLGR 1992, 222.

---

[*]*Epigrammatta Graeca*, 308, *WLGR,* 1992, 217.

[**]ILS7804, No. 370, *WLGR,* 1992, 264.

SUGGESTED READINGS

MacMullen, Ramsay. "Women in Public in the Roman Empire." *Historia* 29 (1980): 208–15.

Pomeroy, Sarah B. "The Relationship of the Married Woman to Her Blood Relatives in Rome." *Ancient Society* 7 (1976): 215–27.

Tregiari, Susan. "Domestic Staff at Rome in the Julio-Claudian Period: 27 B.C. to A.D. 68." *Histoire Sociale, Revue Canadienne* 6: 41–55.

Sources Cited

Chart 11–3 Meeks, Wayne. *The First Urban Christians: The Social World of the Apostle Paul.* New Haven and London: Yale University Press, 1983. 54.

Dio Cassius, Octavian's Generosity to Livia; Tiberius's Resentment of Livia; Livia's Legacy Is Influenced by Tiberius, *Roman History.* Translated by Earnest Carey. Loeb Classical Library. Cambridge and London: Harvard University Press, 1925. Vol. VII, LVI.32.1–4; 42, 1–4; 46.1–47.1.

Macrobius. Julia's Wit. *Saturnalia,* 2.5.1–10. No. 266. Translated by H. Lloyd-Jones. In *Women's Life in Greece and Rome.* Edited by Mary R. Lefkowitz and Maureen B. Fant. Baltimore: Johns Hopkins University Press, 1992. 195.

Dio Cassius. "Caenis, Concubine of the Emperor Vespasian." *Roman History.* Translated by Earnest Carey. Loeb Classical Library, Cambridge and London: Harvard University Press, 1925. vol. VIII, 65.14.1–5.

"Flavia Publicia Nicomachis. Phocaea," Asia Minor. *Pleket 19.* No. 198. Translated by M.R. Lefkowitz. In *Women's Life in Greece and Rome.* Edited by Mary R. Lefkowitz and Maureen B. Fant. Baltimore: Johns Hopkins University Press, 1992. 160

"Modia Quintia. Africa Proconsularis." CIL VIII.23888. No. 199. Translated by Maureen B. Fant. In *Women's Life in Greece and Rome.* Edited by Mary R. Lefkowitz and Maureen B. Fant. Baltimore: Johns Hopkins University Press, 1992. 160.

Aurelia Leite, Female Benefactor. *Pleket 31.* No. 200. Translated by Mary R. Lefkowitz. In *Women's Life in Greece and Rome.* Edited by Mary R. Lefkowitz and Maureen B. Fant. Baltimore: Johns Hopkins University Press, 1992. 160.

Pamphile, A Learned Woman. The Suda 23, 3.520, *Fragmenta Historicorum Graecorum,* 1841–1870.

Gaius. Gaius on the Guardianship of Women. *Institutes of Gaius.* Translated by W.M. Gordon and O.F. Robinson. Ithaca, NY: Cornell University Press, 1988. 1.144–5, 190–1

A Law Requiring Men to Marry. *Women's Life in Greece and Rome.* Edited by Mary R. Lefkowitz and Maureen B. Fant. Baltimore: Johns Hopkins University Press, 1992. 103.

Dio Cassius. Rewards for Marrying and Producing Children. *Roman History,* Translated by Earnest Carey. Loeb Classical Library, Cambridge and London: Harvard University Press, 1917. vol. VI, 54–16.1–2.

Julius Paulus. The Consequences of Adultery. *The Civil Law, Opinions.* Translated by S.P. Scott. New York: AMS Press, 1932 2.26.1–8, 10–12, 14–17

Lolliane, Mother of Three, Requests Legal Autonomy. *Oxyrhynchus Papyrus,* 1896. 1467.

Lucius Apuleius. *The Transformation of Lucius,* from *The Transformation of Lucius: Otherwise Known as the Golden Ass.* Translated by Robert Graves. New York: Farrar, Straus & Giroux, 1951. 263–265.

Apuleius. Rituals of Initiation. *The Transformation of Lucius: Otherwise Known as the Golden Ass.* Translated by Robert Graves. New York: Farrar, Straus & Giroux, 1951.

Ovid. On the Worship of the Goddess Vesta. *Fasti.* Translated by Sir James George Frazer. Loeb Classical Library. Cambridge and London: Harvard University Press, 1982. 5, 339–343.

Musonius Rufus. On the Education of Women. 3, 4, 13a. No. 75. *Women's Life in Greece and Rome.* Edited by Mary R. Lefkowitz and Maureen B. Fant. Baltimore: Johns Hopkins University Press, 1992. 50.

Apollonia. In *Epigraphica II, Pleket 30.* No. 221. *Women's Life in Greece and Rome.* Edited by Mary R. Lefkowitz and Maureen B. Fant. Baltimore: Johns Hopkins University Press, 1992. 169.

Euphrosyne, A Roman Philosopher. CIL VI. 33898 = ILS 7783. No. 222. *Women's Life in Greece and Rome.* Edited by Mary R. Lefkowitz and Maureen B. Fant. Baltimore: Johns Hopkins University Press, 1992. 169.

"A Female Commentator on Religious Ritual." Fouilles de Delphes 4 79. No. 192. *Women's Life in Greece and Rome.* Edited by Mary R. Lefkowitz and Maureen B. Fant. Baltimore: Johns Hopkins University Press, 1992. 158.

Phile, A Female Magistrate and Civic Benefactor. *Pleket 5.* No. 194. *Women's Life in Greece and Rome.* Edited by Mary R. Lefkowitz and Maureen B. Fant. Baltimore: Johns Hopkins University Press, 1992. 158.

"Amemone, a Bar-Maid." CIL XIV. 3709 = ILS 7477. No. 326. *Women's Life in Greece and Rome.* Edited by Mary R. Lefkowitz and Maureen B. Fant. Baltimore: Johns Hopkins University Press, 1992. 220.

Actress from the Theatre at Aquileia. *Epigrammatta Graeca (Kaibel 609).* No.308. *Women's Life in Greece and Rome.* Edited by Mary R. Lefkowitz and Maureen B. Fant. Baltimore: Johns Hopkins University Press, 1992. 217.

Chapter 12

Christian Origins

The present chapter examines the burgeoning sectarian movement in Judaism that emerged in the first century C.E. among followers of a young prophet and sage from the Judean countryside. It traces the history of Christ's origins to the close of the fourth century, when Christianity had become the state religion of the Roman Empire. By the time the empire in the West had succumbed to the Gauls and Visigoths, Christianity had spread throughout the Near East and the Mediterranean basin and included foundations in the British Isles, Northern Africa, and Western Europe. In the Eastern provinces, the Church continued to prosper throughout the Byzantine Era.

Sacred texts and their critics, as well as analysis of social/historical contexts, provide the primary data about women in Christian origins (first to third century C.E.). Such texts and analyses therefore serve as the principal lens through which this chapter views women's experience during the first 300 hundred years of the common era. Within this somewhat narrow focus there is an unexpected breadth of information that disputes and calls into question androcentric interpretations of Christian texts and traditions that have promoted the subjugation of women and ignored or denied women's leadership roles in Christian origins.

Chapters 9, 10 and 11 of this volume lay the foundations of a social context for representing women in Christian origins. Patriarchal cultural norms were dominant, yet, those few opportunities for women that appear to have become available in the Hellenistic period, and continued into the early Empire became significant factors for women's participation in culture. Urbanization and voluntary associations, for example, that emerged in the Hellenistic period and persisted during the Empire afforded some wealthy women both inside and outside the nobility opportunities to achieve prestigious status as patrons and administrators within their communities. Such women, especially among freedwomen and non-citizen residents (*metoikoi*) were often status inconsistent. That is, they were women who had acquired or accumulated wealth but were prohibited from upward mobility by social class and order. Trade, commerce, and mystery religions also continued to flourish in the Empire and provided numerous opportunities for women to achieve status within their communities. Among women in Roman Palestine, Syria, and the Mediterranean Basin there were women who emerged as teachers, preachers, missionaries, deacons, presbyters, prophets, priests, and even bishops as a burgeoning Christianity first began to spread across the Empire. Some of these women would, necessarily, have been literate and educated.

The majority of the reading selections in this chapter, with two or three possible exceptions, were written by males, from the perspective of male experience. When, however, we reconstruct the social and cultural context of women in texts that represent Christian origins, by analogy with other women in the Greco-Roman world, we find compelling evidence for women's leadership roles in Christianity's formative generations. By the time that the religion was fully institutionalized the status of women was diminished, controlled by the patriarchal hierarchy, and must be discussed from radically different perspectives.

THE WOMEN AROUND JESUS

In the Hebrew Bible, the prophet Elijah and the prophet Samuel anointed the heads of kings of Israel with oil as a ritual of investiture of their kingly office. In the Christian Testament there are three texts in which Jesus is anointed by a female disciple. The most frequently quoted passage refers to a female prostitute who anoints Jesus' feet with her tears and dries his feet with her hair. The two passages that attest to a woman who anointed the head of Jesus with oil are seldom quoted. The gesture of the woman standing above Jesus' head and anointing him with oil, a gesture that Jesus identified as a prophetic preparation for his burial, evokes an image of female authority. Prophetic authority from female prophets has roots in the historical period, as we have seen, from the time of the female prophets of Ishtar and the female prophets at Mari (Chapter 3) who received oracles for King Zimri-Lim and in Ancient Israel among Miriam, Deborah, and Huldah. Prophetic utterance in a time-honored ritual gesture, performed by a female was acceptable to the world view of Jesus as Jesus was portrayed by the authors of the Gospels of Matthew and Mark. Such authority attributed to a female has not been favored by androcentric biblical commentators whose interpretations have informed succeeding generations.

PROPHETIC GESTURE: A WOMAN WHO ANOINTED JESUS' HEAD[*]

> Now while Jesus was at Bethany in the house of Simon the leper, a woman came to him with an alabaster jar of very costly ointment, and she poured it on his head as he sat at the table. But when the disciples saw it, they were angry and said, "Why this waste? For this ointment could have been sold for a large sum, and the money given to the poor." But Jesus, aware of this, said to them, "Why do you trouble the woman? She has performed a good service for me, for you always have the poor with you, but you will not always have me. By pouring this ointment on my body she has prepared me for burial. Truly I tell you, wherever this good news is proclaimed in the whole world, what she has done will be told in remembrance of her."

WOMAN WHO ANOINTED JESUS' HEAD[**]

> It was two days before the Passover and the festival of Unleavened Bread. The chief priests and the scribes were looking for a way to arrest Jesus, by stealth and kill him; for they said, "Not during the festival, or there may be a riot among the people."
>   While he was at Bethany in the house of Simon the leper, as he sat at the table, a woman came with an alabaster jar of very costly ointment of nard, and she broke

*NRSV, 1991, Matthew 26:6–13.
**NRSV, 1991, Mark 14:1–9.

open the jar and poured the ointment on his head. But some were there who said to one another in anger, "Why was the ointment wasted in this way? For this ointment could have been sold for more than three hundred denarii, and the money given to the poor." And they scolded her. But Jesus said, "Let her alone; why do you trouble her? She has performed a good service for me. For you always have the poor with you, and you can show kindness to them whenever you wish; but you will not always have me. She has done what she could; she has anointed my body beforehand for its burial. Truly I tell you, wherever the good news is proclaimed in the whole world, what she has done will be told in remembrance of her."

Mary of Magdala

Among women in the biblical world, with the exception of Mary the mother of Jesus, perhaps none evokes a greater spark of recognition among Christians than Mary of Magdala. This enigmatic woman is the only person mentioned by name in all four Gospels as present at the death and resurrection of Jesus. She traveled with Jesus and was one of several women who provided material support for him and for his followers. She was present at the single most significant event in the Christian tradition, the resurrection, yet her name is not found in the canon of scripture outside of the four Gospels.

There are however, several other texts from the biblical world in the first two centuries C.E. that reference Mary Magdalene and attest to her status as a confidant of Jesus and as among his most trusted disciples. It was Mary Magdalene that Jesus sent to tell the other disciples about his resurrection. As one who accompanied Jesus in ministry, who witnessed the resurrection and as the person mentioned that Jesus first sent to "go and tell . . ." about his resurrection, Mary Magdalene is the first Apostle and the "Apostle to the Apostles," a title by which she is known in texts and iconography up through the Middle Ages.

Many scholars believe there was a situation in the early church in which some people saw Mary Magdalene as having apostolic authority just as others saw Peter in that capacity.

Mary Magdalene is featured in several early Christian writings. Texts and traditions that represent early phases of the post-resurrection period attest to her spiritual wisdom and her trusted relationship with Jesus. The nature of the relationship between Jesus and Mary Magdalene implies her authority within the community. Later, traditions in the Middle Ages refer to Mary Magdalene as a great teacher and preacher. There are also traditions suggesting that at the end of her life she became a hermit and devoted herself to a life of love and contemplation of her beloved Jesus.

In later centuries traditions about the Magdalene conflate her stories with biblical figures such as the woman taken in adultery and ascribe to her the status of sinner and penitent. Such ascriptions appear nowhere in the scriptural texts. We provide this lengthy introduction because the various and varied traditions about Mary Magdalene provide an excellent example of the manner in which stories about female leaders in the Church have been advanced and have distorted, ignored, and misrepresented authoritative women in Christian origins.

MARY MAGDALENE AMONG WOMEN WHO PROVIDED FOR JESUS[*]

Soon afterwards he went on through cities and villages, proclaiming and bringing the good news of the kingdom of God. The twelve were with him, as well as some women who had been cured of evil spirits and infirmities: Mary, called Magdalene,

*NRSV, 1991, Luke 8:1–6.

from whom seven demons had gone out, and Joanna, the wife of Herod's steward Chuza, and Susanna, and many others, who provided for them out of their resources.

THE MAGDALENE AT THE RESURRECTION IN LUKE'S GOSPEL[*]

But on the first day of the week, at early dawn, they came to the tomb, taking the spices that they had prepared. They found the stone rolled away from the tomb, but when they went in, they did not find the body. While they were perplexed about this, suddenly two men in dazzling clothes stood beside them. The women were terrified and bowed their faces to the ground, but the men said to them, "Why do you look for the living among the dead? He is not here, but has risen. Remember how he told you, while he was still in Galilee, that the Son of Man must be handed over to sinners, and be crucified, and on the third day rise again." Then they remembered his words, and returning from the tomb, they told all this to the eleven and to all the rest.

[*Mary Magdalene was the first named among those who was an apostle to the apostles*]

Now it was Mary Magdalene, Joanna, Mary, the mother of James, and the other women with them who told this to the apostles. But these words seemed to them an idle tale, and they did not believe them. But Peter got up and ran to the tomb; stooping and looking in, he saw the linen cloths by themselves; then he went home, amazed at what had seen.

MARY MAGDALENE IN JOHN'S PASSION NARRATIVE[**]

. . . Meanwhile, standing near the cross of Jesus were his mother, and his mother's sister, Mary the wife of Clopas and Mary Magdalene.

Early on the first day of the week, while it was still dark, Mary Magdalene came to the tomb and saw that the stone had been removed from the tomb. So she ran and went to Simon Peter and the other disciple, the one whom Jesus loved, and said to them, "They have taken the Lord out of the tomb, and we do not know where they have laid him.". . .

[*The disciples, came to the tomb, disbelieved Mary's story and after they had returned to their homes she wept*]

But Mary stood weeping outside the tomb. As she wept, she bent over to look into the tomb; and she saw two angels in white, sitting where the body of Jesus had been lying, one at the head and the other at the feet. They said to her, "Woman, why are you weeping?" She said to them, "They have taken away my Lord, and I do not know where they have laid him." When she had said this, she turned around and saw Jesus standing there, but she did not know that it was Jesus. Jesus said to her, "Woman, why are you weeping? Whom are you looking

---

[*]NRSV, 1991, Luke 24:1–10.

[**]NRSV, 1991, John 19:25, 20:1–2, 11–18. See also he Gospels of Matthew (27:50–28:10) and Mark (15:40–16:8).

for?" Supposing him to be the gardener, she said to him, "Sir, if you have carried him away, tell me where you have laid him, and I will take him away." Jesus said to her, "Mary!" She turned and said to him in Hebrew, "Rabbouni!" (which means teacher). Jesus said to her, "Do not hold on to me, because I have not yet ascended to the Father. But go to my brothers and say to them, 'I am ascending to my Father and your Father, to my God and your God.' Mary Magdalene went and announced to the disciples, "I have seen the Lord"; and she told them at he had said these things.

This next text comes from a collection of documents that were written in the late first or early second century C.E. In the fourth century, they had been buried in the desert near the monastery of St. Pachomius at Nag Hammadi in Egypt. The texts were discovered and excavated in 1947, translated from the Coptic language and published for the public in 1977. These documents are writings of early Christians whose theology was represented in complex and often confusing texts containing secret sacred knowledge (gnosis). The following section from the Gospel of Phillip recounts a conversation about the relationship between Mary Magdalene and Jesus.

GOSPEL OF PHILLIP PRESENTS MARY MAGDALENE AS JESUS' COMPANION*

There were three who always walked with the Lord: Mary his mother and her sister and Magdalene, the one who was called his companion. His sister and his mother and his companion were each a Mary. "The Lord went into the dye works of Levi. He took seventy-two different colors" and threw them into the vat. He took them out all white. And he said, "Even so has the Son of Man come [as] a dyer." As for the Wisdom who is called "the barren," she is the mother [of the] angels. And the companion of the [Savior is] Mary Magdalene. [But Christ loved] her more than [all] the disciples [and used to] kiss her [often] on her [mouth]. The rest of [the disciples were offended] by it [and expressed disapproval]. They said to him, "Why do you love her more than all of us?" The Savior answered and said to them, "Why do I not love you like her?" When a blind man and one who sees are both together in darkness, they are no different from one another. When the light comes, then he who sees will see the light, and he who is blind will remain in darkness.

The Gospel of Mary is another of the Gnostic documents found at Nag Hammadi, along with The Gospel of Phillip just presented. The earliest known fragment of this particular text dates back to the third century C.E. This post-resurrection dialogue includes Jesus speaking with his female and male disciples. When Jesus instructs the disciples to preach the Good News and they respond with a lack of courage, Mary Magdalene gives them strength. She also relates teachings of Jesus that he had given to her privately. The conflict that arises when some of the disciples resent Mary's close relationship to Jesus indicates that although in this Gnostic community a woman taught with Jesus' authority there were members of the community who found her authority difficult to accept.

*Gospel of Phillip II, 3, The Nag Hammadi Library In English, edited by James M. Robinson, San Francisco and Cambridge: Harper and Row, 1977, 135.

THE GOSPEL OF MARY[*]

. . . When Mary had said this, she fell silent, since it was to this point that the Savior had spoken with her. But Andrew answered and said to the brethren, "Say what you (wish to) say about what she has said. I at least do not believe that the Savior said this. For certainly these teachings are strange ideas." Peter answered and spoke concerning these same things. He questioned them about the Savior: "Did he really speak privately with a woman (and) not openly to us? Are we to turn about and all listen to her? Did he prefer her to us?"

Then Mary wept and said to Peter, "My brother Peter, what do you think? Do you think that I thought this up myself in my heart, or that I am lying about the Savior?" Levi answered and said to Peter, "Peter, you have always been hot-tempered. Now I see you contending against the woman like the adversaries. But if the Savior made her worthy, who are you indeed to reject her? Surely the Savior knows her very well. That is why he loved her more than us. Rather let us be ashamed and put on the perfect man, and separate as he commanded us and preach the gospel, not laying down any other rule or other law beyond what the Savior said." When [. . .] and they began to go forth [to] proclaim and to preach.

MARTHA

In the events leading up to Jesus' raising of Lazarus from the dead, Martha is the first woman to confess Jesus as the Christ. She is confident in her identity, she meets and relates to Jesus as one who is accepted as person, beyond the limitations assigned to her gender. The freedom to be authentic that Martha experiences in relationship to Jesus points to the gender equality in the early Jesus movement.

JOANNA[**]

Joanna is seldom mentioned among women in the New Testament. She left her position at the court of King Herod where her husband Chuza, was an officer and senior official. Joanna is a woman from the aristocracy who left the material security of life at court to share in the life and ministry of a young prophet and sage who was also considered a social revolutionary. Despite texts that name Joanna among women who anointed Jesus for burial, in the context of patriarchal values Joanna's leaving of her husband made her a scandalous woman.

Soon afterwards he went on through cities and villages, proclaiming and bringing the good news of the kingdom of God. The twelve were with him, as well as some women who had been cured of evil spirits and infirmities: Mary, called Magdalene, from whom seven demons had gone out, and Joanna, the wife of

---

[*]*NHLE,* 1977, "Gospel of Mary," 472–474.
[**]NRSV, 1991, Luke 8: 5–6, 24:10.

Herod's steward Chuza, and Susanna, and many others, who provided for them out of their resources.

But on the first day of the week, at early dawn, they came to the tomb, taking the spices that they had prepared. They found the stone rolled away from the tomb, but when they went in, they did not find the body. While they were perplexed about this, suddenly two men in dazzling clothes stood beside them. The women were terrified and bowed their faces to the ground, but the men said to them, "Why do you look for the living among the dead? He is not here, but has risen. Remember how he told you, while he was still in Galilee, that the Son of Man must be handed over to sinners, and be crucified, and on the third day rise again." Then they remembered his words, and returning from the tomb, they told all this to the eleven and to all the rest. Now it was Mary Magdalene, Joanna, Mary the mother of James, and the other women with them who told this to the apostles. . . .

Female Prophets

Anna the prophet, portrayed by the author of Luke's Gospel would have been a contemporary of historical Jewish female ascetics such as the Theraputae, the Virtuous Women among the Essenes (4Q 502), and the fictional Judith. In this selection, she forsees Jesus as a redeemer.

ANNA THE PROPHET[*]

And the child's father and mother were amazed at what was being said about him. Then Simeon blessed them and said to his mother Mary, "This child is destined for the falling and the rising of many in Israel, and to be a sign that will be opposed so that the inner thoughts of many will be revealed, and a sword will pierce your own soul too." There was also a prophet, Anna the daughter of Phanuel, of the tribe of Asher. She was of a great age, having lived with her husband seven years after her marriage, then as a widow to the age of eighty-four. She never left the temple but worshiped there with fasting and prayer night and day. At that moment she came, and began to praise God and to speak about the child, to all who were looking for the redemption of Jerusalem.

FOUR SISTERS ARE PROPHETS[**]

. . . The next day we left and came to Caesarea; and we went into the house of Philip the evangelist, one of the seven, and stayed with him. He had four unmarried daughters who had the gift of prophecy.

[*]NRSV, 1991, Luke 2:36-38.
[**]NRSV, 1991, Acts 21:9.

WOMEN IN THE APOSTOLIC CHURCH

Teachers

In this account it is clear that the female teacher and missionary Priscilla, sometimes referred to as Prisca, teaches Apollos as does her husband Aquila. It is significant as well that in this account of Prisca as a teacher she is correcting inferior or incorrect teaching that Apollos had received in Alexandria.

PRISCILLA AND AQUILA[*]

> Now there came to Ephesus a Jew named Apollos, a native of Alexandria. He was an eloquent man, well-versed in the scriptures. He had been instructed in the Way of the Lord; and he spoke with burning enthusiasm and taught accurately the things concerning Jesus, though he knew only the baptism of John. He began to speak boldly in the synagogue; but when Priscilla and Aquila heard him, they took him aside and explained the Way of God to him more accurately. And when he wished to cross over to Achaia, the believers encouraged him and wrote to the disciples to welcome him. On his arrival he greatly helped those who through grace had become believers, for he powerfully refuted the Jews in public, showing by the scriptures that the Messiah is Jesus.

Female Missionaries and Leaders at Rome

Among important leaders in burgeoning Christianity, Phoebe receives the titles *diakonos* (deacon) of the Church at Cenchreae and *prostasis* (president, leading officer). Schussler-Fiorenza (E.Schussler-Fiorenza, *In Memory of Her*, 1983) suggests it may be that in Phoebe's designated role of leadership in Cenchreae she had traveled to Rome to defend the interests of her community.

PHOEBE: DEACON AND PROSTASIS AT CENCHREAE[**]

> I commend to you our sister Phoebe, a deacon of the church at Cenchreae, so that you may welcome her in the Lord as is fitting for the saints, and help her in whatever she may require from you, for she has been a benefactor of many and of myself as well.

In the text that follows we see Prisca (Priscilla) mentioned again in Rome. She and her husband had homes in Corinth and Ephesus as well as Rome. The fact the Prisca's name precedes that of her husband indicates that her status is the more prestigious of the two. It could be that Aquila is a freed man.

[*]NRSV, 1991, Acts 18:24–28.
[**]NRSV, 1991, Romans 16:1–2.

PRISCA: MISSIONARY, LEADER OF A CHURCH, TEACHER[*]

> Greet Prisca and Aquila, who work with me in Christ Jesus, and who risked their
> necks for my life, to whom not only I give thanks, but also all the churches of the
> Gentiles. Greet also the church in their house.

MARY: A WORKER IN THE CHURCH AT ROME[**]

> Greet Mary, who has worked very hard among you.

Although quite clearly Mary Magdalene is the first apostle, Junia is the only female cited specifically as an apostle in the New Testament canon.

JUNIA, APOSTLE[†]

> Greet Andronicus and Junia, my relatives who were in prison with me; they are
> prominent among the apostles, and they were in Christ before I was.

Tryphaena, mentioned here by Paul as a worker in the Lord, is presented in a much broader portrait in the Acts of Thecla. In the Acts of Thecla, this historical figure is Queen Tryphaena, widow of King Cotys of Thrace. Tryphaena, in addition to her many other endeavors in the burgeoning church, cares for and supports the female missionary Thecla during very difficult times in Thecla's ministry.

TRYPHAENA; TRYPHOSA: WORKERS IN THE LORD[††]

> Greet those workers in the Lord, Tryphaena and Tryphosa.

THE MOTHER OF RUFUS: A MOTHER TO PAUL[‡]

> Greet the beloved Persis, who has worked hard in the Lord. Greet Rufus, chosen in
> the Lord; and greet his mother—a mother to me also. Greet Asyncritus, Phlegon,
> Hermes, Patrobas, Hermas, and the brothers and sisters who are with them.

JULIA: THE SISTER OF NEREUS; OLYMPAS: SAINTS IN THE CHURCH AT ROME[‡‡]

> Greet Philologus, Julia, Nereus and his sister, and Olympas, and all the saints who are
> with them. Greet one another with a holy kiss. All the churches of Christ greet you.

[*]NRSV, 1991, Romans 16:3–5.

[**]NRSV, 1991, Romans 16:6.

[†]NRSV, 1991, Romans 16:7.

[††]NRSV, 1991, Romans 16:12.

[‡]NRSV, 1991, Romans 16:13–14.

[‡‡]NRSV, 1991, Romans 16:15.

WOMEN IN THE POST-APOSTOLIC CHURCH

Female Priests among Thracians

This selection affirms the ministry of female priests in the early Christian church and affirms an early date for communities that express special reverence for Mary the mother of Jesus. Note in particular the reference to baking special breads to honor Mary. The reader may recall that this practice was found among worshipers of Astarte, the Queen of Heaven, whose breads were baked in molds shaped as a likeness of the Goddess. In later periods one of the Virgin Mary's epithets includes The Queen of Heaven. Note how disturbing the male author of this selection finds the practice of the priestesses who honor Mary.

ARABIAN CHRISTIAN WOMEN OF THRACIAN DESCENT WHO BAKE CAKES TO THE VIRGIN MARY AND FUNCTION AS PRIESTS[*]

> For it is related that some women in Arabia, who come from the region of Thrace, put forward this silly idea: they prepare a kind of cake in the name of the ever-Virgin, assemble together, and in the name of the holy Virgin they attempt to undertake a deed that is irreverent and blasphemous beyond measure—in her name they function as priests for women. Now all this is gross and irreverent, a degeneration from the proclamation of the Holy Spirit, all of it a diabolic device and the teaching of an unclean spirit. In their regard the saying is fulfilled: "Some will separate themselves from the sound teaching, clinging to myths and demonic teachings" [I Tim. 4:11]. They will be worshipers of the dead, even as they (the dead) were worshiped in Israel. But the glory given to God by the Saints each in his proper time has become as good as error to those who do not see the truth.

Montanus was converted to Christianity in 155 C.E. Some time after his conversion he prophesied that he had been possessed by the Holy Spirit. Two women, Priscilla and Maximilla, who were members of his congregation, also began to be recognized as prophets. Montanists claimed that their movement was the beginning of the age of the Spirit and required of believers a more rigorous moral life. The emerging Church experienced Montanism as a movement that diminished the significance of events in the New Testament and thus followers of Montanus came to be considered heretical. Tertullian, a famous Christian apologist, was attracted by the more intense emphasis on morality and became, himself, a Montanist. Tertullian, whose writings most often have an androcentric perspective praises this female visionary.

A MONTANIST VISIONARY SUBMITS HER REVELATION TO CAREFUL SCRUTINY[**]

> We have now amongst us a sister whose lot it has been to be favoured with gifts of revelation, which she experiences in the Spirit by ecstatic vision amidst the sacred rites of the Lord's Day in the church; she converses with angels, and sometimes even

---

[*]Epiphanius. *Medicine Box* 78.23, 4th century C.E.," translated by Carolyn Osick. In *Maenads, Martyrs, Matrons, Monastics,* edited by Ross S. Kraemer, 50, No. 29. Philiadelphia: Fortress Press, 1988.

[**]Tertullian. In *On the Soul,* No. 101, 224. A Select Library of the Nicene and Post Nicene Fathers of the Christian Church. New York and Grand Rapids, MI: Christian Literary Company; William B. Eardmans (Reprint), 1886–1900, 1952–1963.

with the Lord; she both sees and hears mysterious communications; some men's hearts she discerns, and she obtains directions for healing for such as need them. Whether it be in the reading of the Scriptures, or in the chanting psalms, or in the preaching of sermons, or in the offering up of prayers, in all these religious services matter and opportunity are afforded her of seeing visions. Perchance, while this sister of ours was in the Spirit, we had discoursed on some topic about the soul. After the people are dismissed at the conclusion of the sacred services, she is in the regular habit of reporting to us whatever things she may have seen in vision; for all her communications are examined with the most scrupulous care, in order that their truth may be probed. "Amongst other things," she says, "there was shown to me a soul in bodily shape, and a spirit appeared to me; not, however, a void and empty illusion, but such as would offer itself to be even grasped by the hand, clear and transparent and of an ethereal colour, and in form resembling that of a human being in every respect." This was her vision, and for her witness there was God; and the apostle is a fitting surety that there were to be Spiritual gifts in the Church.

Hippolytus' response to these female Montanists prophets differs quite substantially from that of Tertullian. What issues seem to be central for Hippolytus, another Christian apologist? What are the implications of Hippolytus' interpretation for the future of females as bearers of the prophetic voice in Western Christianity?

THE MONTANIST PROPHETS MAXIMILLA AND PRISCILLA[*]

But there are others who themselves are even more heretical in nature [than the foregoing], and are Phrygians by birth. These have been tendered victims of error from being previously captivated by [two] wretched women, called a certain Priscilla and Maximilla, whom they supposed [to be] prophetesses. And they assert that into these, the Paraclete Spirit had departed; and antecedently to them, they in like manner consider Montanus as a prophet. And being in possession of an infinite number of their books, [the Phrygians] are overrun with delusion; and they do not judge whatever statements are made by them, according to the criterion of reason; nor do they give heed unto those who are competent to decide; but they are heedlessly swept onwards, by the reliance which they place on these [impostors]. And they allege that they have learned something more through these, than from law, and prophets, and the Gospels. But they magnify these wretched women above the Apostles and every gift of Grace, so that some of them presume to assert that there is in them a something superior to Christ. These acknowledge God to be the Father of the universe, and Creator of all things, similarly with the Church, and [receive] as many things as the Gospel testifies concerning Christ. They introduce, however, the novelties of fasts, and feasts, and meals of parched food, and repasts of radishes, alleging that they have been instructed by women.

*Hippolytus. In *Refutation of All Heresies*. NPNFCC, 1952–1963, No. 102, 225.

In this selection, from the fourth century C.E. we discover further evidence for female prophets, presbyters, and bishops in the early church. Note in this text that despite the reference in canonical scripture to legitimate female religious leaders this writer's perspective is shaped by theologies and traditions some 200–300 years later. He, clearly, is opposed to the idea. Note to what authority he appeals for his argument against women in religious offices.

WOMEN BISHOPS, PRESBYTERS, AND PROPHETS AMONG THE FOLLOWERS OF QUINTILLA AND PRISCILLA*

... These Cataphrygians or Priscillians say that in Pepuza either Quintilla or Priscilla, I am not sure which, but one of them, was, as they said, sleeping in Pepuza when Christ came to her and lay beside her in the following fashion.... "In a vision," she said, "Christ came to me in the form of a woman in a bright garment, endowed me with wisdom, and revealed to me that this place is holy, and it is here that Jerusalem is to descend from heaven." Because of this they say that even to this day some women and men engage in incubation on the spot waiting to see Christ. Some women among them are called prophetesses, but I do not clearly know whether among them or among the Cataphrygians. They are alike and have the same way of thinking.

They use both the Old and New Testament and also speak in the same way of a resurrection of the dead. They consider Quintilla together with Priscilla as founder, the same as the Cataphrygians. They bring with them many useless testimonies, attributing a special grace to Eve because she first ate of the tree of knowledge. They acknowledge the sister of Moses as a prophetess as support for their practice of appointing women to the clergy. Also, they say, Philip had four daughters who prophesied. Often in their assembly seven virgins dressed in white enter carrying lamps, having come in to prophesy to the people. They deceive the people present by giving the appearance of ecstasy; they pretend to weep as if showing the grief of repentance by shedding tears and by their appearance lamenting human life. Women among them are bishops, presbyters, and the rest, as if there were no difference of nature. "For in Christ Jesus there is neither male nor female." These are the things we have learned. They are called Artotyritai because in their mysteries they use bread and cheese and in this fashion they perform their rites.

Images of the Female Principle of the Divine in Early Christian Gnostic Communities

Although there were in the ancient world Jewish, pagan, and Christian Gnostics (from the Greek *gnosis* or "knowledge") whose spiritual path was informed by secret sacred knowledge. The text selected is among writings of early Christians whose theology was expressed in a complex and often perplexing manner said to contain secret sacred knowledge.

Gnostic texts are customarily dualistic, in the Thunder, however, we note that all dualisms are abolished, and the Thunder embodies *all* aspects of being.

---

*Epiphanius, *The Panarion of St. Epiphanius, Bishop of Salamis,* translated by Philip R. Amidon, New York: Oxford University Press, 1990.

THE THUNDER PERFECT MIND[*]

Date uncertain

I was sent forth from [the] power,
   and I have come to those who reflect
      upon me,
   and I have been found among those
      who seek after me.
Look upon me, you (pl.) who reflect
   upon me,
   and you hearers, hear me.
   You who are waiting for me, take me
      to yourselves.
And do not banish me from your
   sight.
   And do not make your voice hate me,
      nor your hearing.
   Do not be ignorant of me anywhere
      or any time. Be on your guard!
   Do not be ignorant of me.
For I am the first and the last.
I am the honored one and the scorned
   one.
I am the whore and the holy one.
I am the wife and the virgin.
I am (the mother) and the daughter.
I am the members of my mother.
I am the barren one
   and many are her sons.
I am she whose wedding is great,
   and I have not taken a husband.
I am the midwife and she who does
   not bear.
I am the solace of my labor pains.
I am the bride and the bridegroom,
   and it is my husband who begot me.
I am the mother of my father
   and the sister of my husband,
   and he is my offspring.
I am the slave of him who prepared
   me.
I am the ruler 14 of my offspring.
   But he is the one who [begot me] be-
   fore the time on a birthday.

And he is my offspring [in] (due)
      time, and my power is from him.
Be on your guard!
Do not hate my obedience
   and do not love my self-control.
In my weakness, do not forsake me,
   and do not be afraid of my power.
For why do you despise my fear
   and curse my pride?
But I am she who exists in all fears
   and strength in trembling.
I am she who is weak,
   and I am well in a pleasant place.
I am senseless and I am wise.

Why have you hated me in your counsels?
For I shall be silent among those who
   are silent,
   and I shall appear and speak.
Why then have you hated me, you Greeks?
   Because I am a barbarian among
      [the] barbarians?
For I am the wisdom [of the] Greeks
   and the knowledge of [the]
      barbarians.
I am the judgment of [the] Greeks and
   of the barbarians.
[I] am the one whose image is great in
   Egypt
   and the one who has no image among
      the barbarians.
I am the one who has been hated
   everywhere
   and who has been loved everywhere.
I am the one whom they call Life,
   and you have called Death.
I am the one whom they call Law,
   and you have called Lawlessness.
I am the one whom you have pursued,
   and I am the one whom you have
      seized.

*NHLE, 1977, 271.

I am the one whom you have scattered,
    and you have gathered me together.
I am the one before whom you have
      been ashamed,
    and you have been shameless to me.
I am she who does not keep festival,
    and I am she whose festivals are many.
I, I am godless,
    and I am the one whose God is great.
I am the union and the dissolution.
I am the abiding and I am the dissolving.
I am the one below,
    and they come up to me.
I am the judgment and the acquittal.
I, I am sinless,
    and the root of sin derives from me.
I am lust in (outward) appearance,
    and interior self-control exists within
      me.
I am the hearing which is attainable to
      everyone
    and the speech which cannot be
      grasped.
I am a mute who does not speak,
    and great is my multitude of words.

Hear me in gentleness, and learn of me
      in roughness.
I am she who cries out,
    and I am cast forth upon the face of
      the earth.
I prepare the bread and my mind within.
I am the knowledge of my name.
I am the one who cries out,
    and I listen.
I appear and [. . .] walk in [. . .] seal of
    my [. . .].
I am [. . .] the defense [. . .].
I am the one who is called Truth,
    and iniquity [. . .].

You honor me [. . .] and you whisper
    against [me].
[. . .] victorious over them.
Judge them before they give judgment
    against you,
      because the judge and partiality exist
      in you.

If you are condemned by this one, who
      will acquit you?
    Or if you are acquitted by him, who
      will be able to detain you?
For what is inside of you is what is out-
      side of you,
    and the one who fashions you on the
      outside
      is the one who shaped the inside of
      you.
    And what you see outside of you,
      you see inside of you;
      it is visible and it is your garment.
Hear me, you hearers,
    and learn of my words, you who
      know me.
I am the hearing that is attainable to
      everything;
    I am the speech that cannot be
      grasped.
I am the name of the sound
    and the sound of the name.
I am the sign of the letter
    and the designation of the division.

Look then at his words
    and all the writings which have been
      completed.
Give heed then, you hearers
    and you also, the angels and those
      who have been sent,
    and you spirits who have arisen from
      the dead.
For I am the one who alone exists,
    and I have no one who will judge me.

For many are the pleasant forms which
      exist in
    numerous sins,
    and incontinencies,
    and disgraceful passions,
    and fleeting pleasures,
      which (men) embrace until they
        become sober
      and go up to their resting-place.
And they will find me there,
    and they will live,
    and they will not die again.

Female Heroes in Second and Third Century Apocryphal Acts of the Apostles

Analysis of these texts convinces several scholars in the present day that many of the stories about women that appear in the Apocryphal Acts of the Apostles were indeed written by women. Among characteristics that prompt this conclusion are delineations of male characters that commit sins of lust, greed, abuse of power, and oppression of women. Female characters display uncommon valor, heroism, virtue, honesty, chastity, devotion to Christ, and an abundance of faith in impossible situations. Whether they are penned by male or female authors, the female characters in the selections that follow demonstrate heroic feats that are unequaled in Christian literature up to this time.

The rather lengthy selection that follows is presented in an extensive excerpt because it so exemplifies this genre. Commentators on the text agree that, regardless of miraculous "embellishments," Thecla's story would have served as a great model for Christian women of her own and succeeding generations.

THE ACTS OF THECLA[*]

And while Paul was speaking so in the middle of the assembly in the house of One-siphorus, a certain Virgin named Thecla (her mother was Theocleta) who was engaged to a man named Thamyris, sat at a nearby window in her house and listened night and day to what Paul said about the chaste life. And she did not turn away from the window but pressed on in the faith, rejoicing exceedingly. Moreover, when she saw many women and virgins going in to Paul she wished that she too be counted worthy to stand before Paul and hear the word of Christ, for she had not yet seen Paul in person but only heard him speak.

. . . [Thamyris] said to Paul, "You have corrupted the city of the Iconians, and my fiancee so that she does not want me. Let us go to governor Castellius!"

Paul lifted up his voice and said, ". . . I proclaim and teach that in [Christ] humanity has hope, fear of God, knowledge of dignity, and love of truth. If then I teach the things revealed to me by God, what wrong do I do, Proconsul?" When the governor heard this, he commanded Paul to be bound and to be led off to prison until he could find a convenient time to give him a more careful hearing.

But during the night Thecla removed her bracelets and gave them to the doorkeeper, and when the door was opened for her she headed off to the prison. Upon giving a silver mirror to the Jailer, she went in to Paul and sitting at his feet she heard about the mighty acts of God. And Paul feared nothing but continued to live with the confidence in God; and her faith also increased, as she kissed his fetters.

But when Thecla was sought by her own people and by Thamyris, they pursued her through the streets as if she were lost, and one of the doorkeeper's fellow slaves made it known that she had gone out during the night. And they questioned the doorkeeper, and he told them that she had gone to the stranger in prison. And they went just as he had told them and found her, so to speak, united with him in loving affection. And they left there, rallied the crowd about them, and relayed this to the governor.

[The governor] ordered Paul to be brought to the judgment seat . . . and commanded that she [Thecla] too be brought to the judgment seat. . . . The governor gladly listened to Paul concerning the holy works of Christ. When he had taken

*The Acts of Paul *The Apocryphal New Testament*, M. R. James, Oxford, Clarendon Press, 1924 (7–47).

counsel he called Thecla, saying, "Why do you not marry Thamyris according to the law of the Iconians?" But she just stood there looking intently at Paul. And when she did not answer, Theocleta, her mother, cried out, saying, "Burn the lawless one! Burn her who is no bride in the midst of the theater in order that all the women who have been taught by this man may be afraid!"

And the governor was greatly moved. He had Paul whipped and threw him out of the city, but Thecla he sentenced to be burned. And immediately the governor arose and went off to the theater, and all the crowd went out to the inevitable spectacle. . . .

Now, the young men and the virgins brought wood and straw for burning Thecla. And as she was brought in naked, the governor wept and marveled at the power in her. The executioners spread out the wood and ordered her to mount the pyre, and making the sign of the cross she mounted up on the wood pile. They put the torch underneath the pile, and although a great fire blazed up, the flame did not touch her. For God in compassion produced a noise below the earth, and a cloud above full of water and hail overshadowed (the theater), and all its contents poured out, so that many were in danger and died. The fire was extinguished, and Thecla was saved.

And Thecla [sought] Paul [and said to him], "I shall cut my hair short and follow you wherever you go." But he said, "The time is horrible, and you are beautiful. May no other temptation come upon you worse than the first and you not bear up but act with cowardice." And Thecla said, "Only give me the seal in Christ, and temptation will not touch me."

[*When Thecla and Paul entered Antioch, she was assaulted by a leading citizen. Thecla humiliated the man so that he brought her before the governor.*]

. . . When she confessed that she had done these things, he sentenced her to the beasts. But the women were horrified and cried out before the judgement seat, "An evil judgment! An impious judgment!" Thecla begged the governor that she might remain pure until her battle with the beasts. And a wealthy woman named Tryphaena, whose daughter had died, took her into custody and found comfort in her.

When the beasts were led in procession, they bound her to a fierce lioness, and the queen Tryphaena followed her. And as Thecla sat upon the lioness's back, the lioness licked her feet, and all the crowd was astounded. . . .

And after the procession, Tryphaena took her again, for her daughter Falconilla, who was dead, had spoken to her in a dream: "Mother, the desolate stranger Thecla you will have in my place in order that she may pray for me and I be translated to the place of the righteous."

. . . [Tryphaena] said, "Thecla, my second child, come and pray for my child, that she may live forever; for this I saw in my dreams." And without hesitation she lifted up her voice and said, "My God, Son of the Most High, who is in heaven, give to her according to her wish, that her daughter Falconilla may live forever!" And when Thecla said this, Tryphaena grieved to think that such beauty was to be thrown to the beasts.

And when it was dawn, . . . the governor sent soldiers in order that Thecla might be brought. Tryphaena, however, did not stand aside but, taking her hand, led her up herself, saying, "My daughter Falconilla I brought to the tomb, but you, Thecla, I bring to battle the beasts." . . .

Now, when Thecla was taken out of Tryphaena's hands, she was stripped, given a girdle, and thrown into the stadium. And lions and bears were thrown at her, and a fierce lioness ran to her and reclined at her feet. Now, the crowd of women shouted loudly. And a bear ran up to her, but the lioness ran and met it, and ripped the bear to shreds.

. . . Then they sent in many beasts while she stood and stretched out her hands and prayed. And when she had finished her prayer, she turned and saw a great ditch full of water and said, . . . "In the name of Jesus Christ, I baptize myself on the last day!" . . . even the governor wept that such a beauty was going to be eaten by seals. So then she threw herself into the water in the name of Jesus Christ, ... About her there was a cloud of fire so that neither could the beasts touch her nor could she be seen naked.

[*After several other remarkable feats*] . . .

The governor summoned Thecla from among the beasts and said to her, "Who are you? And what have you about you that not one of the beasts touched you?" She answered, "I am a servant of the living God. . . . For to the storm-tossed he is a refuge, to the oppressed relief, to the despairing shelter; in a word, whoever does not believe in him shall not live but die for ever."

When the governor heard this, he ordered clothing to be brought and said, . . . "I release to you Thecla, the God-fearing servant of God." So all the women cried out with a loud voice and as with one mouth gave praise to God, saying, "One is God who has saved Thecla!" so that all the city was shaken by the sound.

And when Tryphaena was told the good news, she came to meet her with a crowd. She embraced Thecla and said, "Now I believe that the dead are raised up! Now I believe that my child lives! Come inside, and I will transfer everything that is mine to you." So Thecla went in with her and rested in her house for eight days, instructing her in the word of God, so that the majority of the female servants also believed. And there was great joy in the house.

Yet Thecla longed for Paul and sought him, sending all around in every direction. And it was made known to her that he was in Myra. So taking male and female servants, she got herself ready, sewed her chiton into a cloak like a man's, and headed off to Myra. She found Paul speaking the word of God and threw herself at him. . . .

And taking her by the hand, Paul led her into the house of Hermias and heard everything from her, so that Paul marveled greatly and those who heard were strengthened and prayed on behalf of Tryphaena. And standing up, Thecla said to Paul, "I am going to Iconium." So Paul said, "Go and teach the word of God!" Now, Tryphaena sent her a lot of clothing and gold, so it could be left behind for Paul for the ministry of the poor.

So Thecla herself headed off to Iconium . . .

And she found Thamyris dead, but her mother alive. And calling her mother to her, she said to her, "Theocleta, my mother, are you able to believe that the Lord lives in the heavens? For whether you desire money, the Lord will give it to you through me, or your child, behold, I am standing beside you."

And when she had given this witness she headed off to Seleucia, and after enlightening many with the word of God, she slept with a fine sleep.

PERPETUA'S ACCOUNT OF HER PERSECUTION[*]

A few days later we were imprisoned. I was terrified because never before had I experienced such darkness. What a terrible day! Because of crowded conditions and rough treatment by the soldiers the heat was unbearable. My condition was aggravated by my anxiety for my baby. Then Tertius and Pomponius, those kind deacons who were taking care of our needs, paid for us to be moved for a few hours to a better part of the prison where we might refresh ourselves. Leaving the dungeon we all went about our own business. I nursed my child, who was already weak from hunger. In my anxiety for the infant I spoke to my mother about him, tried to console my brother, and asked that they care for my son. I suffered intensely because I sensed their agony on my account. These were the trials I had to endure for many days. Then I was granted the privilege of having my son remain with me in prison. Being relieved of my anxiety and concern for the infant, I immediately regained my strength. Suddenly the prison became my palace, and I loved being there rather than any other place.

Then my brother said to me, "Dear sister, you already have such a great reputation that you could ask for a vision indicating whether you will be condemned or freed." Since I knew that I could speak with the Lord, whose great favors I had already experienced, I confidently promised to do so. I said I would tell my brother about it the next day. Then I made my request and this is what I saw.

There was a bronze ladder of extraordinary height reaching up to heaven, but it was so narrow that only one person could ascend at a time. Every conceivable kind of iron weapon was attached to the sides of the ladder: swords, lances, hooks, and daggers. If anyone climbed up carelessly or without looking upwards, he/she would be mangled as the flesh adhered to the weapons. Crouching directly beneath the ladder was a monstrous dragon who threatened those climbing up and tried to frighten them from ascent.

Saturus went up first. Because of his concern for us he had given himself up voluntarily after we had been arrested. He had been our source of strength but was not with us at the time of the arrest. When he reached the top of the ladder he turned to me and said, "Perpetua, I'm waiting for you, but be careful not to be bitten by the dragon." I told him that in the name of Jesus Christ the dragon could not harm me. At this the dragon slowly lowered its head as though afraid of me. Using its head as the first step, I began my ascent.

At the summit I saw an immense garden, in the center of which sat a tall, grey-haired man dressed like a shepherd, milking sheep. Standing around him were several thousand white-robed people. As he raised his head he noticed me and said, "Welcome, my child." Then he beckoned me to approach and gave me a small morsel of the cheese he was making. I accepted it with cupped hands and ate it. When all those surrounding us said "Amen," I awoke, still tasting the sweet cheese. I immediately told my brother about the vision, and we both realized that we were to experience the sufferings of martyrdom. From then on we gave up having any hope in this world.

[*]*The Martyrdom of Saints Perpetua and Felicitas,* Early 3rd century C.E., from *A Lost Tradition: Women Writers of the Early Church,* edited by P. Wilson-Kastner, Lanham, MD; University Press of America, 1981, 20–22, 24–25: © held by G. Ronald Kastner.

A few days later there was a rumor that our case was to be heard. My father, completely exhausted from his anxiety, came from the city to see me, with the intention of weakening my faith. "Daughter," he said, "have pity on my grey head. Have pity on your father if I have the honor to be called father by you, if with these hands I have brought you to the prime of your life, and if I have always favored you above your brothers, do not abandon me to the reproach of men. Consider your brothers; consider your mother and your aunt; consider your son who cannot live without you. Give up your stubbornness before you destroy all of us. None of us will be able to speak freely if anything happens to you."

These were the things my father said out of love, kissing my hands and throwing himself at my feet. With tears he called me not daughter, but woman. I was very upset because of my father's condition. He was the only member of my family who would find no reason for joy in my suffering. I tried to comfort him saying, "Whatever God wants at this tribunal will happen, for remember that our power comes not from ourselves but from God." But utterly dejected, my father left me.

One day as we were eating we were suddenly rushed off for a hearing. We arrived at the forum and the news spread quickly throughout the area near the forum, and a huge crowd gathered. We went up to the prisoners' platform. All the others confessed when they were questioned. When my turn came my father appeared with my son. Dragging me from the step, he begged: "Have pity on your son!"

Hilarion, the governor, who assumed power after the death of the proconsul Minucius Timinianus, said, "Have pity on your father's grey head; have pity on your infant son; offer sacrifice for the emperors' welfare." But I answered, "I will not." Hilarion asked, "Are you a Christian?" And I answered, "I am a Christian." And when my father persisted in his attempts to dissuade me, Hilarion ordered him thrown out, and he was beaten with a rod. My father's injury hurt me as much as if I myself had been beaten, and I grieved because of his pathetic old age. Then the sentence was passed; all of us were condemned to the beasts. We were overjoyed as we went back to the prison cell. Since I was still nursing my child who was ordinarily in the cell with me, I quickly sent the deacon Pomponius to my father's house to ask for the baby, but my father refused to give him up. Then God saw to it that my child no longer needed my nursing, nor were my breasts inflamed. After that I was no longer tortured by anxiety about my child or by pain in my breasts.

[*During her stay in prison Perpetua then has two more visions, both of her dead brother. Her fourth and final vision is of her coming martyrdom, during which she sees herself transformed into a man.*]

The day before the battle in the arena, in a vision I saw Pomponius the deacon coming to the prison door and knocking very loudly. I went to open the gate for him. He was dressed in a loosely fitting white robe, wearing richly decorated sandals. He said to me, "Perpetua, come. We're waiting for you!" He took my hand and we began to walk over extremely rocky and winding paths. When we finally arrived short of breath, at the arena, he led me to the center saying, "Don't be frightened! I'll be here to help you." He left me and I stared out over a huge crowd which watched me with apprehension. Because I knew that I had to fight with the beasts, I wondered why they hadn't yet been turned loose in the arena. Coming towards me was some type of Egyptian, horrible to look at, accompanied by fighters who were to help defeat me. Some handsome young men came forward to help and encourage me. I was stripped of my clothing, and suddenly I was a man. My assistants began to rub me with oil as was the custom before a contest, while the Egyptian was on the opposite side rolling in the sand. Then a certain man appeared, so tall that he towered above the amphitheater. He wore a loose purple robe with two parallel stripes across the chest; his sandals were richly decorated with gold and silver. He carried a rod like that of an athletic trainer, and a green branch on which were golden apples. He motioned for silence and said, "If this Egyptian wins, he will kill her with the sword; but if she wins, she will receive this branch." Then he withdrew.

We both stepped forward and began to fight with our fists. My opponent kept trying to grab my feet but I repeatedly kicked his face with my heels. I felt myself being lifted up into the air and began to strike at him as one who was no longer earthbound. But when I saw that we were wasting time, I put my two hands together, linked my fingers, and put his head between them. As he fell on his face I stepped on his head. Then the people began to shout and my assistants started singing victory songs. I walked up to the trainer and accepted the branch. He kissed me and said, "Peace be with you, my daughter." And I triumphantly headed towards the Sanavivarian Gate. Then I woke up realizing that I would be contending not with wild animals but with the devil himself. I knew, however, that I would win. I have recorded the events which occurred up to the day before the final contest. Let anyone who wishes to record the events of the contest itself, do so.

SUGGESTED READINGS

Engelsman, Joan Chamberlin. *The Feminine Dimension of the Divine.* Philadelphia: The Westminster Press, 1979.

Journal of Feminist Studies in Religion. Atlanta: Scholars Press, 1985 to present.

King, Karen L. editor, *Images of the Feminine in Gnosticism.* In *Studies in Antiquity and Christianity,* Philadelphia: Fortress, 1988.

Kraemer, Ross S. and Mary Rose D'Angelo, editors, *Women in Christian Origins.* New York and Oxford: Oxford University Press, 1999.

Maisch, Ingrid. *Between Veneration and Contempt, Mary Magdalen: The Image of a Woman Through the Centuries.* Collegeville, MN: The Liturgical Press, 1998.

Malvern, Marjorie M. *Venus in Sackcloth: The Magdalen's Origins and Metamorphoses.* Carbondale, IL: Southern Illinois University Press, 1975.

Pagels, Elaine. *The Gnostic Gospels.* 2d ed. New York: Vintage Books, 1989.

Schussler-Fiorenza, Elisabeth. *In Memory of Her: A Feminist Re-Construction of Christian Origins.* New York: Crossroad, 1983.

Torjesen, Karen Jo. *When Women Were Priests.* San Francisco: Harper San Francisco, 1993.

Sources Cited

"Prophetic Gesture: A Woman Who Anointed Jesus' Head, The Gospel According to Matthew." In *The New Oxford Annotated Bible,* edited by Bruce M. Metzger and Roland E. Murphy. New Revised Standard Edition, New York: Oxford University Press, 1991. Matthew 26:6–13.

"Woman Who Anointed Jesus' Head, Mark." In *The New Oxford Annotated Bible,* edited by Bruce M. Metzger and Roland E. Murphy. New Revised Standard Edition, New York: Oxford University Press, 1991. Mark 14:3–9.

"Mary Magdalene among Women Who Provided for Jesus as Recorded in Luke's Gospel." In *The New Oxford Annotated Bible,* edited by Bruce M. Metzger and Roland E. Murphy. New Revised Standard Edition, New York: Oxford University Press, 1991. Luke 8:1–6.

"The Magdalene at the Resurrection in Luke's Gospel." In *The New Oxford Annotated Bible,* edited by Bruce M. Metzger and Roland E. Murphy. New Revised Standard Edition, New York: Oxford University Press, 1991. Luke 24:1–10.

"Mary Magdalene in John's Passion Narrative." In *The New Oxford Annotated Bible,* edited by Bruce M. Metzger and Roland E. Murphy. New Revised Standard Edition, New York: Oxford University Press, 1991. John 19:25, 20:1–2, 11–18.

"Gospel of Phillip Presents Mary Magdalene as Jesus' Companion," translated by Members of the Coptic Gnostic Library Project of the Intstitute for Antiquity and Christianity. In *The Nag Hammadi Library in English,* edited by James M. Robinson, San Francisco and Cambridge: Harper and Row, 1977. 135.

"The Gospel of Mary," translated by George W. MacRae and R. Mc L. Wilson. In *The Nag Hammadi Library in English,* edited by Douglas M. Parrot, San Francisco and Cambridge: Harper and Row, 1977, 472–74.

"Joanna." In *The New Oxford Annotated Bible,* edited by Bruce M. Metzger and Roland E. Murphy. New Revised Standard Edition, New York: Oxford University Press, 1991 Luke 8:5–6, 24:10.

"Anna the Prophet." In *The New Oxford Annotated Bible,* edited by Bruce M. Metzger and Roland E. Murphy. New Revised Standard Edition. New York: Oxford University Press, 1991. Luke 2:36–38.

"Four Sisters Are Prophets, Acts, Priscilla and Aquila, Acts." In *The New Oxford Annotated Bible,* edited by Bruce M. Metzger and Roland E. Murphy. New Revised Standard Edition. New York: Oxford University Press, 1991, Acts 21:8–9.

"Priscilla and Aquila." In *The New Oxford Annotated Bible,* edited by Bruce M. Metzger and Roland E. Murphy. New Revised Standard Edition, New York: Oxford University Press, 1991. Acts 18:24–28.

"Phoebe, Deacon and Prostasis at Cenchrae, Patron of Paul and Other Missionaries." In *The New Oxford Annotated Bible,* edited by Bruce M. Metzger and Roland E. Murphy. New Revised Standard Edition, New York: Oxford University Press, 1991. Acts 21:8–9, 18:24–28.

"Mary: A Worker in The Church at Rome; Junia: Female Apostle; Tryphaena; Tryphosa: Workers in the Lord; The Mother of Rufus: A Mother to Paul; Julia: The Sister of Nereus; Olympas: Saints in the Church at Rome, Romans 16." In *The New Oxford Annotated Bible,* edited by Bruce M. Metzger and Roland E. Murphy. New Revised Standard Edition. New York: Oxford University Press, 1991. Romans 16:1–16, 18:24–28.

Epiphanius. "Arabian Christian Women of Thracian Descent Who Bake Cakes to the Virgin Mary and Function as Priests." *Medicine Box* 78.23, translated by Carolyn Osick. In *Maenads, Martyrs, Matrons, Monastics,* Edited by Ross S. Kraemer, Philiadelphia: Fortress Press, 1988. 50, No. 29.

Tertullian. "A Montanist Visionary Who Submits Her Revelation to Careful Scrutiny." In *On the Soul.* A Select Library of the Nicene and Post Nicene Fathers of the Christian Church. New York; Grand Rapids, MI: Christian Literary Company; William B. Eardmans (Reprint), 1886–1900, 1952–1963. No. 101, 224.

Hippolytus. "The Montanist Prophets Maximilla and Priscilla." In *Refutation of All Heresies.* A Select Library of the Nicene and Post Nicene Fathers of the Christian Church. New York; Grand Rapids, MI: Christian Literary Company; William B. Eardmans (Reprint), 1886–1900, 1952–1963. No. 102, 225.

Epiphaneus. "Women Bishops, Presbyters, and Prophets among the Followers of Quintilla and Priscilla." *The Panerion of St. Epiphaneus* 48, translated by Philip R.Amidon, New York, Oxford University Press, 1990.

"Sayings Atributed to Maximilla." Epiphaneus, *Medicine Box* translated by Ross S. Kraemer, MMMM, 1988. 230.

"Sayings of the Montanist Priscilla." Epiphaneus, *Medicine Box* translated by Ross S. Kraemer, MMMM, 1988. 230.

The Thunder, Perfect Mind, translated by George W. MacRae. In *The Nag Hammadi Library in English,* edited by Douglas M. Parrot, San Francisco and Cambridge: Harper & Row, 1977. 271.

Acts of Paul. In *The Apocryphal New Testament,* edited by M.R. James, Oxford: Clarendon Press, 1924. 272–81.

"Mygonia Embraces Her Faith with Her Life." In *The Apocryphal New Testament,* edited by M.R. James, Oxford: Clarendon Press, 1924, 420–25.

"Perpetua's Account of Her Persecution." In *A Lost Tradition: Women Writers of the Early Church,* edited by P. Wilson-Kastner. Lanham, MD: University Press of America, 1981, 20–22, 24–25: © held by G. Ronald Kastner.

Chapter 13

Late Antiquity

The present chapter functions as a transition from the Ancient World to the early Middle Ages (ca. fourth through seventh centuries). For many reasons, including the decline and destruction of the Roman Empire in the West, few primary sources (literary, philosophical, artistic, epigraphic, inscriptive, or legal) concerning women have survived from this time period. A wide enough array of sources does exist, however, to clarify that the oppression, agency, and self-understanding of women in Late Antiquity were shaped and defined by myriad circumstances and predilections. The structure adopted for Chapter 13 is a loose compilation of primary source selections that represent some of these motifs in women's lives during an era of major transformation in cultural and societal realities.

Historians have most often presented the history of civilizations from the point of view of shifts in power won by military might among major contending patriarchal societies. More sensitive, reflective, and inclusive renditions of events, however, do sometimes prevail. This has frequently been the case with historical accounts of the end of the Roman Empire in the West where the origin and impetus for decline clearly emerged from within institutional structures. By the end of the third century C.E., despite the *Pax Romana* and numerous worthwhile accomplishments, the Western factions of the Roman Empire sustained major changes that are outlined in Chart 13–1.

The texts selected for this chapter, therefore, are intended to represent a collection of examples that demonstrate women's oppression, their coping strategies, and their courage in maintaining their integrity despite formidable odds. Our selections represent women's participation in, and contributions to culture emanating from geographic locations that extend from Rome to northern Africa,

---

Chart 13–1   Major Transitions in the Roman Empire, Third to Sixth Centuries C.E.

1. Crumbling economic and bureaucratic stability in the West
2. Vulnerability to invasions by peoples from the North and East that threatened the safety of Roman citizens
3. Establishment of Constantinople as the capital of the empire
4. Beginning of a division of the Roman Empire into Eastern and Western realms
5. Emergence of a small sectarian movement in Judaism that by the fourth century became the state religion of the Roman Empire

---

Celtic Ireland, Britain, and Wales, to the Byzantine world and the deserts and cities of Egypt. The cultural orientation and social locations of these women vary extensively. Even though the model of the noble Roman matron as the paragon of virtue remained intact, cultural diffusion was inevitable. Many customs, traditions, art forms, foods, and fashions that were identified as Roman no longer reflected an Italian heritage. Nevertheless, some women during these centuries identified themselves primarily in terms of their "insider/outsider" relationship as citizens of the Roman Empire. Self-understanding among other women was more closely associated with a particular ethnic/cultural or political identity or religious affiliation.

In the pages that follow we sometimes transgress chronological boundaries to highlight a particular woman or women whose stories are significant to the objectives of the chapter, for example Jewish women in the very early Rabbinic period. As we demonstrate in each section of this chapter and in the remaining chapters of Volume One, some women persisted in challenging oppressive and dehumanizing cultural norms that were fostered by patriarchal political and religious hierarchies. Other women found ways and means to "work within the system" with a modicum of compromise to their own integrity. The great majority of women continued to be oppressed by social structures and institutions that did not recognize them as possessing equal value, worth, and dignity as persons. We begin with texts about women whose principal identification resided in their self-understanding as Roman citizens.

ROMAN WOMEN

Women in the empire whose self-definition was shaped in large measure by their social location and status within the empire were found among patricians and upwardly mobile equestrians as well as among women in the lower strata of society, including female slaves. The public persona of the empress portrayed as epitomizing the virtuous matron persisted, but was, on occasion, circumscribed by an empress whose intervention in matters of the state was perceived as interference rather than accomplishment. There were a few aristocratic women whose wisdom, beneficence, and influence in matters related to the state were held in high regard. One such woman was the Empress Julia Domna. With the exception of continued evidence of wealthy Roman women as patrons of the arts, initiators of construction of public buildings, and private benefactors, there are few primary sources about Roman women during this period that are particularly notable.

The insider/outsider paradigm continued throughout this period and had many levels of meaning, as was exemplified in Chapter 11, "The Roman Empire," within the very household of Emperor Octavian Augustus. There we found references to his wife Livia, who clearly was "inside" at every level. We also found references for his daughter Julia, who, although she had value as a political pawn, came to be considered so much an "outsider" that her father humiliated her and had her exiled from Rome. The objectification (treating as object) of women in the aristocracy as pawns in politically expedient marriages did, however, ensure that most married women were insiders on the basis of their social status.

The insider/outsider model was not limited to the aristocracy but also was retained among female slaves in the Empire. Women, for example, who worked in close association with members of an aristocratic Roman household as scribes, hairstylists, personal attendants, child-care givers, or even wet nurses had explicit opportunities to be "insiders" in ways that female slaves who picked olives or grapes or carded wool and made sheaves of wheat did not. Female slaves of patrician families who had been manumitted and became entrepreneurs may have been better connected to sources of prestige and power than plebian women whose entrepreneurial activities prospered solely on the basis of their own ingenuity. We begin the present survey among patrician women.

Ummidia Quadratilla

The fact that Ummidia's patronage to her community was extravagant and was immortalized with inscriptions that celebrate her generosity indicates that she was a Roman "insider" in the provincial city of Casinum in central Italy. We would have to know a great deal more about her than we do to determine whether her lineage would have placed her among patrician families from Rome, or whether her patronage relied on her success and that of her family as it flourished in a less-than-significant Roman city. Among her contributions in Casinum were a temple, an amphitheater, and patronage of a troupe of actors. Pliny the Younger was a friend of the dowager Ummidia and when she was in her late seventies, he counseled her concerning the education of her grandson.

UMMIDIA AND HER GRANDSON[*]

Ummidia Quadratilla is dead, having almost attained the age of seventy-nine and kept her powers unimpaired up to her last illness, along with a sound constitution and sturdy physique which are rare in a woman. She died leaving an excellent will; her grandson inherits two-thirds of the estate, and her granddaughter the remaining third. I scarcely know the latter, but the grandson is a close friend of mine. He is a remarkable young man who inspires a sort of family affection among people in no way related to him. In the first place, though conspicuous for his good looks, he spent his youth and early manhood untouched by scandal; then he married before he was twenty-four and would have been a father had his prayers been granted. He lived in his grandmother's house, but managed to combine personal austerity with deference to her sybaritic tastes. She kept a troupe of pantomime actors whom she treated with an indulgence unsuitable in a lady of her high position, but Quadratus never watched their performances either in the theatre or at home, nor did she insist on it. Once when she was asking me to supervise her grandson's education she told me that as a woman, with all a woman's idle hours to fill, she was in the habit of amusing herself playing draughts or watching her mimes, but before she did either she always told Quadratus to go away and work: which, I thought, showed her respect for his youth as much as her affection.

   This incident will surprise you as it did me. The last Sacerdotal Games were opened by a performance of mime, and as we left the theatre together Quadratus said to me: "Do you realize that today was the first time I have seen any of my grandmother's freedmen dancing?" So said her grandson; but meanwhile people who were nothing to Quadratilla were running to the theatre to pay their respects to her—though "respect" is hardly the word to use for their fawning attentions—jumping up and clapping to show their admiration, and then copying every gesture of their mistress with snatches of song. Today there is only a tiny bequest as a gratuity for their hired applause, which they will receive from the heir who never watched them perform.

   I have told you this because you are usually glad to hear of any news, and also because I like to dwell on my pleasure by writing about it. It is a joy to witness the family affection shown by the deceased and the honour done to an excellent young man, and I am happy to think that the house which once belonged to Gaius Cassius, the founder

*Pliny the Younger, *Letters*, LCL, 1975. VII 24.15.

of the Cassian School of jurisprudence, will have a master no less distinguished. For my friend Quadratus will adorn it by his presence and restore its former grandeur, fame, and glory by issuing from it to be as great an orator as Cassius was a jurist.

Asclepigenia of Athens

The young female philosopher Asclepigenia taught at the Platonic Academy at Athens in the late fourth and early fifth centuries. Neo-Platonic thought (Platonic thought from the Hellenistic period forward) had taken various forms with distinctly different emphases as it was traditioned and transformed through the centuries. The particular philosophical direction of the Academy at Athens in the early fifth century C.E. valued mystical union with the *One* as a principal objective. This goal represented one of many responses to the turmoil that prevailed throughout the Western regions of the empire. A desire to resolve disparate premises of Platonic and Aristotelian philosophical principles and to achieve mystical union with the *One* characterized the philosophical theories of Asclepigenia's father, Plutarch the Younger. He was director of the Platonic Academy until his death, and he appointed his daughter Asclepigenia, her brother, and a favorite pupil as his successors. The theme of fathers who mentor and encourage their daughters, as did Sargon of Akkad with Enheduanna in the second millennium B.C.E. (Chapter 2) and Plutarch the Younger in the fourth century C.E. appears again and again throughout the two volumes of this reader.

In her treatise on Asclepigenia, philosopher Mary Ellen Waithe discusses the philosophical/mystical developments of Proclus, Asclepigenia's most widely known pupil. Waithe establishes the distinct differences in the thinking of Plotinus and Proclus and argues for specific influences of Asclepigenia on Proclus's thought (Waithe, 1987, 200). To prove her argument Waithe quotes Marinus, a philosopher who related Proclus's philosophy specifically to the teachings of Asclepigenia.

ASCLEPIGENIA'S INFLUENCE[*]

> [Proclus] went to Chaldaic gatherings and (prayer) meetings, employed divine silent tops for strophalemancy, and in general practiced various things of this kind. He learned their significance and use from Asclepigenia, the daughter of Plutarch; for she alone had preserved from (her grandfather) Nestorius, and through the intermediary of her father, the knowledge of the (religious) orgies and the whole theurgic science.
>
> The precise, well-defined levels of the Asclepigenian theurgic program are designed to lead the philosopher into and through the mysteries that are beyond the scope of metaphysics alone. These steps, as outlined by Proclus are:
>
> 1. a life of purging one's consciousness so that one becomes freed of the senses,
> 2. an illumination, consisting of climbing a ladder towards greater and greater levels of abstraction,
> 3. unification with the One.
>
> For Asclepigenia and her pupil, Proclus, knowledge of the One is a cognitive (philosophical), mystical (psychological), and physical (magical) experience. As such, knowledge of the One is not possible by divorcing the philosophical from the psychological and magical/theurgical.

---

[*]Excerpts from *Life of Proclus*, AHWP, 1987, pp. 201–205.

JEWISH WOMEN

Late antiquity marked a period in which conflicts concerning the establishment or preservation of ethnic identity were paramount among the Jews. The culmination of Rome's war against Israel from 68–70 C.E. was the destruction of the Jerusalem Temple, the end of the state, and the expulsion of Jews from Israel. At the close of the Jewish revolt led by Bar Kochba in 135 C.E., Rome established final hegemony over Israel, and all hopes for the people of Israel to return to a "working relationship" as subjects of Rome were forever severed. These realities and the diaspora (dispersion of the citizens to areas outside their homeland) that ensued when all Jews were exiled from Israel marked perhaps the most critical chapters in Jewish history.

By far the majority of families in the Jewish diaspora of the first century C.E. were displaced and dispossessed of home and homeland and were faced with constructing new lives. Often new lifestyles had to be forged within cultures that differed radically from their own. The complexities and particularities of life among women in this category are rarely documented in narrative form. The evidence for their existence has, however, been preserved in a variety of categories. A few scholars are beginning to retrieve some of the information concerning Jewish women in the diaspora in late antiquity and to classify that information in a systematic manner. The following selections provide a sampling of categories in which some Jewish women in the diaspora maintained and/or created a degree of agency and self-definition.

Queen Helena of Adiabene

The Jewish historian Josephus recounts this tale in his *Antiquities.* When Queen Helena of Adiabene and her husband realized that their son Izates was destined to greatness, Izates was sent to live in the household of the king of Charax Spasini with the understanding that when his father died he was to succeed his father as king of Adiabene.

In Charax Spasini the youthful Izates was tutored in the Jewish tradition by a merchant named Ananias. In Adiabene, Queen Helena also happened to be undergoing training in the ways of Judasim. By virtue of a series of curious events not only did Queen Helena of Adiabene and her son Izates became converts to Judaism, but the family and the king of Adiabene were also sustained by their faith in the God of Israel. The selection that follows demonstrates Queen Helena's generosity and gratitude expressed toward the people of Israel during a time of their great distress.

QUEEN HELENA[*]

Helena, the mother of the king, saw that peace prevailed in the kingdom and that her son was prosperous and the object of admiration in all men's eyes, even those of foreigners, thanks to the prudence that God gave him. Now she had conceived a desire to go to the city of Jerusalem and to worship at the temple of God, which was famous throughout the world, and to make thank-offerings there. She consequently asked her son to give her leave. Izates was most enthusiastic in granting his mother's request, made great preparations for her journey, and gave her a large sum of money. He even escorted her for a considerable distance, and she completed her journey to the city of Jerusalem. Her arrival was very advantageous for the people of

---

[*]From Josephus, *Antiquities of the Jews,* H. St. Thackeray, R. Marcus, A. Wikgren and L. Feldman, 1926–1965. LCL, 1965. vol. XIII, XX.49.

Jerusalem, for at that time the city was hard pressed by famine and many were perishing from want of money to purchase what they needed. Queen Helena sent some of her attendants to Alexandria to buy grain for large sums and others to Cyprus to bring back a cargo of dried figs. Her attendants speedily returned with these provisions, which she thereupon distributed among the needy. She has thus left a very great name that will be famous forever among our whole people for her benefaction.

Babata, a Wealthy Female Entrepreneur

The Babata archives are documents belonging to a twice-married Jewish widow named Babata. They were discovered in the 1960s and were published in 1989. The archives attest to Babata's considerable wealth, to the properties she bought and sold, and to various lawsuits that were either initiated by her or directed against her. Among witnesses, officials, sellers, buyers, and recipients whose names are included in the documents are Romans, Nabateans, and Jews. In addition to information about the specific lands and properties that constituted her wealth, the documents include marriage contracts, dowry settlements, sales of properties, leases of lands, purchases of crops, deposits, loans, receipts, and a petition to a Nabatean governor.

EXCERPTS FROM THE BABATA ARCHIVES[*]

Babtha (as her name is spelled here) declares, for a provincial census ordered by the Roman governor, her ownership of four groves of date palms at Maoza; two of the groves are described as running right down to the Dead Sea. Listed for each grove are an identifying place name, the size of the grove, the taxes paid on it in kind and in money, and two of the abutters (presumably those on east and west: cf. 11.4–6n.).

I, Babtha daughter of Simon, of Maoza in the Zoarene [district] of the Petra administrative region, domiciled in my own private property in the said Maoza, register what I possess (present with me as my guardian being Judanes son of Elazar, of the village of En-gedi in the district of Jericho in Judaea, domiciled in his own private property in the said Maoza), viz. within the boundaries of Maoza a date orchard called Algiphiamma, the area of sowing one saton three kaboi of barley, paying as tax, in dates, Syrian and mixed fifteen sata, "splits" ten sata, and for crown tax one "black" and thirty sixtieths, abutters a road and the Sea; within the boundaries of Maoza a date orchard called Algiphiamma, the area of sowing one kabos of barley, paying as tax a half share of the crops produced each year, abutters *moschantic* estate of our lord Caesar and the Sea; within the boundaries of Maoza a date orchard called Bagalgala, the area of sowing three sata of barley, paying as tax, in dates, Syrian and Noaran(?) one koros, "splits" one koros, and for crown tax three "blacks" and thirty sixtieths, abutters heirs of Thesaios son of Sabakas and Iamit son(?) of Manthanthes; within the boundaries of Maoza a date orchard called Bethphaaraia, the area of sowing twenty sata of barley, paying as tax, in dates, Syrian and Noaran(?) three kaboi, "splits" two koroi, and for crown tax eight "blacks" and forty-five sixtieths, abutters Tamar daughter of Thamous and a road.

---

[*] *The Documents from the Bar Kochba Period in the Cave of Letters,* Greek Papyri, ed. by Napthali Lewis, Israel Exploration Society Series. Jerusalem: The Hebrew University of Jerusalem, 1989. 65, 67–68.

Translation of subscription: I, Babtha daughter of Simon, swear by the *genius* of our lord Caesar that I have in good faith registered as has been written above. I, Judanes son of Elazar, acted as guardian and wrote for her. [2nd hand] Translation of subscription of the prefect: I, Priscus, prefect of cavalry, received [this] on the day before the nones of December in the consulship of Gallicanus and Titianus.

On the back, individual signatures	*right edge*
'Abdu son of Muqimu, witness	Babatha
Manthanta son of Amru, witness	
'Awd'el son of _____, witness	
Yohana son of 'Abd'obdat Makhoutha,	
witness Shahru son of _____,	
witness.	

Female Leaders in Synagogues

Feminist historian of religions Bernadette Brooten was the first scholar to explore in depth 19 inscriptions from the ancient world that memorialize female leaders of ancient synagogues. The inscriptions are dated from the first century B.C.E. to the sixth century C.E. and come from a variety of sites in the Mediterranean Basin. The titles ascribed to the women in the inscriptions include the head of synagogue, elder, presbyter, mother of the synagogue, and priest. Numerous inscriptions of female donors to synagogues are also included in Brooten's work. Given the broad range of factors to consider in ascertaining the job description of the various positions, it is important to either accept the reconstructions as historically plausible, or to refute them altogether.

Thorough and detailed research on available data concerning the office of head of synagogue undergirds Bernadette Brooten's reconstruction of the functions of women heads of synagogues. A very brief synopsis of her findings includes the following: They [the women] would have been active in administration and exhortation, and in order to teach and exhort others in its precepts they would have had knowledge of Torah.

HEADS OF SYNAGOGUES: SOPHIA AND THEOPEMPTE[*]

SOPHIA

Sophia of Gortyn, elder and head of the synagogue of Kisamos (lies) here. The memory of the righteous one for ever. Amen.

THEOPEMPTE

[From Th]eopempte, head of the synagogue, and her son Eusebios.

Three inscriptions identifying two female Jewish priests have been discovered. If the term refers to what would be the equivalent of the traditional rabbinic *kohenet* (priest), Brooten reminds us that there would be no question of *orthodoxy* because such designations had no administrative or cultic religious function (Brooten 1982, 98). If, however, the term pertains to ritual/cultic functions related to worship

*Bernadette Brooten, *WLAS*, 1982, 11, 13.

within the synagogue, factoring these women into the equation would necessitate altering the traditional understanding of "priest." When we consider the vast number of references to female priests in the Greco-Roman world that are attested to in the present volume, Brooten's recommendation of caution in considering the possibilities of these inscriptions for female Jewish priests seems wise.

PRIESTS: MARIA AND GAUDENTIA*

MARIA

> Sara, daughter of Naimia, mother of the priest, Lady Maria, lies here
> And Sara, daughter of Naimia and mother of the priest Maria.

GAUDENTIA

> Here lies Gaudentia, priest, (aged) 24 years. In peace be her sleep!

Two of the following inscriptions are representative of donations to the synagogue made by many women who had the agency and the funds to make them. They also apparently had the legal right to do so without a guardian's permission. The third is a donation for the daughter of a female rabbi.

DONORS TO SYNAGOGUES: ALEXANDRA, EUPITHIS, AND HALIPHO**

> Alexandra made 100 feet, in fulfillment of a vow, for the salvation of all (her) relatives.
>
> Eupithis made 100 feet, in fulfillment of a vow, for the salvation of all (her) relatives.

> May Halipho, daughter of Rabbi Saphra, who has gained much merit in this holy place, be of good memory. Amen.

RABBINIC JUDAISM

The Judaism of the present day had its formal origins in the diaspora among a group of Jewish teachers and scholars who, when the Jerusalem Temple was destroyed in 70 C.E., had a plan for defining and continuing their lives as committed Jews. Tradition tells us that they were given permission by the Roman general Vespasian to start a small academy in Palestine in the coastal town of Yavneh. There these scholars and teachers settled and proceeded to determine the canon of scripture for the Hebrew Bible (ca. 90 C.E.) and to transmit the Oral Torah (oral interpretations of the Torah that were shaped in differing cultural contexts over the centuries) in a written document called the Mishnah that was completed by ca. 200 C.E.

Another genre of Jewish texts called Haggadah (that includes stories, myths, legends, and instructions for rituals) such as the Beruriah selection that follows, provides a keener sense of interpretations of women within the Rabbinic tradition who crossed boundaries of that tradition. We also note the wit and wisdom of women who conformed to the norms that were defined for them by the men in their lives.

*Brooten, *WLAS*, 75, 76, 77.
**Brooten, *WLAS*, 158, 160, 161.

Beruriah's place in the history of women in Judaism is revered by all women and men who value women as intelligent, wise, and equally capable of studying and interpreting the Law. Professor David Goodblatt's study of the Beruriah traditions indicates that from the stories about this figure we can gain significant insights into customs about some women in early Rabbinic Judaism (Goodblatt 1977). Beruriah was the wife of a rabbi. She was literate, educated in the study of the Torah, and was recognized as having wisdom that exceeded that of many of the most learned rabbis. Her passion for the study of the Law and her commitment to pursue her passion resulted in a variety of stories about her that were designed to undermine her authority as a scholar and a woman of wisdom.

BERURIAH[*]

Rabbi Simlai came before Rabbi Yohanan and said to him, "Let the master teach me the Book of Genealogies (*sefer yuhasin*)." He said to him, "Where are you from?" He answered, "From Lod." "And where is your residence?" "In Nehardea." He said to him, "One engages in discussion neither with Lodites nor with Nehardeans. How much more so with you who are from Lod and whose residence is in Nehardea." He pressed him, and he consented. He [Simlai] said to him, "Let the master teach me [the material] in three months." He [Yohanan] picked up a clod, threw it at him, and said to him, "If Beruriah, the wife (*devethu*) of Rabbi Meir, the daughter of Rabbi Hananyah ben Teradyon, learned 300 traditions in a day from 300 masters, and even so did not fulfill her obligations in three years—how can you say in three months?" As he [Simlai] was getting up to go he said to him, "Master, what is [the difference] between 'for its own sake' and 'not for its own sake,' [between] 'for those who eat it' and 'not for those who eat it' [referring to Mishnah Pesahim 5:2–3]?" He said to him, "Since you are a disciple of the masters (*surba merabbanan*), come and I will tell you. . . . "

It once happened that Rabbi Meir was sitting and lecturing in the house of study on Sabbath afternoon, and his two sons died. What did their mother do? She laid the two of them on the bed and spread a sheet over them. After the departure of the Sabbath, Rabbi Meir came home from the house of study. He said to her, "Where are my two sons?" She said, "They went to the house of study." He said, "I was watching the house of study, and I did not see them." She gave him a cup for *havdalah*, and he recited the *havdalah* prayer. He again said, "Where are my two sons?" She said to him, "They went to another place and will soon come." She set food before him, and he ate and blessed. After he blessed, she said, "Master, I have a question to ask you." He said to her, "Ask your question." She said to him, "Master, some time ago a man came and gave me something to keep for him. Now he comes and seeks to take it. Shall we return it to him or not?" He said to her, "Daughter, whoever has an object in trust must return it to its owner." She said to him, "Master, I would not have given it to him without your knowledge." What did she do? She took him by the hand and led him up to the room. She led him to the bed and removed the sheet that was on them. When he saw the two of them lying dead on the bed, he began to cry and say, "My sons, my sons. . . ." At that time she said to Rabbi Meir, "Master, did you not say

*Excerpts from David Goodblatt, "The Beruriah Traditions" in *Persons and Institutions in Early Rabbinic Judaism*, William Scott Green, ed. Missoula, MT: Scholars Press, 1977. 208–209, 217–218.

to me that I must return the trust to its master?" He said, "The Lord gave and the Lord has taken away; blessed be the name of the Lord (Job 1:21)."

R. Hanina said, "In this way she comforted him, and his mind was set at ease.

BYZANTINE WOMEN

As we have noted by the third century the vast and unwieldy Roman Empire was disintegrating in the face of internal strife, economic troubles, weak leadership, and invasions by tribes from northern Europe and Persians from the East. Emperor Constantine, in the fourth century, temporarily reversed that process during his reign (324–337 C.E.) when he restored imperial control, but, he also inadvertently paved the way for the permanent East-West division of the empire. When Constantine built a new capital, Constantinople, on the site of the ancient city of Byzantium, he shifted the center of the old Roman Empire to the East. The new capital was a vibrant intellectual and artistic center that blended classical culture with Christian beliefs and iconography, Roman law, and artistic influences from the East. Byzantine culture, as it quickly became known, enjoyed a golden age between 324 and 632, particularly under the leadership of Constantine and, later, the Emperor Justinian (r. 527–565) and the Empress Theodora. Constantinople remained the greatest city in the Christian world and a flourishing cultural center until it was conquered by the Turks in 1453. Meanwhile, the West disintegrated, and in 476, a Germanic chieftain deposed the last Roman emperor. Although Emperor Justinian temporarily restored Byzantine control over Italy and other parts of the West, his effort to reunite the empire ultimately failed, and the East-West division became permanent.

As the following excerpt suggests, Helen, the mother of Constantine, was in large measure responsible for her son's awareness of Christianity. Helen was a great patron of the Church and was personally responsible for the construction of some of the first actual churches that were erected. Before this time congregations had convened in the homes of fellow Christians and had gathered in synagogues and meeting halls.

HELEN, MOTHER OF CONSTANTINE[*]

For she [Helen], having resolved to discharge the duties of pious devotion to the God, the King of kings, and feeling it incumbent on her to render thanksgivings with prayers on behalf both of her own son, now so mighty an emperor, and of his sons, her own grandchildren, the divinely favored Caesars, though now advanced in years, yet gifted with no common degree of wisdom, had hastened with youthful alacrity to survey this venerable land; and at the same time to visit the eastern provinces, cities, and people, with a truly imperial solicitude. As soon, then, as she had rendered due reverence to the ground which the Savior's feet had trodden, according to the prophetic word which says "Let us worship at the place whereon his feet have stood," she immediately bequeathed the fruit of her piety to future generations.

For without delay she dedicated two churches to the God whom she adored, one at the grotto which had been the scene of the Savior's birth; the other on the

---

*From Eusebius, *Life of Constantine, NPNF,* 1886–1900, vol. I, 530–31.

mount of his ascension. For he who was "God with us" had submitted to be born even in a cave of the earth, and the place of his nativity was called Bethlehem by the Hebrews. Accordingly the pious empress honored with rare memorials the scene of her travail who bore this heavenly child, and beautified the sacred cave with all possible splendor. The emperor himself soon after testified his reverence for the spot by princely offerings, and added to his mother's magnificence by costly presents of silver and gold, and embroidered hangings. And farther, the mother of the emperor raised a stately structure on the Mount of Olives also, in memory of his ascent to heaven who is the Savior of mankind, erecting a sacred church and temple on the very summit of the mount. . . . Thus did Helena Augusta, the pious mother of a pious emperor, erect over the two mystic caverns these two noble and beautiful monuments of devotion, worthy of everlasting remembrance, to the honor of God her Savior, and as proofs of her holy zeal, receiving from her son the aid of his imperial power. Nor was it long ere this aged woman reaped the due reward of her labors. After passing the whole period of her life, even to declining age, in the greatest prosperity, and exhibiting both in word and deed abundant fruits of obedience to the divine precepts, and having enjoyed in consequence an easy and tranquil existence, with unimpaired powers of body and mind, at length she obtained from God an end befitting her pious course, and a recompense of her good deeds even in this present life.

For on the occasion of a circuit which she made of the eastern provinces, in the splendor of imperial authority, she bestowed abundant proofs of her liberality as well on the inhabitants of the several cities collectively, as on individuals who approached her, at the same time that she scattered largesses among the soldiery with a liberal hand. But especially abundant were the gifts she bestowed on the naked and unprotected poor. To some she gave money, to others an ample supply of clothing: she liberated some from imprisonment, or from the bitter servitude of the mines; others she delivered from unjust oppression, and others again, she restored from exile.

While, however, her character derived luster from such deeds as I have described, she was far from neglecting personal piety toward God. She might be seen continually frequenting his Church, while at the same time she adorned the houses of prayer with splendid offerings, not overlooking the churches of the smallest cities. In short, this admirable woman was to be seen, in simple and modest attire, mingling with the crowd of worshipers, and testifying her devotion to God by a uniform course of pious conduct.

And when at length at the close of a long life, she was called to inherit a happier lot, having arrived at the eightieth year of her age, and being very near the time of her departure, she prepared and executed her last will in favor of her only son, the emperor and sole monarch of the world, and her grandchildren, the Caesars his sons, to whom severally she bequeathed whatever property she possessed in any part of the world. Having thus made her will, this thrice blessed woman died in the presence of her illustrious son, who was in attendance at her side, caring for her and held her hands: so that, to those who rightly discerned the truth, the thrice blessed one seemed not to die, but to experience a real change and transition from an earthly to a heavenly existence, since her soul, remolded as it were into an incorruptible and angelic essence, was received up into her Savior's presence.

Hypatia of Alexandria

Hypatia of Alexandria was without question one of the most remarkable women in the ancient world. She, not unlike Sappho (Chapter 6), Aspasia (Chapter 7), Beruriah, earlier in this chapter, and others, was praised, disparaged, honored, and denounced during her lifetime and in the historical record. So far as is known, however, no other woman discussed in this volume met with such an untimely and brutal death.

The city of Alexandria in the fourth and fifth centuries was an intellectual and cultural center that was unparalleled in late antiquity. There is substantive evidence attesting that Hypatia was recognized as a virtuous spokesperson in social, political, and cultural matters in Alexandria. She was respected and admired among the city's intellectuals for her accomplishments as a mathematician, scholar and philosopher. Like her father, Theon, Hypatia was a Neo-Platonist who subscribed to the writings of Plotinus and had teaching residencies both in Athens and Alexandria where she was appointed director of the famous library.

Existing sources related to Hypatia that provide the most information about her are from dignitaries and political and religious leaders, many of whom had been her pupils. The conspiracy that resulted in her premature and violent death had its roots in the religious politics of Cyril, the Bishop of Alexandria who generated a massive campaign to rid the city of "heretics." Hypatia became vulnerable to Cyril's zealous "purge" because she sustained her friendship with Orestes, the prefect of Egypt who had opposed the Bishop's decrees.

THE MURDER OF HYPATIA[*]

There was a woman at Alexandria named Hypatia, daughter of the philosopher Theon, who made such attainments in literature and science, as to far surpass all the philosophers of her own time. Having succeeded to the school of Plato and Plotinus, she explained the principles of philosophy to her auditors, many of whom came from a distance to receive her instructions. On account of the self-possession and ease of manner, which she had acquired in consequence of the cultivation of her mind, she not infrequently appeared in public in presence of the magistrates. Neither did she feel abashed in coming to an assembly of men. For all men on account of her extraordinary dignity and virtue admired her the more. Yet even she fell a victim to the political jealousy which at that time prevailed. For as she had frequent interviews with Orestes, it was calumniously reported among the Christian populace, that it was she who prevented Orestes from being reconciled to the bishop. Some of them therefore, hurried away by a fierce and bigoted zeal, whose ringleader was a reader named Peter, waylaid her returning home, and dragging her from her carriage, they took her to the church called *Caesareum,* where they completely stripped her, and then murdered her with tiles. After tearing her body in pieces, they took her mangled limbs to a place called Cinaron, and there burnt them. This affair brought not the least opprobrium, not only upon Cyril, but also upon the whole Alexandrian church. And surely nothing can be farther from the spirit of Christianity than the allowance of massacres, fights, and transactions of that sort. This happened in the month of March during Lent, in the fourth year of Cyril's episcopate, under the tenth consulate of Honorius, and the sixth of Theodosius.

[*]From Socrates, Sozomenus, *Church History,* vol. 2. *NPNF,* 1979. p. 160.

Empress Theodora

Theodora was the daughter of a circus performer. This remarkable woman's rise to power as a co-ruler of the Roman Empire with her husband, the Emperor Justinian, is the subject of several novels that do an excellent job of fleshing out the story that primary sources can only suggest. Theodora was a brilliant young woman who actively pursued knowledge about increasingly complex and multifaceted issues that interested her. She brought an inquisitive mind and a keen intuition to bear upon matters of government, law, religious doctrine, women's rights, and public policy. Theodora was a staunch defender of women's rights, and a powerful voice in the Church. Her monophysite theology was still considered heretical by the orthodox. Theodora's theology directly contested the rulings of the Church at the Council of Chalcedon that required the sanction of her husband.

CHRISTIAN WOMEN IN LATE ANTIQUITY: EAST AND WEST

Political developments in the fourth to seventh centuries had important consequences for Christianity. Throughout this period, there were myriad, well-established religions and cults that had co-existed peacefully for generations. During the years that Christianity was becoming the state religion of the Empire, it was clear that all citizens and *metoikoi* (non-citizen residents) would be required to renounce their former traditions to become exclusively Christian. There were also schisms among a number of sectarian movements within Christianity that contended for authoritative doctrinal positions. Christians continued to experience persecution periodically from secular officials as well as religious rivals. Christian leaders themselves occasionally persecuted nonbelievers and minority Christian sects with whom they disagreed. Nevertheless, through a series of imperial edicts, Christianity became the official religion of the empire by the end of the fourth century.

As Christianity spread and enjoyed governmental support, the patriarchs or church leaders began to formalize its organization, define its core beliefs, and standardize religious practices and church rules. The loosely structured early Jesus movement and diverse forms of worship of the early churches gave way to a formal religion governed by male bishops located throughout the empire, and eventually headed by the bishop of Rome in the West and the Byzantine Emperor in the East. In the fifth century, divisions in the Church intensified. These schisms were perhaps inevitable considering the vast distance from the Patriarch at Rome to the four Patriarchs of Constantinople, Antioch, Jerusalem, and Alexandria. Eventually, the ecclesia was divided into the Eastern (Byzantine) Church and the Western (Roman Catholic) Church. The division reflected sharp cultural, linguistic, political, doctrinal, and structural differences between the East and West.

It is important to note that despite Christianity's new status, hundreds of thousands of citizens and non-citizens of the empire tenaciously resisted the new religion of the state. Yet, in the West, with few exceptions, until the late twentieth to early twenty-first centuries C.E. when texts concerning women in Islam (from the seventh century) have gradually been introduced, the majority of translated texts concerning women that survive, from the fifth century forward into the Middle Ages, tend to relate to Christianity. Male and female converts to Christianity continued to spread the new religion and explore diverse ways of living out their faith. Women explored ascetic life in the desert just as did their Christian brothers. There they could embody self-denial to enhance their spiritual growth. They created new communities (monasteries) where they could work, live, and pray together as they defined what it meant to be a Christian. These women and men developed spiritual literature, rituals, and iconography.

Women were important participants and leaders in each of these endeavors, despite the increasingly patriarchal character of the official Church. Inevitably, they also sometimes found themselves at odds with official dogma and male leaders. As we will see, for many such women the institutionalization of celibacy in the Church meant that the cost of achieving personal agency frequently included the renunciation of intimate expression of their sexuality. The implications of this renunciation are many, not all of which are obvious, and they are considered as we proceed.

Origins of Female Monasticism in the East

Gregory of Nyssa, a revered theologian in the Eastern Orthodox Church, writes a biography of his beloved and pious sister Macrina (327–379 C.E.). Macrina was the eldest child in this family of nine children, four of whom would be recognized by the Church as saints. She was also certainly among the first women to be recognized as foundress of a formal religious community for women and later a community for men. This selection provides insight into the daily-life experience of women in Macrina's community. Note that the emphasis on poverty, equanimity, and living a life in common among the women demands that women of higher social status renounce the comforts of wealth.

SAINT MACRINA, FOUNDRESS, ABBESS, TEACHER[*]

In a variety of ways, therefore, her mother was distracted by worries. (By this time her father had left this life.) In all of these affairs, Macrina was a sharer of her mother's toils, taking on part of her cares and lightening the heaviness of her griefs. . . . When there was no longer any necessity for them to continue their rather worldly way of life, Macrina persuaded her mother to give up her customary mode of living and her more ostentatious existence and the services of her maids, to which she had long been accustomed, and to put herself on a level with the many by entering into a common life with her maids, making them her sisters and equals rather than her slaves and underlings. . . .

[*Some years after Gregory was summoned to Macrina's bedside.*]

When the prayer and blessing were finished and the women had responded to the blessing by bowing their heads, they removed themselves from our presence and went off to their own quarters. Since not one of them remained with me, I correctly surmised that their Superior [Macrina] was not among them. An attendant led me to the house where the Superior was and opened the door, and I entered that sacred place. She was already very ill. . . . When she saw me standing at the door, . . . she stretched out her hand to God and said: "You have granted me this favor, O God, and have not deprived me of my desire, since you have impelled your servant to visit your handmaid." And in order not to disturb me, she tried to cover up . . . the difficulty she had in breathing, and, through it all, she adjusted herself to the brighter side. She initiated suitable topics of conversation and gave me an opportunity to speak by asking me questions. . . . She rehearsed such arguments, explaining the human situation through natural principles and disclosing the divine plan hidden in misfortune, and she spoke of certain aspects of the future life as if she was inspired by the Holy Spirit, so that my soul almost seemed to be lifted up out of its human sphere by what she said and, under the direction of her discourse, take its stand in the heavenly sanctuaries.

. . . although the fever was burning up all her energy and leading her to death, she was refreshing her body as if by a kind of dew, she kept her mind free in the contemplation of higher things and unimpeded by the disease. . . . she was lifted up by her discourse on the soul; how she explained the reason for life in the flesh, why man exists; how he is mortal, whence death comes; and what release there is from death back again into life. In all of this, she went on as if inspired by the power of the Holy Spirit, explaining it all clearly and logically. Her speech flowed with complete ease, just as a stream of water goes down a hill without obstruction.

Desert Mothers and Harlots of the Desert

Records from the fifth century provide strikingly different models descriptive of women who went to the desert to express their devotion to Jesus. Just as males, following the example of St. Antony, made their way to the deserts of Egypt to adopt an ascetic lifestyle, so we find records of women who made that same commitment. Like their brothers, their harsh life of fasting and prayer also included battling against sins and "temptations of the flesh and the devil." By this time, philosophical precepts based on Platonic dualisms had become foundational to much of Christian theology and spiritual practice. Any aspect of life that embraced nature and the body was, from this theological perspective, perceived as antithetical to the Spirit.

The first two readings are quotations from two of the desert mothers, Amma Sarah and Amma Syncletica. These two women are exemplary figures in the literature whose perseverance against evil was legendary and whose pursuit of God so tenacious that they embodied great Wisdom and served as counselors to many monks.

AMMA SARAH INSTRUCTS HOLY MEN*

1. It was related of Amma Sarah that for thirteen years she waged warfare against the demon of fornication. She never prayed that the warfare should cease but she said, "O God, give me strength."
3. It was said concerning her that for sixty years she lived beside a river and never lifted her eyes to look at it.
4. Another time, two old men, great anchorites, came to the district of Pelusia to visit her. When they arrived one said to the other, "Let us humiliate this old woman." So they said to her, "Be careful not to become conceited thinking of yourself: 'Look how anchorites are coming to see me, a mere woman.'" But Amma Sarah said to them, "According to nature I am a woman, but not according to my thoughts."
8. Some monks of Scetis came one day to visit Amma Sarah. She offered them a small basket of fruit. They left the good fruit and ate the bad. So she said to them, "You are true monks of Scetis."
9. She also said to the brothers, "It is I who am a man, you who are women."

*From *Sayings of the Desert Fathers,* translated by H. Wadell. London: Constable and Co., 1936.

Amma Syncletica Teaches Perseverance and Humility*

1. Amma Syncletica said, "In the beginning there are a great many battles and a good deal of suffering for those who are advancing towards God and afterwards, ineffable joy. It is like those who wish to light a fire; at first they are choked by the smoke and cry, and by this means obtain what they seek (as it is said: 'Our God is a consuming fire' [Heb. 12.24]): so we also must kindle the divine fire in ourselves through tears and hard work."

5. Blessed Syncletica was asked if poverty is a perfect good. She said, "For those who are capable of it, it is a perfect good. Those who can sustain it receive suffering in the body but rest in the soul, for just as one washes coarse clothes by trampling them underfoot and turning them about in all directions, even so the strong soul becomes much more stable thanks to voluntary poverty."

8. She also said, "If illness weighs us down, let us not be sorrowful as though, because of the illness and the prostration of our bodies we could not sing, for all these things are for our good, for the purification of our desires. Truly fasting and sleeping on the ground are set before us because of our sensuality. If illness then weakens this sensuality the reason for these practices is superfluous. For this is the great asceticism: to control oneself in illness and to sing hymns of thanksgiving to God."

11. She also said, "Imitate the publican, and you will not be condemned with the Pharisee. Choose the meekness of Moses and you will find your heart which is a rock changed into a spring of water."

14. She also said, "Those who are great athletes must contend against stronger enemies."

16. She also said, "As long as we are in the monastery, obedience is preferable to asceticism. The one teaches pride, the other humility."

19. Amma Syncletica said, "There are many who live in the mountains and behave as if they were in the town, and they are wasting their time. It is possible to be a solitary in one's mind while living in a crowd, and it is possible for one who is a solitary to live in the crowd of his own thoughts."

26. She also said, "Just as one cannot build a ship unless one has some nails, so it is impossible to be saved without humility."

Female Deacons and the Order of Widows

As early as the third century the Church made economic provisions for women in communities such as the female deacons and widows who gave their lives to the service of Christ. It is instructive, however, to compare the proscriptions required for their lifestyles, personal agency, and freedom with the female Christian Montanist prophets, priests, and bishops (see earlier) and the Naditu priestesses in the Ancient Near East in the second millenium B.C.E. (see Chapter 2). The following selections present regulations and proscriptions that describe relationships with the male hierarchy among women who formally consecrated their lives to service in the Church. Note specifically the distinctions between Phoebe's vocation as a deacon in the first century (see earlier) and the ministry of the deaconesses described here in the fourth century. The first text firmly establishes the lines of authority under which the female deacons were to fall. It also, however, reveals considerable respect for female deacons. The Order of Widows was, by the fourth century, formally instituted with clear-cut regulations concerning

*From *Sayings of the Desert Fathers,* 1936, 53 b-f.

status, dress, comportment, areas in which women were forbidden to minister, and lines of authority and submission to males in the Church's hierarchy.

REGULATIONS FOR DEACONESSES[*]

Let the Bishop, therefore, preside over you as one honored with the authority of God, which he is to exercise over the clergy, and by which he is to govern all the people. But let the deacon minister to him as Christ doth to his Father, and let him serve him unblamably in all things, as Christ doeth nothing of himself, but doeth always those things that please his Father. Let also the deaconess be honored by you in the place of the Holy Ghost, and not do nor say any thing without the deacon; as neither doth the Comforter say nor do any thing of himself, but giveth glory to Christ by waiting for his pleasure. And as we cannot believe on Christ without the teaching of the Spirit, so let not any woman address herself to the deacon or to the Bishop without the deaconess. Let the presbyters be esteemed by you to represent us the apostles, and let them be the teachers of divine knowledge; since our Lord, when he sent us, said, *Go ye, and make disciples of all nations, baptizing them in the name of the Father, and of the Son, and of the Holy Ghost; teaching them to observe all things whatsoever I have commanded you.* Let the widows and orphans be esteemed as representing the altar of burnt-offering; and let the virgins be honored as representing the altar of incense, and the incense itself.

REGULATIONS FOR CHRISTIAN WIDOWS[**]

3. OF WHAT CHARACTER THE WIDOWS OUGHT TO BE, AND HOW THEY OUGHT TO BE SUPPORTED BY THE BISHOP

But the true widows are those who have had only one husband, having a good report among the generality for good works; *widows indeed,* sober, chaste, faithful, pious, who have brought up their children well, and have *entertained strangers* unblamably; who are to be supported, as devoted to God.

Besides, do thou, O Bishop, be mindful of the needy, both reaching out thy helping hand, and making provision for them, as the steward of God, distributing seasonably the oblations to every one of them, to the widows, the orphans, the friendless, and those who are tried with affliction.

Origins of Monasticism in the West

In the early fifth century in the West at Rome, "Marcella's circle" constituted a less formal, but nonetheless intentional formation of women in Christian community. Jerome is quick to allude to Marcella's status as a Patrician woman, well born, but eager to denounce her wealth and to embrace a life of poverty and simplicity of life. Marcella's commitment to study, interpretation of scripture, and prayer set a precedent that would continue among religious women in the West.

[*]From Irah Chase, *The Work Claiming to Be the Constitutions of the Holy Apostles, Including the Canons.* New York: D. Appleton, 1848. II. 26.

[**]From Chase, *Work Claiming to Be the Constitutions of the Holy Apostles,* 1848, III.3.

JEROME PRAISES MARCELLA AND HER *CIRCLE* OF HOLY WOMEN[*]

1. You have besought me often and earnestly, Principia, virgin of Christ, to dedicate a letter to the memory of that holy woman Marcella, and to set forth the goodness long enjoyed by us for others to know and to imitate. I am so anxious myself to do justice to her merits that it grieves me that you should spur me on and fancy that your entreaties are needed when I do not yield even to you in love of her. In putting upon record her signal virtues I shall receive far more benefit myself than I can possibly confer upon others. If I have hitherto remained silent and have allowed two years to go over without making any sign, this has not been owing to a wish to ignore her as you wrongly suppose, but to an incredible sorrow which so overcame my mind that I judged it better to remain silent for a while than to praise her virtues in inadequate language. Neither will I now follow the rules of rhetoric in eulogizing one so dear to both of us and to all the saints, Marcella the glory of her native Rome. I will not set forth her illustrious family and lofty lineage, nor will I trace her pedigree through a line of consuls and practorian prefects. I will praise her for nothing but the virtue which is her own and which is the more noble, because forsaking both wealth and rank she has sought the true nobility of poverty and lowliness.

5. In those days no highborn lady at Rome had made profession of the monastic life, or had ventured—so strange and ignominious and degrading did it then seem—publicly to call herself a nun. It was from some priests of Alexandria, and from pope Athanasius, and subsequently from Peter, who, to escape the persecution of the Arian heretics, had all fled for refuge to Rome as the safest haven in which they could find communion—it was from these that Marcella heard of the life of the blessed Antony, then still alive, and of the monasteries in the Thebaid founded by Pachomius, and of the discipline laid down for virgins and for widows. Nor was she ashamed to profess a life which she had thus learned to be pleasing to Christ. Many years after her example was followed first by Sophronia and then by others, of whom it may be well said in the words of Ennius:

> Would that ne'er in Pelion's woods
> Had the axe these pinetrees felled.

My revered friend Paula was blessed with Marcella's friendship, and it was in Marcella's cell that Eustochium, that paragon of virgins, was gradually trained. Thus it is easy to see of what type the mistress was who found such pupils.

The unbelieving reader may perhaps laugh at me for dwelling so long on the praises of mere women; yet if he will but remember how holy women followed our Lord and Saviour and ministered to Him of their substance, and how the three Marys stood before the cross and especially how Mary Magdalen—called the tower from the earnestness and glow of her faith—was privileged to see the rising Christ first of all before the very apostles, he will convict himself of pride sooner than me of folly. For we judge of people's virtue not by their sex but by their character, and hold those to be worthy of the highest glory who have renounced both rank and wealth.

[*]From Jerome, *Letters,* LCL, 1933. 127 1–7.

The following document is a rare example of a text written by a woman in the fifth century C.E. In contrast to the overwhelming number of texts written by males about women, Egeria records her own interpretation of her experiences. Unfortunately, the only information we have about Egeria comes from her journal entries. They reveal a woman of the nobility, who was, apparently, like Paula and Marcella, also a member of a group of women who were devoted to Christ.

EGERIA'S ACCOUNT OF HER PILGRIMAGE TO JERUSALEM[*]

Then on Sabbath we went up the mountain, and coming to some monastic cells, where the monks living there received us very hospitably, providing us every courtesy. A church with a presbyter is there. There we remained for the night, and on the morning of the Lord's Day, with the priests and monks who lived there, one by one we began to climb the mountain.

These mountains are climbed with infinite labor, because you do not go up them very slowly in a circular path, as we say "in a spiral," but you go straight up the whole way as if climbing over a wall. Then one must directly descend each one of these mountains until you reach the very base of the central mountain which is called Sinai. So by the will of Christ our God, helped by the prayers of holy men who were going with us, and with great labor, it was done. I had to go up on foot because one cannot go straight up riding. Nonetheless one does not feel the labor, because I saw the desire which I had being completed through the will of God.

At the fourth hour we arrived at the top of the holy mountain of God, Sinai, where the Law was given, in the place where the majesty of God descended on that day when the mountain of God smoked. [Ex. 19:18] Now in this place the summit of the mountain is not very large. Nonetheless the church itself is very graceful. When therefore by the help of God we had ascended to the height and arrived at the door of the church, there was the presbyter assigned to that church coming to meet us from his monastic cell. He was a healthy old man, and, as they say here, an "ascetic," and—what more can I say—quite worthy to be in this place. Then also other presbyters met us, and all the monks who live around the mountain, that is, if they were not prevented by age or weakness. In fact no one stays on the summit of the central mountain, for there is nothing there except the church and the cave where Saint Moses was. [Ex. 33:22] The reading in this place was all from the book of Moses, the Oblation was made in due order and here we communicated. Now as we left the church the presbyters gave us eulogia from this place, fruits which grow on this mountain. Even though the holy mountain Sinai is all rocky, not having even a bush, still there is a bit of earth down by the foot of these mountains, both around the central one and those which surround it. There the holy monks through their diligence put bushes and establish orchards or cultivated plots, and next to them their dwellings, so that they may seem to gather fruits from the soil of the mountain itself, but nonetheless they have cultivated it with their own hands.

[*]"Egeria Records Her Travels Throughout the Holy Land for Holy Women in Her Circle at Home," *A Lost Tradition: Women Writers of the Early Church*, edited by Patricia Wilson-Kastner, et al., Washington DC, University Press of America, 1981. 86–88, 91–92: © held by G. Ronald Kastner.

After we had communicated and the holy men had given us the eulogia and we had come through the church door, then I immediately asked them to show us each place. The holy men kindly agreed to show us all the sites. They pointed out to us the cave where Saint Moses was when he ascended into the mountain of God that he might receive again the tables of the Law, after he had broken the first one when the people had sinned. [Ex. 34; 32:19] Then they showed us other places which we wanted to see, and also ones which they knew better than we.

But I would like you to know, venerable ladies my sisters, that from the place where we were standing, the area around the church, the summit of the middle, it seemed to us that those mountains which we had first ascended with difficulty were like little hills. Nonetheless they seemed boundless and I do not think that I have seen any higher, except for the middle mountain which greatly exceeds them. From that place we saw Egypt, Palestine, the Red Sea, and the Parthenian Sea which goes all the way to Alexandria, and finally the infinite Saracen lands. It is scarcely possible to believe it, but these holy men pointed out each place to us.

THE CELTS

Like any ethnographic study of an ancient culture, descriptions of Celtic culture vary considerably depending upon the sources referenced, when they were written, by whom and why they were written, and by whom and for whom they were disseminated. Studies written to examine the Celtic warrior, for example, provide one perspective, whereas, studies written from the point of view of Celtic religious specialists (Druids and later Celtic Christians) present a different picture. Gender markings among the Celts also reveal Celtic women whose image as women warriors were threatening and offensive to Roman sensibilities.

The earliest Celts (ca. second millennium B.C.E.) were pastoralists, nomadic, warring people whose social organization was patriarchal with a chief/warrior/king at the head of a hierarchy that included a priestly class, a warrior class, peasants, and serfs. Southern migrations included settled Neolithic towns and villages of Old Europe, settlements in the Black Sea area, throughout the Alps and northern Europe, and west to Ireland and the British Isles. Celtic tribes from the Alps also migrated into Mediterranean regions to conquer Etruscan settlements and they ultimately came against Rome in 390 B.C.E. Stories and bits of history about the warring Celts, both male and female, are reminiscent of theories about "invasions" into settlements in Old Europe during the Neolithic (see Chapter 1, "Paleolithic, Neolithic, and Proto-Historic Cultures").

The greatest military victories that the Celts achieved took place in the first millennium B.C.E., after which they came increasingly under Roman domination. A last stronghold of Celtic culture persists into the present day in Ireland, Scotland, Wales, and Brittany where Celtic languages continue to be spoken. Studies reveal that Celts were literate and had knowledge of astronomy and mathematics. Among other achievements of the Celts were the intricately worked weaponry and jewelry with nature motifs that are both terrifying (gargoyles) and beautiful (intertwining vines and leaves that might grace the handle of a dagger). Fabrics woven in bright colors and plaids and checks that were appropriated by different clans also constituted a notable cultural contribution that persists in fashion in the present.

Inconsistent with the martial aspect of Celtic culture are the mythical and mystical dimensions expressed in its poetry, music, song, and dance. The deep appreciation of, and reverence for, all aspects of nature are definite characteristics of Celtic culture and are integral to the arts and expressions of the Sacred. The Gods and Goddesses of the Celts were described and portrayed as a combination of the descriptions of the Goddess we spoke of in Chapter 1 in Old Europe. The female deities in this patriarchal culture, however, included Goddesses that had a fierce warrior image, not unlike Anath in Canaan, Hathor in Egypt, and the Amazons described by Herodotus. Love of nature, reverence for independence, and a keen sense of the mystical in all of life are characteristics of Celtic spirituality that were integral to the traditions of Celtic Christianity as it developed from the fifth century C.E.

Women Warriors

We include here two examples from Celtic mythology that illustrate the blurring lines between mythology, legend, and history. The Horse Goddess Rhiannon and the story of Maedb continue as part of the woman warrior tradition in Celtic culture.

The story of Rhiannon appears in the earliest known manuscript of *The Mabinogion,* a collection of Welsh tales that dates from the early fourteenth century. The oral tradition of which these tales are representative tends to combine myth, legend, history, and a fair amount of other-worldly magical inspiration. By the fourteenth century they had also come to include some elements that are distinctly Christian. Rhiannon, the protagonist of the tale, is a Goddess of horses, yet she, like her counterparts in other pantheons, marries a human king. Mythographers suggest that the element of marriage between the human male and the divine female may point to or be meant to explain or compliment historical women whose prowess and expertise are recognized and admired within their culture.

RHIANNON, THE HORSE GODDESS[*]

They [Pwyll and Rhiannon] ruled the land successfully that year and the next. But in the third year, the men of the land began to feel sad within themselves at seeing the man they loved so much as their lord and foster-brother without an heir. And they summoned him to them. It was in Presseleu in Dyfed that they met.

"Lord," they said, "we know that you are not the same age as some of the men in this land, and we are afraid that you might not have an heir from the woman who is with you. So for that reason, take another wife that you may have an heir from her. You will not last forever, and though you would like to remain as you are, we will not tolerate it from you."

"Well," said Pwyll, "we have not been together long, and much may happen yet. Be patient with me until the end of the year: we will arrange to meet a year from now, and I will act according to your advice."

The appointment was made, but before the time was up, a son was born to him, and in Arberth he was born. On the night of his birth, women were brought in to watch over the boy and his mother. What the women did, however, was sleep, and Rhiannon, the boy's mother, too. Six was the number of women brought in. They kept vigil for a part of the night, but then, however, before midnight, each fell asleep; toward dawn they awakened. When they awoke, they looked where they had put the boy, but there was no sign of him there.

"Och!" exclaimed one of the women, "the boy is surely lost!"

*From *Mabinogion and Other Welsh Tales,* translated by Patrick A. Ford. Berkeley, Los Angeles, CA and London: University of California Press, 1977. 186–187.

"Indeed," said another, "it would be a small punishment to burn us or slay us on account of the boy."

"Is there any counsel in the world for that?" one of them asked.

"There is," said another, "I have good counsel."

"What is it?" they asked.

"There is a staghound bitch here," she said, "and she had puppies. Let us kill some of the pups, smear Rhiannon's face and hands with the blood, cast the bones before her, and swear that she herself has destroyed her son. And our affirmation will not yield to her own."

They decided on that. Toward day Rhiannon awoke and said, "Ladies, where is my boy?"

"Lady," they said, "don't ask us for your son. We have nothing but bruises and blows from struggling with you, and we have certainly never seen ferocity in any woman as much as in you. But it did us no good to fight with you; you have destroyed your son yourself, so do not seek him from us."

"You poor things!" exclaimed Rhiannon, "for the sake of the Lord God who knows all things, don't lie to me! God, who knows everything, knows that's a lie. If it is because you are afraid, I confess to God, I will protect you."

"God knows," they said, "we would not suffer harm to befall us for anyone in the world."

"Poor things," she said, "you'll suffer no harm for telling the truth."

But despite what she would say either in reason or with emotion, she would get only the same answer from the women.

Thereupon Pwyll Pen Annwfn rose, along with the retinue and the hosts; it was impossible to conceal what had happened. The news went through the land, and every nobleman heard it. The nobles met and sent emissaries to Pwyll, to ask him to divorce his wife for having committed an outrage as reprehensible as she had done.

"They have no cause to request that I divorce my wife, save that she bear no children," Pwyll told them. "I know she has children, and I will not divorce her. If she has done wrong, let her be punished for it."

Rhiannon, for her part, summoned to her teachers and men of wisdom. And when it seemed more appropriate to her to accept her penance than to haggle with the women, she accepted her punishment. This was the punishment handed down to her: to be in that court in Arberth for seven years, to sit beside the mounting block that was outside the gate each day, to tell her story to all who came whom she thought might not know it, and to offer to those guests and distant travellers who would allow it to carry them on her back to the court; only rarely would one allow himself to be carried. And thus she spent a part of the year.

At that time, Teyrnon Twrf Liant was lord over Gwent Is Coed, and he was the best man in the world. In his house was a mare, and there was neither stallion nor mare fairer than she in his kingdom. On the eve of every May day she would foal, but no one knew what became of her foal. One night, Teyrnon conversed with his wife.

"Wife," he said, "we are remiss in allowing our mare to bear issue each year without us getting any of them."

"What can be done about it?" she asked.

"God's vengeance on me," said he, "if I do not find out what destruction is carrying off the colts: tonight is May eve."

He had the mare brought into the house, armed himself, and began the night's vigil. As night fell, the mare gave birth to a large, handsome colt; it stood immediately. Teyrnon rose to inspect the stoutness of the colt, and as he was so engaged, he heard a great commotion, and after the commotion, a great claw came through the window, and grasped the colt by the mane. Teyrnon drew his sword and cut off the arm from the elbow, so that that part of the arm and the colt remained inside with him. At the same time, he heard a roar and wail together. He opened the door and rushed headlong in the direction of the noise, but he could see nothing because of the night's darkness. He pursued the sound, following it. Then he remembered having left the door open, and went back. At the door there was a small boy all wrapped up in a mantle of silk brocade! He took the boy to him and, indeed, the boy was strong for his age!

The story of Queen Maedb (pronounced Maeve) is a part of the Irish epic entitled the *Tain Bo Cuailnge* (Cattle Raid of Cuailnge). This epic is one of many cattle-raiding stories that can be identified from the Steppes to India to Ireland and any culture in which cattle and horses were a crucial element in the subsistence mode of a culture. The custom of "bride price" is often an integral feature of cattle-raiding stories. Again, this story, like the tale about Rhiannon, had its origins in oral tradition going back as early as the first century C.E. The earliest version in print is from the twelfth century. In the *Tain*, Queen Maedb (the daughter of the king of Ireland) is one of many powerful females who are part of the nobility in the aristocratic warrior society of Ulster in Ireland. Although the hero of the story is Cuchulainn, his adversary Maedb is the female protagonist who sets the story in motion and whose desire to own the "brown bull" of Ulster propels the action. Maedb's keen sense of confidence and self assurance is clear from the opening of the epic. In the brief excerpt that follows, called the "pillow talk" Maedb is engaged in a boasting contest with her husband Ailill. [In the brief excerpt Maedb also indicates her values and the importance of choosing a mate whose personality is compatible with her own.]

MAEDB, WOMAN WARRIOR[*]

I outdid them in grace and giving and battle and warlike combat. I had fifteen hundred soldiers in my royal pay, all exiles sons, and the same number of freeborn native men, and for every paid soldier I had ten more. . . .

My father gave me a whole province of Ireland, this province ruled from Cruachan, which is why I am called "Maeb of Cruachan" . . . they came from Finn the King of Leinster, Rus Ruad's son, to woo me, and from Coirpre Niafer, the king of Temair . . . from Conchobor, king of Ulster and they came from Fochaid Bec, and I would not go. For I asked a harder wedding gift than any woman ever asked before from a man in Ireland . . . the absence of meanness and jealousy and fear. . . . If I married a mean man the union would be wrong because I am full of grace and giving . . . if my husband was a timid man our union would be wrong because I thrive . . . on all kinds of trouble . . . and it is an insult for a wife to be more spirited than her husband. So I got the kind of man I wanted: Rus Ruad's other son . . . yourself, Ailill, from Leinster.

*From *The Tain*, translated by Thomas Kinsella. Oxford: Oxford University Press in Association with The Dolman Press, Dublin, 1969. 52, 53.

Celtic Christian Saints

Celtic Christianity retained many of the mystical elements of spirituality from its former traditions. Central among these elements were the primacy of nature, an understanding that the Holy is in all things, and the value of the spiritual path of the individual. Christianity that emerged among the Celts boasted one of the richest expressions of monastic life and ascetic practices that were very much akin to the desert fathers and mothers in Egypt. The artwork that was created and produced at the great abbeys and monasteries, especially the art of illumination among scribes who generated prayer books, psalters, and copies of the Bible, is unrivaled in Christendom. The short selections from Nigel Pennick's *The Celtic Saints* that follow give examples of Celtic Christian saints, some of whom have legends that are combined with the stories of their ancient predecessors in legend and mythology.[*]

St. Non

According to Rhygyfarch's work, *The Life of St. David,* and traditions preserved in the former service book of her church at Altarnon, St. Non was the daughter of Anna, daughter of Gwrthefyr Fendigaid. On her father's side, she was also of noble birth, being the daughter of Cynyr of Caer Gawch. Like many Celtic saints, St. Non, who has the epithet Bendigaid, "Blessed," is also known by other names. In Britain, she appears as Nonna and Nonnita, and in Brittany as Melaria. St. Non is revered mainly because she was the mother of St. David, who eventually became the patron saint of Wales. Her most sacred place is at St. Non's Head in Pembrokeshire, west Wales. According to Rhygyfarch's account, one day a wandering monk, called Sant, was out hunting. Sant was no ordinary monk however, for he was the former king of Ceredigion and had abdicated to take up the religious life. By the River Teifi, Sant experienced some typical Celtic hunting omens. He chased a stag along the riverbank, and through the chase, discovered a colony of bees in a tree. He killed the stag, took the honey, and caught a fish in the river. The result of his hunt was that he had the produce of the beasts of the earth, water, and air. Having collected together his spoils, an angel, a being of fire, appeared to him, and told him that he must give a portion of his takings to the nearby monastery of Ty Gwyn at Maucan. These offerings, the angel said, represented the virtues of a son whom he would father.

Non was a student at the school of Ty Gwyn, one of the monasteries where women were permitted to study. There, Sant made Non pregnant. Shortly afterward, the traveling preacher, Gildas, came to the church of Ty Gwyn, and tried to conduct a service. But he was disempowered, and could not speak. The pregnant Non was hidden inside the church and, when Gildas called for any concealed persons to show themselves, she came out of her hiding place and left the church. Then Gildas discovered that his power of concentration was restored. The holy presence of the as yet unborn St. David had overwhelmed him. Non, pregnant with David, was threatened by "a certain man in the district, accounted a tyrant," so she left the monastic school and went to live in a cottage among the standing stones on the clifftop beyond Bryn y Garn.

[*]Nigel Pennick, ed., *The Celtic Saints.* New York: Sterling Publishing Co., 1997. 27–28, 30–31, 90–91.

Non gave birth to the baby at the standing stones during a thunderstorm. In addition to the thunder and lightning, other omens accompanied the birth of the baby, for the stone on which St. Non lay to give birth was split with the force of the birth, leaving the imprint of her hands upon it. One part of the stone remained behind St. Non's head and the other stood upright at her feet. This stone was later used as the altar slab in the chapel of St. Non. Another legend tells how, when the megalith was split, a spring welled up. This is the origin of the spring of St. Non, that is revered to this day for its curative powers. Writing of the holy well in 1811, the author Fenton noted, "The fame this consecrated spring had obtained is incredible, and still it is resorted to for many complaints. In my infancy . . . I was often dipped in it, and offerings, however trifling, even of a farthing or a pin, were made after each ablution, and the bottom of the well shone with votive brass. The spring . . . is of a most excellent quality, is reported to ebb and flow, and to be of wondrous efficacy in complaints of the eye."

According to legend, St. David was born dead, but St. Ailbe, who was present at the birth, resuscitated the baby, and baptized him in the spring. Then, the baby was taken away to be fostered by the bishop, and grew up to be one of the greatest Welsh churchmen. At the request of her sister, St. Gwen, St. Non later left Wales and went to Cornwall, where she founded the church of Altarnon. Like her original holy place in Pembrokeshire, the sacred enclosure of Altarnon was located at a holy well with healing properties. Like so many British saints, she also visited Brittany. She is remembered there by several church dedications and a mystery play of her life, Buhez Santes Nonn, that was performed for many years at her pardon at Dirinon.

St. Melangell

The most potent instance of Celtic harmony with nature is the story of St. Melangell, the daughter of an Irish king. Renouncing her status as princess for the religious life, she became a nun, but despite this, was ordered to marry the man of her father's choice. In order to escape this forced marriage, she fled eastward across the Irish Sea and settled at Pennant, in Wales. She is considered a protectress because of an incident that took place during a hunt in the year 604, conducted by the prince of Powys, Brochwel Ysgithrog. While his hounds were chasing a hare, the prince came across Melangell, praying devoutly in a bramble thicket. The hare was hiding inside the sleeve of Melangell's garment, and looked out at the dogs. Prince Brochwel called to the dogs to catch the hare, but they retreated in fear from the saint, and ran off. The prince had never experienced anything like this before, so he asked the woman her name, and what she was doing there. After she had told him, Brochwel acknowledged her holy power as "a hand-maiden of the true God, and most sincere worshiper of Christ."

Because God had enabled her to protect the wild hare from the vicious hunting dogs, Brochwell gave her the lands across which his hunt had come. After that, the lands of Pennant Melangell became a sanctuary under her guardianship. She lived there for another thirty-seven years, during which time no animal was killed on her land. The wild animals living there became tame and humans too, could claim sanctuary from persecution at Pennant Melangell. After her death, St. Melangell became the tutelary saint of hares, which are called *wyn Melangell,* "Melangell's Lambs." To kill a hare in Melangell's parish was an act of sacrilege. St. Melangell is recognized today as the Celtic patroness of animals and the natural environment. According to the Celtic Christian philosophy, because the natural environment is the manifestation of God's will on earth, those who destroy it are not only threatening the continuance of all life on earth, but also going counter to "the protection and favor of the Creator."

As we leave Late Antiquity and enter the Middle Ages, we will shift our attention from the Mediterranean world and return to the region where we began our exploration of women and culture, Western Europe. This is the focus of Chapter 14, "Medieval Culture: The Religious Context," and Chapter 15, "Medieval Culture: The Secular Context," of Volume I.

SUGGESTED READINGS

Brooten, Bernadette. *Women Leaders in the Ancient Synagogues.* Vol. 36 of Brown Judaic Studies 36. Chico, CA: Scholars Press, 1982. 11, 13.

Davies, Wendy, "Celtic Women in the Early Middle Ages," in *Images of Women in Antiquity.* Edited by Averil Cameron and Amelie Kuhrt. London and Canberra, Croom Helm, 1983.

Images of Women in Antiquity. Edited by Averil Cameron and Amelie Kuhrt. London and Canberra: Croom Helm, 1983.

On Being a Jewish Feminist: A Reader. Edited by Susannah Heschel. New York: Schocken Books, 1983.

Sources Cited

Pliny the Younger. Ummidia and Her Grandson. *Letters.* Translated by Radice. Loeb Classical Library, Cambridge, London: Harvard University Press 1975. VII 24.15, abridged.

Marinus of Flavia Neopolis, Asclepigenia's Influence. *Life of Proclus.* London, 1972. In *A History of Women Philosophers,* 1987. Edited by M.E. Waithe. Excerpts from 201–205.

Josephus. Queen Helena. *Antiquities of the Jews.* H. St. Thackeray, R. Marcus, A. Wikgren, and L. Feldman. 1926–1965. Loeb Classical Library, Cambridge, London: Harvard University Press, 1965. 5th imprint. Vol. XIII. XX. 49. Excerpts.

Excerpts from the Babata Archives. *The Documents from the Bar Kochba Period in the Cave of Letters,* Greek Papyri. Edited by Napthali Lewis. Israel Exploration Society Series. Jerusalem: The Hebrew University of Jerusalem, 1989. 65, 67–68.

Brooten, Bernadette. *Women Leaders in the Ancient Synagogues,* Brown Judaic Studies 36. Chico, CA: Scholars Press, 1982. 11, 13. Excerpts.

Goodblatt, David. Beruriah. "The Beruriah Traditions" in *Persons and Institutions in Early Rabbinic Judaism.* Edited by William Scott Green. Missoula, MT: Scholars Press, 1977. 208–209; 217–218.

Eusebius. Helen, Mother of Constantine. *Life of Constantine.* Translated by Arthur C. Mc Giffert in *A Select Library of Nicene and Post Nicene Fathers of the Christian Church,* Vol. 1 of Second Series. Buffalo and New York. 1886–1900. 530–531.

Socrates, Sozomenus. The Murder of Hypatia. *Church History,* Vol.2. *A Select Library of Nicene and Post Nicene Fathers of the Christian Church,* Vol. 2 of Second Series. Buffalo and New York: 1979. 160.

Gregory of Nyssa. Saint Macrina, Foundress, Abbess, Teacher. "The Life of St. Macrina," *Saint Gregory of Nyssa: Ascetical Works.* Translated by V.W. Callahan in *The Fathers of the Church,* Vol.58. Washington DC: Catholic University of America Press, 1967. 58–59.

Amma Sarah Instructs Holy Men. *Sayings of the Desert Fathers.* Translated by H. Wadell. London: Constable and Co. 1936. Excerpts.

Amma Syncletica Teaches Perseverance and Humility. *Sayings of the Desert Fathers.* Translated by H. Wadell, London: Constable and Co. 1936. 53 b-f. Excerpts.

"Regulations for Deaconesses," *The Work Claiming to Be the Constitutions of the Holy Apostles, Including the Canons.* Translated by Irah Chase. New York: D. Appleton, 1848. II. 26.

"Regulations for Christian Widows," *The Work Claiming to Be the Constitutions of the Holy Apostles, Including the Canons.* Translated by Irah Chase. New York: D. Appleton, 1848. III.3.

Jerome. Jerome's Letter Praises Marcella and Her "Circle" of Holy Women. *Letters.* Translated by F. A. Wright. Loeb Classical Library, Cambridge, London: Harvard University Press, 1933. 127 1–7. Excerpts.

Egeria's Account of Her Pilgrimage to Jerusalem. From "Egeria Records Her Travels Throughout the Holy Land for Holy Women in Her Circle at Home," *A Lost Tradition: Women Writers of the Early Church.* Edited by Patricia Wilson-Kastner, et. al., Washington DC: University Press of America, 1981. 86–88, 91–92: © held by G. Ronald Kastner.

"Rhiannon, the Horse Goddess," *The Mabinogion and Other Welsh Tales.* Translated by Patrick A. Ford. Berkeley, CA: University of California Press, 1977. 186–187.

"Maedb, Woman Warrior," *The Tain.* Translated by Thomas Kinsella, Oxford: Oxford University Press in association with The Dolman Press, Dublin. 1969. 52, 53.

"St. Non," *The Celtic Saints.* Edited by Nigel Pennick. New York: Sterling Publishing Co. Inc., 1997. 27–28.

"St. Melangell," *The Celtic Saints.* Edited by Nigel Pennick. New York: Sterling Publishing Co. Inc., 1997, 90–91.

Chapter 14

Medieval Culture:
The Religious Context

The early Middle Ages, particularly the seventh and eighth centuries, has been called a "golden age" for female monasticism. The earliest women's monasteries were established in Britain and France in the sixth century. During the seventh century, nearly 33 percent of new monastic houses founded in France, Belgium, and Britain were for women; 12 percent of new houses were for women in the eighth century. Most women's houses were founded by queens and noble women or by fathers or brothers at a woman's request. The founding mothers of Anglo-Saxon and Frankish monasteries include Queen Ethelburga of Barking; Etheldreda of Ely; Hilda of Whitby; Queen Balthild of Chelles; Caesaria of Arles; and Queen Radegund of Poitiers. All but Radegund and Balthild served as abbess or head of their communities. The Church rewarded all these founding mothers with sainthood. (Schulenburg 1989, 268)

Women played important roles in the spread of Christianity in this formative period. Queens and noblewomen, who were often the first converts, converted their husbands whose subjects then became Christian. Their wealth also helped underwrite the missionary efforts of the Church. Women's monasteries served as supply bases and staging locales for male missionaries in frontier areas and functioned as missionary outposts themselves, converting those in surrounding areas and educating converts in their schools. Abbesses exercised many of the powers reserved for priests and monks elsewhere in Christendom. They heard confessions and gave absolution and benediction to Christians, although they were not permitted to serve communion.

Double monasteries were popular in the Western European countryside as they had been in the desert communities of early Christianity and the Theraputae of early Judaism. As they had in the first double and triple monasteries, men and women worked together and enjoyed an intellectual and spiritual partnership. Most double monasteries were governed by abbesses, or by an abbess and abbot jointly. In some cases of joint governance, the abbess had the superior authority.

Monastic life was attractive to noble women and their families throughout most of the medieval period for many reasons. (Only the nobility, it should be noted, could afford the dowry required to enter a monastery.) It was an acceptable and less costly alternative to an arranged marriage, and, in a culture that placed spiritual above secular concerns and stressed preparation for salvation, monastic life enabled religious women to devote their lives to their faith. More importantly, monasteries were the libraries or repositories of available knowledge. One of their functions was to preserve that knowledge by copying the texts that had come into their possession after the collapse of the Roman Empire. As a result, monastic women received a basic education and training in the arts of manuscript illumination and calligraphy, as well as needlework and music. Indeed, for most of the Middle Ages, monasteries were the primary source of both basic female literacy and of the small number of highly educated women. Finally, monastic life gave women, especially abbesses, stature and often authority that extended into the secular arena.

Invasions, the rise of the papacy, and the expansion of feudalism weakened the female monastic movement in much of Europe beginning in the ninth century. The Church abolished most double monasteries and restricted the economic activities of women's monasteries and the power of abbesses. In the secular realm, as noble families sought to protect and increase family holdings, women lost the power to control their own estates and became increasingly valuable as marriage pawns. As a result, they were less able to support monastic communities.

Although there was a revival of women's monastic life and even of double monasteries, particularly in Germany, in the twelfth century, the overall trend was not reversed. Intellectual currents and the religious ferment that began in the twelfth century hastened the pattern of decline. A more negative, indeed misogynist, view of women emerged within the Church as it became more institutionalized and confronted new challenges from heretics. Women were further marginalized with the founding of universities and the emergence of scholastic thought.

Beginning in the twelfth century, as a renewed religious fervor swept Europe and the revival of towns and trade drew people off the land, women pursued new ways to live out their faith. They were active in all the religious movements, from the Crusades to the new religious sects that emerged, and some chose to live their faith independent of any institution. In keeping with the growing secularization of Western culture, moreover, many sought to pursue their faith in the secular world. Women from artisan and working groups, not just the nobility, were participants in these religious phenomena.

The readings in this chapter illustrate the achievements and cultural contributions of talented religious women throughout the Middle Ages and the factors that fostered and inhibited their creativity. They reveal some of the strategies women employed to make their voices heard and the considerable authority that they were able, at times, to wield. The documents also demonstrate the ways in which women both reenforced and challenged prevailing gender ideology and patriarchal structures and power.

MONASTIC LIFE AND FEMALE CREATIVITY

Radegund of Poitiers (520–587)

Saint Radegund was one of the founding mothers of Western monasticism. Her early life illustrates the chaos that engulfed Western Europe after the fall of Rome and the changes that accompanied the spread of Christianity. She was born in the kingdom of Thuringia, ruled jointly by her father and his brothers. In 531, Thuringia was brutally sacked by two sons of Clovis, the king of the Franks. One of them, Clothar, won Radegund and her brother as part of his share of the spoils of war and took them to his kingdom. Clothar placed the 12-year-old girl in a convent to be educated as a Christian and prepared for marriage. In 540, Clothar married Radegund to legitimize his claim to the kingdom of Thuringia. Like other early Christian kings, he had concubines and numerous wives. When the king had her brother murdered, she bribed a bishop to consecrate her as a deaconess, and, with Clothar in pursuit, fled to Poitiers. Persuaded by the bishop to give the queen her freedom, Clothar donated the buildings in Poitiers in which she founded her monastery of Notre Dame.

Radegund was a model of piety and asceticism and a wise leader. She gave her wealth to the monastery, went on fasts, sometimes mortified her flesh, and followed a rigid daily regimen. She

gained fame as a healer who cared for the needy. Hoping to buffer her convent from the wars and political intrigues of the sixth century, she collected early Christian relics. After obtaining fragments of
the Holy Cross, she renamed her monastery St. Croix. The relics enhanced the fame, wealth, and security of her monastery which eventually numbered 1,200 nuns and became a major intellectual center.
Radegund was a writer, a patron of letters, and she had a close partnership with Venantius Fortunatus,
a respected scholar and literary figure. She also inspired two biographies: the first by Fortunatus, and
the second by a nun, Baudonivia, who was assigned by the abbess to write a life of Radegund 20 years
after her death. Baudonivia's biography is the first known book about a woman written by a woman,
and is thus a marker in the birth of women's history.

This excerpt from Radegund's elegy, *The Fall of Thuringia,* is a poignant memoir of her life. It also
provides a female perspective on war that differs markedly from most literature that celebrates the
heroics of male warriors. Her comparison between her land's fate and the fall of Troy reveals her
knowledge of classical languages and familiarity with Greek literature.

THE FALL OF THURINGIA[*]

The harsh nature of war! The malevolent fate of all things! How proud kingdoms
fall, suddenly in ruins! Blissful housetops that held up for long ages now lie torched,
consumed beneath a huge devastation.

This hall that once flourished in imperial splendor is covered no longer with
vaulted arches but with wretched cinders. A pall of pale ashes buries the steep shining roof that long ago gleamed with red-gold metal. Its potentate has been sent into
captivity, subject to an enemy lord. Its former glory has fallen into lowliness. The attendant crowd of striving retainers, all of whom served together, lies filthy in the
dust of death. Their life is over. The brilliant throng, the circle of court dignitaries,
lies unsepulchered, deprived of the honors due to the dead.

My beloved father's sister lies stretched on the ground, her milk-white body
outshining the flame-spewing, red-gold glow of her hair. Ah, the foully unburied
corpses have covered the field, and so the whole nation lies in one tomb.

No longer may Troy be the only city to lament her ruin. The land of Thuringia has
endured an equal massacre. From this place the married woman bound in chains was
dragged by her mangled hair, not able to bid a sad farewell to the gods of her hearth.
The captive was not allowed to imprint kisses on his doorpost, or turn his eyes once
more to the places he would never see again. The wife walked barefoot through her husband's blood, and the tender sister stepped over her fallen brother. The child, torn from
his mother's embrace, still hung on her lips, and there was no one to accord them a
flood of mourning tears. It was not enough that harsh fate deprived her of her child's
life. The mother, all her breath gone, had also lost her son's affectionate weeping.

But I, a barbarian woman, cannot weep enough, even though in all my wretched-
ness I were to swim in a lake of tears. Each person had an individual lament. I alone
pour forth laments for all, since the public grief is a private grief for me. Fortune took
care of those men whom the enemy forces cut down. But I endure as a sole survivor

in order to mourn for them all. I am forced to weep not only for dear ones slain; I weep as well for those whom kindly, life has preserved. Often I press my eyes shut, my face wet with tears. My sighs lie quelled, but my cares are not silent!

Eagerly I look to see whether a breeze will carry some greeting. Yet not a single shadow from among all my kinsmen comes to me. Unfriendly fate has torn from my embrace the one whose look used to console me with tender love.

Since you are so far from me, doesn't my grief torment you? . . . At least remember, Hamalafred, how from your earliest years of youth I used to be your Radegund, and how much you loved me when you were a sweet baby and the son of my father's brother, beloved cousin. You alone were for me what my dead father, what my mother, what my sister or brother could be considered. . . . [After their father was killed, she and her brother were raised with Hamalafred.]

Now the East hides you too in the shadows, as the West hides me. . . . A world separates those whom no lands had parted before. All that earth holds forces loving ones asunder. . . .

Be more fortunate, however, there where the good wishes of your family are keeping you, more fortunate than the land of Thuringia allowed you to be!

Here, on the contrary, I am tormented, burdened by strong griefs. Why are you unwilling to send me any sign of yourself? If only a letter would arrive to paint the features of him I long for but do not see! . . .

Why, cousin, do I avoid mentioning my brother, and why do I put off my weeping? . . . Unhappy me, I begin my weeping afresh when I remember his death, and suffer again while I speak of these grievous things.

Because he feared hurting me, he now becomes the reason for my grief. A tender downy-bearded boy, he is slain. I, his sister, being absent, did not see his terrible death. Not only did I lose him, but I did not close his dear eyes, nor did I throw myself upon him, nor did I speak words of farewell. . . . Life was denied him—why could not his dying breath as a brother be caught from his lips and be given to his sister? . . . All I was to him was the cause of his death, and I did not provide him a sepulcher!

I who left my homeland once have twice been captured, for when my brother lay cut down, I suffered the enemy again. This sorrow has returned so that I may weep for father and mother, uncle and kindred at their tomb. After my brother's death there is no day free of tears, for he has taken my joy with him to the dwelling of the shades.

Was it for this that my sweet kinsmen—wretched woman that I am—achieved the highest honors, for this their royal blood and birth descended in an unbroken line? . . . fair cousin, I ask that your letter may hasten now, so that your kind utterance may soothe my heavy grief.

Hrotswitha of Gandersheim (ca. 935–1001)

Hrotswitha (also spelled Hrosvitha or Hroswitha) was a noblewoman and canoness at the Benedictine monastery of Gandersheim in Saxony. She is the first woman playwright in Western culture, and the first playwright to appear in the Middle Ages. No other dramas with the same level of sophistication would appear for another two hundred years. Although best known for her six Latin dramas, she also wrote poems, eight legends of saints' lives, and two Latin historical epics, *The Deeds of Otto* and *The Founding of the Monastery of Gandersheim*. She called herself the "strong voice of Gandersheim" (St. John 1966, xxvi). She lived during the reigns of Otto I and Otto II (936–983), an era called the "Ottonian Renaissance," and a time when female monasticism flourished in Saxony. The court of Otto I (crowned Roman Emperor in 936) was a cosmopolitan center of Christianity and culture. After his son Otto II (955–983) married Theophano, daughter of the Byzantine emperor, the court was enriched by Byzantine influences.

Gandersheim was one of the first female monasteries founded in Saxony after its conversion to Christianity. It was founded in 852 by Duke Liudolf, the great-grandfather of Otto I, at the request of his Frankish wife Oda and her mother Aeda. As an imperial monastery, its abbesses were usually women of the royal family. Gandersheim admitted both nuns, who took vows of chastity and obedience, and canonesses who did not take vows. In 947, Emperor Otto I removed Gandersheim from imperial rule and vested the abbess with supreme authority. Thus, during Hrotswitha's lifetime, the monastery was an independent principality ruled by women. The abbess had full power over her lands and her vassals, and had a seat in the Imperial Diet.

Hrotswitha and the others at Gandersheim shared a rich intellectual and religious life similar to that enjoyed by Radegund's circle. The abbey had an excellent library and, as Hrotswitha's writings reveal, its women studied music, classical and Christian writers, Latin and perhaps Greek, and probably astronomy and mathematics. They also interacted with the learned men who gathered at the court.

Hrotswitha's plays were modeled after the comedies by the Roman playwright Terence, however she retold the stories from both a gynocentric and a Christian perspective. Angry at his negative stereotypes of women as weak, licentious, and shrewish, and his negative portrayals of Christians, she reversed his characterizations of men and women, pagans and Christians. Her plays and legends address similar themes: chastity, rape and illicit sexuality, redemption and salvation through faith, and the power of martyrdom. Her plays included stage directions and were probably performed at the convent for the emperor and empress. The plays were rediscovered in the late nineteenth century and translated into English (ca. 1912) by a woman, Christopher St. John.

The *Dulcitius* is based on a famous story from the *Acts of the Christian Martyrs* in the fourth century at the height of Rome's persecutions of Christians. Three young virgins from a prominent Roman family that has converted to Christianity are brought before the emperor. Exercising his power over his subjects, Diocletian proposes to "save" the girls by marrying them off. As you read the excerpts, compare Hrotswitha's portrayal of the male and female characters and note which of her themes appear in this play.

DULCITIUS OR THE MARTYRDOM OF THE HOLY VIRGINS AGAPE, CHIONE, AND IRENA*

[*Main characters:* Emperor Diocletian, Agape, Chiona, Irena, Dulcitius, Count Sisinnius]

SCENE I: [Emperor is seated on his throne; the girls, dressed in white, stand before him]

Diocletian: The pure and famous race to which you belong and your own rare beauty make it fitting that you should be wedded to the highest in our court. Thus we decree, making the condition that you first promise to deny your Christ and sacrifice to the gods.

---

*Excerpts from *Dulcitius*, in *The Plays of Roswitha*, Christopher St. John, Medieval Library Series, Sir Israel Gollancz, gen. ed. (London: Chatto & Windus, 1923), pp. 35–47.

Agape: We beg you not to concern yourself about us, and it is useless to make preparations for our marriage. Nothing can make us deny that Name which all should confess, or let our purity be stained.

Diocletian: What does this madness mean? . . .

Agape: In what way are we mad?

Diocletian: Is it not madness to give up practising an ancient religion and run after this silly new Christian superstition?

Agape: You are bold to slander the majesty of Almighty God. It is dangerous.

Diocletian: Dangerous? To whom?

Agape: To you, and to the state you rule.

Diocletian: The girl raves. Take her away. [guards remove her from the room]

Chionia: My sister does not rave. She is right.

Diocletian: This [one] seems even more violent than the other! Remove her also from our presence, and we will question the third. [guards return with Irena]

Irena: You will find her as rebellious and as determined to resist.

Diocletian: Irena, you are the youngest in years. Show yourself the oldest in dignity.

Irena: Pray tell me how.

Diocletian: Bow your head to the gods, and set an example to your sisters. It may rebuke and save them.

Irena: Let those who wish to provoke the wrath of the Most High prostrate themselves before idols! I will not dishonour this head which has been anointed with heavenly oil by abasing it at the feet of images. . . .

Diocletian: Enough of this presumptuous chatter. The rack shall put an end to it!

Irena: That is what we desire. We ask nothing better than to suffer the most cruel tortures for the love of Christ.

Diocletian: Let these obstinate women who dare to defy our authority be laden with chains and thrown into a dungeon. Let them be examined by Governor Dulcitius.

SCENE II: [soldiers stand outside the "prison," Dulcitius peers in the window] . . .

Dulcitius: Ye Gods, but these girls are beautiful! What grace, what charm! . . . I am enraptured! . . . Do you think they will fall in love with me?

Soldiers: From what we know, you will have little success. . . .

Dulcitius: A few sweet words will work wonders!

Soldiers: They despise flattery.

Dulcitius: Then I shall woo in another fashion with torture!

Soldiers: They would not care. . . .

Dulcitius: Lock them in the inner room—the one leading out of the passage where the pots and pans are kept.

Soldiers: Why there?

Dulcitius: I can visit them oftener. [he leaves] . . .

SCENE III: [A well-dressed Dulcitius returns and addresses the guards] . . .

Dulcitius: Take your torches, and guard the doors. I will go in and enjoy myself in those lovely arms! . . .

SCENE IV: [The room where the girls are held. Irena sees Dulcitius enter the kitchen]

Agape: What noise is that outside the door?

Irena: It is that wretch Dulcitius.

Chionia: Now may God protect us! . . . There is more noise! It sounds like the clashing of pots and pans and fire-irons.

Irena: I will go and look. Come quick and peep through the crack of the door. . . . Oh, look! He must be out of his senses I believe he thinks that he is kissing us. . . . Now he presses the saucepans tenderly to his breast, now the kettles and frying-pans! He is kissing them hard! . . . His face, his hands, his clothes! They are all as black as soot. He looks like an Ethiope.

Agape: I am glad. His body should turn black to match his soul, which is possessed of a devil.

Irena: Look! He is going now. Let us watch the soldiers and see what they do when he goes out.

SCENE V: [Soldiers are playing cards. Dulcitius rushes out.]

Soldiers: What's this? Either one possessed by the devil, or the devil himself. Let's be off!

Dulcitius: Soldiers, soldiers! Why do you hurry away? Stay, wait! Light me to my house with your torches.

Soldiers: The voice is our master's voice, but the face is a devil's. Come, let's take to our heels! This devil means us no good. [they exit.]

Dulcitius: I will hasten to the palace. I will tell the whole court how I have been insulted.

SCENE VI: [Two men guard the entrance to the emperor's quarters]

Dulcitius: Ushers, admit me at once. I have important business with the Emperor.

Ushers: Who is this fearsome, horrid monster? Coming here in these filthy rags! Come, let us beat him and throw him down the steps. Stop him from coming further.

Dulcitius: Ye gods, what has happened to me? Am I not dressed in my best? Am I not clean and fine in my person? And yet everyone who meets me expresses disgust at the sight of me and treats me as if I were some foul monster! I will go to my wife. She will tell me the truth. But here she comes. Her looks are wild, her hair unbound, and all her household follow her weeping.

SCENE VII:

Wife: My lord, my lord, what evil has come on you? Have you lost your reason, Dulcitius? Have the Christ-worshippers put a spell on you?

Dulcitius: Now at last I know! Those artful women have made an ass of me! . . . Those impudent wenches shall be stripped and exposed naked in public. They shall have a taste of the outrage to which I have been subjected.

SCENE VIII: [a public square; guards are struggling to rip the clothes off the three girls]

Soldiers: Here we are sweating like pigs and what's the use? Their clothes cling to their bodies like their own skin. . . . We will go to the Emperor and tell him all that has passed.

SCENE IX: [Imperial Palace Court, as in Scene I]

Diocletian: I grieve to hear of the outrageous way in which the Governor Dulcitius has been insulted and hoaxed! But these girls shall not boast of having blasphemed our gods with impunity, or of having made a mock of those who worship them. I will entrust the execution of my vengeance to Count Sisinnius.

SCENE X: [a public room with guards; Count Sisinnius enters]

Sisinnius: Soldiers, where are these impudent hussies who are to be put to the torture?

SCENE XI: [Guards return with the two older girls] . . .

Sisinnius: Agape, and you, Chionia, take my advice.

Agape: And if we do, what then?

Sisinnius: You will sacrifice to the gods.

Agape: We offer a perpetual sacrifice of praise to the true God, the eternal Father, to His Son, co-eternal, and to the Holy Ghost.

Sisinnius: I do not speak of that sacrifice. That is prohibited on pain of the most severe penalties.

Agape: You have no power over us, and can never compel us to sacrifice to demons.

Sisinnius: Do not be obstinate. Sacrifice to the gods, or by order of the Emperor Diocletian I must put you to death.

Chionia: Your Emperor has ordered you to put us to death, and you must obey, as we scorn his decree. If you were to spare us out of pity, you also would die.

Sisinnius: Come, soldiers! Seize these blasphemers and fling them alive into the flames.

Soldiers: We will build a pyre at once. The fierceness of the fire will soon put an end to their insolence. [They tie the girls to a stake; girls begin to pray]

Agape: O Lord, we know Thy power! It would not be anything strange or new if the fire forgot its nature and obeyed Thee. But we are weary of this world, and we implore Thee to break the bonds that chain our souls, and to let our bodies be consumed that we may rejoice with Thee in heaven. [They die in the flames.]

Soldiers: O wonderful, most wonderful! Their spirits have left their bodies, but there is no sign of any hurt. Neither their hair, nor their garments, much less their bodies, have been touched by the flames! [They fall to their knees.] . . .

SCENE XII: [Sisinnius is in his official seat; two guards bring Irena in]

Sisinnius: Irena, take warning from the fate of your sisters, and tremble, for if you follow their example you will perish.

Irena: I long to follow their example, and to die, that I may share their eternal joy.

Sisinnius: Yield, yield!

Irena: I will yield to no man who persuades me to sin.

Sisinnius: If you persist in your refusal, I shall not grant you a swift death. . . . every day I shall increase and renew your torments.

Irena: The greater my pain, the greater my glory!

Sisinnius: You are not afraid of being tortured, I know, but I can use another means that will be abhorrent to you.

Irena: By Christ's help I shall escape from all you can devise against me.

Sisinnius: I can send you to a house of ill-fame, where your body will be abominably defiled.

Irena: Better far that my body should suffer outrage than my soul.

Sisinnius: When you are dishonoured and forced to live among harlots, you can no longer be numbered among the virgins.

Irena: The wage of sin is death; the wage of suffering a crown. If the soul does not consent, there is no guilt.

Sisinnius: In vain I try to spare her, and show pity to her youth! . . . I will show her no more mercy. . . . [Guards,] . . . drag her to the lowest brothel you can find.

Irena: They will never take me there.

Sisinnius: Indeed! What can prevent them?

Irena: The power that rules the world.

Sisinnius: We shall see. . . . [Soldiers take her away.]

SCENE XIII: [Sisinnius' official room, several hours later]

Sisinnius: Who are these men hurrying towards us? They cannot be the soldiers who took away Irena. Yet they resemble them. Yes, these are the men! Why have you returned so suddenly? Why are you panting for breath?

Soldiers: We ran back to find you.

Sisinnius: Where is the girl?

Soldiers: On the crest of the mountain.

Sisinnius: What mountain?

Soldiers: The mountain yonder, nearest this place.

Sisinnius: O fools, madmen! Have you lost your senses? . . . Fools! Did I not tell you to take this rebellious girl to a brothel?

Soldiers: That is so, but while we were on the way up came two young strangers and told us you had sent them to take Irena to the summit of the mountain. . . .

Sisinnius: What were these strangers like?

Soldiers: They were gorgeously dressed and looked like people of rank. . . .

Sisinnius: What did they do?

Soldiers: They placed themselves one on each side of Irena, and told us to hasten and tell you what we had seen.

Sisinnius: Then there is nothing to do but for me to mount my horse and ride to the mountain to discover who has dared to play us this trick. . . .

SCENE XIV: [Sisinnius and soldiers are at the foot of the mountain; Irena stands on a ledge above.]

Sisinnius: What has happened to me? These Christians have bewitched me. I wander blindly round this hill, and when I stumble on a path I can neither follow it nor return upon my steps.

Soldiers: We are all the sport of some strange enchantment. We are exhausted. If you let this madwoman live an hour longer it will be the death of us all.

Sisinnius: Take a bow one of you, bend it as far as you can, and loose a shaft that shall pierce this devilish witch. . . .

Irena: You wretched Sisinnius! Do you not blush for your shameful defeat? Are you not ashamed that you could not overcome the resolution of a little child without resorting to force of arms?

Sisinnius: I accept the shame gladly, since now I am sure of your death.

Irena: To me my death means joy, but to you calamity. For your cruelty you will be damned in Tartarus. But I shall receive the martyr's palm, and, adorned with the crown of virginity, I shall enter the azure palace of the Eternal King, to Whom be glory and honour for ever and ever! [She raises her arms and dies as the arrows strike.]

Hildegard of Bingen (1098–1179)

Hildegard of Bingen is perhaps the most remarkable woman of the Middle Ages—a true "Renaissance woman." She was influential and widely known in her extended lifetime and for several centuries after her death. Hildegard was a powerful abbess who preached across Germany and served as a political and theological advisor to some of the most powerful men of her day. She was a mystic, philosopher, composer, and poet. She wrote three books of visions, theological treatises, two saints' biographies, two books on a secret language she developed, the texts and music for 77 sacred songs, a morality play, and a *kyrie* for mass. She was also a scientist and healer and author of books on natural history and medicine.

When she was eight, Hildegard was placed in a Benedictine convent at Disibodenberg, under the tutelage of her aunt, Abbess Jutta. The convent, a double monastery, was one of a number of strong female monasteries flourishing in Germany at the time. Jutta nourished Hildegard's talents with a regimen of study that included Latin, German, theology, philosophy, and music. In 1136, she succeeded Jutta as abbess.

At age 15, Hildegard began to have the intense religious experiences or visions that would occur throughout her life. Fearing they were signs of God's displeasure, she kept them secret for years. In 1140, however, she had a vision in which a voice from Heaven explained why she had been tested with her revelations, and commanded: "Speak therefore of these wonders, and, being so taught, write them and speak" (Hildegard 1990, 59). Assured of their validity, she began to dictate her visions to a monk, Volmar, her friend and secretary. He convinced her to submit her work to their abbot, and from him the manuscript made its way to Pope Eugenius, who, at the Council at Trier, ruled that her visions were authentic prophesies from God. Fortified with papal approval, her creative energies were unleashed. In 1150, she moved her monastery to Mount St. Rupert near the town of Bingen. In 1157, she completed her first book of visions, which became a "best seller." Her visions were the basis of her subsequent religious and political authority. Hildegard was able to maximize her independence and power by capitalizing on divisions within the Church and the Holy Roman Empire, and the struggle between the pope and emperor for control over the bishops and their lands. Still, she always had to function within the confines of a patriarchal church and culture that remained resistant to powerful, independent women.

As Hildegard's fame spread, people all over Germany and Europe wrote to her, seeking advice on everything from politics, military rivalries, church reform, and theological points to health and fertility. Her correspondents included Henry II of England, Eleanor of Aquitaine, and Byzantine Empress Irene; four popes; Holy Roman Emperors Konrad III and Frederick Barbarossa; three archbishops; abbots, abbesses, nuns, and lay persons. The letter that follows is typical in its tone and language of some she wrote to powerful men, including Emperor Barbarossa.[*]

HILDEGARD TO POPE ANASTASIUS, 1153–54

O you who are the estimable defense and the bulwark of a beautifully adorned city, which has been established as the bride of Christ, hear Him who is eternal and does not grow weary.

You, O man, who are too tired, in the eye of your knowledge, to rein in the pomposity of arrogance among those placed in your bosom, why do you not call back the shipwrecked who cannot rise from the depths without help? And why do you not cut off the root of evil which is choking out the good and beneficial plants of sweet taste and delightful aroma? You are neglecting the King's daughter who was entrusted to you, that is, heavenly Justice herself. You are allowing this King's daughter to be thrown to the ground: her beautiful crown and tunic torn asunder by the crudeness of those hostile people who bark like dogs and who, like chickens trying to sing at night, raise up their ineffectual voices. They are charlatans, crying out, ostensibly, for peace, but, all the while, biting each other in their hearts, like a dog that wags its tail among those known to him, but bites the honorable knight indispensable to the king's household. . . .

Wherefore, O man, you who sit on the papal throne, you despise God when you embrace evil. For in failing to speak out against the evil of those in your company, you are certainly not rejecting evil. Rather, you are kissing it. And so the whole world is being led astray through unstable error, simply because people love that which God has cast down.

And you, O Rome, when you are lying at the point of death, you will be so shaken that the strength of your feet, upon which you have stood so far, will no longer sustain you. For you do not love the King's daughter, that is, Justice, with a blazing passion, but with a dull sloth, so that, in fact, you banish her from your presence. Indeed, she is ready to flee from you, if you do not call her back. . . . Beware, therefore, of becoming entangled in pagan rites, lest you fall. Now, hear Him who lives and will never die. The world is now lascivious, and will later become sad. Then will come such great terror that people will not care whether they are killed or not. . . .

Therefore, you, O man, stand on the strait path, and God will save you and bring you back into the abode of blessing and election, and you will live forever.

Hildegard is the first woman scientist whose complete works have survived to the present day. She has been called one of the most original medical writers of the twelfth century and "the most distinguished naturalist" in Western Europe in the twelfth century (Alic 1986, 74, 198 n. 14). Her scientific writings were among the first that showed familiarity with the scientific knowledge that Arabs were bringing to Europe. Between 1150 and 1160, she wrote a natural history encyclopedia, *Physica,* in which she described 230 plants (and their medical application), 60 trees, and the fish, birds, reptiles, mammals, and metals of Germany. Her last major work, *Causea et Curae,* is a blend of medical and biological theory and remedies. She stressed hygiene, diet, and exercise; and was the first writer to note the importance of boiling drinking water (Alic 1986, 66, 73–74). In her version of the medieval cosmology of the macrocosm (universe) and microcosm (man or particular earthly things), she also taught that the four elements or humours of the universe affected corresponding humours in the body (microcosm), determining such things as physical ailments, conception, and character traits.

Excerpts from *Causae et curae*[*]

[*On Reproduction*]

When the man approaches the woman, releasing powerful semen and in a true cherishing love for the woman, and she too has a true love for the man in that same hour, then a male child is conceived, for so it was ordained by God. Nor can it be otherwise, because Adam was formed of clay, which is a stronger material than flesh. And this male child will be prudent and virtuous.

But if the woman's love is lacking in that hour . . . and if the man's semen is strong, a male child will still be born, because the man's cherishing love predominates. But that male child will be feeble and not virtuous. . . If the man's semen is thin, and yet he cherishes the woman lovingly and she him, then a virtuous female child is procreated. . . .

If the man's semen is powerful but neither the man nor the woman cherish each other lovingly, a male child is procreated . . . but he will be bitter with his parents' bitterness; and if the man's semen is thin and there is no cherishing love on either side in that hour, a girl of bitter temperament is born.

As late as 1987, Hildegard's musical achievements were not mentioned in the standard writings on medieval music, yet she is the first woman composer with a substantial body of work for whom we have both music and text. Her morality play *Ordo virtutum* is the first full drama by a woman to appear since Hrotswitha's plays 200 years earlier, and it predates other liturgical morality plays by two centuries (Yardley 1987, 28, 36 n. 54). It is also the first drama set to music. She was, according to Barbara Newman, the "first Christian thinker to deal seriously and positively with the feminine." Through her reflections on Eve, Mary, Ecclesia, and a visionary form "she called Sapientia or caritas: holy Wisdom and Love divine," Hildegard "developed a theology of the feminine" (Newman 1987, xvii–xviii). Fifteen of her 77 songs are about the Virgin Mary, 13 are about virgins in the Church, and others celebrate Wisdom (Sophia) and Ecclesia. The imagery in the songs and the vision that follow reveal much about her theology. Compare her image of Wisdom with early Judaism's Sophia (see Chapter 5, "Ancient Israel").

*Excerpts from Peter Dronke, *Women Writers of the Middle Ages: A Critical Study of Texts from Perpetua (203) to Marguerite Porete (1310)* (Cambridge: Cambridge University Press, 1984), pp. 175, 177. Copyright © 1984 by Cambridge University Press. Reprinted with the permission of Cambridge University Press.

SONGS FROM *SYMPHONY OF THE HARMONY OF CELESTIAL REVELATIONS**

19. SONG TO THE VIRGIN

Never was leaf so green,
  for you branched from the spirited
  blast of the quest
  of the saints.
When it came time
  for your boughs to blossom
  (I salute you!)
  your scent was like balsam
  distilled in the sun.
And your flower made all spices
  fragrant
  dry though they were:
  they burst into verdure.
So the skies rained dew on the grass
  and the whole earth exulted,
  for her womb brought forth wheat,
  for the birds of heaven
  made their nests in it.
Keepers of the feast, rejoice!

The banquet's ready. And you
  sweet maid-child
  are a fount of gladness.
But Eve?
  She despised every joy.
  Praise nonetheless,
  praise to the Highest.

24. ANTIPHON FOR THE HOLY SPIRIT

The Spirit of God
  is a life that bestows life,
  root of the world-tree
  and wind in its boughs.
Scrubbing out sins,
  she rubs oil into wounds.
She is glistening life
  alluring all praise,
  all-awakening,
  all-resurrecting.

VISION NINE: 15 WISDOM AND HER APPEARANCE FROM SCIVIAS**

And on top of this dome you see a very beautiful figure standing. This is to say that this virtue was in the Most High Father before all creatures, giving counsel in the formation of all the creatures made in heaven and earth; so that she is the great ornament of God and the broad stairway of all the other virtues that live in Him, joined to Him in sweet embrace in a dance of ardent love. And *she is looking out at the people in the world;* for she protects and guides the people who want to follow her, and keeps with great love those who are true to her. And this figure represents the Wisdom of God, for through her all things are created and ruled by God. . . .

MANUSCRIPT ILLUMINATIONS

As we have seen, the daily work of monastic men and women included the important task of copying classical and sacred writings. Because all work was supposed to be for the glory of God, manuscripts grew increasingly elaborate and the work became specialized. Some only copied texts but excelled in

*Reprinted from Hildegard of Bingen, Barbara Newman (ed. and trans.). *Symphonia. A Critical Edition of the Symphonia armonie celestium revelationum,* pp. 127, 141. Copyright © 1989 by Cornell University. Used by permission of the publisher, Cornell University Press.

**Excerpts from *Scivias* by St. Hildegard of Bingen. Columba Hart and Jane Bishop, trans., (New York: Paulist Press, 1990), Book Three, p. 465. Copyright © 1990, Paulist Press. Used with permission of Paulist Press. *www.paulistpress.com*

calligraphy. *Rubricators* specialized in elaborate lettering and created the first letter of a paragraph or section. Others, trained as *illuminators* or painters, created borders and illustrations for the text. Most manuscripts were copied and decorated anonymously in keeping with the humility expected of religious women and men, so we know the names of few artists. The first woman artist we can identify for certain is En or Ende who did nearly all the illuminations in a Spanish manuscript, known as the *Beatus Apocalypse,* 975. She identified herself as *En depintrix* (paintress) and *Dei aiutrix* (servant of God) at the end of the manuscript (Miner 1974, 9).

Other known women illuminators were products of the cultural renaissance of the Ottonian empire and the wealthy female monastic communities that flourished through the mid-thirteenth century. The works of women illuminators include an astronomical treatise, psalters, saints' lives, and cosmological treatises. *Hortus Deliciarium,* an encyclopedia of knowledge compiled by Herrad of Landsberg (1130–1195), had about 630 superb miniature illustrations. Herrad, abbess of Hohenburg, a prosperous convent near Strasbourg, worked closely with the nuns who did the artwork. Known illuminators include a Bavarian nun Diemud, who illustrated 45 known books, and Claricia, whose dress suggests she was a lay student in her Augsburg convent (Chadwick 1990, 44–48). Claricia's self-portrait (Fig. 14–1) shows she had a sense of humor.

One of the most remarkable illuminated works by religious women was Hildegard's *Scivias* (*Know Thou the Ways of God*), a compilation of her visions, each of which is described in vivid detail with an accompanying illumination. Hildegard is often shown in the bottom corner of the illustration writing down the vision that is reproduced exactly as she received it. Some illuminations show her receiving

Figure 14–1   From a Psalter, Claricia swinging on the Tail of Q. *Detail from a* Psalter. *W.26, folio 64. German, 1200. The Walters Art Museum, Baltimore*

the vision in the form of fire entering her head from above. Circles, egg-shaped forms, and elements of nature are common in her visions. *Man at the Center of the Universe* (Fig. 14–2) depicts her belief in the human as microcosm of the macrocosm.

VARIETIES OF FEMALE PIETY

Between the twelfth and fourteenth centuries Europe was engulfed in tremendous religious ferment as men and women sought new ways to express their faith. One of the most popular manifestations of religious fervor in these centuries was *mysticism*. Mystics (male and female) had intense inner experiences in which knowledge came in a sudden revelation, followed by an overwhelming sense of union with the Divine. One prepared for a mystical experience by purging the body, meditation and prayer, and emptying the mind of all thoughts. Because the ascetic and meditative practices that opened one to a mystical experience could be taught, we find clusters of female mystics in certain regions, monasteries, and communities that valued this inner life.

Mysticism had special appeal for women. It was a personal, individual experience, totally independent of male-defined rituals, rules, and teachings. Equally important, it was a way uneducated women and secular or laywomen, as well as nuns, could express their piety. Barred from the religious roles men enjoyed, women welcomed this alternative way to express their faith. Their revelations enabled some to assume male roles as mediators, preachers, and leaders.

Figure 14–2   Man at the center of the Universe.
Codex latinum 1942 by St. Hildegard, fol. 9r. Copyright Scala/Art Resource, NY. Biblioteca Statale, Lucca, Italy

Concurrently, hundreds of thousands of women in France, the Rhineland, the Low Countries, and Switzerland joined the *beguines,* an independent women's religious movement that flourished in urban areas, particularly in towns where women outnumbered men. Beguines were laywomen who took no formal religious vows, but committed themselves to lives of chastity, poverty, prayer, and charitable works. Most lived in groups, worshiped communally, and met regularly to assess their spiritual growth. Beguines were generally of "middle-class" origins, worked in a variety of female occupations to support themselves and their charitable causes, and congregated in cheap housing in artisan districts.

As their numbers grew, beguines became a matter of concern to both religious and secular authorities because they were independent of male authority. By the fourteenth century, regulations imposed by cities and guilds began to undermine their ability to make a living. Then, in 1312, the Council of Vienne condemned beguines as suspected heretics and the Church brought them under the control of Franciscan or Dominican monasteries, thus destroying the movement's vitality. Some communities, however, continued to exist into the twentieth century.

In the readings that follow, note how each woman experienced the Divine, the context in which each lived her life, and how each was received by her contemporaries.

Mechthild of Magdeburg (ca. 1210–ca. 1282): Mystic and Beguine

Mechthild began having visions when she was 12. At 23, she left her family to take up a religious life as a beguine in Magdeburg. There she wrote six books of her prayers, meditations, and visions. In 1268, after her visions and criticisms of local clergy prompted accusations of heresy, she fled Magdeburg. She lived the rest of her life in the safety of the Abbey at Helfta, a center of female mysticism. There she completed her seventh book. Her books were published as *Das Fliessende Lict der Gottheit (The Flowing Light of the Godhead).* She also composed sacred music (Yardley 1987, 25). Her imagery of divine love and marriage is typical of thirteenth-century German and Dutch female mysticism.

THE FLOWING LIGHT OF THE GODHEAD*

BOOK III: 5. HOW THE SOUL COMPLAINS THAT SHE HEARS NO MASS NOR HOURS AND HOW GOD PRAISES HER IN TEN THINGS

Thus did a forsaken soul complain when God excluded her from his ecstatic love and loved her by means of great suffering: "Alas, how sulkingly does a rich man bear it when after glorious wealth he is led into great poverty!"
And she says: "Oh, Lord, now I am extremely destitute in my sickly body and am so miserable in my soul which is so lacking in spiritual order that no one recites the hours of the office in my presence and no one celebrates holy mass for me!"
The loving Mouth spoke, the Mouth that wounded my soul so terribly with his sublime words that I never received worthily:
"You are the feelings of love in my desire.
You are a sweet cooling for my breast.

*Excerpts from *Mechthild of Magdeburg. The Flowing Light of the Godhead,* by Frank Tobin, trans., Copyright © 1988 by Frank Tobin (Mahwah, NJ: Paulist Press, 1998), p. 111. Used with permission of Paulist Press. www.paulistpress.com

You are a passionate kiss for my mouth.
You are a blissful joy of my discovery.
I am in you And you are in me.
We could not be closer,

For we two have flowed into one
And have been poured into one mold.
Thus shall we remain forever content."

Marguerite Porete (12??–1310): Mystic and Beguine

The French mystic and beguine Marguerite Porete described her revelations about seven states of grace in a book, *Le Miroir des simples ames (Mirror of Simple Souls)*, written between 1296 and 1306. She preached that in the seventh stage, the soul arrived at a state of perfect grace in which it was totally free. A church court condemned and burned her book in 1306 and prohibited her from spreading her ideas. In 1308 she was brought before the Inquisition because she had defied the court and continued to circulate copies. She was imprisoned for a year and a half, then tried and burned at the stake in Paris.

MIRROR OF SIMPLE SOULS[*]

How this Soul is free, and more free still, and very free. Chapter 85.
  Love. This Soul, says Love, is free, and yet more free, and yet very free, and yet supremely free, in root and stems and every branch, and in every fruit of her branches.
  This Soul has her portion of perfect freedom, and her every side has its full measure. She replies to no-one, if she does not wish, if he is not of her kin, for a man of noble birth would not deign to reply to a churl if he challenged him or sought him out on the battlefield; and therefore no-one who challenges such a Soul finds her. No more do her enemies have reply from her.
  The Soul. That is right and proper, says this Soul; since I believe that God is in me, he must be mindful of me, and his goodness cannot have me lost.
  Love. This Soul, says Love, is flayed by mortification, and burned by the ardor of the fire of charity, and her ashes are strewn by the nothingness of her will upon the high seas. In prosperity she has the nobility of the wellborn, in adversity the nobility of one exalted, in all places, whatever they be, the nobility of the excellent. She who is such no longer seeks God through penance or through any sacrament of Holy Church, not through reflections or words or works, not through any creature here below or through any creature there above, not through justice or mercy or the glory of glories, not through divine knowledge or divine love or divine praise. . . .

Julian of Norwich (b. 1343?): Mystic and Anchorite

One option popular among mystics was to retreat from the world and become a hermit. Julian adopted a variant on that lifestyle and became an anchorite hermit. She lived in three walled-off rooms that were "anchored" to the church at Norwich, England. She had a window that opened into the church, permitting her to receive the sacraments, and a window to the outside that enabled her to speak with people who flocked to her for spiritual advice. She received the first of her six mystical vi-

*From Margaret Porette, *The Mirror of Simple Souls,* trans. Edmund Colledge, J.C. Marler, and Judith Grant (Notre Dame, IN: University of Notre Dame Press, 1999), pp. 109–10. By Permission of University of Notre Dame Press.

sions during a life-threatening illness when she was 31. She later wrote an account of these "showings" entitled *Revelations of Divine Love.* Her theology of God is a significant reconceptualization of the Divine that earned her respect as a theologian.

THE REVELATIONS OF DIVINE LOVE[*]

But Jesus is our true Mother . . .

The mother's service is nearest, readiest and surest; nearest, for it is most like us; readiest, for it is most of love; surest, for it is most of truth. This office no one might nor could ever do to the full, except he alone. We know that all our mothers bear us to pain and to dying; a strange thing, that! But our true Mother Jesus, he alone bears us to joy and to endless living; blessed may he be! Thus he sustains us within him, in love and in travail unto the full time in which he willed to suffer the sharpest throes and most grievous pains that ever were, or ever shall be; and he died at the last. Yet all this might not fully satisfy his marvellous love. And that he showed in these high overpassing words of love: "If I could suffer more, I would suffer more." . . .

Wherefore it behoveth him to feed us; for the very dear love of motherhood hath made him our debtor. The mother can give her child to suck of her milk. But our precious Mother Jesus, he can feed us with himself; and does, full courteously and tenderly, with the Blessed Sacrament, that is the precious food of true life. . . .

The mother can lay her child tenderly to her breast. But our tender Mother Jesus can lead us . . . into his blessed breast, by his sweet open side; and show us there, in part, the Godhead and the joys of heaven, with a ghostly sureness of endless bliss.

This fair lovely word *Mother,* it is so sweet and so kind in itself, that it cannot truly be said to any nor of any, but to him and of him who is very Mother of life and of all. To the property of Motherhood belongs kind love, wisdom and knowing; and it is God. . . .

. . . And though possibly an earthly mother may suffer her child to perish, our heavenly Mother Jesus can never allow us who are his children to perish. For he is almighty, all-wisdom and all-love: and so is none but he. Blessed may he be!

MEDIEVAL IMAGES OF WOMEN: THE EVA/AVE DUALISM

Throughout the Middle Ages, as in centuries past, two very contradictory images of women coexisted. Women, on the one hand, were seen as the "daughters of Eve," the natural inheritors of her traits. Yet, while Eve was responsible for introducing sin and evil into the Garden of Eden, the Virgin Mary, Christians believed, had redeemed mankind. This EVA/AVE paradigm (Ave meant Hail) in essence represented the two faces of woman: one who by nature was like Eve, but who, if she emulated Mary, could be a blessing to mankind.

*From James Walsh, trans., *Julian of Norwich, The Revelations of Divine Love,* (St. Meinrad, IN: Abbey Press, 1974), pp. 163–164, 166–167. By Permission of Paulist Press.

The medieval Church and clergy were instrumental in fostering Eva imagery. Clerical misogyny, as we have seen, was rooted in biblical sources and teachings of the patristics (Church fathers). It was reinforced by the early Church's belief that virginity and celibacy constituted the highest form of human existence, and the accompanying belief that women's sexuality was a temptation that threatened man's attainment of that ideal. It was also reinforced by the philosophical theories of the ancient world that were rediscovered by Europeans in the twelfth century. The next section introduces one influential example of Eva imagery.

Malleus Maleficarum or *The Hammer of Witches,* 1486: Eva Imagery

The *Malleus Maleficarum* or *The Hammer of Witches* was published at the peak of the witch hysteria that emerged in the twelfth century. It was a collection of fifty years of scholarly thought about witchcraft, but it was the first treatise on witchcraft to reach a wide audience. Papal approval assured its impact. Its authors were two well-educated Dominican monks, Heinrich Kramer and Jacob Sprenger, who had worked as inquisitors prosecuting witches in Germany. *Malleus* provided a theological rationale for the prosecution of witches, told how to identify and prosecute witches, and suggested that those denying the existence of witches were heretics. It reflects many of the ideas about women that were pervasive in medieval Europe, and the increasing misogyny of the late Middle Ages. Witch hunts flourished until 1700 and resulted in courts sentencing tens of thousands to death. The majority of victims were older single women.

WHY SUPERSTITION IS CHIEFLY FOUND IN WOMEN
FROM MALLEUS MALEFICARUM*

> . . . Now the wickedness of women is spoken of in *Ecclesiasticus xxv:* There is no head above the head of a serpent: and there is no wrath above the wrath of a woman. . . . And among much which in that place precedes and follows about a wicked woman, he concludes: All wickedness is but little to the wickedness of a woman. . . .
>
> Others again have propounded other reasons why there are more superstitious women found than men. And the first is, that they are more credulous; and since the chief aim of the devil is to corrupt faith, therefore he rather attacks them. . . . The second reason is, that women are naturally more impressionable, and more ready to receive the influence of a disembodied spirit. . . .
>
> The third reason is that they have slippery tongues, and are unable to conceal from their fellow-women those things which by evil arts they know; and, since they are weak, they find an easy and secret manner of vindicating themselves by witchcraft. . . .
>
> . . . since they are feebler both in mind and body, it is not surprising that they should come more under the spell of witchcraft.

*Excerpts from *The Malleus Maleficarum of Heinrich Kramer & Jacob Sprenger.* Edited by Montague Summers. (London: John Rodker, 1928). Reprint edition of original reprinted by New York: Dover Publications, Ind., 1971 (Salem, New Hampshire: Ayer Company Publishers, Inc., 1988), pp. 43–45, 47.

For as regards intellect, or the understanding of spiritual things, they seem to be of a different nature from men. . . .

But the natural reason is that she is more carnal than a man, as is clear from her many carnal abominations. And it should be noted that there was a defect in the formation of the first woman, since she was formed from a bent rib. . . . And since through this defect she is an imperfect animal, she always deceives. . . .

Women also have weak memories; and it is a natural vice in them not to be disciplined, but to follow their own impulses without any sense of what is due. . . .

To conclude. All witchcraft comes from carnal lust, which is in women insatiable. . . . Wherefore for the sake of fulfilling their lusts they consort even with devils. . . .

Ave Imagery: Mariology or the Cult of the Blessed Virgin Mary

Ironically, misogyny peaked at the very time that worship of the Virgin Mary was at its zenith. During the Middle Ages, Mary assumed an increasingly important place in the Christian faith. By the twelfth to thirteenth centuries she was worshiped as a semi-divine figure with special powers. Prayers, legends, and hymns such as Hildegard's "Song to the Virgin" glorified her and cathedrals, such as Notre Dame (Our Lady) in Paris, were built in her honor. Statues, stained glass windows, and paintings depicting her graced churches, cathedrals, and monasteries.

The Church opened the door for the worship of Mary in 431 C.E. when the Third Ecumenical Council, meeting in Ephesus, officially declared Mary the Mother of God. By the sixth century, the Church had five feast days honoring special days in Mary's life. Pope Urban II officially sanctioned the Cult of the Virgin when he launched the First Crusade under her protection. The veneration of Mary was closely linked to pre-Christian religious traditions. Often Mary's feast days fell on days previously devoted to a goddess, and May became the month of Mary, thus co-opting pagan May Day celebrations. Shrines and churches dedicated to her were located on sites of earlier goddess worship.

Mary worship also evolved independently of the Church as people, particularly women, identified in her the characteristics they or perhaps their ancestors had worshiped in a goddess. Women worshiped her as the giver of life and protectress of women in childbirth. Many turned to her because she seemed more accessible than the clergy. In the thirteenth century, concerned about her growing popularity, the pope ruled that while Mary deserved veneration as the Mother of Christ, Christ had given the keys to His kingdom only to his apostles. In short, her status did not confer power in the Church on women.

The Blessed Virgin Mary was venerated by her followers and, within limits, by the Church as the Second Eve, Queen of Heaven, Seat of Wisdom, the Mother of Christ, and Intercessor. The images that follow are representative of some of the countless images of the Virgin Mary enthroned. Many depict her being crowned by Christ. Some portray her as his bride, others as his partner in ruling the divine kingdom. Many, however, show Mary seated alone on a throne or with Jesus on her lap. These are reminiscent of earlier depictions of various goddesses who ruled heaven and embodied wisdom. The tapestry scene *Queen of Heaven/Wisdom* (Fig. 14–3) is noteworthy because it includes the lions that were central to the iconography of the Neolithic goddess, Cybele, who was still worshiped in the Hellenistic era. The tapestry scene and statues such as *Madonna and Child Enthroned* (Fig. 14–4) also honor her as the mother and seat of wisdom, if not wisdom herself.

Figure 14–3   Queen of Heaven/Wisdom from a fourteenth-century tapestry. *14th Century Tapestry, Inventory #26 Altar Frontal of Königsfelden. Bernisches Historisches Museum. Bern, Switzerland*

Figure 14–4   Madonna and Child Enthroned.
Unknown, French, Auvergne, Twelfth Century. North Carolina Museum of Art, Raleigh, Purchased with funds from the State of North Carolina

SUGGESTED READINGS

Beer, Frances. *Women and Mystical Experience in the Middle Ages.* Woodbridge, Suffolk, UK: Rochester, NY: Boydell Press, 1992.

Gold, Penny Schine. *The Lady and the Virgin: Image, Attitude, and Experience in Twelfth-Century France.* Chicago: University of Chicago Press, 1985.

Hamburger, Jeffrey F. *Nuns as Artists: The Visual Culture of a Medieval Convent.* Berkeley: University of California Press, 1997.

Krantz, M. Diane F. *The Life and Text of Julian of Norwich: The Poetics of Enclosure.* New York: P. Lang, 1997.

Newman, Barbara ed. *Voice of the Living Light: Hildegard of Bingen and Her World.* Berkeley: University of California Press, 1998.

Simons, Walter. *Cities of Ladies: Beguine Communities in the Medieval Low Countries, 1200–1565.* Philadelphia: University of Pennsylvania Press, 2001.

Audio Sources

Hildegard of Bingen. *Feather on the Breath of God.* Hyperion, 1993. Compact disc. 66039.

Hildegard, Saint. *Ordo Virtutum (Play of the Virtues).* EMI/Deutsche Harmonia Mundi, 1982. Compact discs (2). CDC 7 49249 2, CDC 7 49250 2; USA only: CDCB 49249.

Web Sites

Women's Early Art: *http://womensearlyart.net.* Use links to *Women's Early Music* and *Historical Women Artists: Illustrations.*

Chapter 15

Medieval Culture:
The Secular Context

The readings in this chapter document the struggles and achievements of talented secular women in medieval Europe. In many respects, finding their creative voices and outlets was more problematic for these women than for those who functioned within a religious context. Lacking the legitimization of divine inspiration or authority, secular women had special difficulty establishing their right to speak or create. Moreover, by and large, they functioned without the nurturing of talent, the emotional support, and the intellectual and artistic stimuli that religious communities provided their members. Above all, like many of the secular women we have encountered earlier in this volume, their personal aspirations were antithetical to societal dictates that they marry and submerge themselves in familial concerns. Such gender role expectations coupled with persistent beliefs in the inherent inferiority of the female sex guaranteed that women who remained in the secular world would be educationally disadvantaged.

As a rule, those women who rose above traditional expectations for their sex did so through a combination of class privilege and luck. Some were educated in convents. Some were reared specifically to govern in the absence of husbands or male heirs. Others had fathers or husbands who recognized their talent and believed in women's education, or, perhaps more importantly, had no son to nurture. Most benefited from the tutelage and patronage of powerful men and other accomplished women. The vast majority of creative women were members of the nobility or, more rarely, had close ties with the ruling elite.

We also find clusters of creative women in certain time periods, geographic locations, and fields of art, indicating that variations in economic and educational structures, the political and legal status of women, and prevailing cultural values and artistic tastes affected female achievements. Among such clusters were the female troubadours (*trobairitzes*) of twelfth-century southern France and the English needleworkers of the tenth to thirteenth centuries.

In the thirteenth century, women artists began appearing among the lower classes in Europe's towns and cities. Most of these women were members of guilds, new craft-based organizations that trained artisans; controlled quality, production, and price; and wielded political influence on behalf of their members. Although the guilds gave lower-class women as well as men access to training previously available only in monasteries or homes of the nobility, they tended to replicate existing gender ideology and labor patterns. Women dominated guilds in traditionally female skills, particularly textiles and the silk industry, but they experienced persistent discrimination in guilds in traditionally male crafts. Some guilds excluded women completely. During the fifteenth century, however, men began systematically excluding women from their guilds and seizing control of the female-dominated textile guilds. By 1500, guilds had largely ceased to be the nurturing ground of female creativity and professionalism. In the Low Countries of northern Europe, however, where both guilds and middle-class patronage remained strong, the numbers of women painters increased in the fifteenth century.

The selections in this chapter reveal the forces that enabled some women to rise above gender restrictions, the strategies they utilized to make their voices heard, and the ways in which they challenged patriarchy indirectly and, sometimes directly, in their lives and work. They also reveal some of the self-doubt that creative women experienced as they moved into the public realm.

WOMEN TROUBADOURS (TWELFTH AND THIRTEENTH CENTURIES)

The troubadours, medieval singer-poets of southern France, are well known, but until recently, few knew of the existence of women troubadours or *trobairitz* as they are called in Provençal. Songs by more than 20 women have been discovered, but the music to only one song, "A Chantar," has survived. The troubadours were noblewomen who helped to popularize a new genre of romantic love poetry and to make vernacular speech acceptable as a language for literary and poetic expression. They are also important as being among the first women poets of the Middle Ages to write in their own voice without apologizing, denying their talent, or claiming to be the instruments of God. As their poetry reveals, they were free-spirited women who expressed themselves openly.

Why did a cluster of women troubadours appear only in the Rhone valley of southern France (a region known as Occitania) in the early twelfth century? Unlike other parts of France and Europe where feudalism consolidated land in men's hands, women still held a number of fiefs in this area. The reasons for this are unclear, and it could have been mere oversight on the part of some families. Quite unintentionally, however, the Crusades gave women a degree of autonomy they had rarely enjoyed except in some monastic communities. In 1095, Pope Urban II launched the First Crusade to recapture the Holy Land from the Muslims whose armies had spread the Islamic empire from the eastern Mediterranean to Spain. Jerusalem fell to the Christians in 1099. From that date on, control of the Holy Land see-sawed as Christians and Muslims fought to recapture Jerusalem. Political and economic as well as religious interests fueled the conflict between Christians and Muslims. Christians regained control during the Second Crusade, 1144–1187, only to lose it in 1187. A Third Crusade, 1189–1192, was unsuccessful, and the Fourth Crusade, launched in 1202 by Pope Innocent III, bogged down in Constantinople. Each effort involved tens of thousands of men, and included some women and children as well. By draining the male population in an already lightly populated region, the Crusades gave noblewomen control over fiefs sometimes as stand-ins, but also as replacements for missing men. The women troubadours emerged from this particular generation of women who benefited from a favorable legal heritage, the Crusades, and their aristocratic lineage.

The artistic genre of courtly love poetry developed by the troubadours of southern France was part of the cultural awakening that followed the First Crusade. Courtly love poetry expressed primarily a romantic as opposed to a sexual love. Troubadours paid homage to a lady of superior rank and declared themselves her servant. Typically, the object of a troubadour's love was the wife of his lord, his employer. She was beautiful, unattainable, unresponsive, and passive; the object of man's affection and worship, not a partner in love. Thus, true love meant endless suffering, and troubadours cursed women for breaking their hearts. The highest expression of love was chastity, which elevated men to a more noble level of existence. Such themes were typical of the love poetry of Moorish Spain, thus it is probable that the troubadour love poetry derived in part from Arab influences.

Troubadour poetry disappeared during the Church's crusade against the Cathars, a group of "heretics" in Occitania. This effort, launched in 1209, was part of the Fourth Crusade. When the Inquisition, created to eliminate "unbelievers" or "enemies" within Christendom, declared courtly love poetry to be heretical, the troubadours were silenced or fled the region. Courtly love poetry was transformed into worship of the ultimate unattainable lady, the Virgin Mary.

At first glance, it appears that the poetry of women troubadours was the same as men's, but closer examination has revealed that they shifted the conventions or themes of the genre in some revealing ways. Their poetry is more direct and personal. In the selections that follow look for other ways the women depart from the themes or conventions of troubadour poetry and perhaps challenge the notion of womanhood idealized by men.

Castelloza (born ca. 1200)

Castelloza was from the Le Puy region of Auvergne. She was probably the wife of a nobleman who fought in the Fourth Crusade. Three of her poems have survived.

CHANSON II*

II. God knows I should have had my fill
   of song—
the more I sing
the worse I fare in love,
and tears and cares
make me their home;
I've placed my heart and soul
in jeopardy,
and if I don't end this poem now
it will already be too long.
      Oh handsome friend, just once
      before I die
of grief, show me
your handsome face;
the other lovers say
you are a beast—
but still, though no joy
comes to me from you,
I'm proud to love you always
in good faith, with an unfickle heart.
      Nor ever from me a treacherous
      heart
toward you will turn—
though I be your inferior,
in loving I excel;

this I believe,
and this I think
even when I ponder your great worth,
and I know well that you deserve
a lady higher born than I.
      Since I first caught sight of you
      I've been
at your command; and yet, friend,
it's brought me naught,
for you've sent neither
messages nor envoys.
And if you left me now,
I wouldn't feel a thing,
for since no joy sustains me
a little pain won't drive me mad.
      Knights there are I know who
      harm themselves
in courting ladies
more than ladies them,
when they are neither
higher born nor richer;
for when a lady's mind
is set on love, she ought
to court the man, if he shows strength
   and chivalry.

*From Meg Bogin, *The Women Troubadours*. (New York: W. W. Norton, 1980), pp. 123, 125, 127. By permission of Magda Bogin.

Lady Almucs, I always
love what's worst for me,
for he who's most deserving
has the heart most fleeting.

Good Name, my love for you
will never cease,
for I live on kindness,
faith and constant courage

La Comtessa de Dia (b. ca. 1140)

We know little about Countess Beatritz de Dia (Die). Some say she was the wife of En Guillen de Poitiers, but that her songs were written for En Raimbaut d'Orange with whom she fell in love. Five of her poems and the music to one, "A Chantar," survive.

ESTAT AI EN GREU COSSIRIER[*]

I. I have been sorely troubled
about a knight I had;
I want it known for all time
how exceedingly I loved him.
Now I see myself betrayed
because I didn't grant my love
to him; I've suffered much distress
from it, in bed and fully clothed.
II. I'd like to hold my knight
in my arms one evening, naked,
for he'd be overjoyed
were I only serving as his pillow,

and I am more pleased with him
than Floris his Blanchaflor.
To him I grant my heart, my love,
my mind, my eyes, my life.
III. Fair, agreeable, good friend,
when will I have you in my power,
lie beside you for an evening
and kiss you amorously?
Be sure I'd feel a strong desire
to have you in my husband's place
provided you had promised me
to do everything as I wished.

Bieiris De Romans

All we know about Bieris De Romans is that she was born in Romans, in Occitania. Her "Chanson to Maria" is unique among the trobairitz genre, for it is the only known chanson written by a woman to another woman. As scholars have recovered more of women's voices throughout history, however, they have found more expressions of romantic and passionate feelings between women. Maria's identity is unknown.

CHANSON TO MARIA[**]

Lady Maria, in you merit and distinction,
joy, intelligence and perfect beauty,
hospitality and honor and distinction,
your noble speech and pleasing
    company,
your sweet face and merry disposition,
the sweet look and the loving expression

that exist in you without pretension
cause me to turn toward you with a pure
    heart.
    Thus I pray you, if it please you
    that true love
and celebration and sweet humility
should bring me such relief with you,

---

*Copyright 2000, 1995. From *Songs of the Women Troubadours* by Matilda Tomaryn Bruckner, Laurie Shepard, Sarah White, eds. and trans. (New York & London: Garland Publishing, Inc., 2000), p. 11. Reproduced by permission of Routledge, Inc., part of The Taylor & Francis Group. With the permission of Matilda Tomaryn Bruckner, Laurie Shepard, and Sarah White.

**From Bogin, *Women Troubadours,* p. 133. By permission of Magda Bogin.

if it please you, lovely woman, then give
     me
that which most hope and joy promises
for in you lie my desire and my heart
and from you stems all my happiness,
and because of you I'm often sighing.
          And because merit and beauty
     raise you high
above all others (for none surpasses you),

I pray you, please, by this which does
     you honor,
Don't grant your love to a deceitful suitor.
          Lovely woman, whom joy and
     noble speech uplift,
and merit, to you my stanzas go,
for in you are gaiety and happiness,
and all good things one could ask of a
     woman.

WOMEN ARTISTS, ARTISANS, AND PATRONS

The Art of Embroidery

Some of the finest works of medieval art consist of exquisitely embroidered religious vestments worked with gold and silver thread, silk, and precious stones for the clergy. As we have seen, women had expressed their creativity through their weaving and needlework since ancient times. During the Middle Ages, women were trained in the art of embroidery and produced fine works in both monastic and secular settings. Nuns and noblewomen alike took pride in their skills and created gifts for the clergy or to honor saints. As demand for luxury items grew in the ninth century, teams of women in some convent and manorial workshops or homes of noblewomen also produced richly decorated textiles for export to Byzantium or neighboring countries for purchase by royalty, the nobility, and the Church. In the early Middle Ages, it is likely that some of this work was done by trained female slaves and peasant women in the *gynaecea* (women's work rooms). The first known example of fine needlework by a woman is a stole and maniple embroidered in gold and precious stones for St. Cuthbert in the seventh century by St. Etheldreda, Abbess of Ely, an English monastery. Other known works include a stole and maniple worked by Queen Aelfflaed, wife of King Edward the Elder, in ca. 910 that is preserved in England's Durham Cathedral and a tapestry embroidered by a noblewoman, Aedelfleda, in 991 for the church at Ely.

The most famous example of medieval needlework and one of the finest examples of secular medieval art is the Bayeux Tapestry (ca. 1070), commissioned by Bishop Odo of Bayeux, France. This 230-ft. by 20-ft. tapestry relates the events surrounding the Norman conquest of England in the Battle of Hastings in over 70 scenes embroidered in eight colors of wool thread on a light brown linen cloth. The borders of the tapestry consist of fanciful pictures, including many animals, from Aesop's fables or perhaps other oral traditions, and some rather erotic images. There is still some debate about where and by whom the tapestry was produced. It seems to be the consensus, however that the tapestry was made either at an English estate or convent, probably by a team of women, because there is no record of male needle workers capable of such intricate work at that time. The scene in Figure 15–1 is the only scene in the tapestry with a woman. Her identity, other than her name, and the reason for her inclusion have been the subject of much speculation.

By the late eleventh century, English needlewomen began to excel in a type of intricate embroidery that became known as *Opus Anglicanum.* Demand for this valuable embroidery grew so rapidly that production was shifted from homes of the nobility to male-controlled guild workshops in London in the thirteenth century. In that setting, skilled female artisans from the lower classes executed the work. The Syon Cope (Fig. 15–2) is one of the finest examples of *Opus Anglicanum.* The work on this exquisite clerical vestment consists of scenes from daily life and the Bible, "drawn" with silk and metal threads, jewels, and gold on linen or velvet.

Figure 15–1 A **Bayeux tapestry:** Harolde, William. Aelfgyva, and Cleric. *Giraudon, Art Resource, New York*

Figure 15–2   The Syon Cope. *V & A Picture Library, The Victoria and Albert Museum, London*

Skilled Textile Workers and Guilds

Women dominated certain highly skilled trades involved in producing luxury textiles such as silk or linen, and fine handwork such as embroidery, beadwork, and fancy headgear. In most cities, women in these trades organized guilds and controlled their craft. Silk workers, for example, ran workshops, trained apprentices, invested funds for raw materials, owned or hired their own spindles, maintained quality control, and set prices. They carefully guarded the secrets of their craft from all but their apprentices. Many worked independently of their husbands, who pursued other trades. In Cologne and Paris, however, husbands or another male relative marketed the products, which were profitable luxury exports.

In Paris, as the selection that follows reveals, silk women enjoyed the benefits of their own guild but were essentially employed by silk merchants (often relatives), who purchased the raw materials and "put out" the silk to the women for spinning and finishing. Men, appointed by city officials, also served as supervisors or overseers of female guilds, whereas male guilds elected their own officials (Kowaleski and Bennett 1989, 480–86; Herlihy 1990, 147–48).

ORDINANCES REGULATING THE PARIS SILK WORKERS GUILD, 1254–71[*]

Whoever wants to be a silk spinster on large spindles at Paris, that is to say to reel spin double and retwist, can do it openly as long as she follows the craft's habits and customs, which are such:

No spinster of silk on large spindles can have more than three apprentices unless they are her children or the children of her husband, born of a legal marriage; she can not take the apprentices under her care either for less than seven years and for a fee of less than 20 Parisian sols, which is due her as their mistress, or for eight years of service without pay; however, the mistress can require more service and more money if she wishes to do so. . . .

[*]Excerpts from Etienne Boileau, *Reglemens sur les arts et metiers de Paris, rediges au XIIIe siecle: et connus sous le nom du Livre des metiers d'Etienne Boileau, publies pour la premiere fois en entier, d'apres les manuscrits de la Bibliotheque du roi et des Archives du royaume/avec des notes et une introduction par G. B. Depping*, (Paris, 1837), Mary K Cooney, trans., pp. 80–82.

No one of the said craft can hire another apprentice or female worker before she [the employee] has perfected and completed her service for the woman to whom she was apprenticed.

If anyone has taken an apprentice for the said craft, she can not take another before the seven years are finished unless the apprentice leaves, dies or renounces the craft forever.

If any apprentice buys her freedom before she has served the said seven years, she can not take an apprentice before she has exercised the said craft for the extent of seven years. . . .

If any female worker from outside of Paris comes to Paris and wants to perform the said craft, she must swear before the two protectors who safeguard the craft that she will practice the said craft properly and faithfully and that she will observe both the habits and customs of the craft.

If anyone of the said craft takes silk from another person and then uses this silk, it is ordained that a fine of five sols will be paid to the King if the person to whom the silk belongs makes a claim. . . .

Anyone who violates any of the above rules will give to the King five sols for each time that she violates them. . . .

London silk workers controlled their craft as other silk women did, but they did not organize a guild. Between 1368 and 1504, they petitioned the mayor or Parliament for protection of their craft from competition six times, and they usually won. In the sixteenth century, the male weavers' guild seized control of silk weaving and forced the London silk women out of the craft by prohibiting guild members from accepting female apprentices (Herlihy 1990, 480, 486).

LONDON SILK WOMEN'S PETITION TO PARLIAMENT, 1455[*]

[Petition from] the silk women and throwsters of the crafts and occupation of silk work within the city of London . . . (Until recently) many a woman lived full honorably, and therewith many households kept, and many gentlewomen and others in great number like as there now be more than a thousand, have been drawn under them in learning the same crafts and occupation. . . . lately divers Lombards [Italians] and other alien strangers imagining to destroy the same crafts and all such virtuous occupations for women within this land, to the intent to enrich themselves and put such occupations to other lands, bring now daily into this land wrought silk, thrown ribbons, and laces falsely and deceivably wrought, and no silk unwrought, to the great hurt of all such as shall wear or occupy the same and the utter destruction of all the same crafts and occupations: The sufferance whereof hath caused and is like to cause great idleness amongst gentlewomen and other women of worship. . . . In reformation whereof [the women urge Parliament to get the King to prohibit all finished silk from entering] this land from beyond the sea.

*From *Rotuli Parliamentorum; ut et petitiones, et placita in parliamento,* vol. 5, collected and arranged by R. Blyke, P. Morant, T. Astle, and John Topham, John Strachey, ed. (London, 1767–77), p. 325.

Manuscript Illuminations

In the thirteenth century, the work of copying and illustrating manuscripts shifted from monasteries to commercial businesses and guilds in northern European cities. This created opportunities for women from outside the nobility to receive artistic training and employment. Although most manuscript illuminators, except for master painters, were anonymous, guild and tax records document the existence of women painters and sculptors. Most women artists probably belonged to male-dominated guilds, but at least one all-female guild of book illuminators and binders existed in Paris in 1270. Records also indicate that female membership in the artist guild of Bruges increased from about 12 percent in 1454 to 25 percent in the 1480s (Chadwick 1990, 57; Miner 1974, 22, 24). Manuscript illuminations of daily life also depict women artists and sculptors at work.

We have more information about two fourteenth-century women artists. Bourgot, "enlumineresse de livres" (illuminator of books), was employed by many important patrons of her day. She was the daughter of Jean Le Noir, a miniaturist, and together they illustrated a Book of Hours for Yolande de Flandre in 1353 and subsequently collaborated to illustrate works for the French king, Charles V, and the Duke of Berry (Miner 1974, 18–19; Meiss 1967, 4). A second French artist, Anastasia, was praised by Christine de Pizan in a section of her *Book of the City of Ladies* on women's contributions to the arts in Western culture.

ANASTASIA[*]

> I know a woman today, named Anastasia, who is so learned and skilled in painting manuscript borders and miniature backgrounds that one cannot find an artisan in all the city of Paris — where the best in the world are found — who can surpass her, nor who can paint flowers and details as delicately as she does, nor whose work is more highly esteemed, no matter how rich or precious the book is. People cannot stop talking about her. And I know this from experience, for she has executed several things for me which stand out among the ornamental borders of the great masters.

Women Book Owners as Patrons

From the twelfth century on, as literacy spread, an increasing number of laywomen (mainly among the nobility) acquired books, and in the fourteenth and fifteenth centuries, bourgeois women also began to purchase books. Books were among the items passed on from mothers to daughters and frequently willed by fathers at their daughters' requests. Women's preferences in books shaped culture in significant ways. The most popular books in women's libraries were devotional works, particularly Books of Hours, compilations of biblical texts, prayers, and devotional readings that the buyer or patron could have custom-made to suit her particular tastes. Mothers ordered Books of Hours as advice books for their daughters on the eve of their marriage. More importantly, women book owners fostered the spread of vernacular literature by purchasing books in their spoken tongue. By the twelfth to the thirteenth centuries, few women, even the most highly educated, knew Latin which had become the language only of the clergy and university men. Women also demanded books with lavish illuminations, decorated borders, and elaborate lettering. Indeed, it seemed to some critics that women acquired garishly illustrated books as status symbols rather than for their literary merits. Nevertheless, their

*From *The Book of the City of Ladies* by Christine de Pizan. Translated by Earl Jeffrey Richards. p. 85. Copyright © 1982, 1998 by Persea Books, Inc. Reprinted by permission of Persea Books, Inc. (New York).

demand fostered the art of illumination and hence the earnings of male and female illuminators and also shaped the artistic themes and styles of their day. Elite women took their books with them when they went abroad to marry, thus spreading artistic trends and culture across political borders (Bell 1982, 742–68).

By the fourteenth century, women book owners had added a new dimension to the iconography of the Virgin Mary. Earlier depictions of the Virgin Mary in her daily role as mother had depicted her weaving or getting water from a well. The new iconography showed Mary reading or with piles of manuscripts close by, particularly during key events in her life. This iconography linked Mary with Wisdom in a new way and made her a new role model for laywomen who were increasingly urged to read devotional texts as preparation for motherhood and salvation (Bell, 1982, 760–62). The illumination in Figure 15–3 is one of several interesting examples of family role reversal.

TWO MAJOR WRITERS OF THE MIDDLE AGES

Marie de France (Twelfth Century): Poet and Social Critic

Marie de France has been praised as the "the greatest woman poet of medieval Europe," and as "'perhaps the greatest woman author of the Middle Ages and certainly the creator of the finest medieval short fiction before Boccaccio and Chaucer'" (Barnstone and Barnstone 1987, 186; Hanning and Ferrante, 1978, 1). One student of her work suggests that she is "one of the great writers of the Middle Ages and one of the greatest of all women writers" (Spiegel 1978, 3). She wrote in three literary genres: *lais, fables,* and haigiographical romances. Her work includes 5 manuscripts consisting of 12 *lais* (narrative

Figure 15–3   The Virgin Mary Reading *Book of Hours.* w.290, folio 69. French, 1400–1500. *The Walters Art Museum, Baltimore*

poems of love and adventure based on medieval legends), 24 manuscripts of fables, and *St. Patrick's Purgatory,* a work which recounts fabulous journeys to the other world undertaken by a saintly hero.

Despite her fame during the Middle Ages, Marie de France was forgotten until the early nineteenth century, when her *lais* revived her literary reputation. Her *Fables,* her most popular work during the Middle Ages, continued to be ignored. Many scholars erroneously dismissed these and *St. Patrick's Purgatory* as merely translations from the Latin, ignoring the creative innovations and original content she added to each, and the significance of her translations from Latin into the vernacular. Sixty-three of her fables had never appeared in print, and it is likely that she collected these from oral sources and wrote them to preserve them for posterity. Thus, she is also important as a folklorist and as a major figure in the development of vernacular literature.

Marie, herself, remains something of a mystery. Based on her statements in the prologues and epilogues to her works, it is agreed that she was born in France but lived and wrote in England and had important patrons though their identity is clouded. Her high level of education, the subject matter of her works, and a contemporary's reference to her as "dame Marie" all indicate she was of noble birth. There seems to be a growing consensus that she was the illegitimate daughter of Geoffrey Plantagenet of Anjou; the half-sister of King Henry II of England; and abbess of Shaftesbury from 1181–1216. Some think it is likely that she spent time at the court of Eleanor of Aquitaine (Henry's estranged wife), a powerful ruler and a patron of learning and the arts. She was more or less a contemporary of Hildegard of Bingen.

France and England experienced political turmoil from intrafamily rivalries and royal conflicts during her lifetime. Concurrently, the social and economic changes of the twelfth century disrupted the old social order of manorialism and feudalism, threatened the status of the nobility, and brought insecurity to those in the emerging middle class. One reaction to these dislocations was a longing for a return to the "good old days." The popularity of the new literary genre of romance reflected that nostalgia for hero worship and social order. Marie clearly perceived that fables were also a genre well suited to an era when traditional codes of conduct had eroded.

Fables are believed to have originated with a Greek slave, Aesop, who lived between ca. 620 and ca. 560 B.C.E. Aesop told clever tales that beneath the humor were scathing critiques of certain people, oppressive social structures, and human behavior. He masked the specific targets of his criticism by using animals and inanimate objects to represent individuals and institutions, but his audience undoubtedly recognized his subjects. Later writers of fables were, like Aesop, persons of marginal status. These included a Roman freedman (noncitizen), a medieval Jew (Nagdam), and Marie, the first woman to re-create the Aesopic fables.

Only half of Marie's fables are Aesopic. The rest are her own versions of oral folk tales, and one-third feature human characters. Most of her fables, like Aesop's, were designed to instruct and to critique weaknesses in society and human behavior. Her main purpose was to insure social stability, but she also demonstrated compassion for the unfortunate and belief in an equitable system of justice. Like Aesop, she began each fable with a *promythium* or introduction and followed most with an *epinythium* in which she highlighted the moral she wanted to impart. Occasionally, she surprises her readers with an unexpected "lesson."

Fables offered persons on the fringes of society a way to comment on, criticize, and perhaps change a society in which they had virtually no voice. They also enabled those who allegedly lacked intelligence and knowledge to demonstrate their wisdom. Many of her lais and fables, as well as the prologue and the epilogue that follow reveal that she was a woman of courage, willing to challenge societal mores and the sexual double standard.

The second fable that follows is among a number that reflect her sensitivity to women's experiences. In each case, she changed parts of the original story to reflect a more gynocentric perspective.

The deities in the original version of "The Peacock" (and in "The Sun Who Wished to Wed"), were gods. Note how her version differs.

Marie de France was one of the first women of the Middle Ages to openly speak of herself as a writer and to demand recognition as a poet and philosopher, and she was an inspiration to many of her sex.

SELECTIONS FROM MARIE'S FABLES*

"PROLOGUE"

Those persons, all, who are well-read,
Should study and pay careful heed
To fine accounts in worthy tomes,
To models and to axioms:
That which philosophers did find
And wrote about and kept in mind.
The sayings which they heard, they wrote,
So that the morals we would note;
Thus those who wish to mend their ways
Can think about what wisdom says.
The ancient fathers did just this.
The emperor, named Romulus,
Wrote to his son, enunciating,
And through examples demonstrating,
How it behooved him to take care
That no one trick him unaware.
Thus Aesop to his master wrote;
He knew his manner and his thought;
From Greek to Latin were transposed
Those fables found and those composed.
To many it was curious
That he'd apply his wisdom thus;
Yet there's no fable so inane
That folks cannot some knowledge gain
From lessons that come subsequent
To make each tale significant.
To me, who must these verses write,
It seemed improper to repeat
Some of the words that you'll find here.
Thus he commissioned me, however—
That one, the flower of chivalry,
Gentility and courtesy.

And when I'm asked by such a man,
I can do nothing other than
Labour with pained exactitude;
Though some may think that I am crude
In doing what he asked me for.
I'll start off with the first, therefore,
Of fables Aesop formulated.
Which, for his master, he related.

"EPILOGUE"

To end these tales I've here narrated
And into Romance tongue translated,
I'll give my name, for memory:
I am from France, my name's Marie.
And it may hap that many a clerk
Will claim as his what is my work.
But such pronouncements I want not!
It's folly to become forgot! . . .

44. "THE PEASANT WHO SAW ANOTHER WITH HIS WIFE"

It's said a peasant lay in wait
And spied within his household gate.
A man in his own bed he sighted
Who there with his own wife delighted.
'Alas!' he said. 'What have I spied!'
And this is how his wife replied:
'Fair lord, dear love, what do you see?'
'Another man! It seems to me
That he embraces you in bed!'
Then angrily the woman said,
'I'm very sure, it is no guess,
    That this is your old foolishness;

*All the selections that follow are from *Marie de France. Fables,* Harriet Spiegel, ed. and trans. (Toronto: University of Toronto Press, 1987), pp. 29, 31; 259; 135, 137; 111. Copyright © 1987 by University of Toronto Press. With permission of University of Toronto Press.

You cling to lies as verity.'
Said he, 'I must trust what I see.'
'You're crazy,' she replied, 'if you
Believe all that you see is true.'
She took him, led him by the hand
Unto a vat of water and
She made him peer into the vat.
The woman next demanded that
He tell her what he saw inside.
He saw his image, he replied. 'Just so.
And you are not,' she said,
            'Inside that vat completely clad.
What you see here is but semblance,

And you ought not to give credence
To eyes which often lies present.'
The peasant said, 'I do repent!
Each one had best believe and know
Whatever his wife says, is so!
And not believe what false eyes see;
            Their vision can be trickery!'
From this example comes this lore:
Good sense and shrewdness are worth
    more—
And will, to many, more help give
Than wealth or any relative. . . .

31. "THE PEACOCK"

Once there was a peacock who
Was discontented, angry too,
Because his voice, he said, was not
Befitting or appropriate.
He told all this to Destiny;
That Lady asked him then if he
Weren't with his beauty satisfied—
Such fine adornment she'd supplied!
His feathers lovelier made she
Than any bird's he'd ever see.
The peacock answered that he feared

He was, of all, the vilest bird,
For he could not sing prettily.
Then she responded, 'Let me be!
Your beauty should suffice for you.'
'Oh, no!' he said. 'I tell you true
Because the nightingale petite
Has finer voice, my shame's complete.'
        This is how many folks behave:
The more they have, the more they
    crave.

Christine de Pizan (1365–ca. 1430–34): Voice for Women and France

Christine de Pizan is considered to be France's first woman author and one of its first professional writers. She is probably the first woman of the Middle Ages to make her living exclusively by writing. She wrote a remarkable variety of works in prose and verse that reflected her mastery of all the literary genres of her time and her creativity in experimenting with new forms. Her works included allegories, devotional works, courtly love romances and ballades, educational treatises, history and political commentary, biographies of Charles V and Joan of Arc, and instructional "handbooks" (akin to Machiavelli's *The Prince*) for both men and women. She also made significant contributions to art. She personally engaged artists to illustrate her works and was one of the first vernacular authors to supervise the copying and illuminating of her books (Meiss 1967, 8, 14, 16, 23, 37–41). She is best known for her works in defense of women, most notably, *The Book of the City of Ladies*. In writing the first systematic defenses of women by a woman, she helped launch the *querelle des femmes*, a debate about the nature, worth, and status of women in society that continues today.

Pizan commanded the respect of leading European intellectuals and citizens. Her works, particularly those in defense and praise of women, were popular in England, Italy, Flanders, Portugal, and

Spain as well as in France and influenced writers in a number of countries. Her patrons were among the most powerful people of her time. They included Charles VI and Queen Isabella, Philip and John of Burgundy, Louis of Orleans, and her major patron, John de Berry. Her books, including *City of Ladies* and *Treasure of the City of Ladies* (often translated as *Treasury*), were read by a number of important women, including Marguerite of Austria, Mary of Hungary, Anne of Brittany, and the queens of France and Portugal (Willard 1984, 340; Meiss 1967, 38–39). Equally important, bourgeois women acquired inexpensive versions of these books. Through the popularity of her books, she remained an intellectual and literary force into the middle of the sixteenth century. Then her works were largely forgotten until their rediscovery in the mid-nineteenth century.

We know a great deal about Pizan because much of her writing was autobiographical. She was born in Venice, but moved to France at the age of three when her father, Thomas, became the personal physician and astrologer of Charles V. Her father educated her well, over the objections of her mother who wanted her to be trained only in womanly things, and he chose a scholar and notary, Etienne de Castel, for her husband. The two were married in 1380 when she was 15 and Etienne was 25. They had a happy marriage that was blessed with a daughter and two sons. Both her father and husband encouraged her intellectual development and brought her into contact with some of the most progressive men of the time. Unfortunately, when Charles V died in 1380, her father lost his position at court and had to depend on Etienne's assistance until his death ca. 1387. Then, Etienne died suddenly in 1390, leaving Pizan the sole support of her mother and three children. In response, she resumed her studies and probably supported her dependents by working as a manuscript copyist. By 1394 she had begun writing verse and soon was attracting patrons. In 1397, her connections enabled her daughter Marie to enter the royal convent of Poissy. The next year, a patron, the earl of Salisbury, took her son Jean to England as a companion for his son. From then on, she focused on her writing.

Her first successes were in the courtly love genre which was popular among those at the court of Louis, duke of Orleans. In 1405, she attracted the patronage of Duke Philip of Burgundy, who commissioned her to write a biography of his late brother Charles V. His support and that of other patrons enabled Pizan to pursue her interests in more serious works. These reflect her concerns about the chaos that engulfed France during her lifetime: the Hundred Years War and invasion by England; civil war between the houses of Orleans and Burgundy; ineffective political leadership; and popular unrest. They also reveal her desire to affect the outcome of public affairs despite her sex and her determination to prove the worth and improve the position of all women. She was a keen observer, and her works provide invaluable insights into the political struggles in France and the lives of men and women of all social strata.

Pizan is best known for her book in defense of women, *The Book of the City of Ladies.* In this thought-provoking work she presents all the negative and harmful stereotypes about women pervasive in Western culture, and then systematically sets out to disprove each, using historical examples of both real and mythical women, Christian and non-Christian, queens, empresses and warriors, prophets, goddesses and biblical heroines, and writers and artists as evidence. Her examples include many whom you have encountered in previous chapters. In the process, she also explains (through the words of Lady Reason) why men devote so much energy into putting women down. The work is a marvelous compendium of women's contributions to society, told from a gynocentric perspective. More importantly, it is a shrewd critique of the patriarchal social structure and ideology we have examined in much of this volume. As you read the following selections, note the literary strategies she employs to involve the reader in thinking about women's experiences. Also observe how she demonstrates the ways in which women internalize and accept male views of their sex, and the impact it has on their self-image.

PIZAN'S DEFENSE OF WOMEN: *THE BOOK OF THE CITY OF LADIES,* 1405[*]

I.1.1 One day as I was sitting alone in my study surrounded by books on all kinds of subjects, devoting myself to literary studies, my usual habit, my mind dwelt at length on the weighty opinions of various authors whom I had studied for a long time. . . . I remembered wanting to examine this book by Matheolus. . . . But just the sight of his book . . . made me wonder how it happened that so many different men—and learned men among them—have been and are so inclined to express both in speaking and in their treatises and writings so many wicked insults about women and their behavior. . . . They all concur in one conclusion: that the behavior of women is inclined to and full of every vice. Thinking deeply about these matters, I began to examine my character and conduct as a natural woman and, similarly, I considered other women whose company I frequently kept. . . . I could not see or realize how their claims could be true when compared to the natural behavior and character of women. Yet I still argued vehemently against women, saying that it would be impossible that so many famous men . . . possessed of such deep and great understanding . . . could have spoken falsely on so many occasions that I could hardly find a book on morals where, even before I had read it in its entirety, I did not find several chapters or certain sections attacking women, no matter who the author was. . . . And I finally decided that God formed a vile creature when He made woman, and I wondered how such a worthy artisan could have deigned to make such an abominable work which . . . is the vessel as well as the refuge and abode of every evil and vice. As I was thinking this, a great unhappiness and sadness welled up in my heart, for I detested myself and the entire feminine sex, as though we were monstrosities in nature.

I.1.2 ". . . Alas, God, why did You not let me be born in the world as a man, so that all my inclinations would be to serve You better, and so that I would not stray in anything and would be as perfect as a man is said to be?" . . . I spoke these words to God in my lament . . . , and in my folly I considered myself most unfortunate because God had made me inhabit a female body in this world.

I.2.1 So occupied with these painful thoughts, my head bowed in shame, my eyes filled with tears, . . . I suddenly saw a ray of light fall on my lap, as though it were the sun. . . . And as I lifted my head to see where this light was coming from, I saw three crowned ladies standing before me, and the splendor of their bright faces shone on me and throughout the entire room. [*Ladies Reason, Rectitude, and Justice*]

I.2.2 Then she who was the first of the three smiled and began to speak, "Dear daughter, do not be afraid, . . . we have come to bring you out of the ignorance which so blinds your own intellect that you shun what you know for a certainty and believe what you do not know . . . or recognize except by virtue of many strange opinions. . . . Do you not know that the best things are the most debated and the most discussed?"

---

[*]Excerpts from *The Book of the City of Ladies* by Christine de Pizan. Translated by Earl Jeffrey Richards. pp. 3–6, 10–11, 16–19, 63, 71, 142, 153–55, 160–61. Copyright © 1982, 1998 by Persea Books, Inc. Reprinted by permission of Persea Books, Inc. (New York).

I.3.3 "There is another greater and even more special reason for our coming which you will learn from our speeches: In fact we have come to vanquish from the world the same error into which you had fallen, so that from now on ladies and all valiant women may have a refuge and defense against the various assailants. . . we three ladies whom you see here, . . . have come to you to announce a particular edifice built like a city wall, strongly constructed and well founded, which has been predestined and established by our aid and counsel for you to build, where no one will reside except all ladies of fame and women worthy of praise, for the walls of the city will be closed to those women who lack virtue." . . .

I.8.1 Then Lady Reason . . . said, "Get up, daughter! Without waiting any longer, let us go to the Field of Letters. There the City of Ladies will be founded on a flat and fertile plain, where all the fruits and freshwater rivers are found and where the earth abounds in all good things. Take the pick of your understanding and dig and clear out a great ditch wherever you see the marks of my ruler, and I will help you carry away the earth on my own shoulders."

I.8.3 [*As Christine began to dig, she spoke to Lady Reason.*] "Lady, . . . please tell me why and for what reason different authors have spoken against women in their books, since I already know from you that this is wrong; tell me if Nature makes man so inclined or whether they do it out of hatred and where does this behavior come from?" Then she replied, ". . . This behavior most certainly does not come from Nature, but rather is contrary to Nature. . . . The causes which have moved and which still move men to attack women . . . are diverse and varied. For some have attacked women with good intentions, that is, in order to draw men who have gone astray away from the company of vicious and dissolute women. . . . "

I.8.4 "Other men have attacked women for other reasons: such reproach has occurred to some men because of their own vices and others have been moved by the defects of their own bodies, others through pure jealousy, still others by the pleasure they derive in their own personalities from slander. Others, in order to show they have read many authors, base their own writings on what they have found in books and repeat what other writers have said. . . . "

I.8.8 "Those men who have attacked women out of jealousy are those wicked ones who have seen and realized that many women have greater understanding and are more noble in conduct than they themselves, and thus they are pained and disdainful." . . .

I.27.1 [*Christine spoke:*] "But please enlighten me again, whether it has ever pleased this God . . . to honor the feminine sex with the privilege of the virtue of high understanding and great learning. . . . I wish very much to know this because men maintain that the mind of women can learn only a little."

She answered, "My daughter, . . . I tell you again . . . if it were customary to send daughters to school like sons, and if they were then taught the natural sciences, they would learn as thoroughly and understand the subtleties of all the arts and sciences as well as sons. And by chance there happen to be such women. . . . [*She speaks of Sappho and others.*]

I.33.1 . . . "Rest assured, dear friend, that many noteworthy and great sciences and arts have been discovered through the understanding and subtlety of women, both in cognitive speculation, demonstrated in writing, and in the arts, manifested in manual works of labor." [*Reason cites Minerva, Queen Ceres, Isis, Thamaris, Sempronia, and others.*]

II.30.1 [*Christine speaks:*] "My lady, I see the endless benefits which have accrued to the world through women and nevertheless these men claim that there is no evil which has not come into the world because of them."

"Fair friend," she answered, "you can see from what I have already said to you that the contrary of what they say is true. For there is no man who could sum up the enormous benefits which have come about through women and which come about every day, and I proved this for you with the examples of the noble ladies who gave the sciences and arts to the world. But, if what I have said about the earthly benefits accruing thanks to women is not enough for you, I will tell you about the spiritual ones. Oh, how could any man be so heartless to forget that the door of Paradise was opened to him by a woman? . . ." [*Reason recounts the deeds of Judith, Esther, and other Biblical heroines.*]

II.36.1 I, Christine, spoke, "My lady, I realize that women have accomplished many good things. . . . Therefore, I am amazed by the opinion of some men who claim that they do not want their daughters, wives, or kinswomen to be educated because their mores would be ruined as a result."

II.36.4 [*Reason responds:*] ". . . not all men . . . share the opinion that it is bad for women to be educated. But it is very true that many foolish men have claimed this because it displeased them that women knew more than they did. Your father, who was a great scientist and philosopher, did not believe that women were worth less by knowing science; rather, as you know, he took great pleasure from seeing your inclination to learning. The feminine opinion of your mother, however, who wished to keep you busy with spinning and silly girlishness, following the common custom of women, was the major obstacle to your being more involved in the sciences. . . ."

II.44.1 Then I, Christine, spoke as follows, ". . . I am certain that there are plenty of beautiful women who are virtuous and chaste and who know how to protect themselves well from the entrapments of deceitful men. I am therefore troubled and grieved when men argue that many women want to be raped and that it does not bother them at all to be raped by men even when they verbally protest."

She answered, "Rest assured . . . chaste ladies who live honestly take absolutely no pleasure in being raped. Indeed, rape is the greatest possible sorrow for them. Many upright women have demonstrated that this is true with their own credible examples, just like Lucretia, the noblest Roman woman, supreme in chastity among Roman women, wife of a nobleman named Tarquin Collatinus." [*Reason recounts the story of Lucretia's rape, her suicide, and its historical impact, then tells the stories of other women of virtue.*] . . .

After completing *Book of the City of Ladies* Pizan wrote *Treasure of the City of Ladies* to help women live virtuous lives and hence merit citizenship in the City of Ladies. The work, however, is more than a handbook for women of her time; it is also an invaluable description of medieval women's real lives and responsibilities. It is unusual in that Pizan includes women of all classes and sectors of society in her account, not merely the nobility. The excerpts that follow cover only a few of the groups of women she discusses in the book. Note the extent to which she accepts or challenges the existing social order and the various instructions she gives to ensure that women from all classes contribute to the welfare of society.

TREASURE OF THE CITY OF LADIES[*]

Part Two: 10. How ladies and young women who live on their manors ought to manage their households and estates.

There is another condition of rank and of life than that of baronesses that pertains to ordinary ladies and young women living on or off their lands outside fine cities. Because barons and still more commonly knights and squires and gentlemen travel and go off to the war, their wives should be wise and sound administrators and manage their affairs well. . . . They should have all the responsibility of the administration and know how to make use of their revenues and possessions. . . .

. . . There is nothing dishonourable about making herself familiar with the accounts. She will see them often and wish to know how they are managed in regard to her vassals so that they are not being cheated. . . . Towards poor people a lady should, out of love for God, be more compassionate than strict.

In addition, she will do well to be a very good manager of the estate and to know all about the work on the land and at what time and in which season one ought to perform what operations. . . .

Part Three: 8. Of the wives of artisans and how they ought to conduct themselves.

. . . All wives of artisans should be very painstaking and diligent if they wish to have the necessities of life. They should encourage their husbands or their workmen to get to work early in the morning and work until late. . . . And besides encouraging the others, the wife herself should be involved in the work to the extent that she knows all about it, so that she may know how to oversee his workers if her husband is absent, and to reprove them if they do not do well. . . . Nor should she go off on these pilgrimages got up for no good reason and involving a lot of needless expense. . . .

10. Of the instruction for prostitutes.

Just as the sun shines on the just and on the unjust, we have no shame in extending our instruction even to the women who are foolish and loose and lead disorderly lives, although there is nothing more abominable. . . . Therefore, for charity and goodness and so that some of them may perhaps retain from our teachings something that may rescue them from their disreputable lives, we will teach them something. . . .

Throughout her life, Pizan wrote letters, treatises, and handbooks for common citizens, knights, and rulers, including manuals of government and military ethics, in an effort to foster social stability and peace. In *Lament on the Evils of the Civil War*, she exhorts the French to put an end to the civil war that broke out between the Armagnac and Burgundian factions in 1409. Note to whom she addresses her plea and why, how compelling it is, and whether her depiction of war differs from most literary and artistic portrayals of warfare.

---

[*]*The Treasure of the City of Ladies* by Christine de Pizan, translated by Sarah Lawson (Penguin, 1985), Copyright © Sarah Lawson, 1985, pp. 130–31, 167–68, 171. By permission of The Penguin Group (UK).

PIZAN'S LAMENT ON THE EVILS OF THE CIVIL WAR, 1410[*]

In the very heart of France! The noble knights and youth of France, all of one nature, one single soul and body, which used to defend the crown and the public good, are now gathered in a shameful battle one against another, father against son, brother against brother, relatives against one another, with deadly swords, covering the pitiful fields with blood, dead bodies, and limbs. Oh, dishonorable victory may be to the one who has it! What glory will Fame give to it? Will it be crowned with laurels? Ah me, it will have to be shamefully bound with back thorns when it sees itself, not as a victor, but as the very killer of its own blood, for whom it is appropriate to wear black, as in the death of kin.

Oh, you, knight who comes from such a battle, tell me, I pray you, what honor did you win there? . . .

And what will follow, in God's name? Famine, because of the wasting and ruining of things that will ensue, and the lack of cultivation, from which will spring revolts by the people who have been too often robbed, deprived and oppressed, their food taken away and stolen here and there by soldiers, subversion in the towns because of outrageous taxes which will have to be levied on the citizens and dwellers to raise the needed money, and above all, the English will obtain checkmate on the side, if Fortune agrees to it; . . .

Is it thus decided? Yes, indeed! So, cry, cry, beat your hands and cry . . . you ladies, damsels, and women of the kingdom of France! Because the swords that will make you widows and deprive you of your children and kin have already been sharpened! . . . Oh, crowned Queen of France, are you still sleeping? Who prevents you from restraining now this side of your kin and putting an end to this deadly enterprise? Revered Princess, who but you can do anything, and who will disobey your sovereignty and authority, if you rightly want to mediate a peace?

Come, all you wise men of this realm, come with *your* queen! What use are you if not for the royal council? Everyone should offer his hand. . . .

People, be firm! And you, pious women, cry mercy for this grievous storm! Ah, France, France, once a glorious kingdom! Alas, what more can I say? . . .

SUGGESTED READINGS

Brown-Grant, Rosalind. *Christine de Pizan and the Moral Defence of Women: Reading Beyond Gender.* Cambridge: Cambridge University Press, 1999.

Erler, M. and Maryann Kowalski, eds. *Women and Power in the Middle Ages.* Athens: University of Georgia Press, 1988.

---

[*]Excerpts from *Christine de Pizan. The Epistle of the Prison of Human Life with an Epistle to the Queen of France and Lament on the Evils of Civil War* by Josette A. Wisman, ed. & tr. (New York, NY: Garland Publishing, Inc., 1984), pp. 87, 89. Copyright 1984. Reproduced by permission of Routledge, Inc., part of The Taylor & Francis Group. With the permission of Josette A. Wisman.

Ferrante, Joan M. *To the Glory of Her Sex: Women's Roles in the Composition of Medieval Texts.* Bloomington: Indiana University Press, 1997.

Kelly, A. *Eleanor of Aquitaine and the Four Kings.* Cambridge, MA: Harvard University Press, 1950.

Richards, Earl Jeffrey ed. with Joan Williamson, Nadia Margolis, and Christine Reno. *Reinterpreting Christine de Pizan.* Athens: University of Georgia Press, 1992.

Warner, Marina. *Joan of Arc: The Image of Female Heroism.* Berkeley: University of California Press, 1981.

Willard, Charity Cannon. *Christine de Pizan: Her Life and Works.* New York: Persea Books, 1994.

Audiovisual and Web Source

Bayeux Tapestry. http://www.sjolander.com/viking/museum. Click *Invasion of England, 1066.*

Bibliography

Aeschylus. *Eumenides*. Trans. G. Thomson. The Laurel Classical Drama Series. New York: Dell, 1965.

Alic, Margaret. *Hypatia's Heritage: A History of Women in Science from Antiquity through the Nineteenth Century*. Boston: Beacon Press, 1986.

Anchor Bible Commentary. (multivolume series) New York: Doubleday, ca. 1972–2003.

Bachofen, Johann Jakob. *Myth, Religion and Mother Right*. New York: Bollingen Foundation. Translated and adapted from *Das Mutterrecht*. Edited by Rudolf Marx. Stuttgart: Alfred Kröner Verlag, 1954. Princeton, NJ: Princeton University Press, 1967.

Baillet, Maurice. "Qumran Grotte 4Q, 502 Rituel de Mariage." In *Discoveries in the Judean Desert 7*, Fragment 17. Oxford, 1982. English trans. L. Bennett Elder.

Barber, Elizabeth. *Women's Work: The First 20,000 Years. Women, Cloth, and Society in Early Times*. New York, London: Norton Publishers, 1994.

Barnard, Mary, trans. *Sappho: Poems*. Los Angeles and London: University of California Press, 1958.

Barnstone, Aliki and Willis Barnstone, eds. *A Book of Women Poets from Antiquity to Now*. New York: Schocken Books, 1987.

Batto, Bernard Frank. *Studies on Women at Mari*. Baltimore, MD: Johns Hopkins University Press, 1974.

Baumgarten, Joseph. "4Q502: Marriage or Golden Age Ritual." *Journal of Jewish Studies* 35.2 (Autumn 1987): 266-69.

Bell, Susan Groag, "Medieval Women Book Owners: Arbiters of Lay Piety and Ambassadors of Culture." *Signs: Journal of Women in Culture and Society* 7, no. 4 (summer 1982).

Biaggi, Cristina. *Habitations of the Great Goddess*. Manchester, CT: Knowledge Ideas and Trends, 1994.

Bickerman, Elias. *Jews in the Greek Age*, 92. Cambridge, MA: Harvard University Press, 1988.

Billigmeier, J. C. and J. A. Turner. "The Socio-Economic Roles of Women in Mycenaean Greece: A Brief Survey from Evidence of the Linear B Tablets."

Bonfante, Larissa. "Etruscans in Their Aristocratic Society." In *Reflections of Women in Antiquity*. Compiled by Helene P. Foley. Philadelphia: Gordon and Breach Science Publications, 1981.

Book of J (The). Trans. David Rosenberg. Interpreted by Harold Bloom. New York: Grove Weidenfield, 1990.

Brenner, Athalyah A., ed. *Feminist Companion to the Old Testament*, Sheffield, UK: Sheffield Academic Press, 1988.

Briffault, Robert. *The Mothers: The Matriarchal Theory of Social Origins*, New York: MacMillan, 1931.

Brooten, Bernadette. *Women Leaders in the Ancient Synagogues*. Vol. 36 of *Brown Judaic Studies*. Chico, CA: Scholars Press, 1982.

Brown, Peter. *Religion and Society in the Age of St. Augustine*. London: Harper and Row, 1972.

Budge, E. A. Wallis. *The Queen of Sheba and Her Only Son Menyelek*. London, Liverpool, Boston: The Medici Society, 1922.

Burstein, Stanley M., ed. and trans. *Hellenistic Age from the Battle of Ipsos to the Death of Kleopatra VII (The)*. Translated Documents of Greece and Rome Series. V. 3. Cambridge; New York: Cambridge University Press, 1985.

Cambridge Ancient History (The). Edited by S.A. Cook, F. E. Baldock and M. P. Charlesworth. Vols. 7, 8, 9, 10. New York: MacMillan, 1928–1934.

Chadwick, Nora. *The Celts*. Harmondsworth England: Penguin Books, 1970.

Chadwick, Whitney. *Women, Art, and Society*. New York and London: Thames and Hudson, 1990.

Conley T. "General Education in Philo Alexandria." Proceedings of the Center for Hermeneutical Studies in Hellenistic and Modern Culture. January, 1975. Berkeley: University of California Press. 1975.

Cook, Joan E. *Hannah's Desire, God's Design*. Supplement Series 282. *Journal for the Study of the Old Testament*. Sheffield: Sheffield Academic Press, 1999.

De Grummond, Nancy T. *The Etruscans, Legacy of a Lost Civilization, From the Vatican Museums*, The Memphis International Cultural Series and the Vatican Museums, Memphis, TN, 1992.

Downing, Marymay. "The Goddess and Technology at Crete." *Journal of Feminist Studies in Religion* 1, no. 1 (1984).

Dupont Summer. Trans. "The Rule Annexe." In *The Essene Writings From Qumran*. Cleveland and New York: The World Publishing Company, 1962.

Dyczek, Piotr. "The Status of Women in Aegean Culture: Some Considerations." In *Studia Aegaea et Balcanica in Honorem Lodovicae Press, Wydawnictwa Uniwersytetu Warszawskiego*. Edited by Anna Lipska, Ewa Niezgoda, and Maria Zabecka, 81–89. Warszawa, 1992.

Ehrenberg, Margaret. *Women in Pre-History*. Norman, London: University of Oklahoma Press, 1989.

Encyclopaedia Judaica. New York: The Macmillan Co., 1971–1972.

Engels, Fredrick. *The Origin of the Family, Private Property, and the State*. New York: International Publishers, 1972.

Fantham, Elaine, et al, eds. *Women in the Classical World*. Oxford: Oxford University Press, 1994.

Farnell, Lewis R. *Cults of the Greek States*. Oxford: Clarendon Press, 1896–1909.

Foley, Helene P. *Reflections of Women in Antiquity*. Philadelphia: Gordon and Breach Science Publications. 1st ed. 1981, 2d ed. 1992.

Gardiner, A. H. "The Gods of Thebes as Guarantors of Personal Property." *Journal of Egyptian Archaeology*, 48 (1962).

Gardner, Jane G. and Thomas Wiedemann, eds. *The Roman Househol: A Sourcebook*. London; New York: Routledge, 1991.

Gero, Joan M. and Margaret W. Conkey, eds. *Engendering Archaeology: Women and Prehistory*. Oxford: Blackwell Publishers, 1991.

Gimbutas, Marija. *Civilization of the Goddess*. San Francisco, CA: Harper, 1991.

Gimbutas, Marija. *Language of the Goddess*. San Francisco, CA: Harper, 1989.

Ginzberg, Louis, ed. *The Legends of the Jews*. Vol.1. Edited by Philadelphia: Jewish Publications Society, 1956.

Goodblatt, David. "The Beruriah Traditions." In *Persons and Institutions in Early Rabbinic Judaism*. Edited by William Scott Green. Missoula, MT: Scholars Press, 1977.

Grimal, Nicolas. *A History of Ancient Egypt*. Trans. Ian Shaw. Oxford, UK; Cambridge, USA: Blackwell, 1992.

Hallett, Judith. *Fathers and Daughters in Roman Society: Women in the Elite Family*. Princeton: Princeton University Press, 1984.

Hallo, William W., ed. *Contexts of Scripture: Canonical Compositions from the Biblical World*. Vols.1 and 2. Leiden, London, Koln: Brill, 1997.

Hallo, William W. and William Kelly Simpson, eds. *The Ancient Near East*. New York, Chicago: Harcourt Brace Javanovich, 1971.

Hanning, Robert and Joan Ferrante, trans. *The Lais of Marie de France*. New York: E. P. Dutton, 1978.

Harlots of the Desert. Trans. Benedicta Ward. Kalamazoo, MI: Cistercian Publications, 1987.

Harrington, Daniel J. "Pseudo-Philo." In *Old Testament Pseudepigrapha*. Vol. II of *Biblical Antiquities*. Edited by James Charlesworth, No. 40. Garden City, NY: Doubleday and Co., 1985.

Harris, Rivkah. "Independent Women in Ancient Mesopotamia." In *Women's Earliest Records: From Ancient Egypt and Western Asia*. Edited by Barbara Lesko. Brown Judaic Studies. Atlanta: Scholars Press, 1989

Harris, Rivkah. "The Naditu Woman," In *Studies Oppenheim*. The Oriental Institute, The University of Chicago, 1965.

Harrison, Jane Ellen. *Prolegomena to the Study of Greek Religion*. 3rd Edition. New York: Meridian, 1922, reprint 1955.

Hawkes, Jacquetta and Sir Leonard Wooley, eds. *Pre-History and the Beginnings of Civilization*. New York: Harper and Row, 1965–1967.

Herlihy, David. *Opera Muliebria: Women and Work in Medieval Europe*. New York: McGraw-Hill, 1990.

Heyob, Sharon Kelly. *The Cult of Isis Among Women in the Greco-Roman World*. Leiden: Brill, 1979.

Hildegard, Saint. *Scivias*. Trans. Columba Hart and Jane Bishop. Classics of Western Spirituality. New York: Paulist Press, 1990.

Hingle, Martin. *Judaism and Hellenism*. Vols 1 and 2. Translated from the German by John Bowden. Philadelphia: Fortress Press, 1974.

Hirsch, Udo. *Environment, Economy, Cult and Culture*. Vol. III in *Goddess from Anatolia*. Edited by James Mellaart, Udo Hirsch, and Belkis Balpinar. Milan: Ezkanazi, 1989.

Hoffman, Michael. *Egypt Before the Pharaohs: The Historical Foundations of Egyptian Civilization*. Revised. Austin: University of Texas Press, 1991.

Hollis, Susan. "Queens and Goddesses in Ancient Egypt." Unpublished paper delivered at the Conference on Goddess Traditions at Claremont College. Claremont, California, 1992.

Iamblichus. *Iamblichus on the Pythagorean Way of Life*. Edited by John Dillon and Jackson Hershbell. Atlanta: Scholars Press, 1991.

Jones, A. H. M. *The Later Roman Empire: 284–602: A Social, Economic and Administrative Survey*. 2 vols. Norman, University of Oklahoma Press, 1964.

Jones, P. and K Sidwell, ed. *The World of Rome*. Cambridge, MA: Cambridge University Press, 1997.

King, Kare L., ed. *Images of the Feminine in Gnosticism*. Studies in Antiquity and Christianity 4. Philadelphia: Fortress Press, 1988.

Kleiner, D. and S. Matheson, eds. *I Claudia, Women in Ancient Rome*. Austin: University of Texas Press, 1996.

Koester, Helmut. *Introduction to the New Testament*. History, Culture and Religion of the Hellenistic Age. Vol. I. Philadelphia: Fortress Press, 1982.

Kowaleski, Maryanne and Judith M. Bennett. "Crafts, Gilds, and Women in the Middle Ages: Fifty Years after Marian K. Dale." *Signs: Journal of Women in Culture and Society* 14, no. 2 (winter 1989).

Kraemer, Ross S. *Her Share of the Blessings: Women's Religions among Pagans, Jews and Christians*. New York: Oxford University Press, 1992.

Kraemer, Ross S. *Maenads, Martyrs, Matrons and Monastics*. Philadelphia: Fortress Press, 1988.

Kramer, Samuel Noah. *The Sumerians: Their History, Culture and Character*. Chicago: University of Chicago Press, 1963.

Kramer, Samuel Noah. *The Sacred Marriage Rite*. Philadelphia: University of Pennsylvania Press, 1969.

Lesko, Barbara, ed. *Women's Earliest Records: From Ancient Egypt and Western Asia*. Brown Judaic Studies. Atlanta: Scholars Press, 1989.

Levine, Amy-Jill, ed. *"Women Like This": New Perspectives on Jewish Women in the Greco-Roman World*. Early Judaism and Its Literature Series, no. 01. Atlanta, GA: Scholars Press, 1991.

Lichtheim, Miriam. *Ancient Egyptian Literature*. Published under the auspices of the Gustave E. von Grunebaum Center for Near Eastern Studies. Berkeley, Los Angeles, London: University of California Press, 1973.

Loeb Classical Library. Cambridge, MA and London: Harvard University Press, ca. 1912–2003.

Mabinogion and Other Welsh Tales (The). Trans. Patrick A. Ford. Berkeley: University of California Press, 1977.

MacMullen, Ramsay. *Paganism in the Roman Empire*. New Haven and London: Yale University Press, 1981.

MacMullen, Ramsay. *Roman Social Relations: 50 B.C.E. to 284 C.E.* New Haven: Yale University Press, 1974.

Macurdy, Grace H. *The Hellenistic Queens: A Study of Woman-Power in Macedonia, Seleucid Syria, and Ptolemaic Egypt*. Chicago: Ares Publishers, 1932.

Marcus, Joyce. *Women's Ritual in Formative Oaxaca: Figurine Making, Divination, Death and the Ancestors*. Ann Arbor, MI: University of Michigan Museum of Anthropology, 1998.

Marinatos, N. "The Minoan Harem: The Role of Eminent Women and the Knossos Frescoes." *Dialogues d'Histoire Ancienne [Hommage a Ettore Lepore]*. 15.2 (1989): 33–50.

Marrou, Henri I. *A History of Education in Antiquity*. Trans. George Lamb. New York: Sheed and Ward, 1956.

Meeks, Wayne A. *The First Urban Christians: the Social World of the Apostle Paul*. New Haven and London: Yale University Press, 1988.

Meiss, Millard. *French Painting in the Time of Jean de Berry; the Late Fourteenth Century and the Patronage of the Duke*. London: Phaidon, 1967.

Mellaart, James. *Catal Huyuk: A Neolithic Town in Anatolia*. New York: McGraw-Hill, 1967.

Menu, Bernadette, "Women in Business Life in the First Millennium B.C." In *Women's Earliest Records: From Ancient Egypt and Western Asia*. Edited by Barbara Lesko. Brown Judaic Studies. Atlanta: Scholars Press, 1989.

Miner, Dorothy Eugenia. *Anastaise and Her Sisters: Women Artists of the Middle Ages*. Baltimore, MD: Walters Art Gallery.

Mishnah (The): A New Translation. Ed. Jacob Neusner. New Haven and London: Yale University Press, 1988.

Nachtigall, H. *Vokerkunde*. Stuttgart 1979.

Nagle, Brendan D. *The Ancient World, A Social Cultural History*, 5th edition, Upper Saddle River, NJ: Prentice Hall, 2002.

Newman, Barbara. *Sister of Wisdom. St. Hildegard's Theology of the Feminine*. Berkeley: University of California Press, 1987.

Newsom, Carol A. and Sharon H. Ringe, eds. *The Women's Bible Commentary*. Louisville, KY: Westminster John Knox Press, 1992.

Nilsson, Martin. *Minoan-Mycenaean Religions*. NP, 1927.

Oppenheimer, A. Leo. *Ancient Mesopotamia: Portrait of a Dead Civilization*. Erica Reiner, Photographs. Chicago: University of Chicago Press, 1977.

Ortner, Sherry. *Making Gender*. Boston: Beacon Press, 1996.

Oxford History of the Roman World (The). Edited by Griffin J. Boardman and O. Murray. Oxford: Oxford University Press, 1986.

Pantel, Pauline Schmitt, ed. *A History of Women: From Ancient Goddesses to Christian Saints*. Cambridge, MA and London: The Belknapp Press of Harvard U. P., 1993.

Patai, Raphael. *The Hebrew Goddess*. 3rd edition. Detroit: Wayne State University Press, 1990.

Philo of Alexandria, ed. and trans. David Winston, p. 52 (VIII)-55 (X). New York and Toronto: Paulist Press, 1981.

Piccione, P.A. "The Status of Women in Ancient Egyptian Society." http://www.library.nwu.edu/class/history/B94/B94women.html. 1995.

Pitor, Michaelowski, ed. *Law Collections from Mesopotamia and Asia Minor*. Writings from the Ancient World Series, Society of Biblical Literature. Atlanta: Scholars Press, 1995.

Pomeroy, Sarah B. *Goddesses, Whores, Wives and Slaves*. New York: Schocken Books, 1975.

Pomeroy, Sarah B. *Women in Hellenistic Egypt: From Alexander to Cleopatra*. New York: Schocken Books, 1984.

Postgate, Nicholas, and Postgate J. N. *Early Mesopotamia: Society and Economy at the Dawn of History*. Routledge Press, 1994.

Pritchard, James B., ed. *Ancient Near East Texts Relating to the Old Testament*. Princeton, NJ: Princeton University Press, 1969.

Robins, Gay. *Women in Ancient Egypt*. Cambridge, MA: Harvard University Press, 1993.

Rosaldo, Michelle Zimbalist and Louise Lamhere, eds. *Woman, Culture and Society*. Stanford, CA: Stanford University Press, 1974.

St. John, Christopher, trans. *The Plays of Roswitha*. New York: Benjamin Blom, 1966.

Sayings of the Desert Fathers. Trans. H. Wadell. London: Constable and Co., 1936.

Schulenberg, Jane Tibbets. "Women's Monastic Communities, 500–1100: Patterns of Expansion and Decline." *Signs: A Journal of Women in Culture and Society* 14, No. 2 (winter 1989).

Schüssler Fiorenza, Elisabeth. *In Memory of Her: A Feminist Re-Construction of Christian Origins*. New York: Crossroad, 1983.

Schüssler Fiorenza, Elisabeth, ed. *Searching the Scriptures: A Feminist Commentary*. 2 vols. Edited by New York: Crossroad, 1994.

Shelton, J. *As the Romans Did: A Sourcebook in Roman Social History*. New York: Oxford University Press, 1988.

Sommer, DuPont, trans. "The Rule Annexe." In *The Essene. Writings from Qumran*. Cleveland and New York: The World Publishing Company, 1962.

Spiegel, Harriet, ed. and trans. *Marie de France. Fables*. Toronto: University of Toronto Press, 1987.

The Tain. Trans. Thomas Kinsella. Oxford: Oxford University Press in association with The Dolman Press, Dublin. 1969.

Townsend, John. "Ancient Education in the Time of the Early Roman Empire." In *The Catacombs and the Colosseum*. Edited by Stephen Benko and John O'Rourke. Valley Forge: Judson Press, 1971.

Tregiari, Susan. "Domestic Staff at Rome in the Julio-Claudian Period: 27 B.C. to A.D. 68." *Histoire Sociale, Revue Canadienne* 6:41–55.

Tyldesley, Joyce. *Daughters of Isis: Women of Ancient Egypt*. London: Penguin, 1994.

Waithe, Mary Ellen, ed. *Ancient Women Philosophers 600 B.C.–500 A.D. In A History of Women Philosophers*. Vol.1. Dordrecht, The Netherlands: Kluwer Academic Publishers, 1987.

Watterson, Barbara. *Women in Ancient Egypt*. New York: St. Martin's Press, 1991.

Willard, Charity Cannon. "The Franco-Italian Professional Writer: Christine de Pizan." In *Medieval Women Writers*. Edited by Katharina Wilson. Athens: University of Georgia Press, 1984.

Wilson-Kastner, Patricia, et. al., ed. *Lost Tradition: Women Writers of the Early Church (A)*. Edited by Washington DC: University Press of America, 1981.

Wilson, Robert R. *Prophecy and Society in Ancient Israel*. Philadelphia: Fortress, 1980.

Witt, R.E. *Isis in the Greco-Roman World*. Ithaca, New York: Cornell University Press, 1977.

Work Claiming to be the Constitutions of the Holy Apostles, Including the Canons (The). Trans. Irah Chase. Vol. II. New York: D. Appleton, 1848.

Yakar, Clak. *Pre-Historic Anatolia: The Neolithic Transformation and the Early Chalcolithic Period*. Tel Aviv: Institute of Archaeology of Tel Aviv University, 1991.

Yardley, Anne Bagnall, "'Ful weel she soong the service dyvyne': The Cloistered Musician in the Middle Ages." In *Women Making Music: The Western Art Tradition, 1150–1950*. Illini Books. Edited by Jane Bowers and Judith Tick. Urbana and Chicago: University of Illinois Press, 1987.